CONTENT PAGE

INTRODUCTION.. PAGE 2

SMALL AND SIMPLE SKULL TATTOOS................... PAGE 3

LARGE AND DETAILED SKULL TATTOOS............ PAGE 18

TRADTIONAL SKULL TATTOOS................................. PAGE 38

SCARY SKULL TATTOOS.. PAGE 53

UNUSUAL SKULL TATTOOS... PAGE 67

FUNNY SKULL TATTOOS.. PAGE 80

SUGAR SKULL TATTOOS.. PAGE 91

TRIBAL SKULL TATTOOS.. PAGE 102

GRIM REAPER SKULL TATTOOS................................. PAGE 113

SERPENT SKULL TATTOOS... PAGE 125

SKULL WITH WINGS TATTOOS.................................. PAGE 136

CELTIC SKULL TATTOOS.. PAGE 147

NATURE SKULL TATTOOS... PAGE 159

GEOMETRIC SKULL TATTOOS.................................... PAGE 171

ANIMAL SKULL TATTOOS.. PAGE 180

ALIEN SKULL TATTOOS... PAGE 189

FINAL THOUGHTS.. PAGE 201

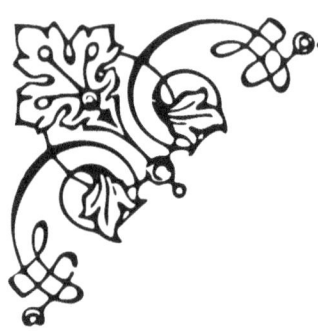
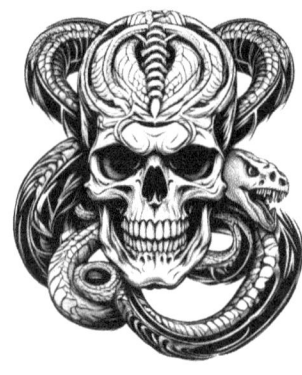

INTRODUCTION:

Thank you for purchasing this book. It's designed to inspire your next skull tattoo.

This book includes many different styles and themes of skull tattoos to choose from, ranging from scary skull tattoos to funny skull tattoos. It's designed to give the reader a vast selection of ideas on the different types of AI skull tattoos, helping to decide your favourite style and design. This 200+ page book includes hundreds of skull tattoos and is designed for both the individual looking to get their next skull tattoo, as well as the tattoo artist looking for new ideas.

HOW TO USE THIS BOOK:

There is a wide range of skull tattoo designs within this book, and I hope it helps the viewer in the process of choosing their next tattoo. These tattoo designs should be used as a guide or tool for the tattoo artist to create their own work from. If you discover a skull tattoo design that you like, (which I'm sure you will!) I would recommend that the tattoo artist you choose, adds his or her own creative style to the design, and makes it their own.

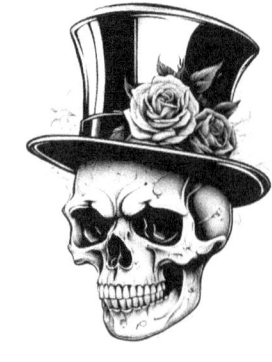

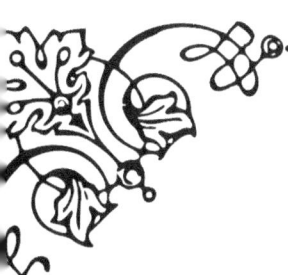
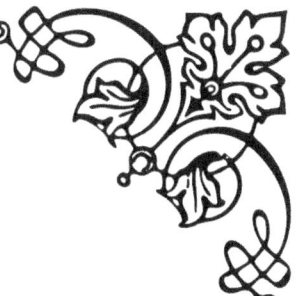

SMALL AND SIMPLE TATTOOS

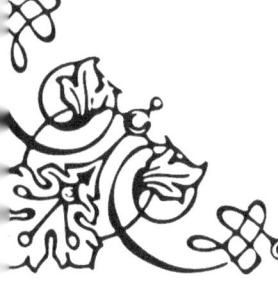

SMALL AND SIMPLE SKULL TATTOOS

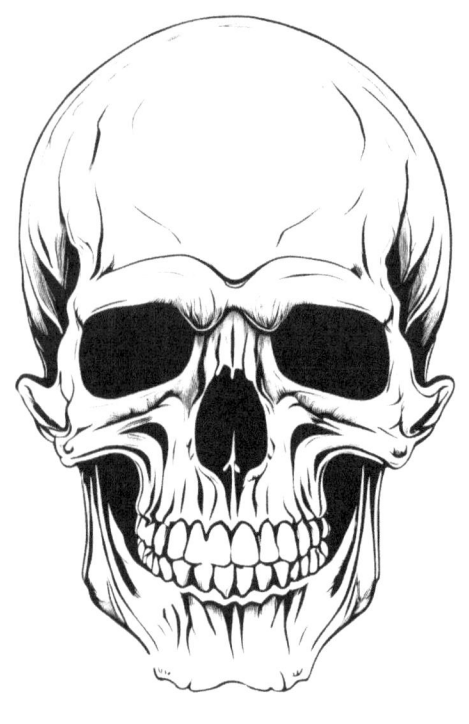
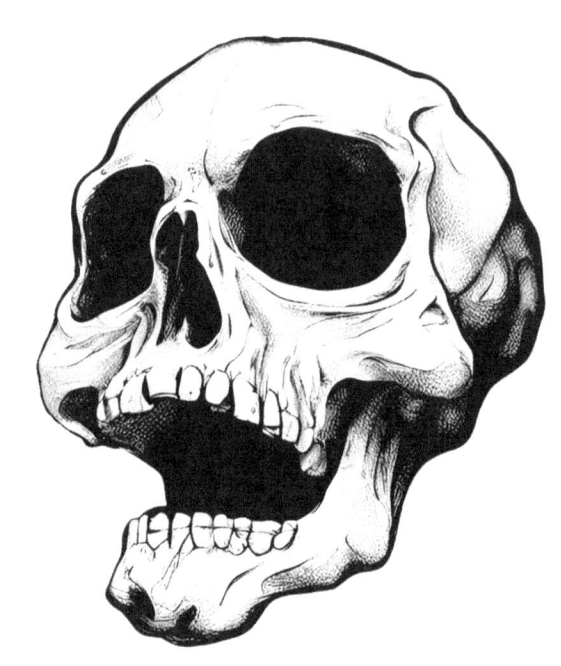
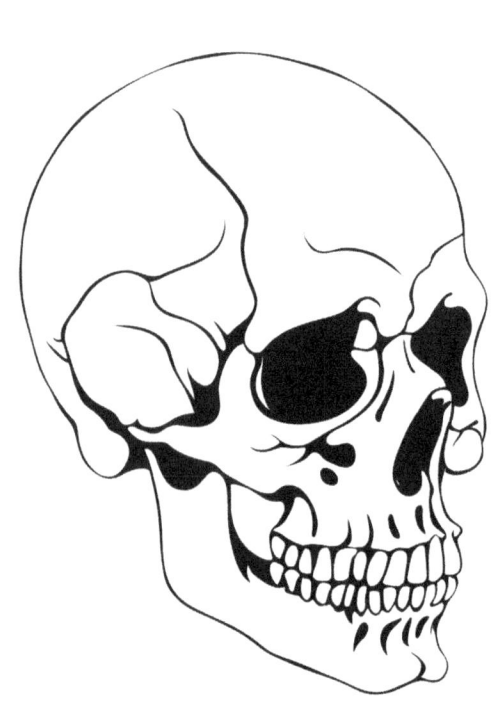
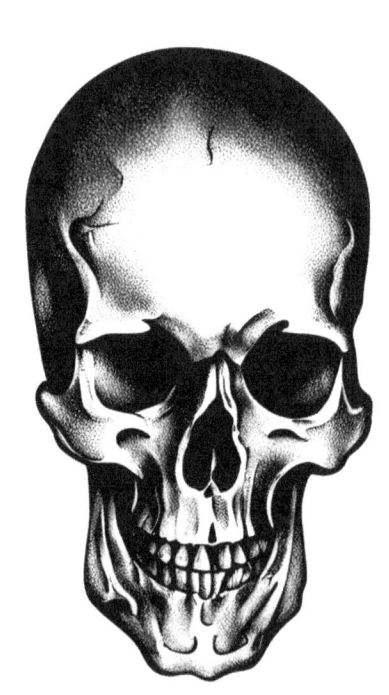

SMALL AND SIMPLE SKULL TATTOOS

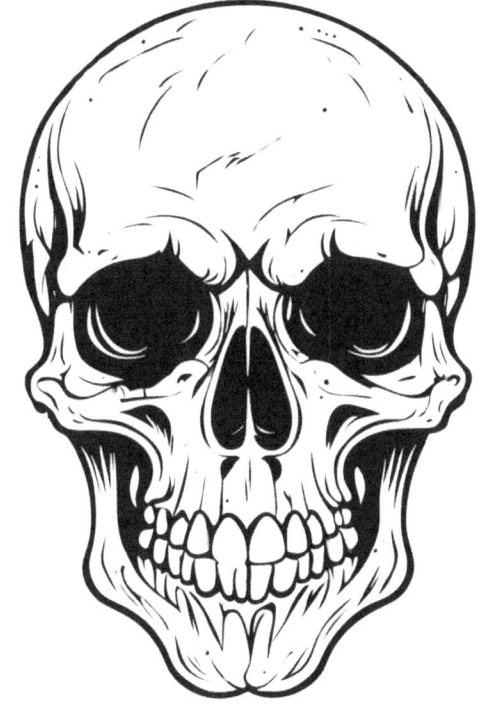
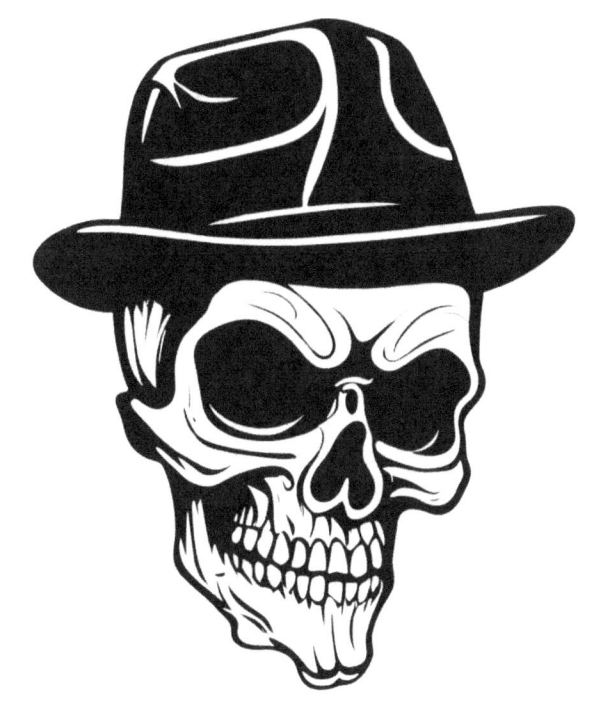
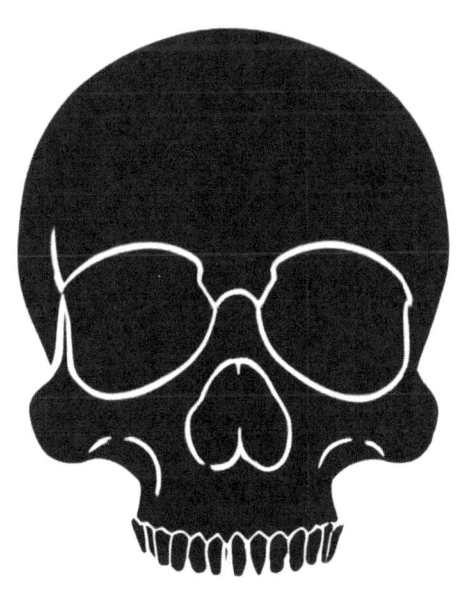
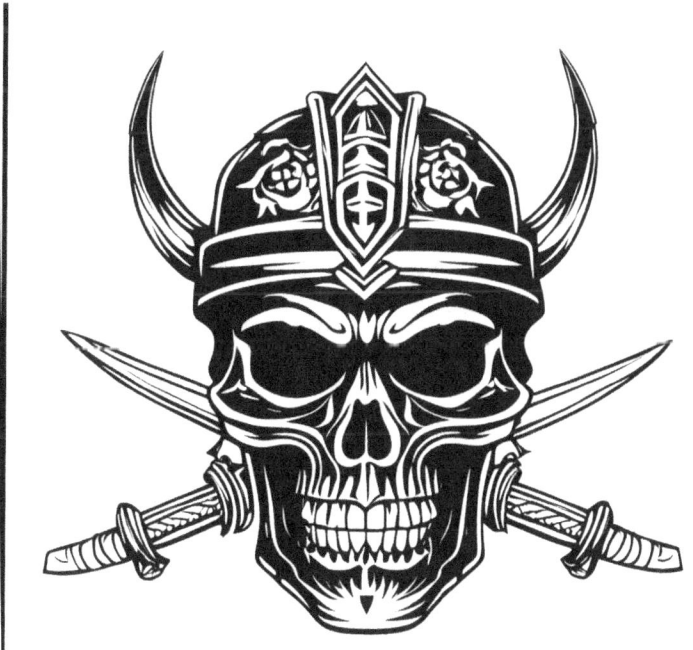

SMALL AND SIMPLE SKULL TATTOOS

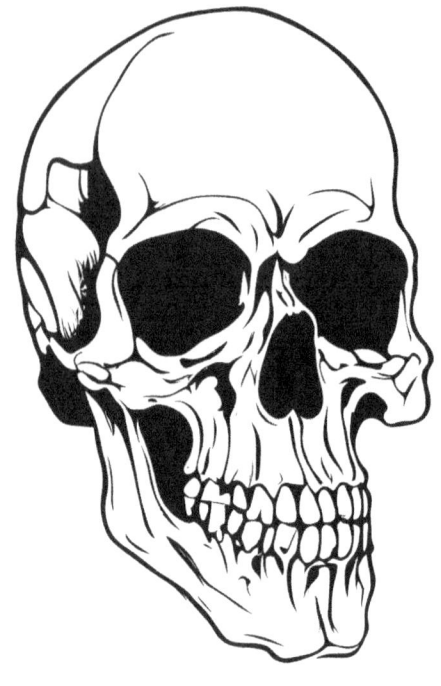
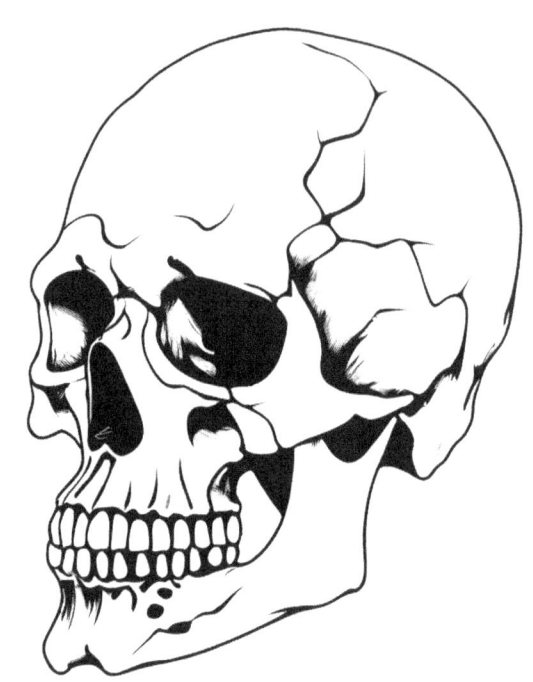
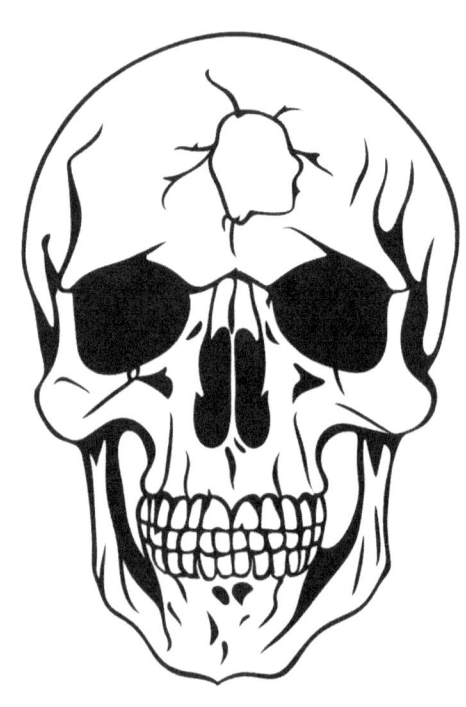
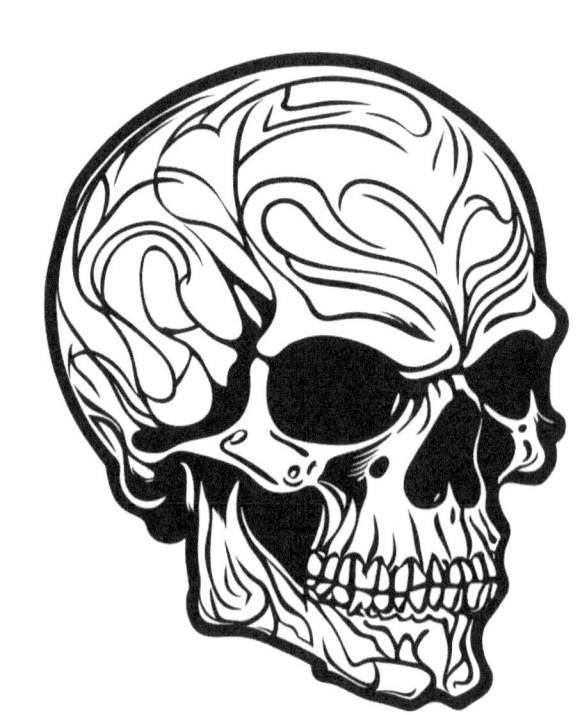

SMALL AND SIMPLE SKULL TATTOOS

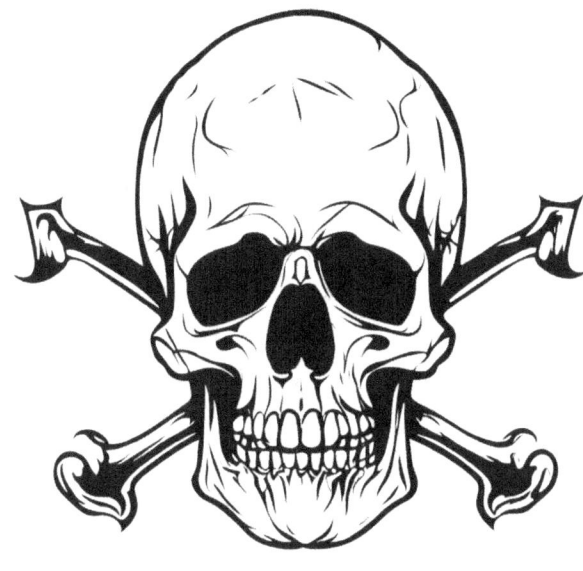
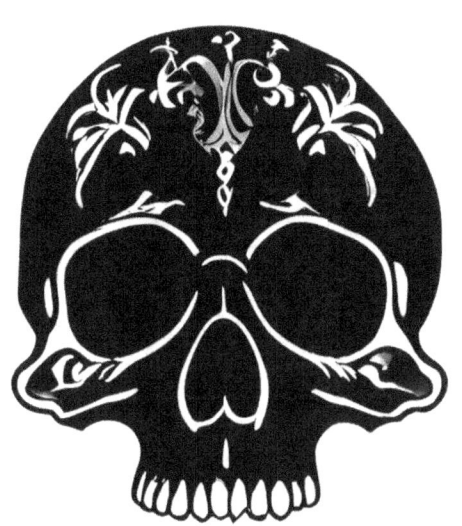
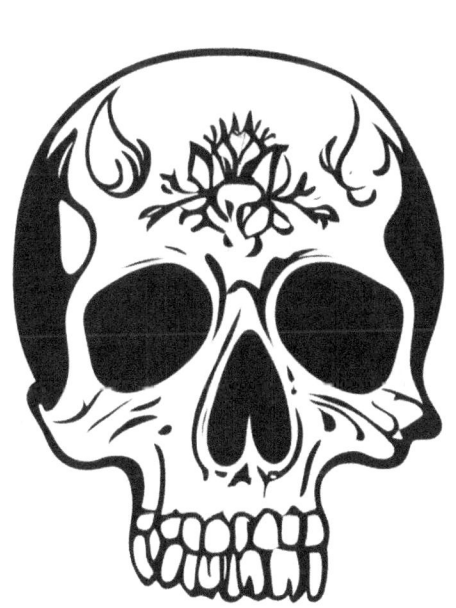
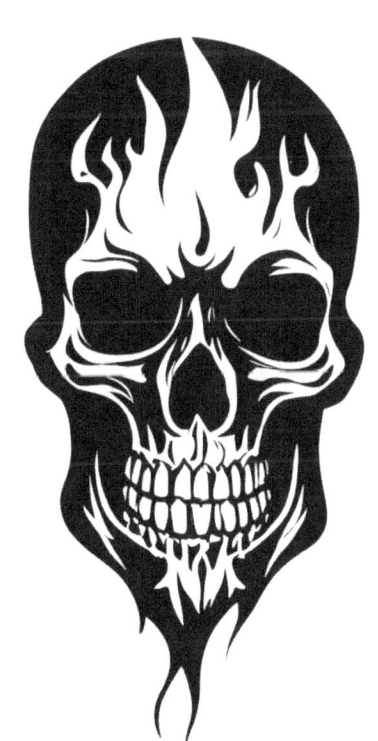

SMALL AND SIMPLE SKULL TATTOOS

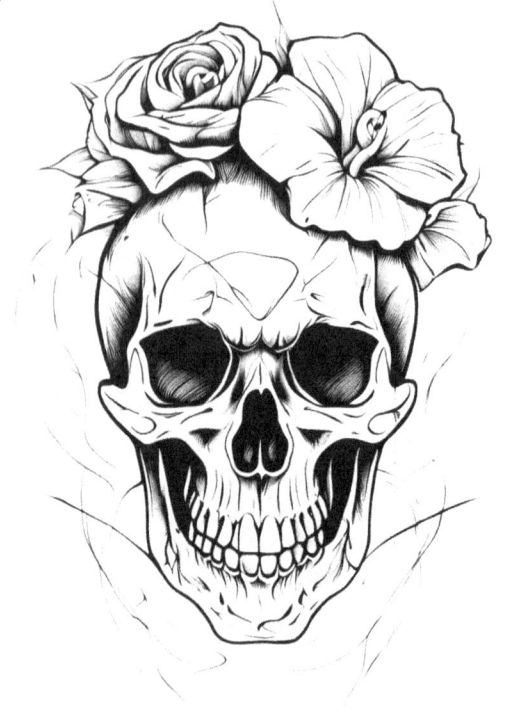
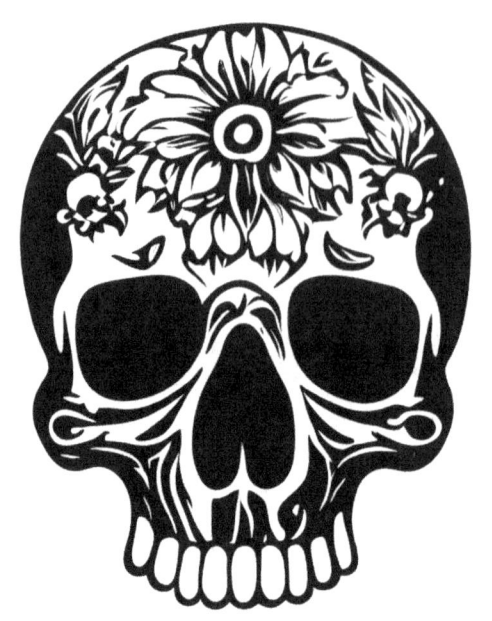
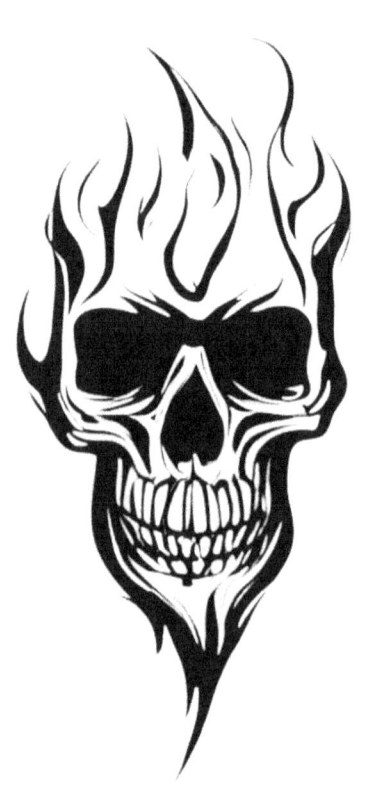
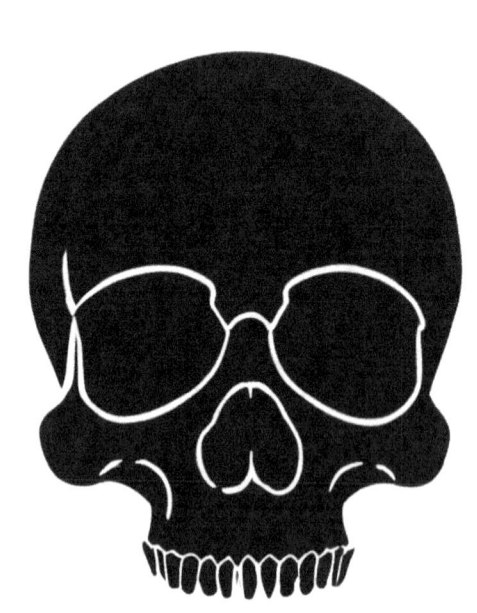

SMALL AND SIMPLE SKULL TATTOOS

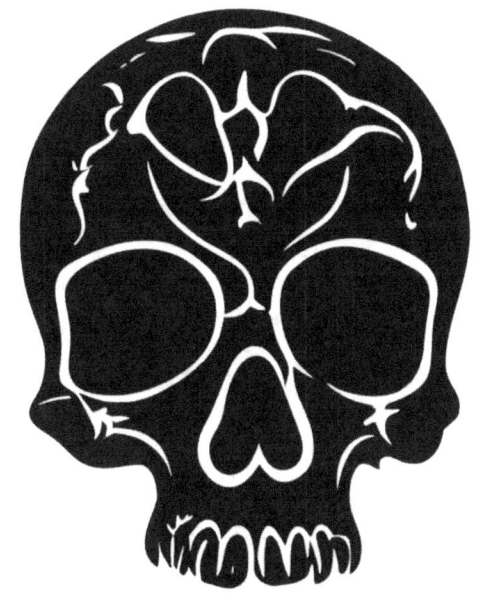
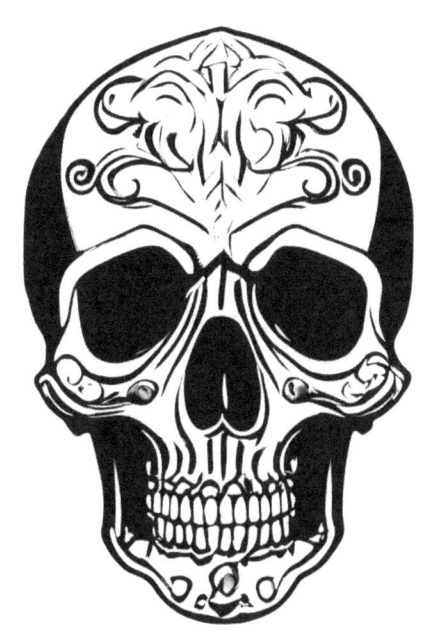
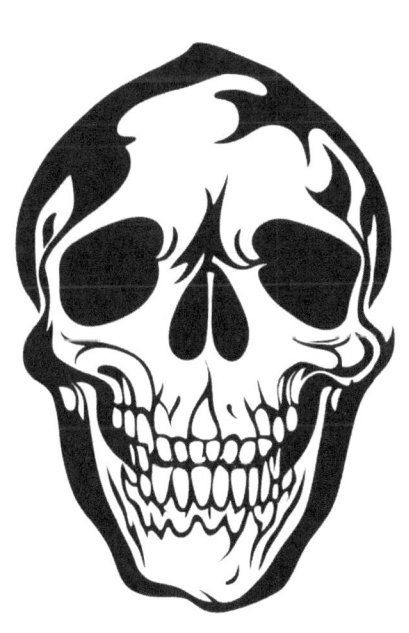
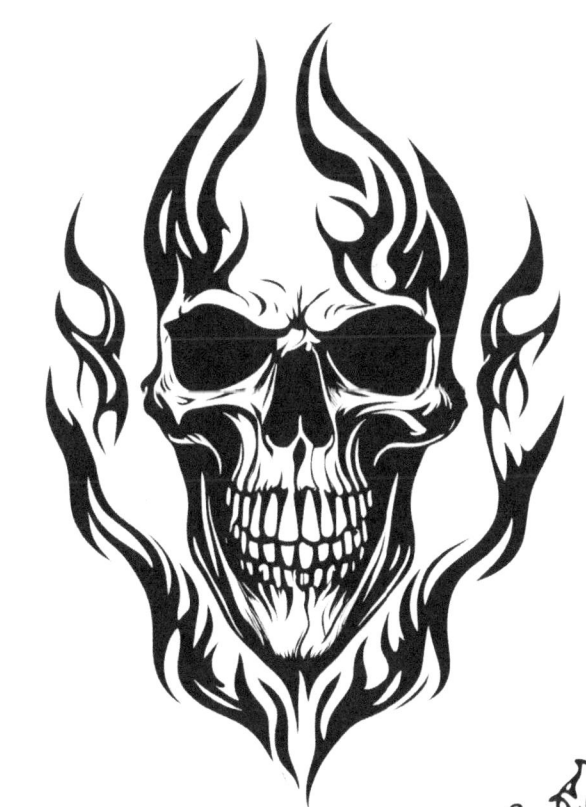

SMALL AND SIMPLE SKULL TATTOOS

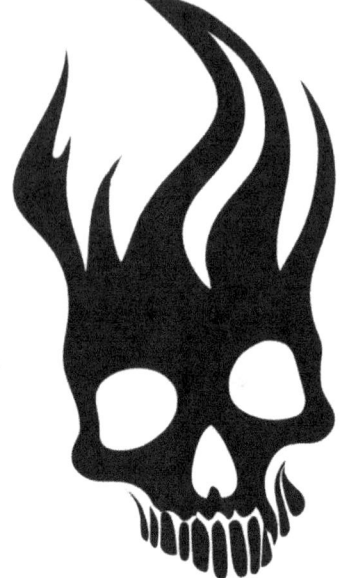
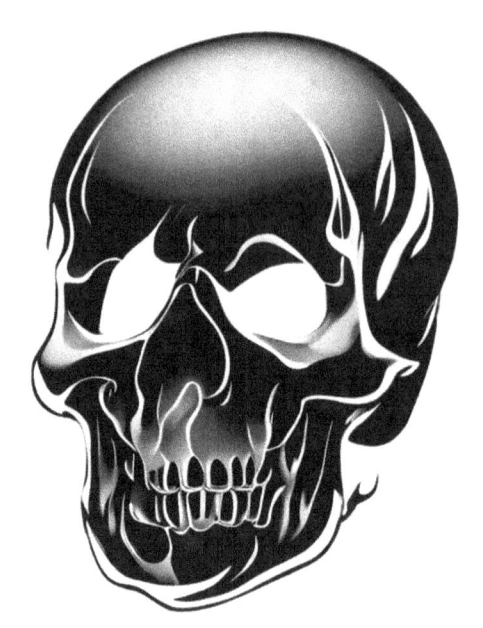
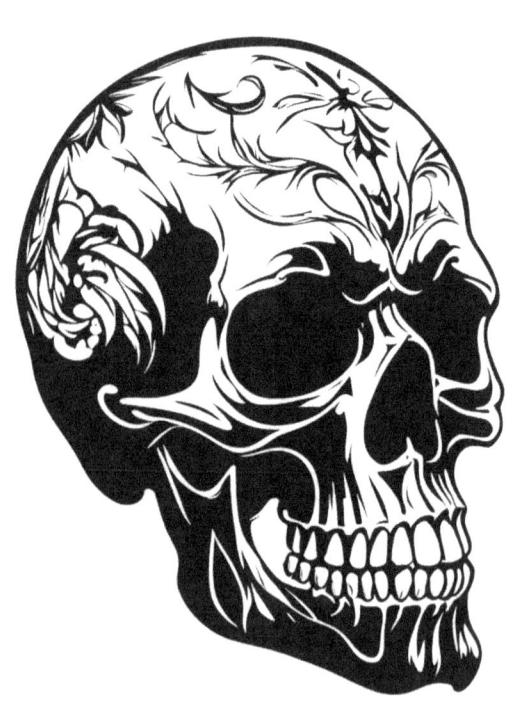
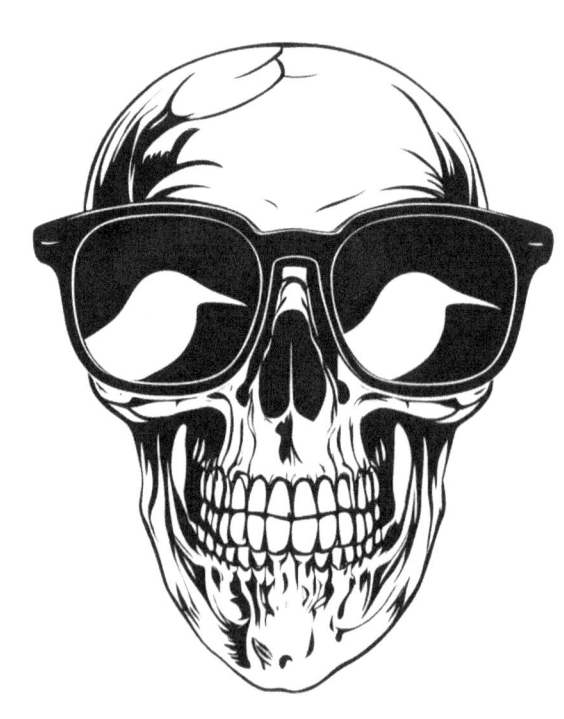

SMALL AND SIMPLE SKULL TATTOOS

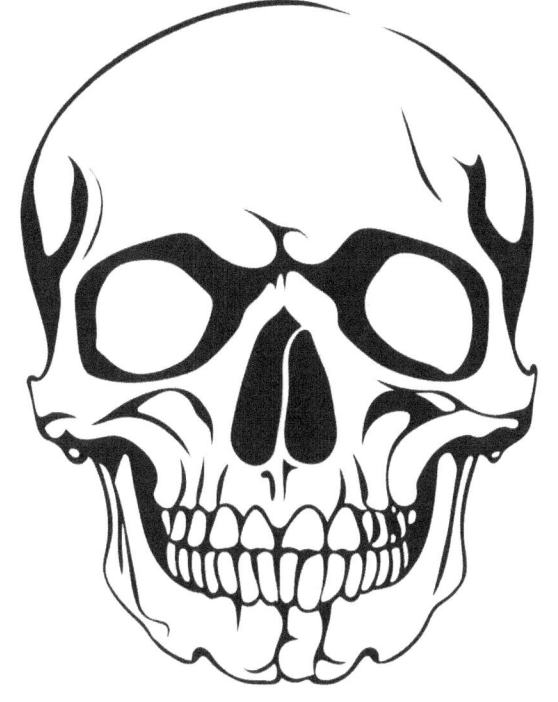
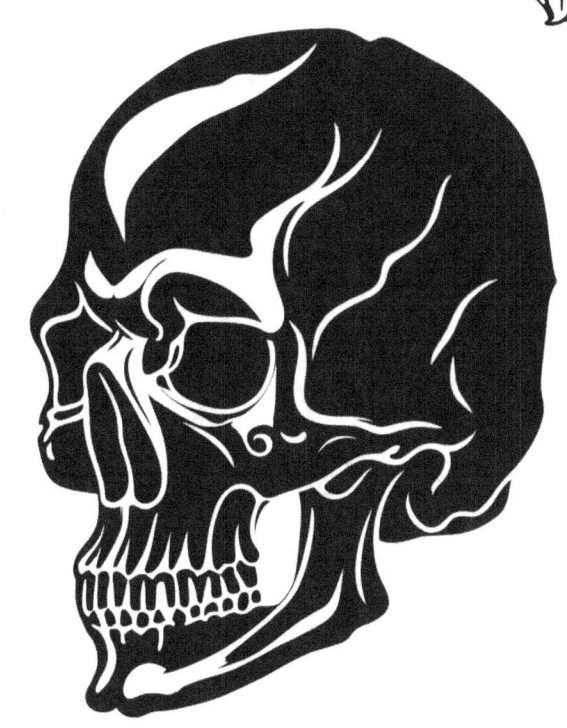
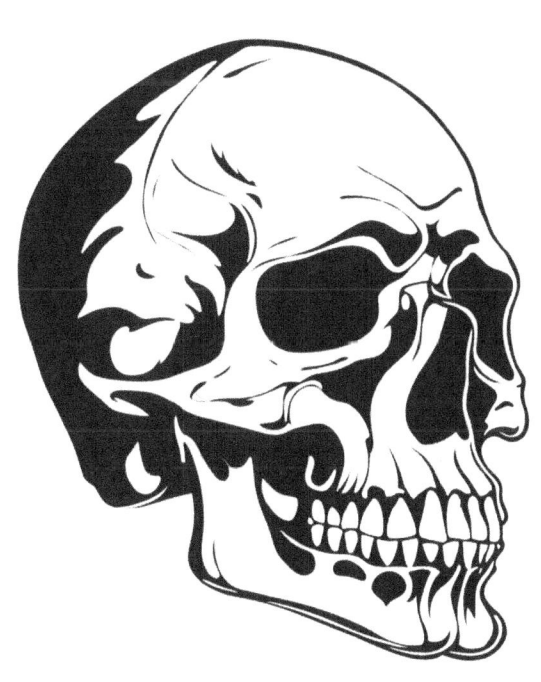
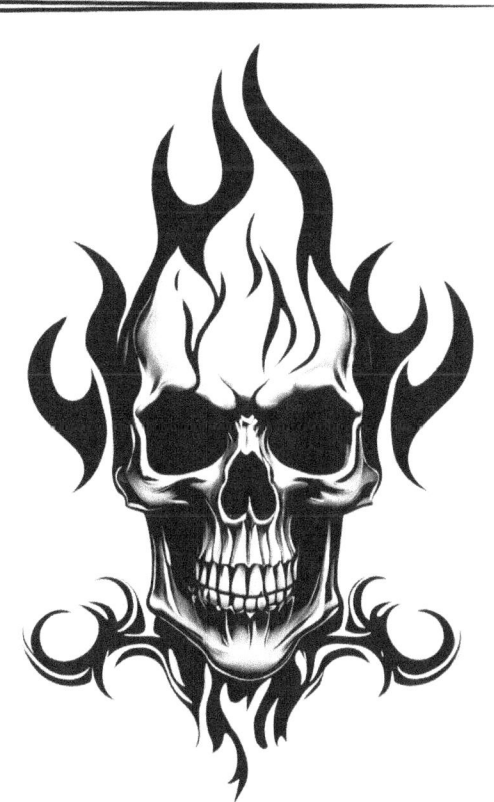

SMALL AND SIMPLE SKULL TATTOOS

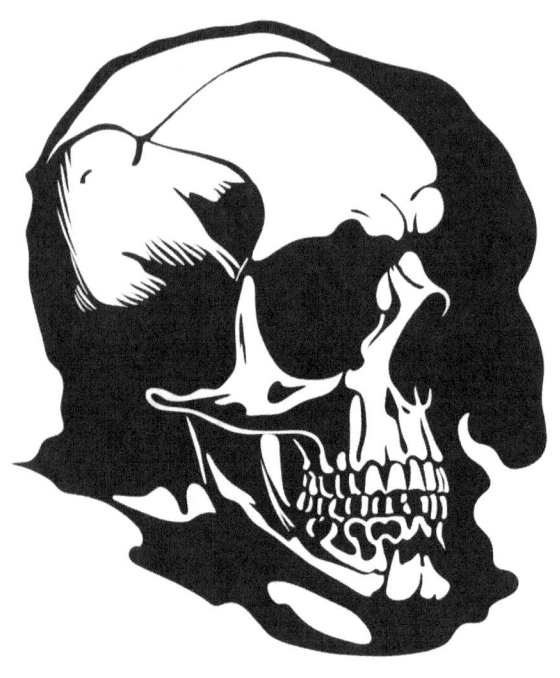
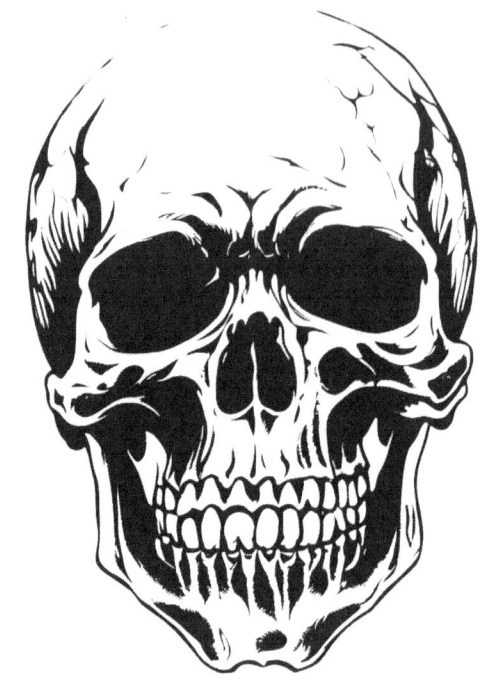
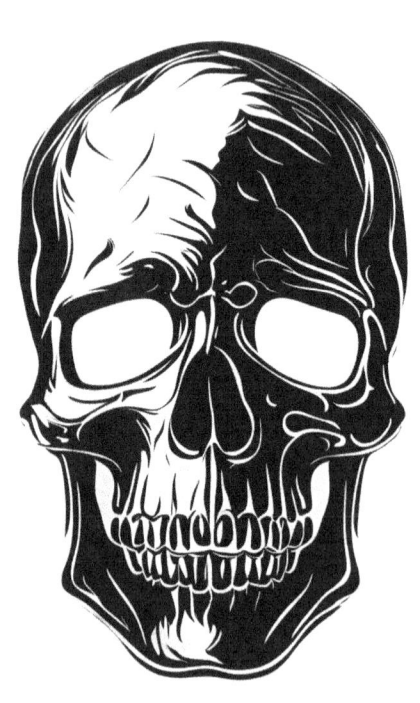
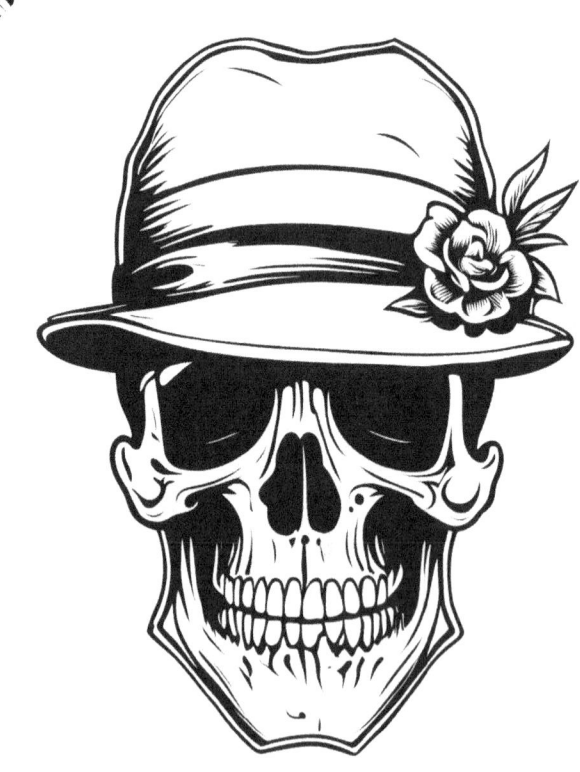

SMALL AND SIMPLE SKULL TATTOOS

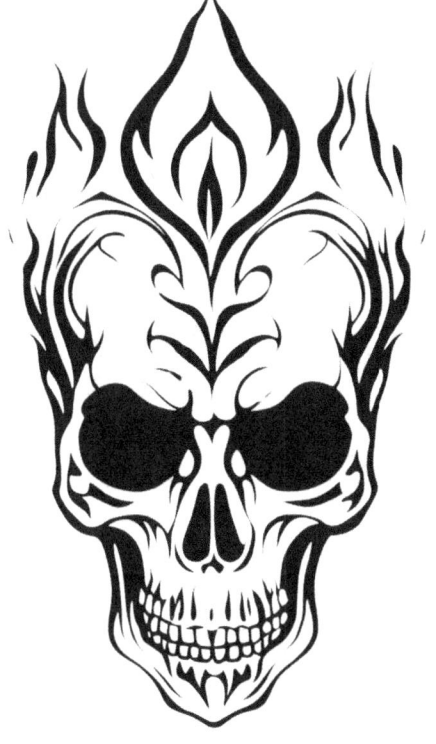
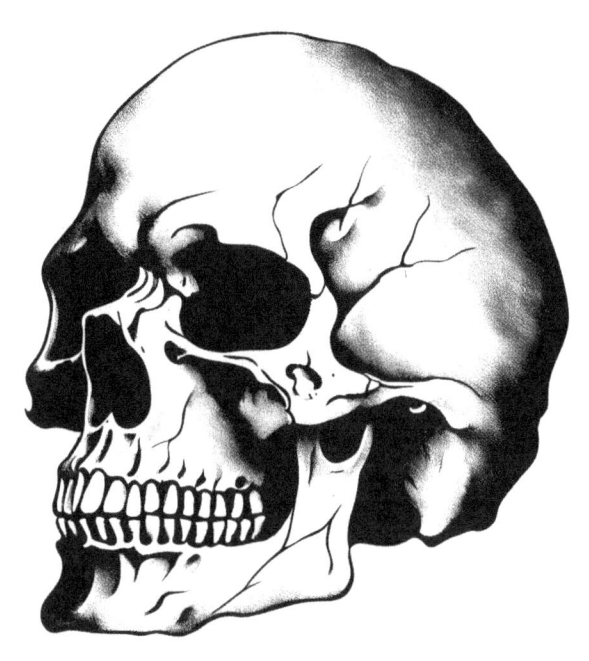
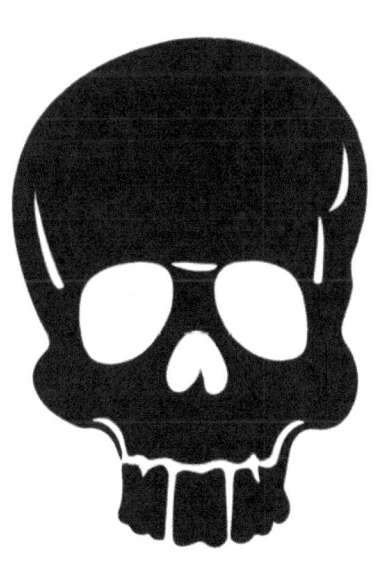
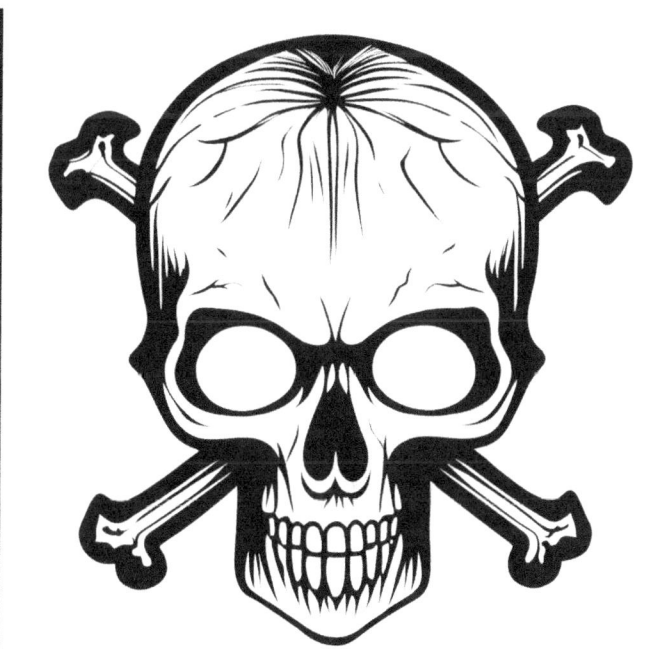

SMALL AND SIMPLE SKULL TATTOOS

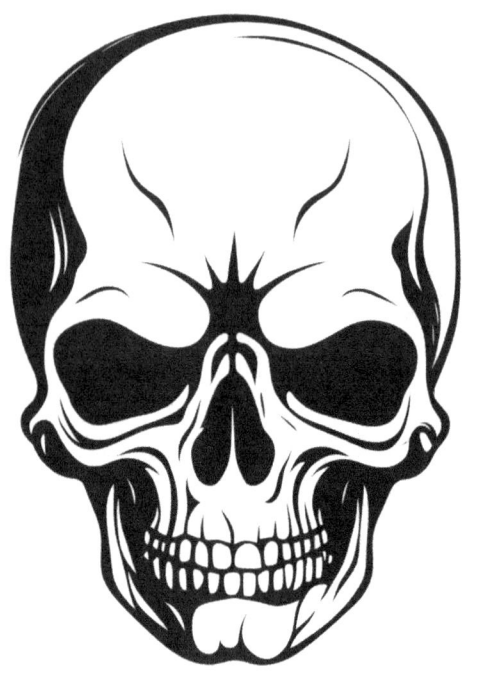
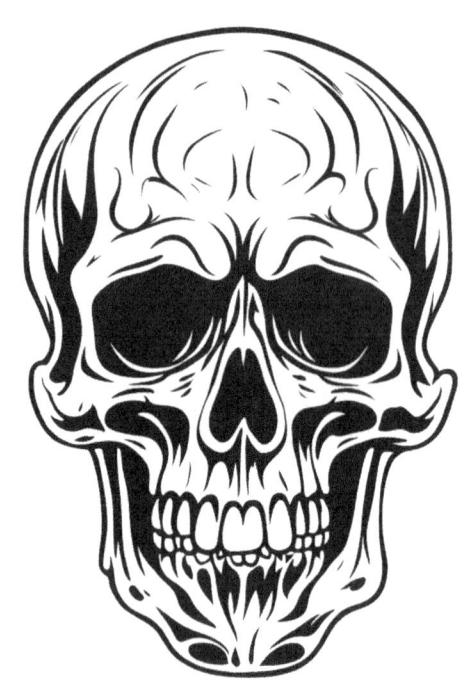
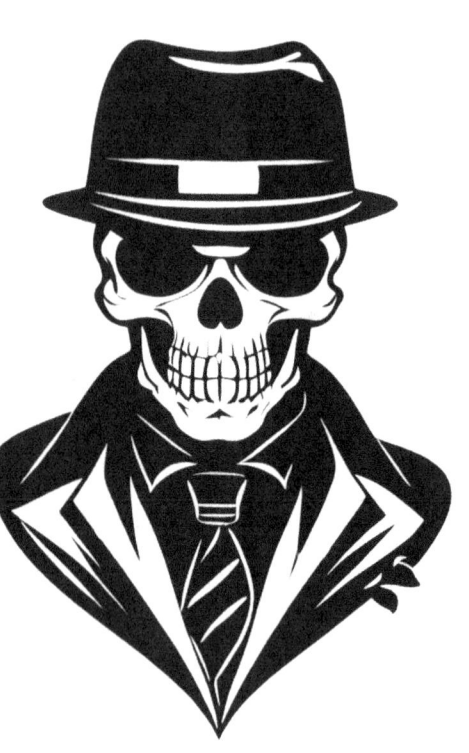
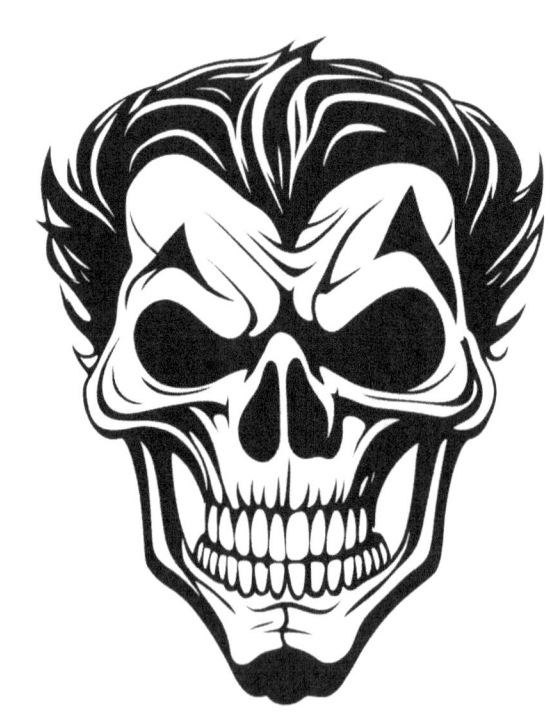

SMALL AND SIMPLE SKULL TATTOOS

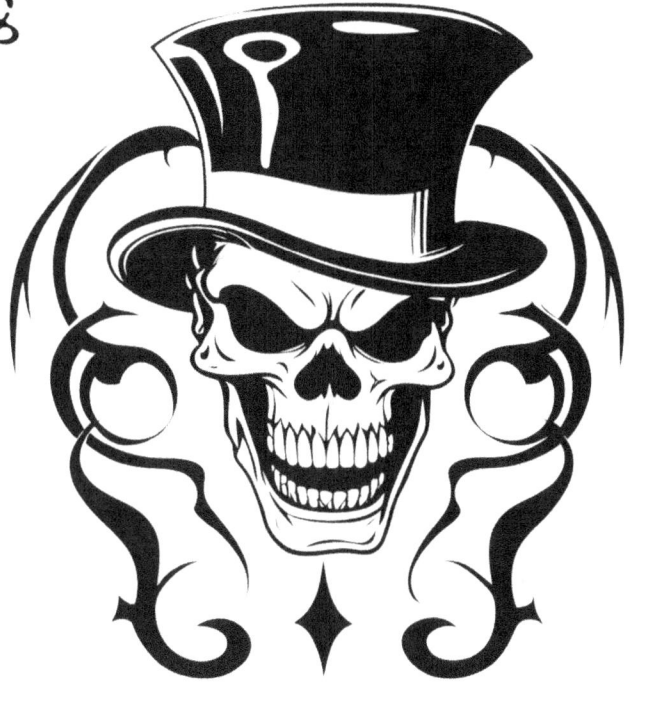
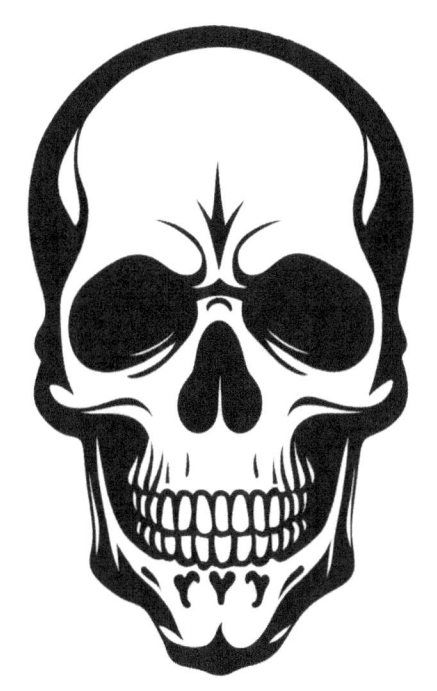
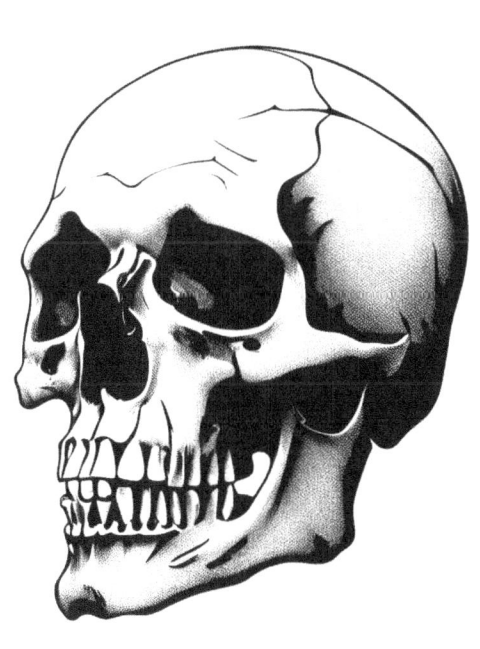
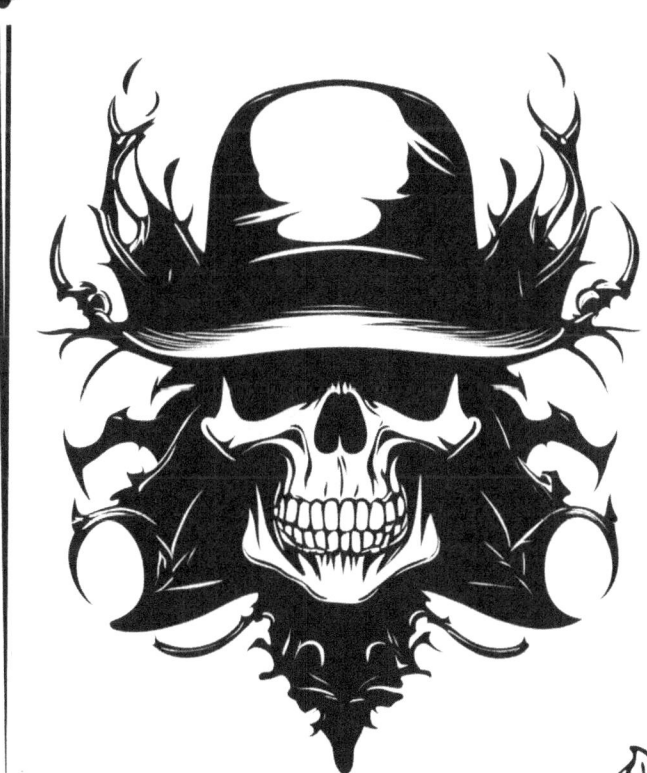

SMALL AND SIMPLE SKULL TATTOOS

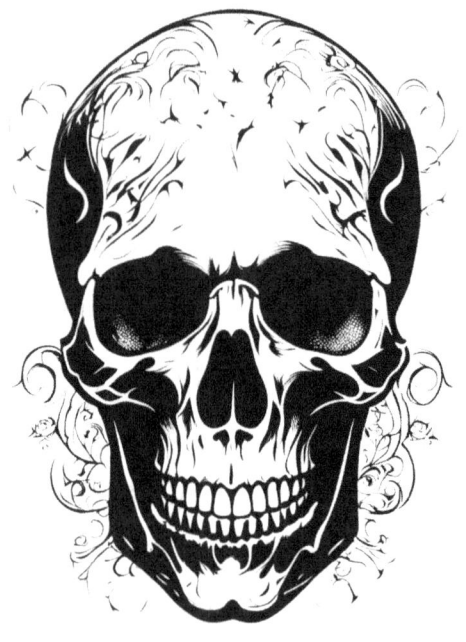
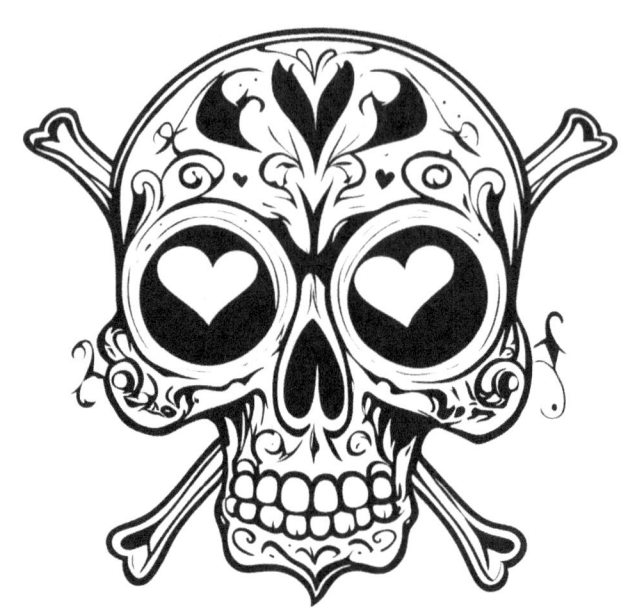
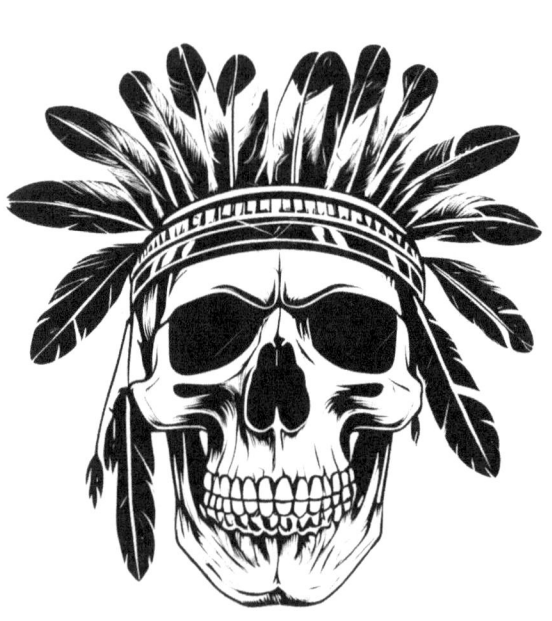
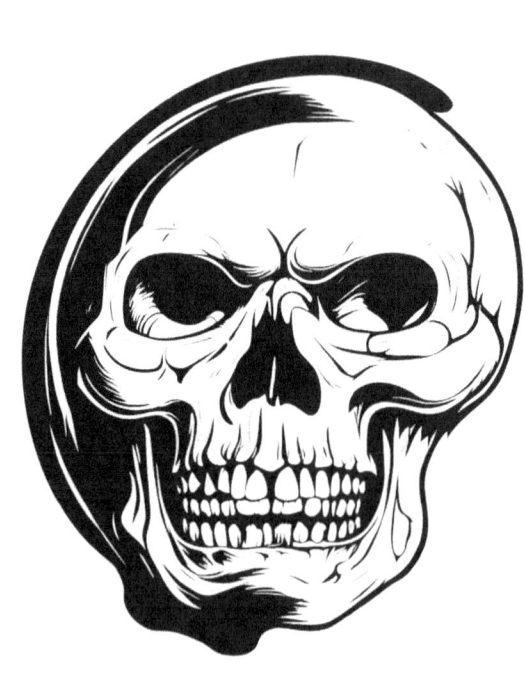

SMALL AND SIMPLE SKULL TATTOOS

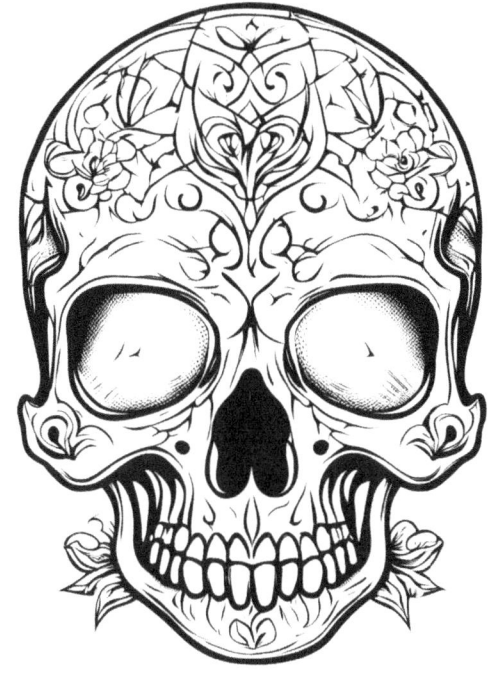
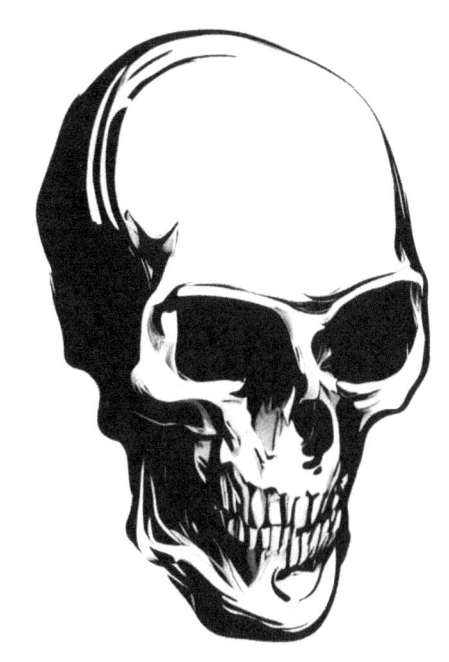
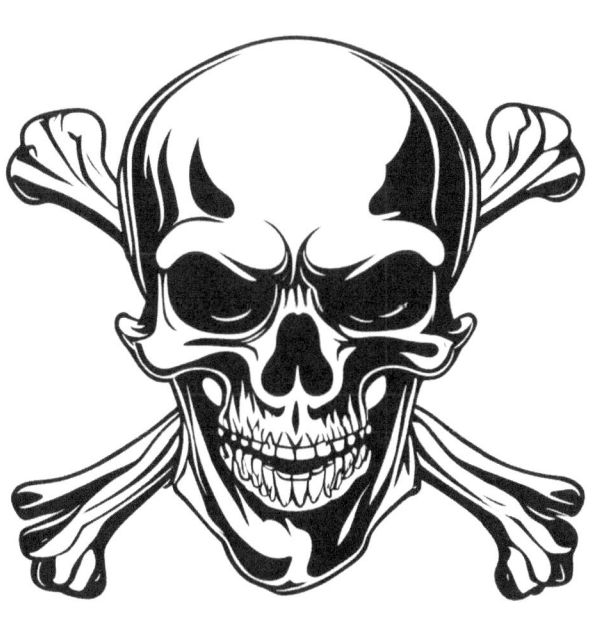
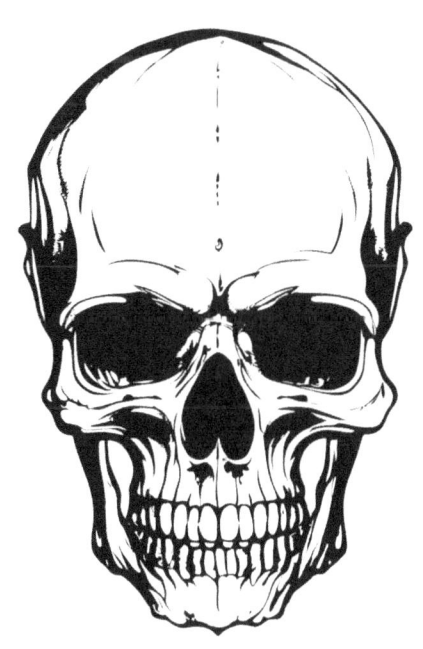

LARGE AND DETAILED SKULL TATTOOS

LARGE AND DETAILED SKULL TATTOOS

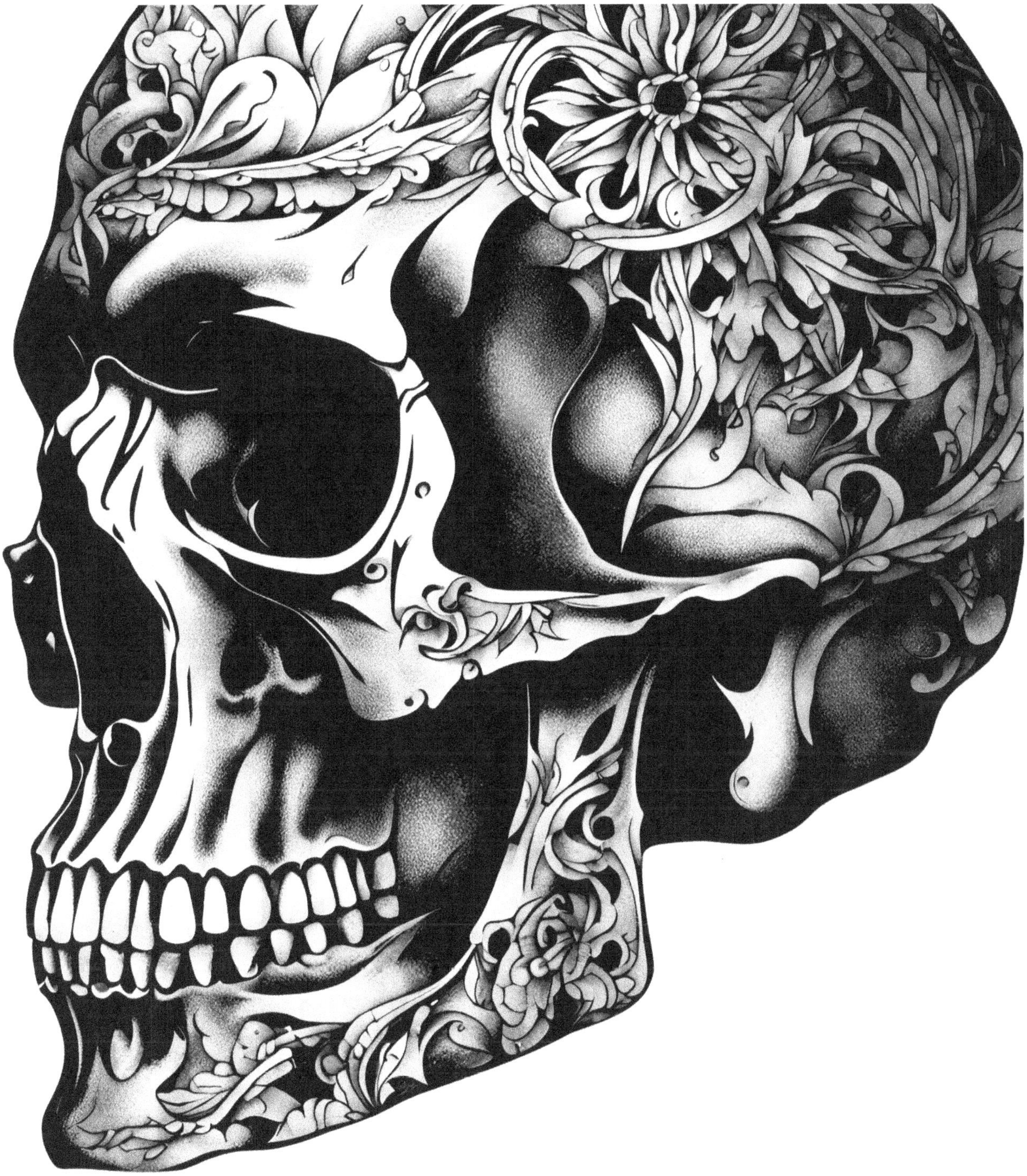

LARGE AND DETAILED SKULL TATTOOS

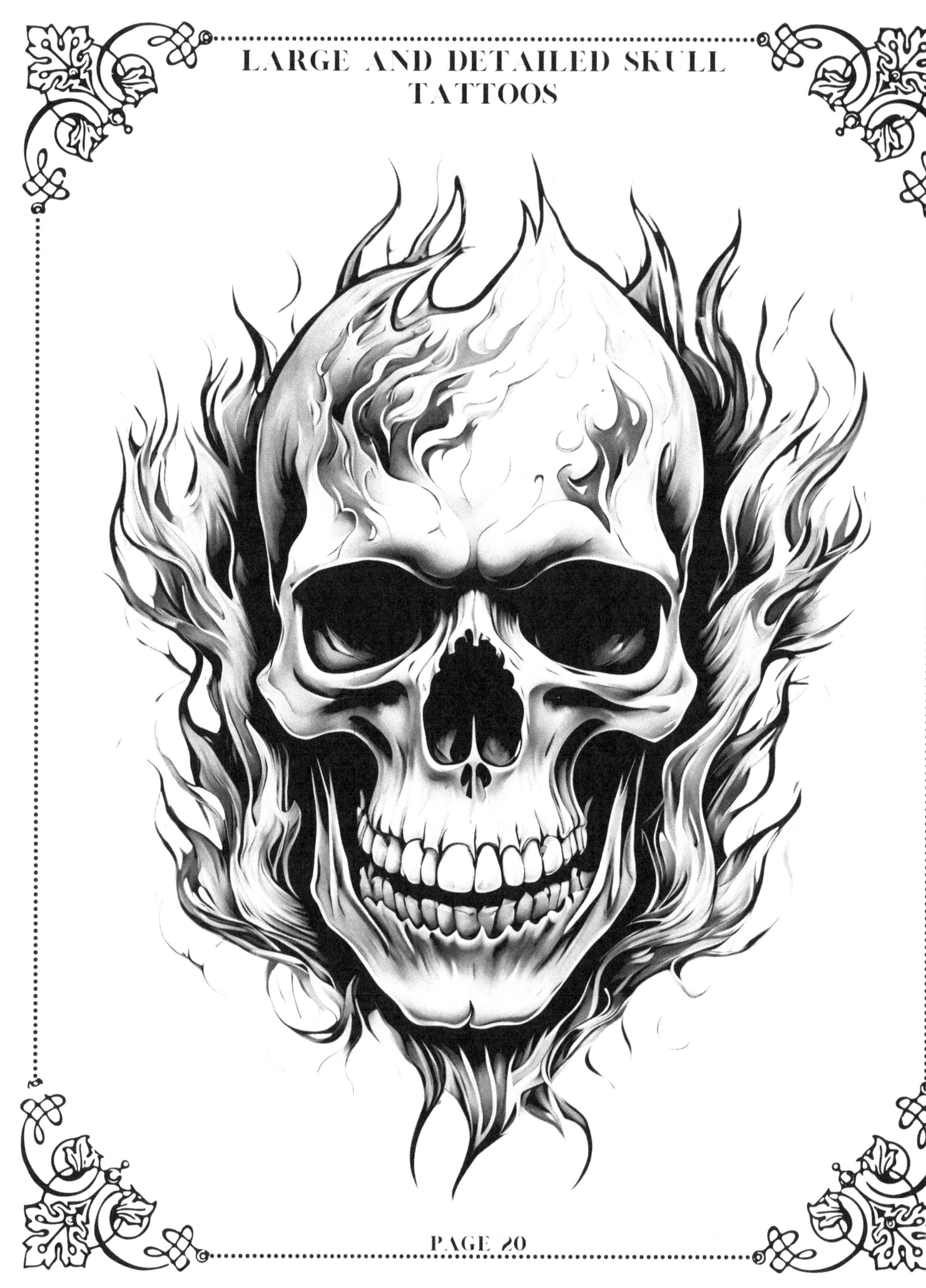

LARGE AND DETAILED SKULL TATTOOS

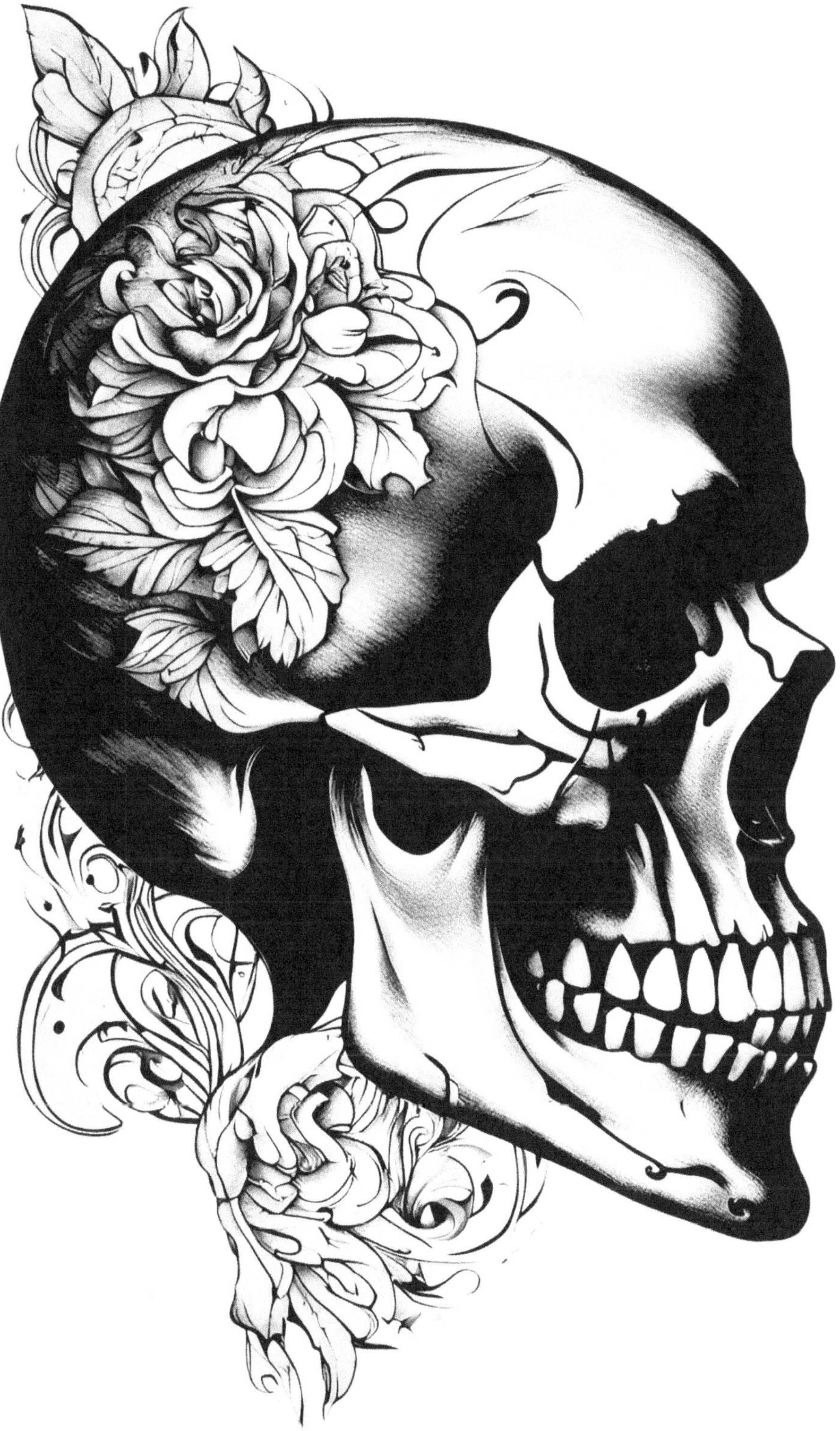

LARGE AND DETAILED SKULL TATTOOS

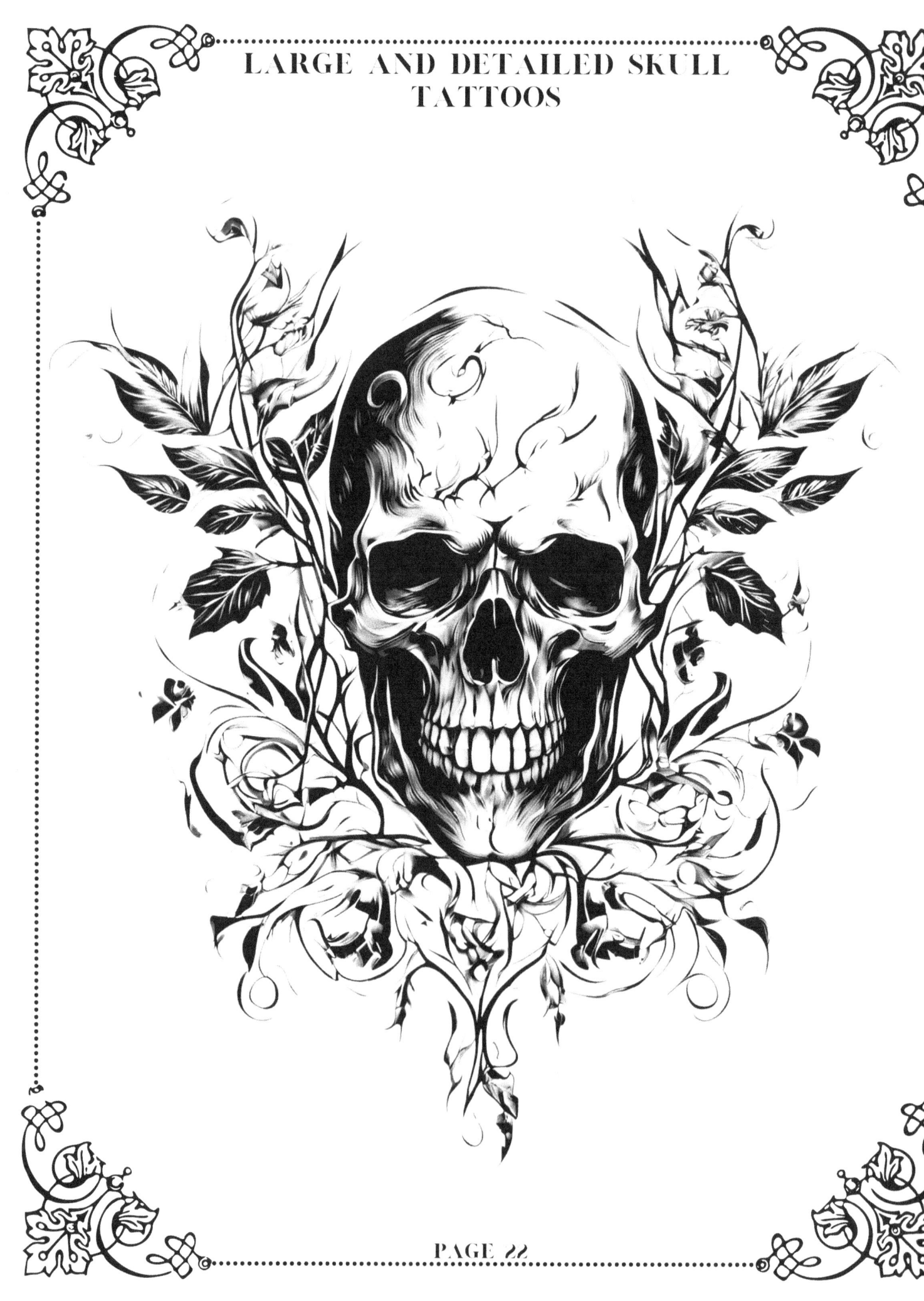

LARGE AND DETAILED SKULL TATTOOS

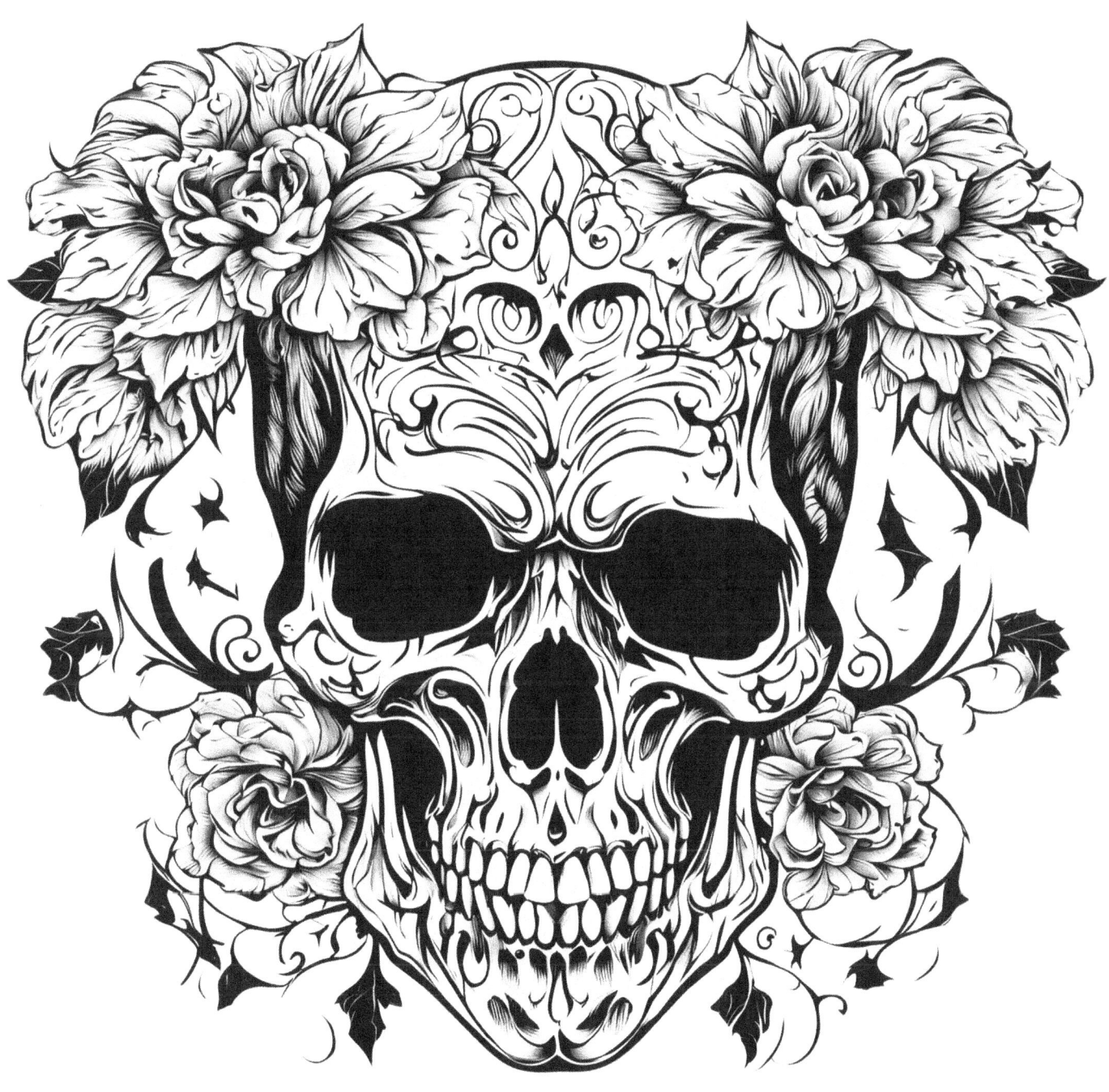

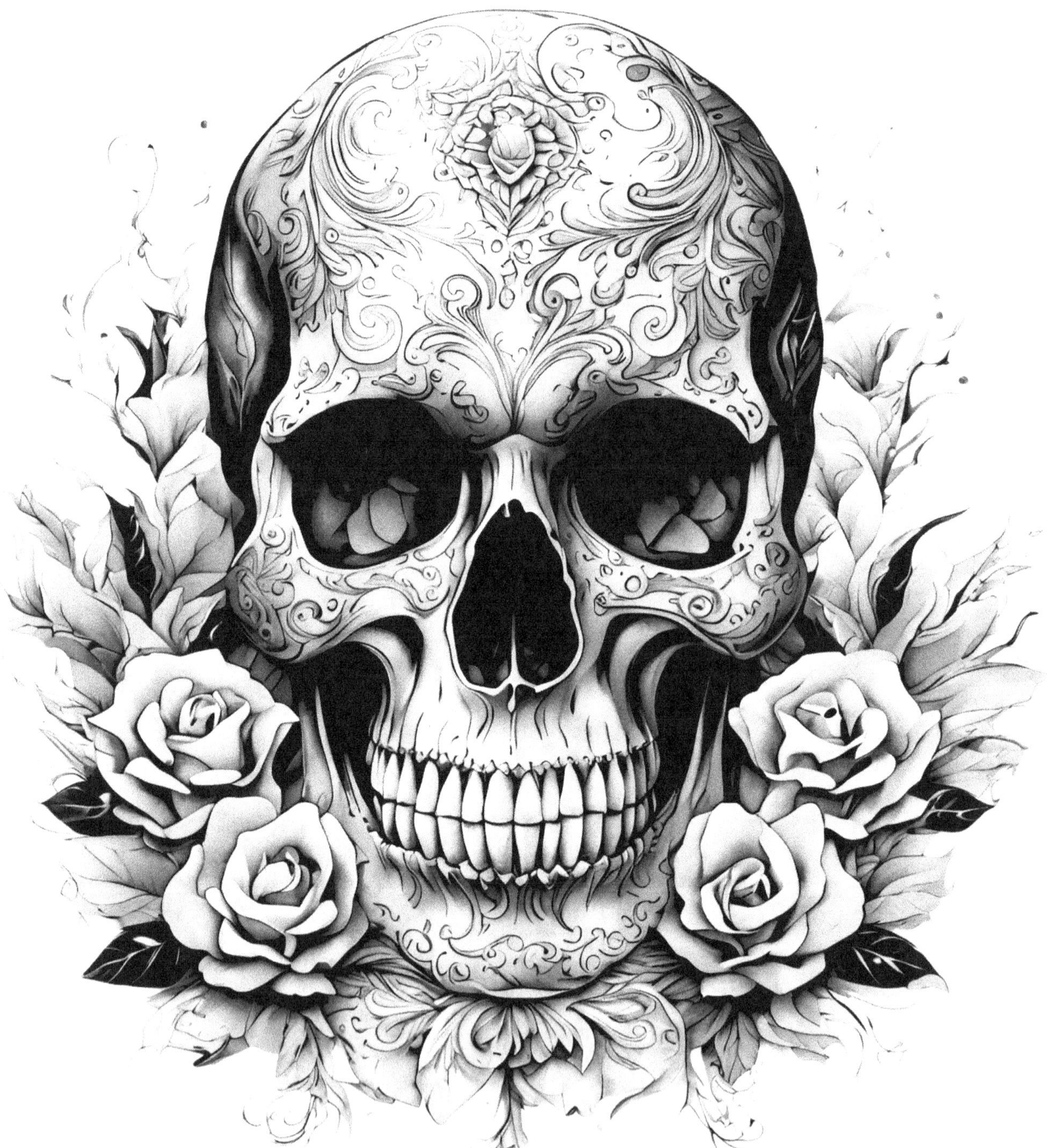

LARGE AND DETAILED SKULL TATTOOS

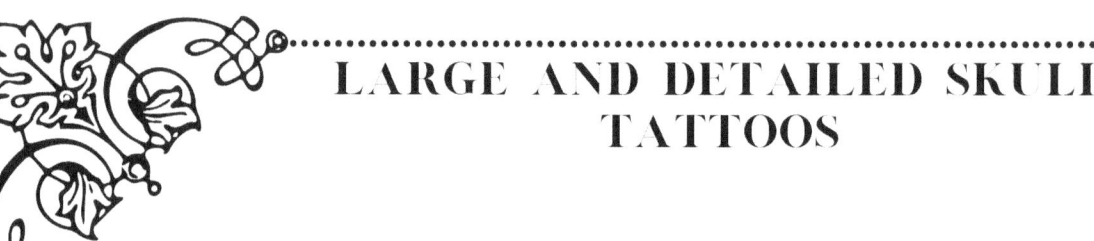

LARGE AND DETAILED SKULL TATTOOS

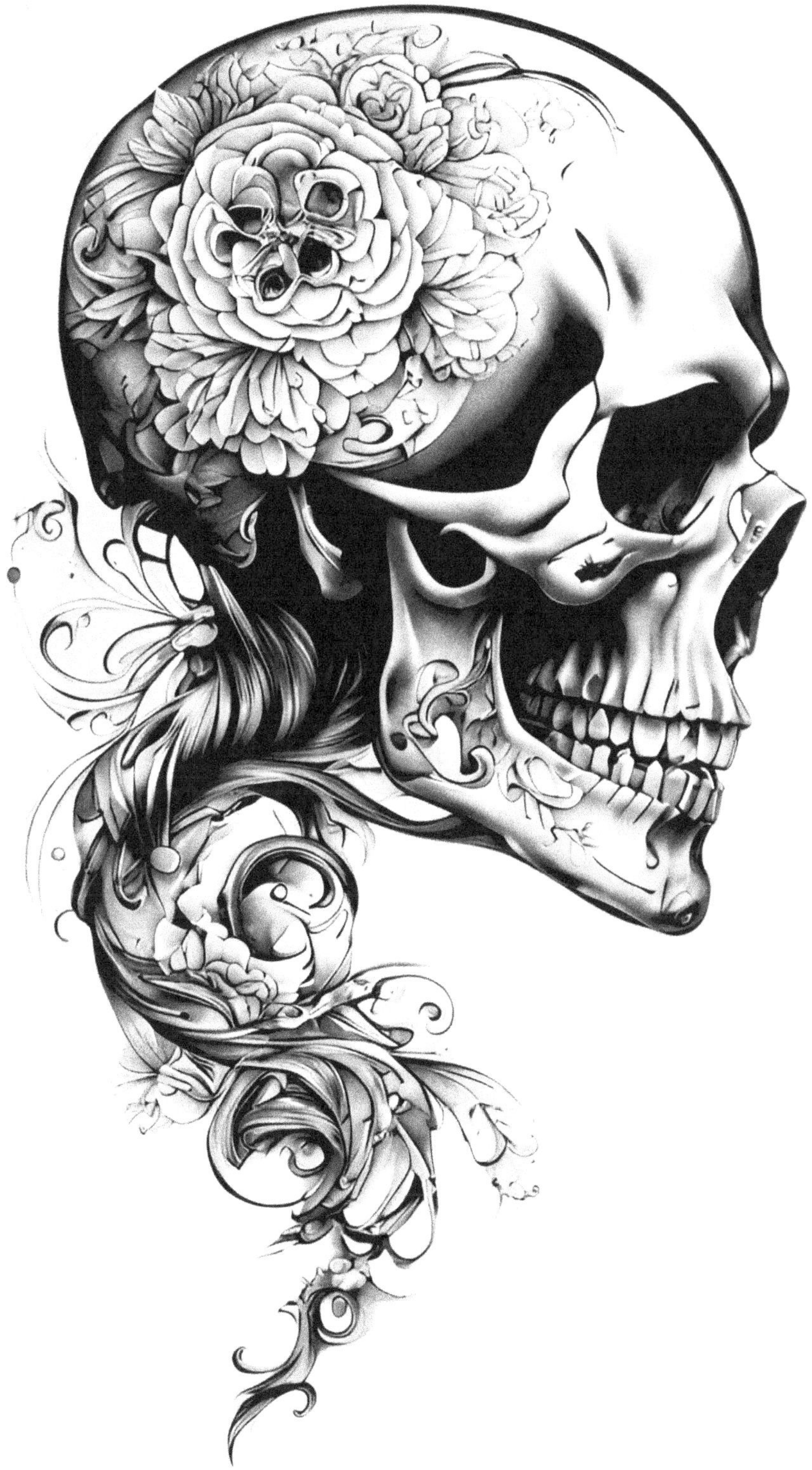

LARGE AND DETAILED SKULL TATTOOS

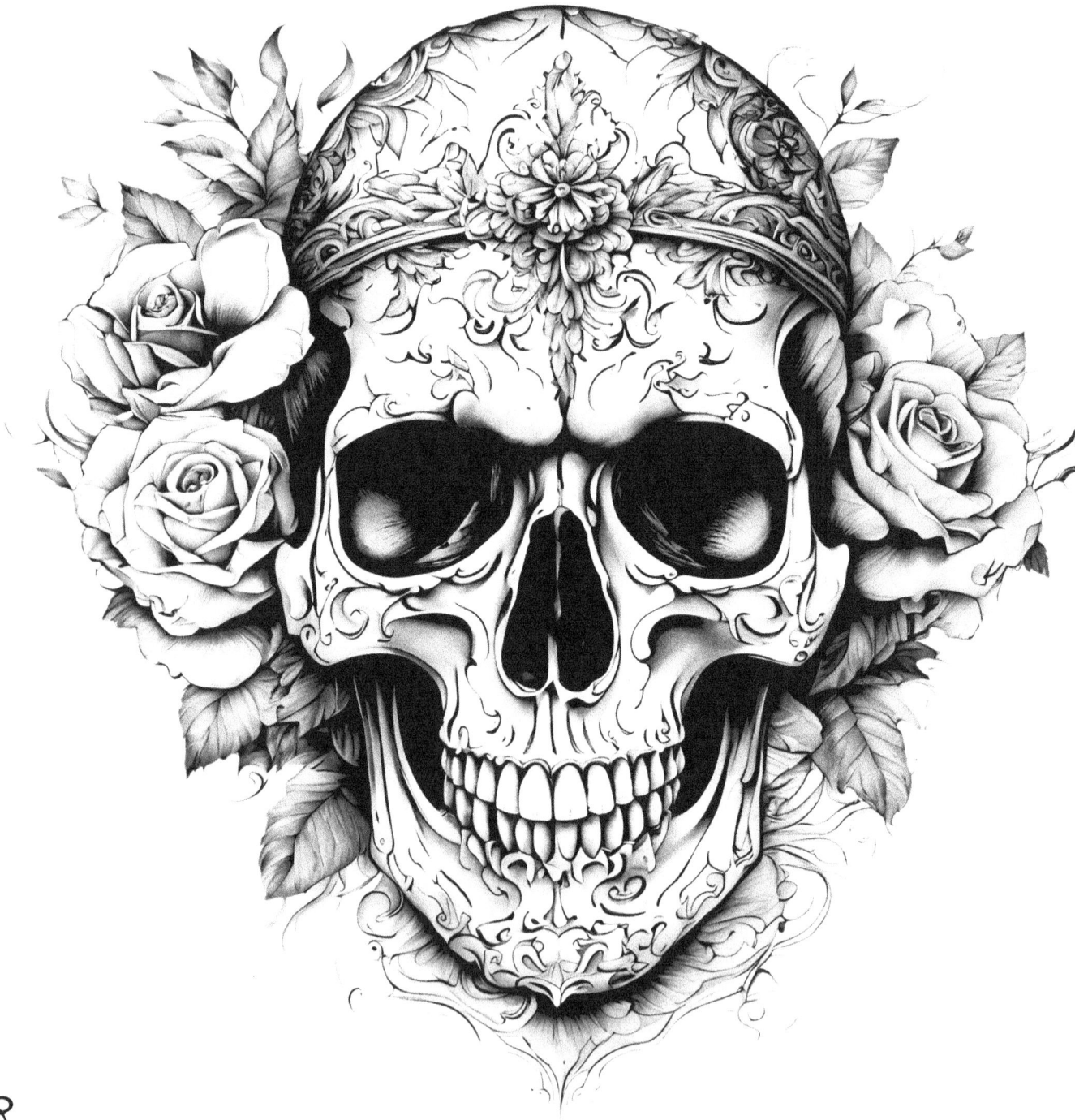

LARGE AND DETAILED SKULL TATTOOS

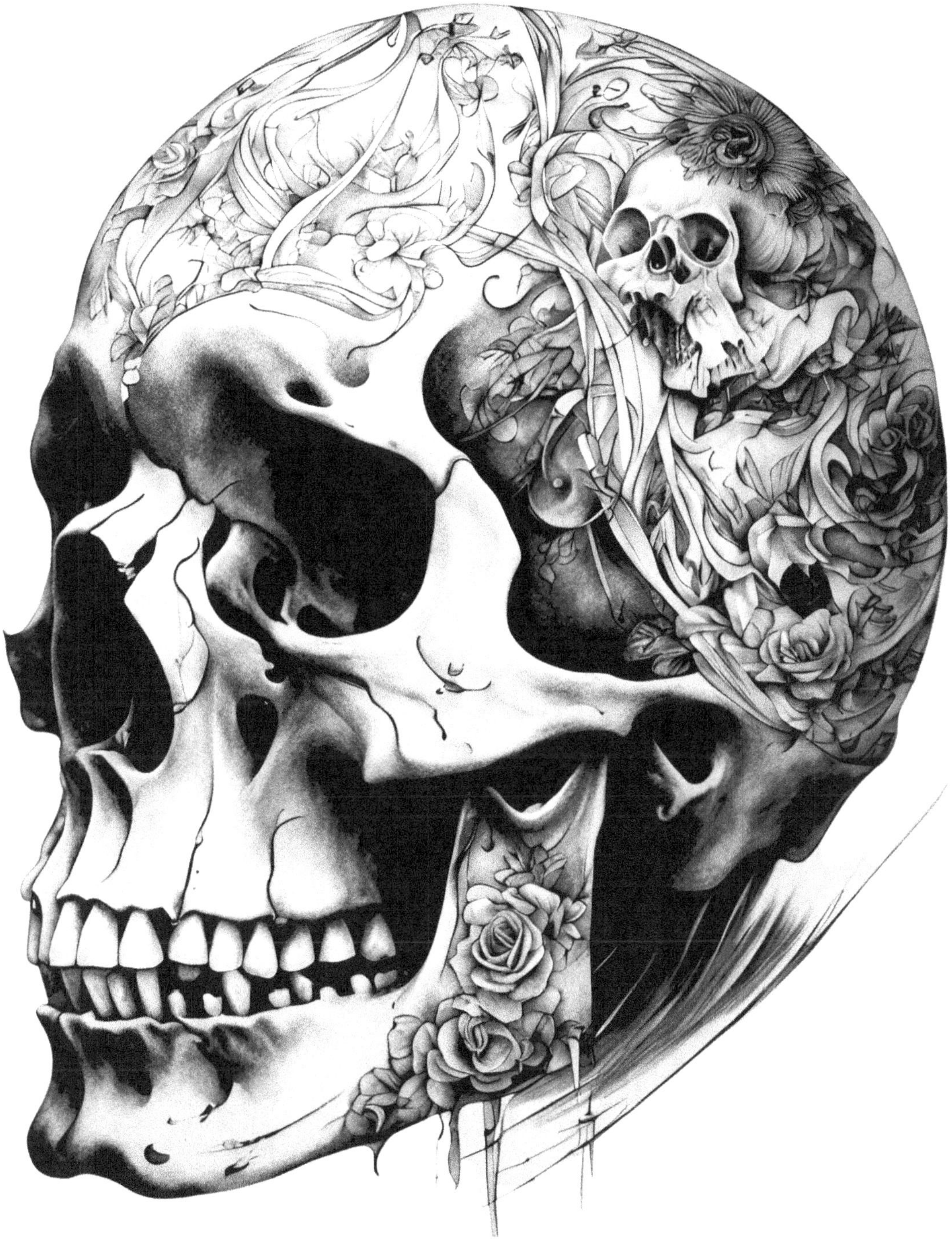

LARGE AND DETAILED SKULL TATTOOS

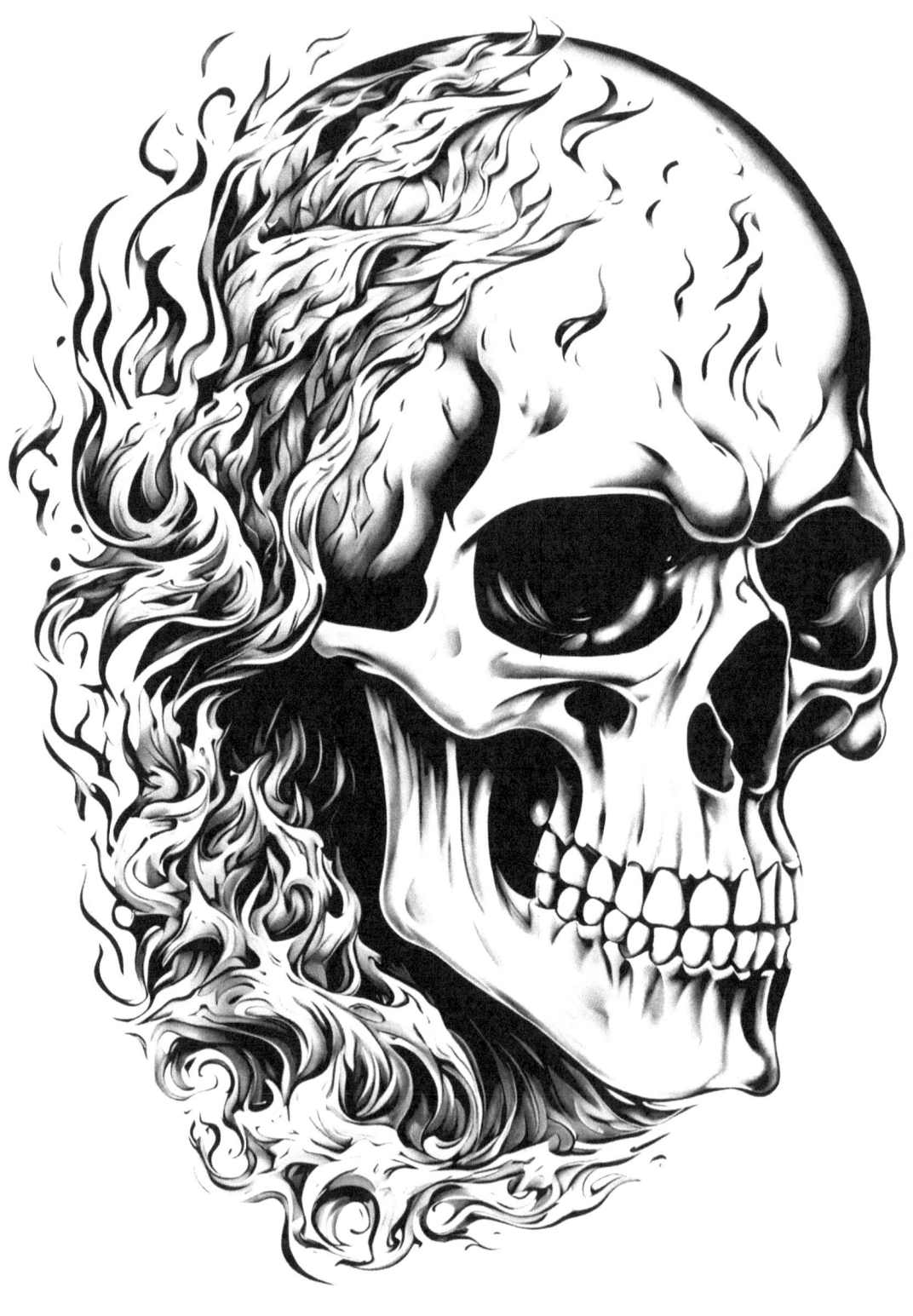

LARGE AND DETAILED SKULL TATTOOS

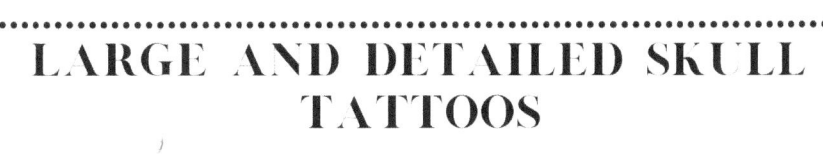

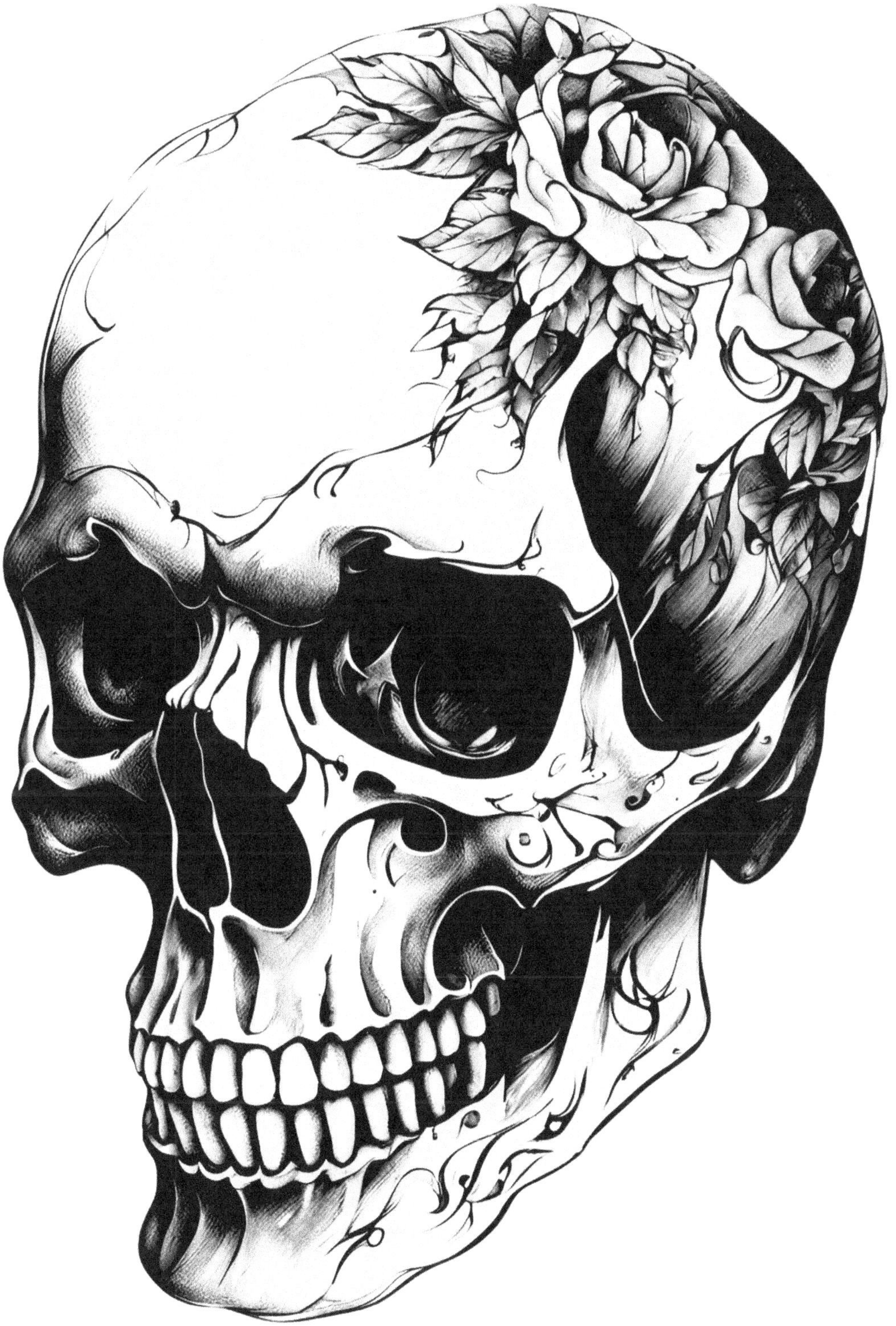

LARGE AND DETAILED SKULL TATTOOS

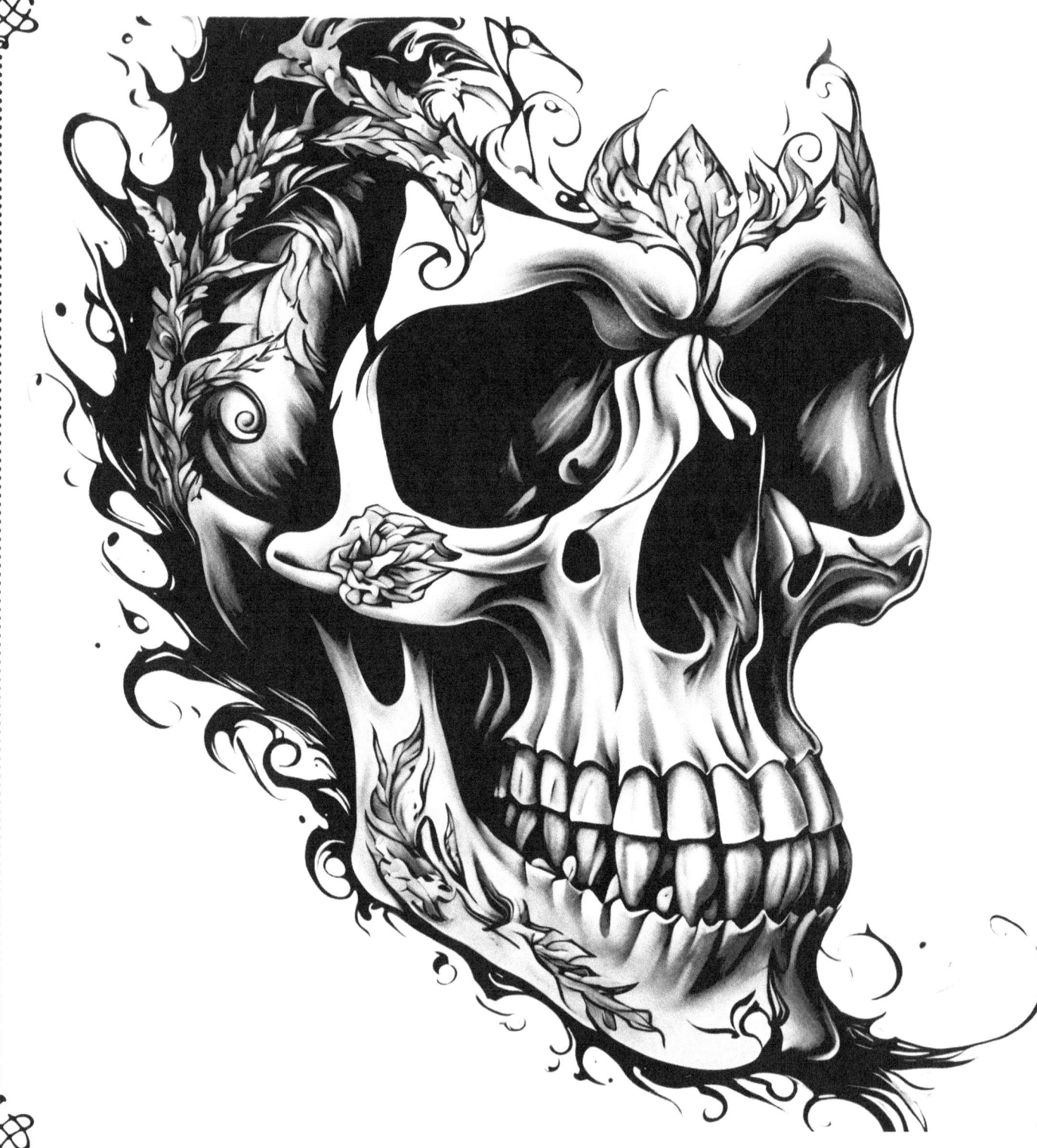

LARGE AND DETAILED SKULL TATTOOS

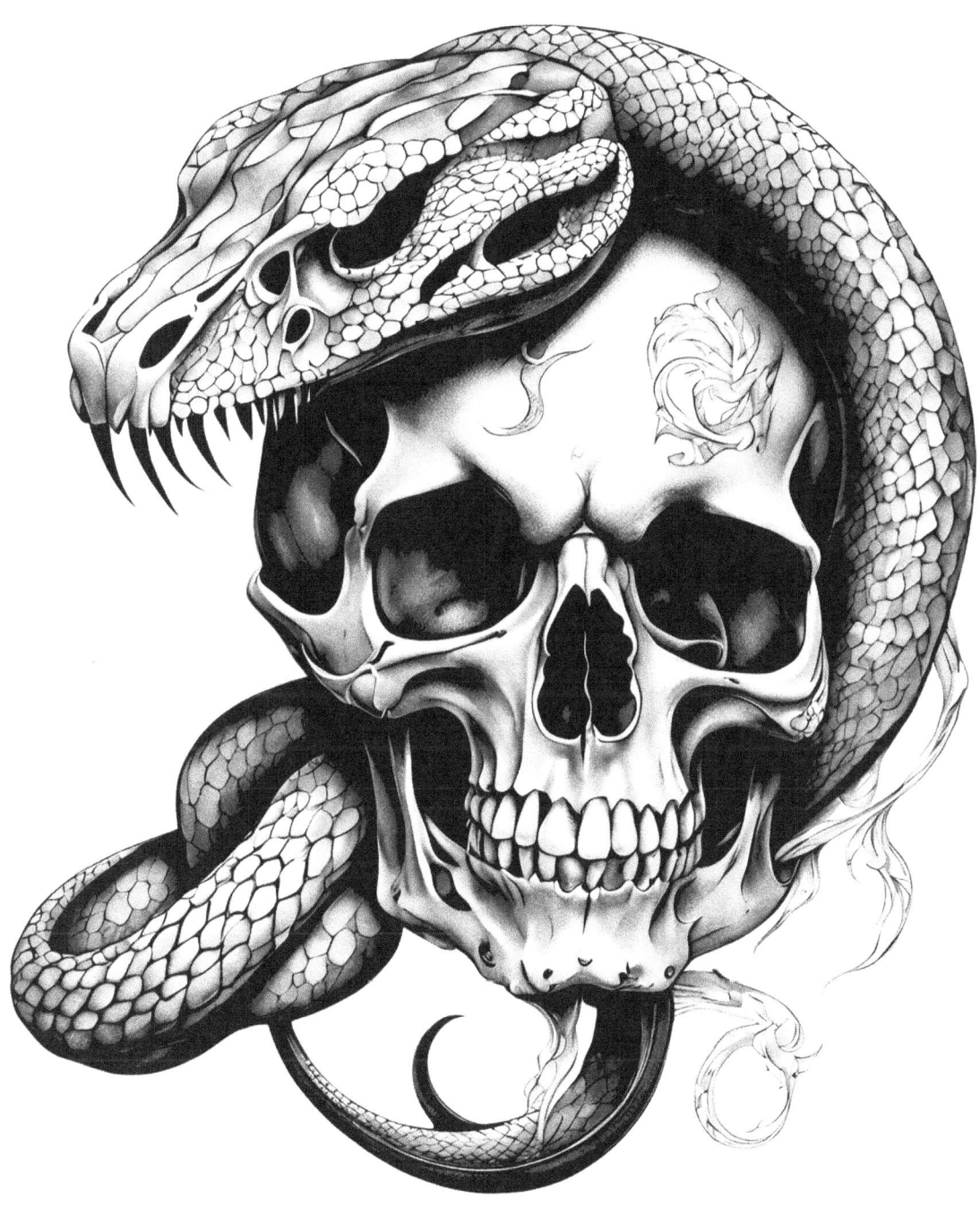

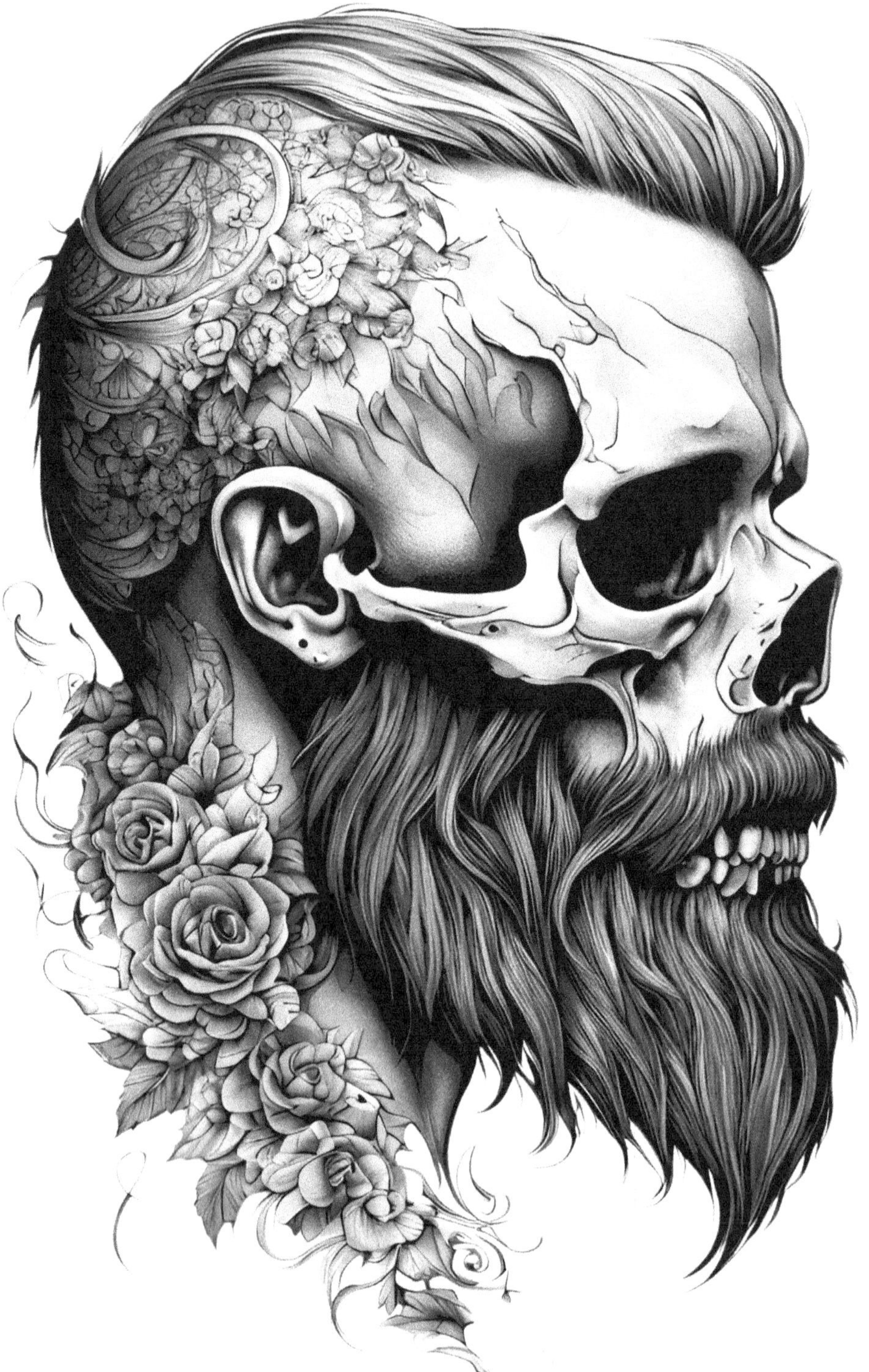

LARGE AND DETAILED SKULL TATTOOS

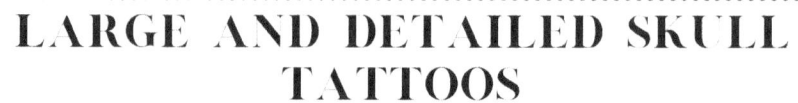

LARGE AND DETAILED SKULL TATTOOS

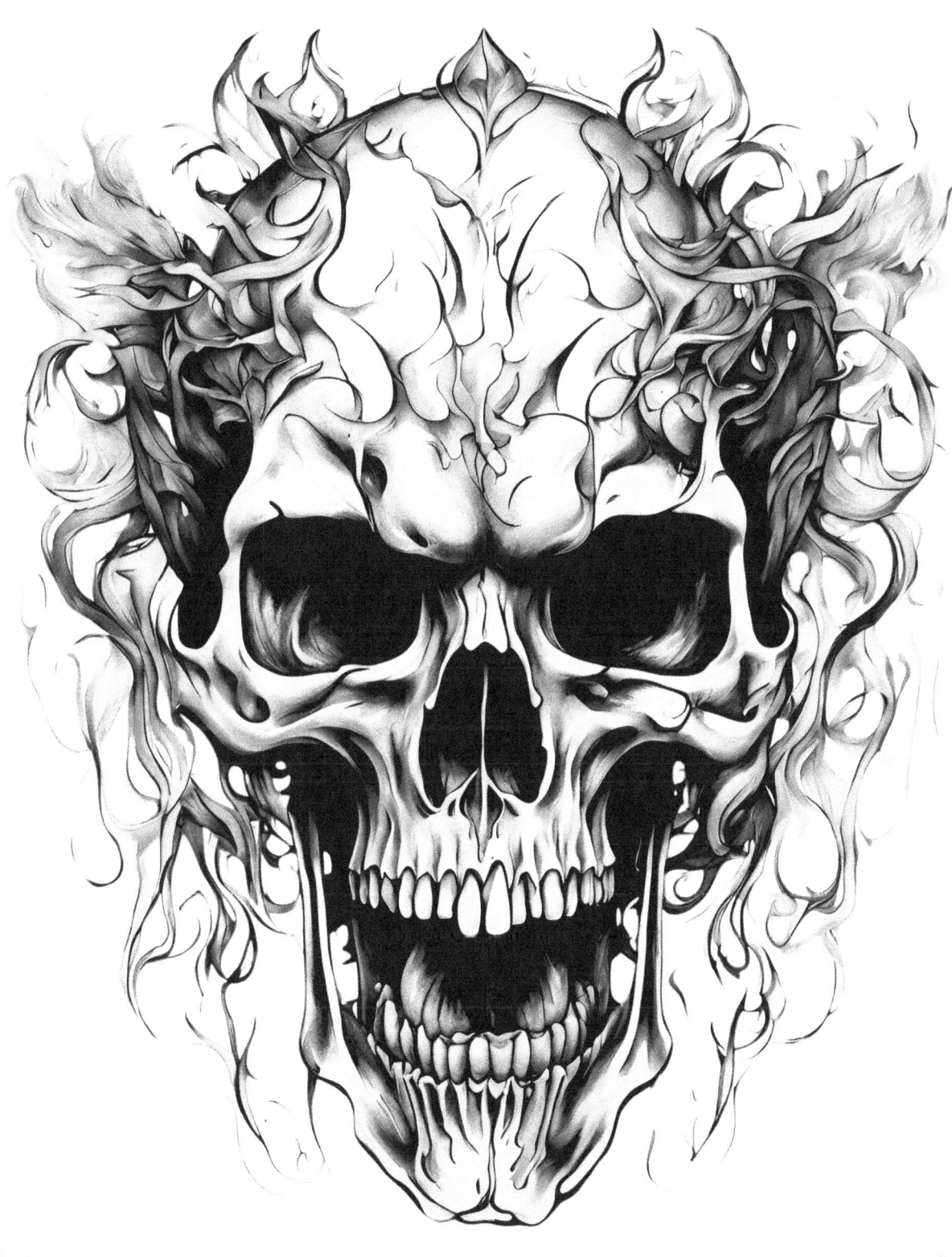

LARGE AND DETAILED SKULL TATTOOS

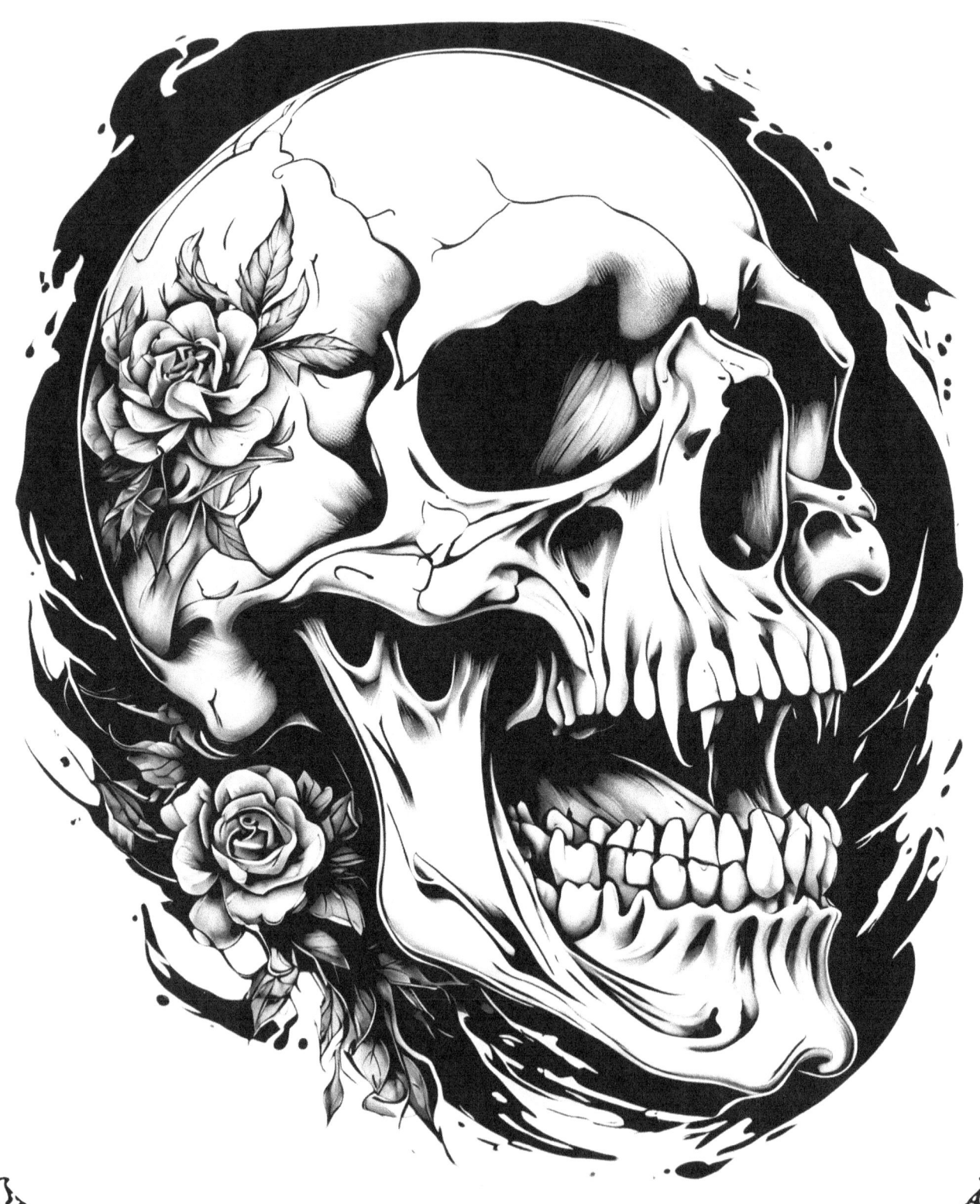

LARGE AND DETAILED SKULL TATTOOS

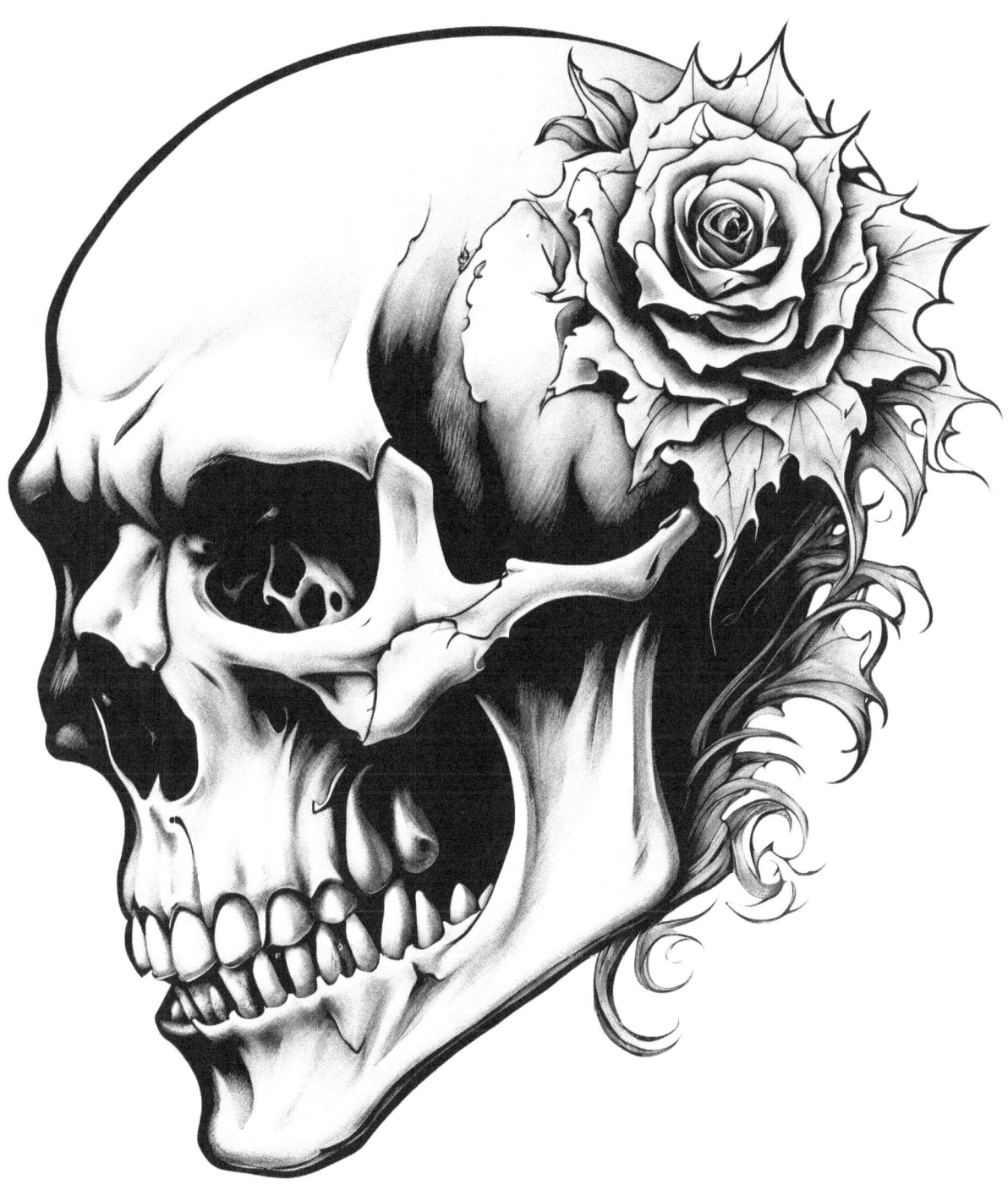

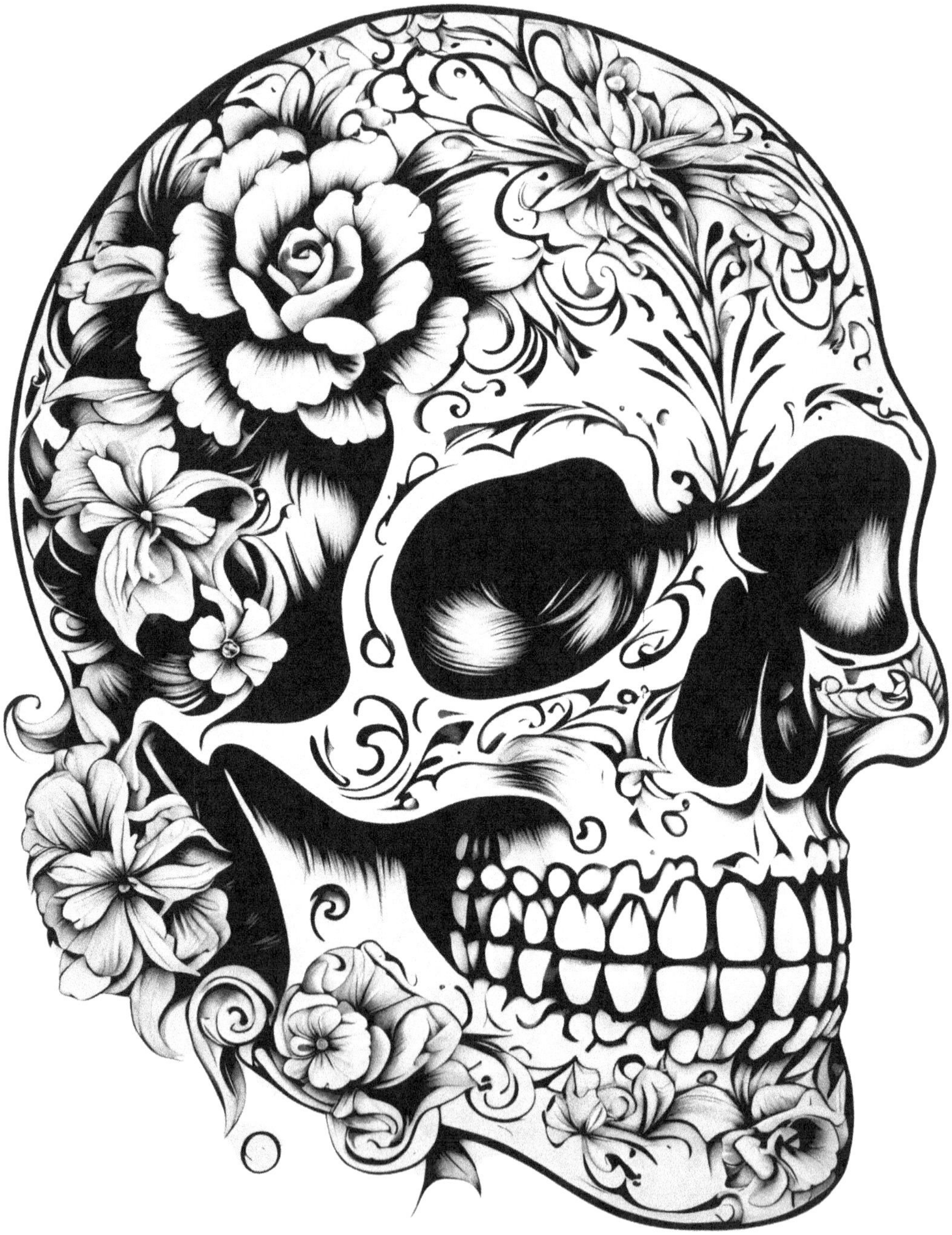

LARGE AND DETAILED SKULL TATTOOS

LARGE AND DETAILED SKULL TATTOOS

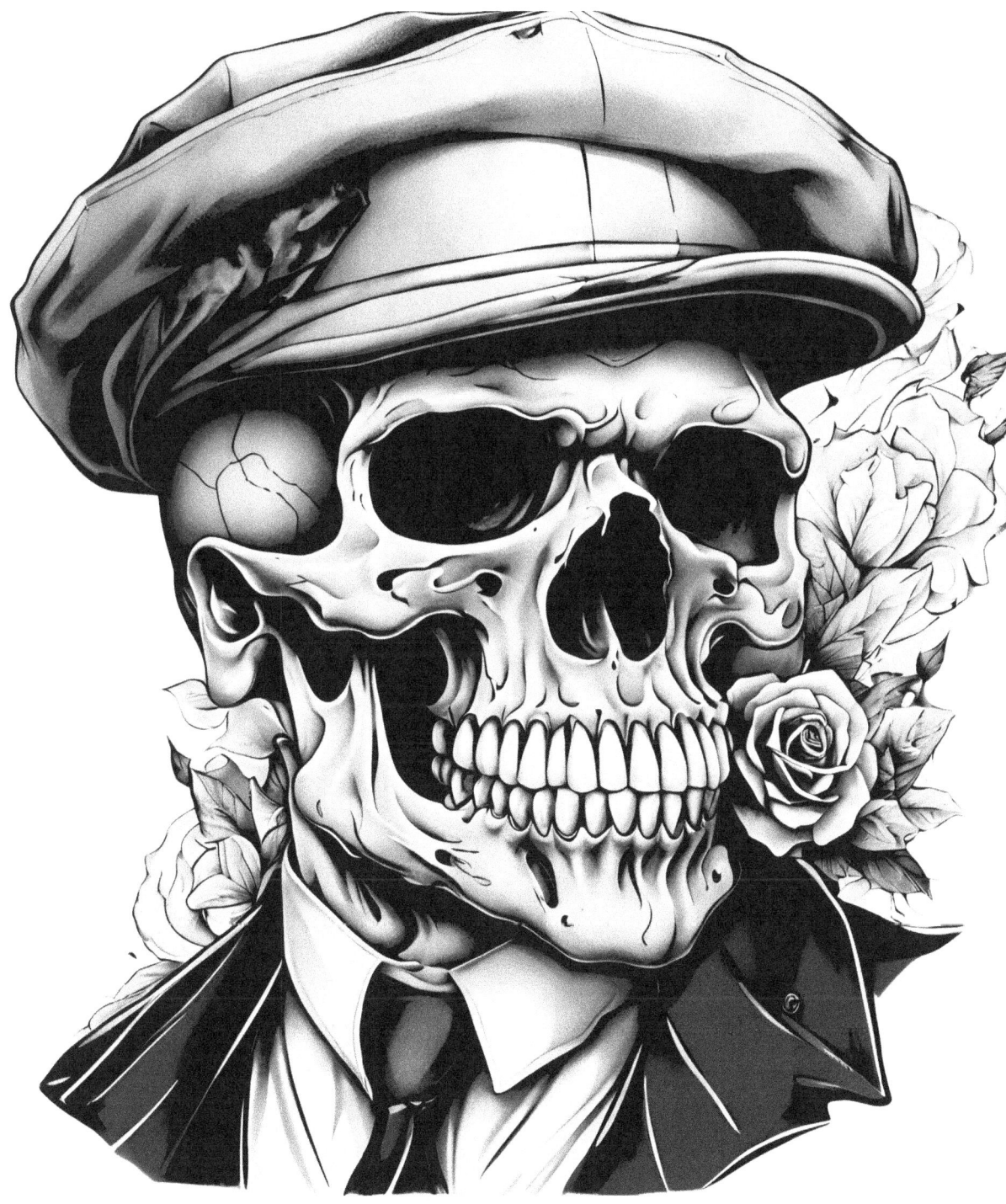

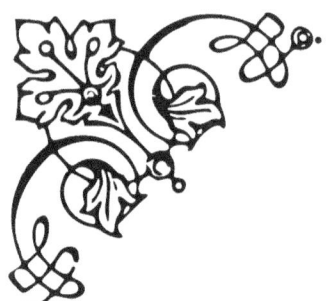
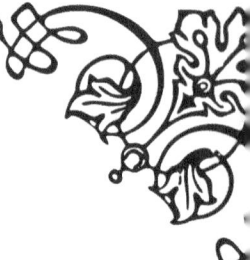

TRADITIONAL SKULL TATTOOS

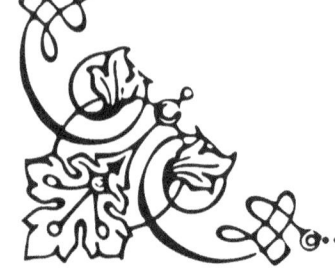
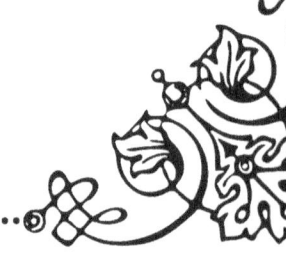

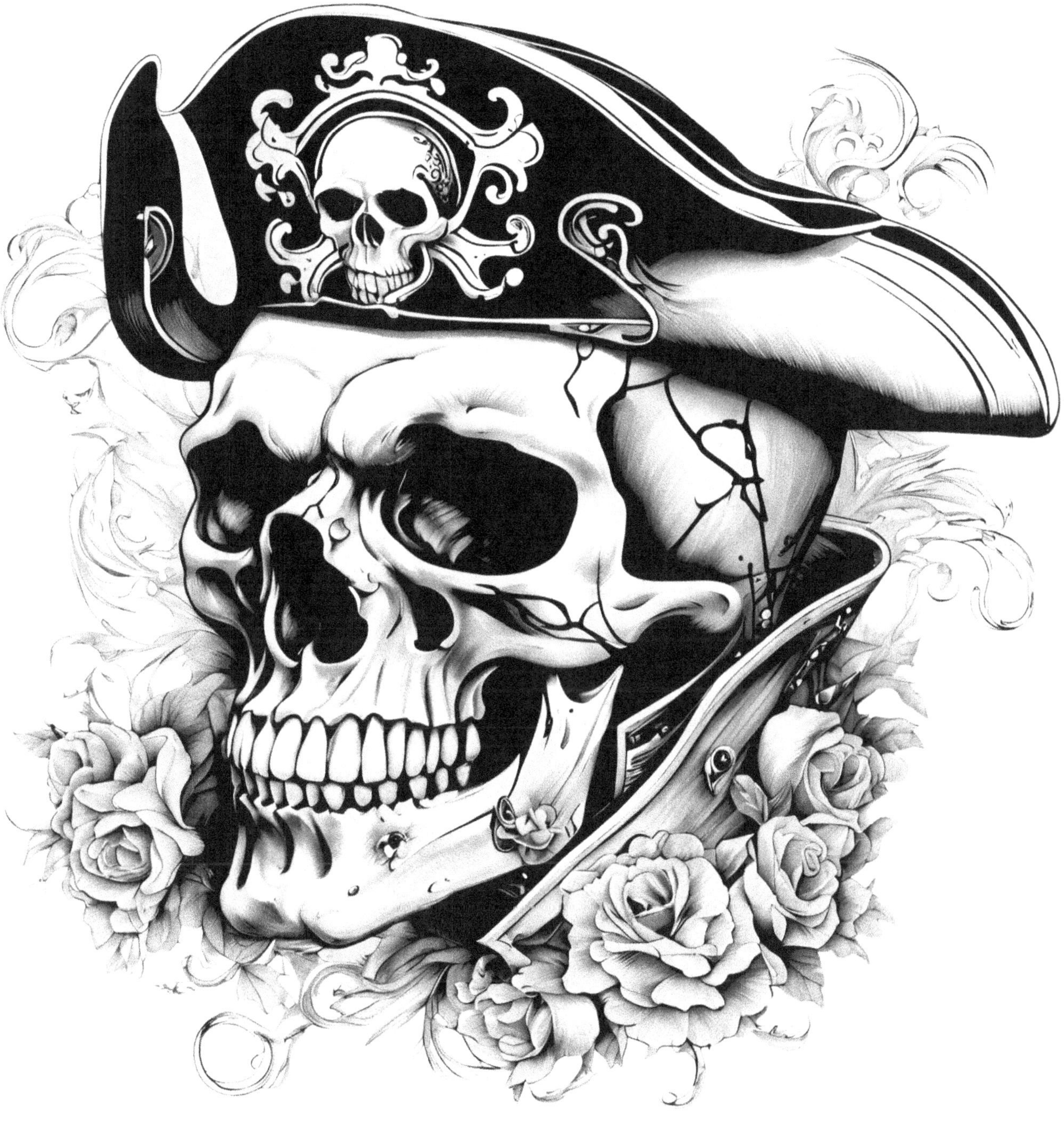

TRADITIONAL SKULL TATTOOS

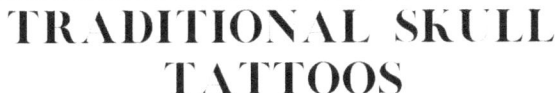

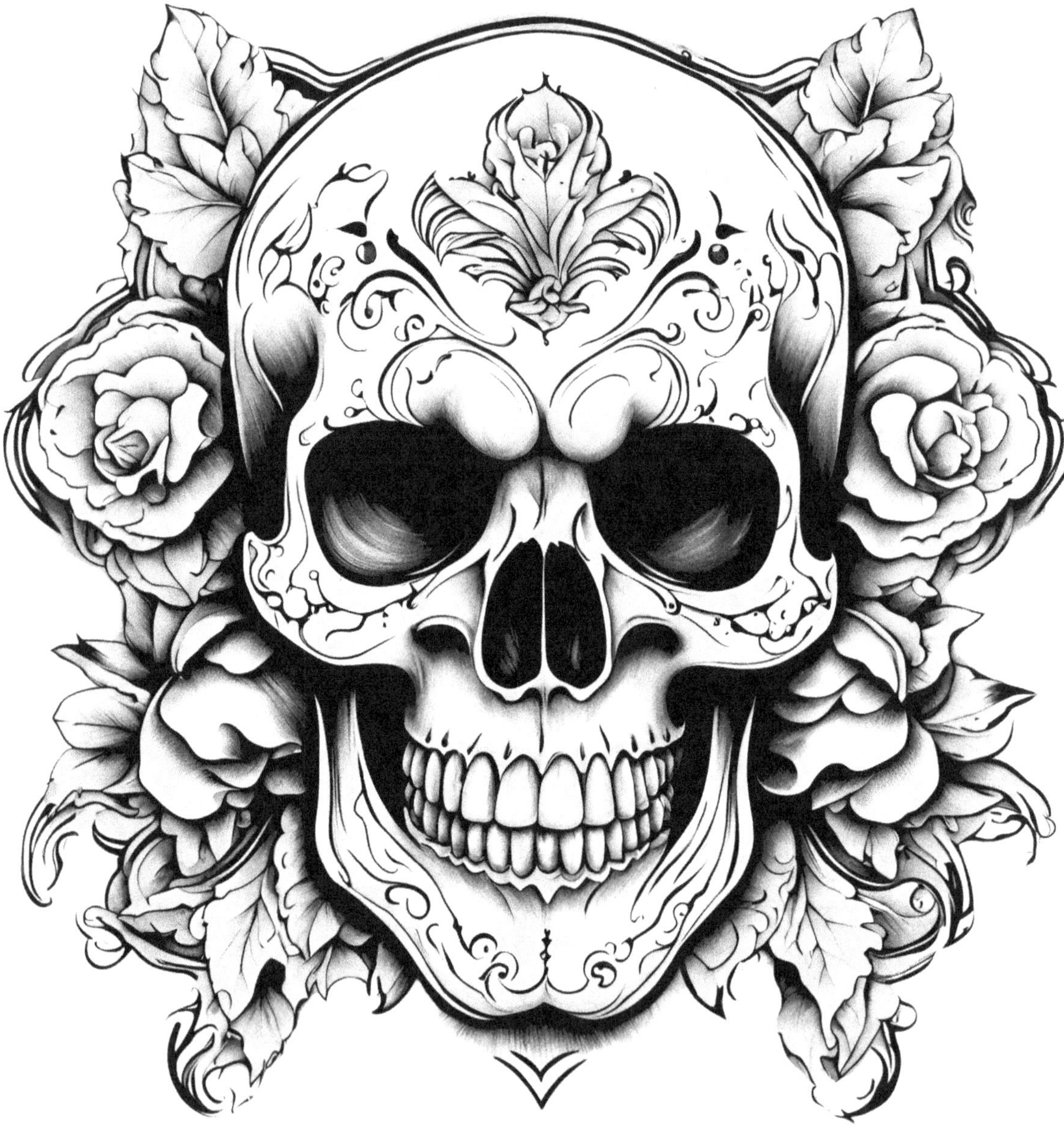

TRADITIONAL SKULL TATTOOS

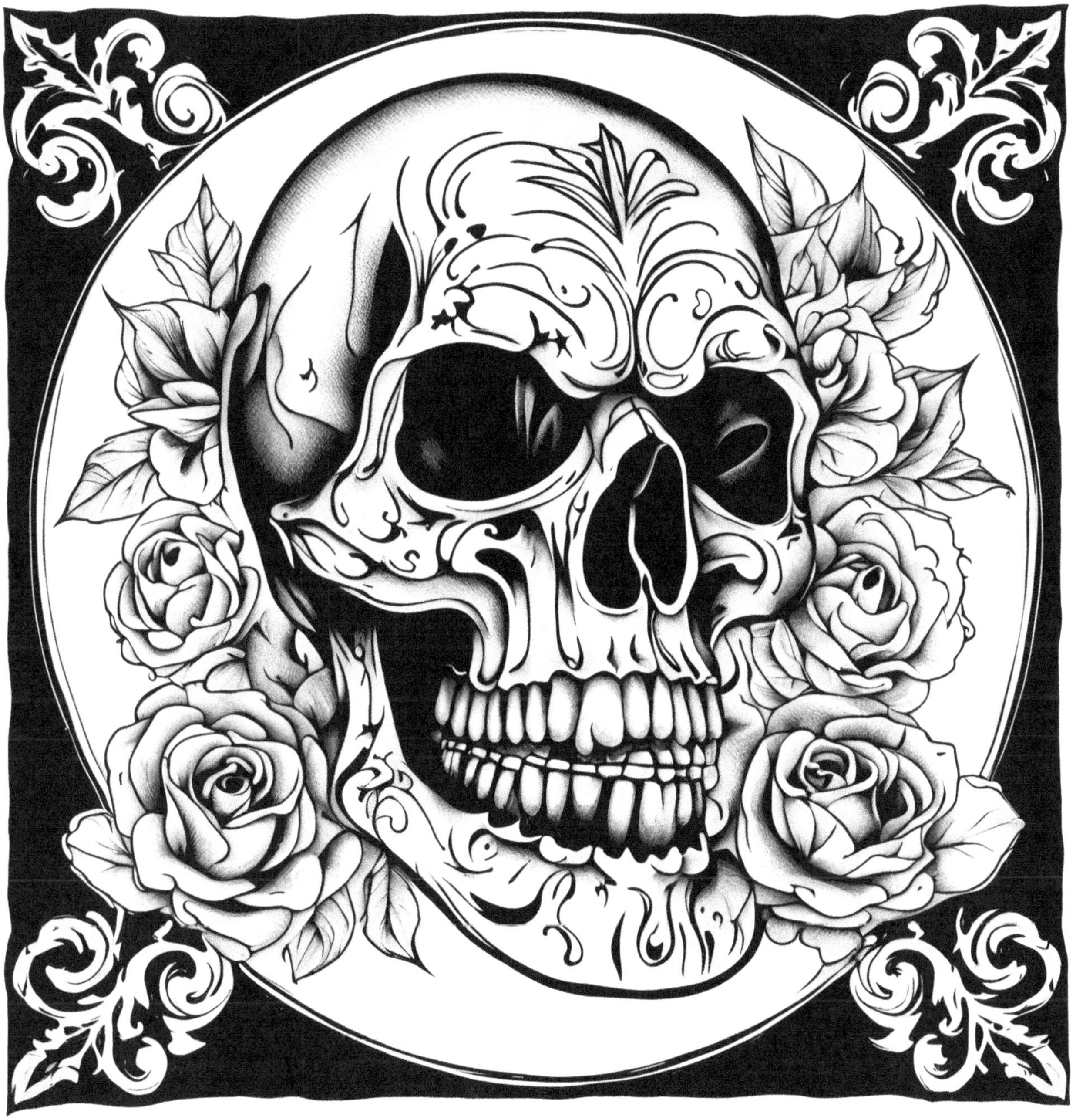

TRADITIONAL SKULL TATTOOS

TRADITIONAL SKULL TATTOOS

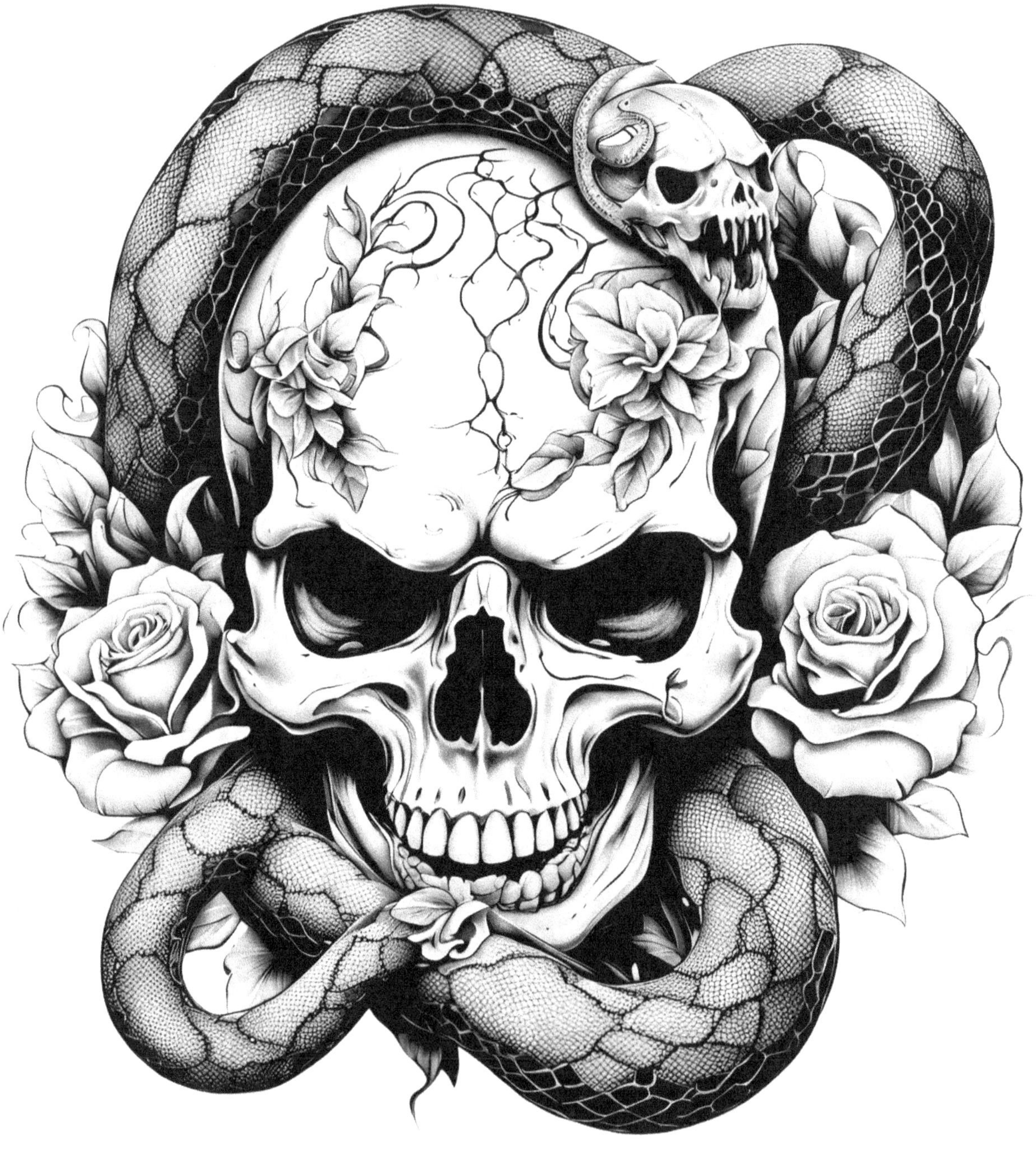

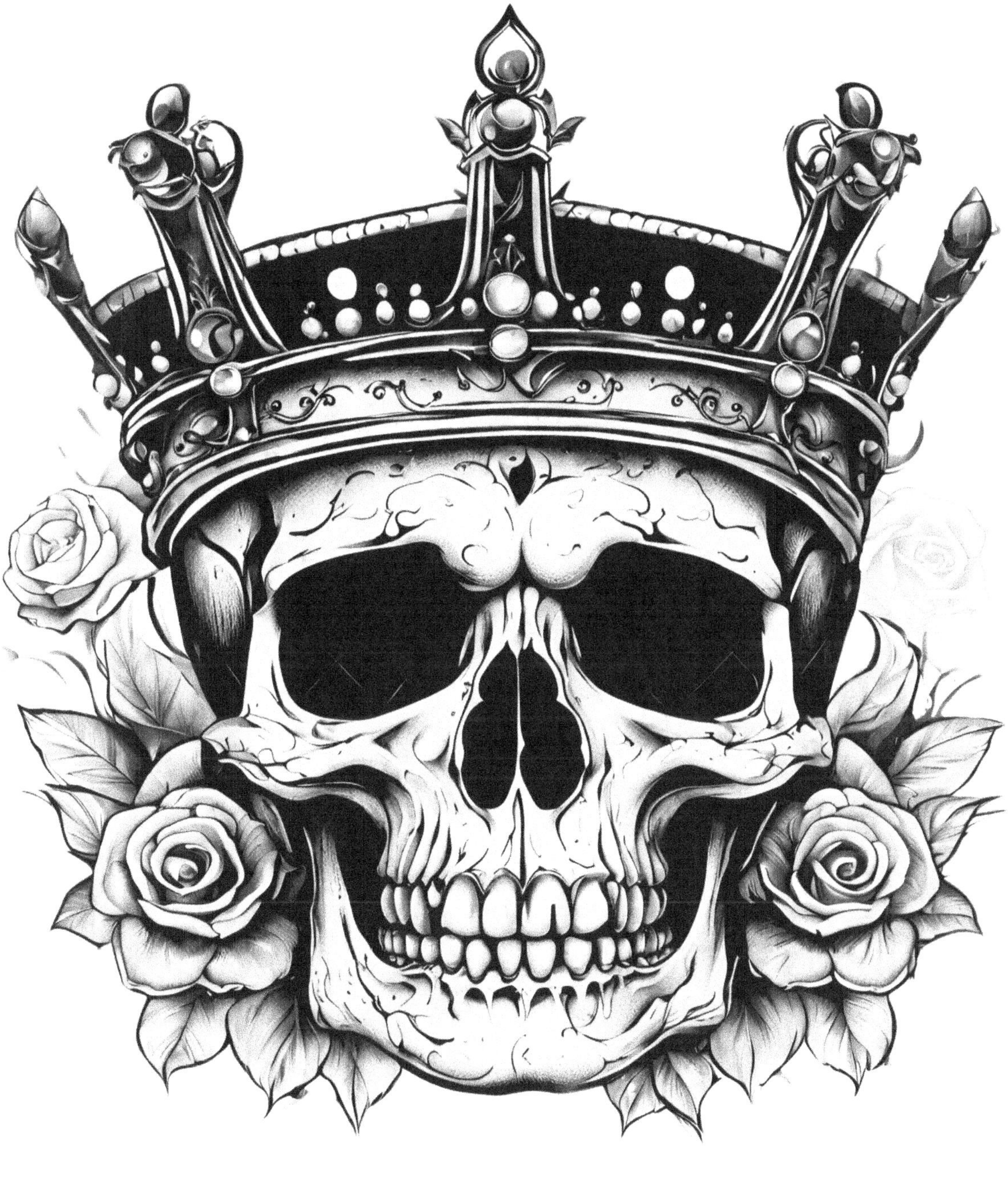

TRADITIONAL SKULL TATTOOS

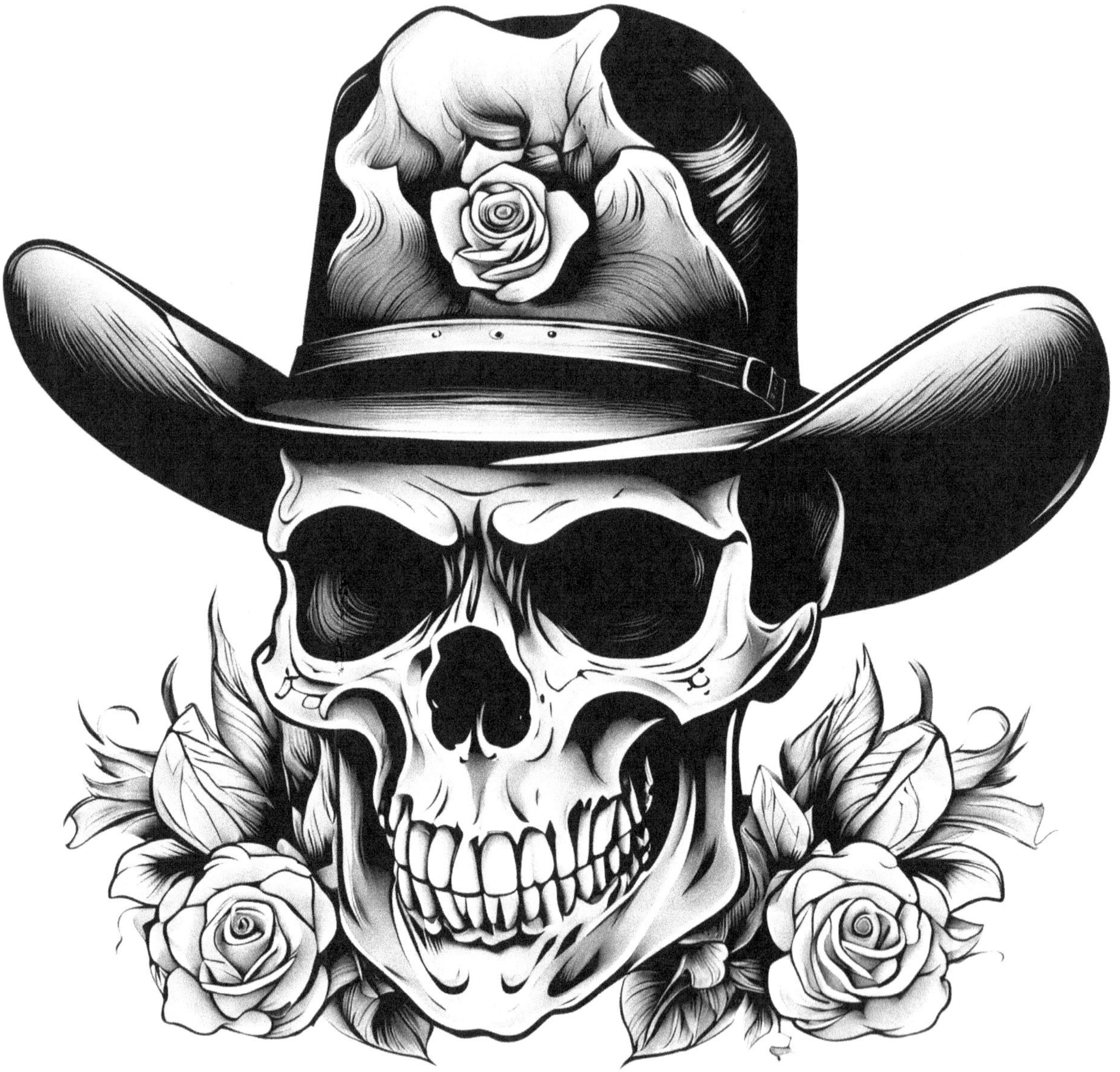

TRADITIONAL SKULL TATTOOS

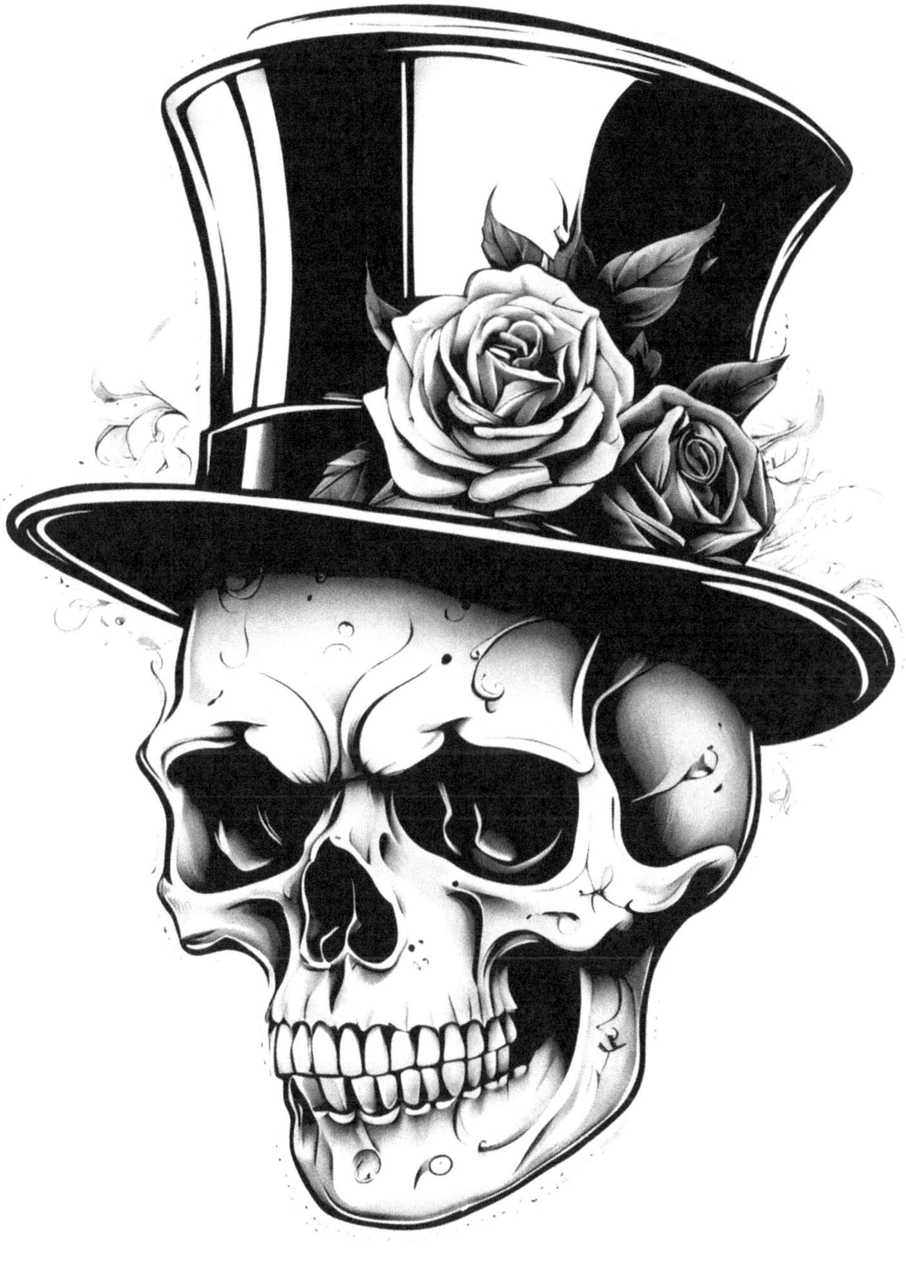

TRADITIONAL SKULL TATTOOS

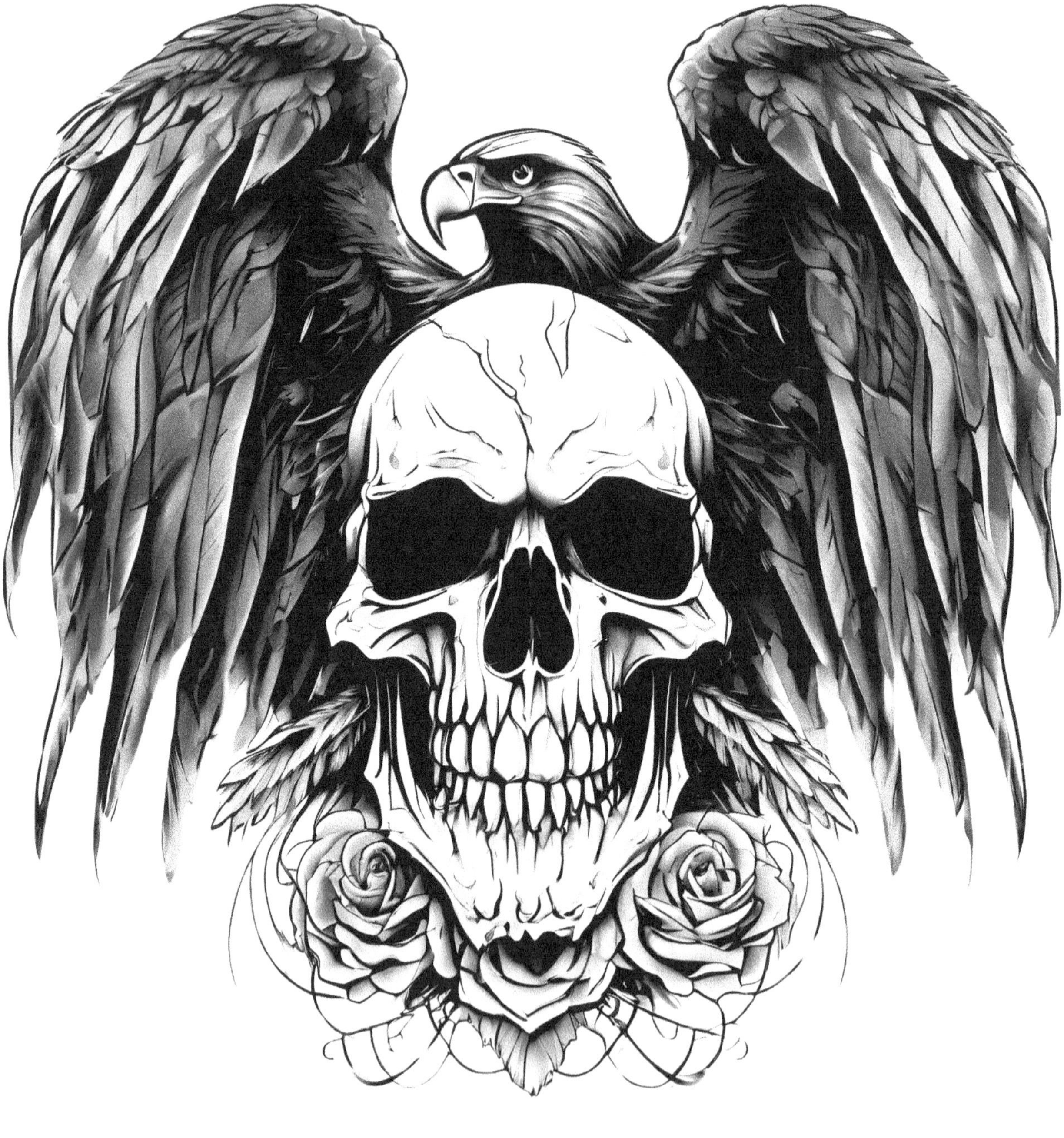

TRADITIONAL SKULL TATTOOS

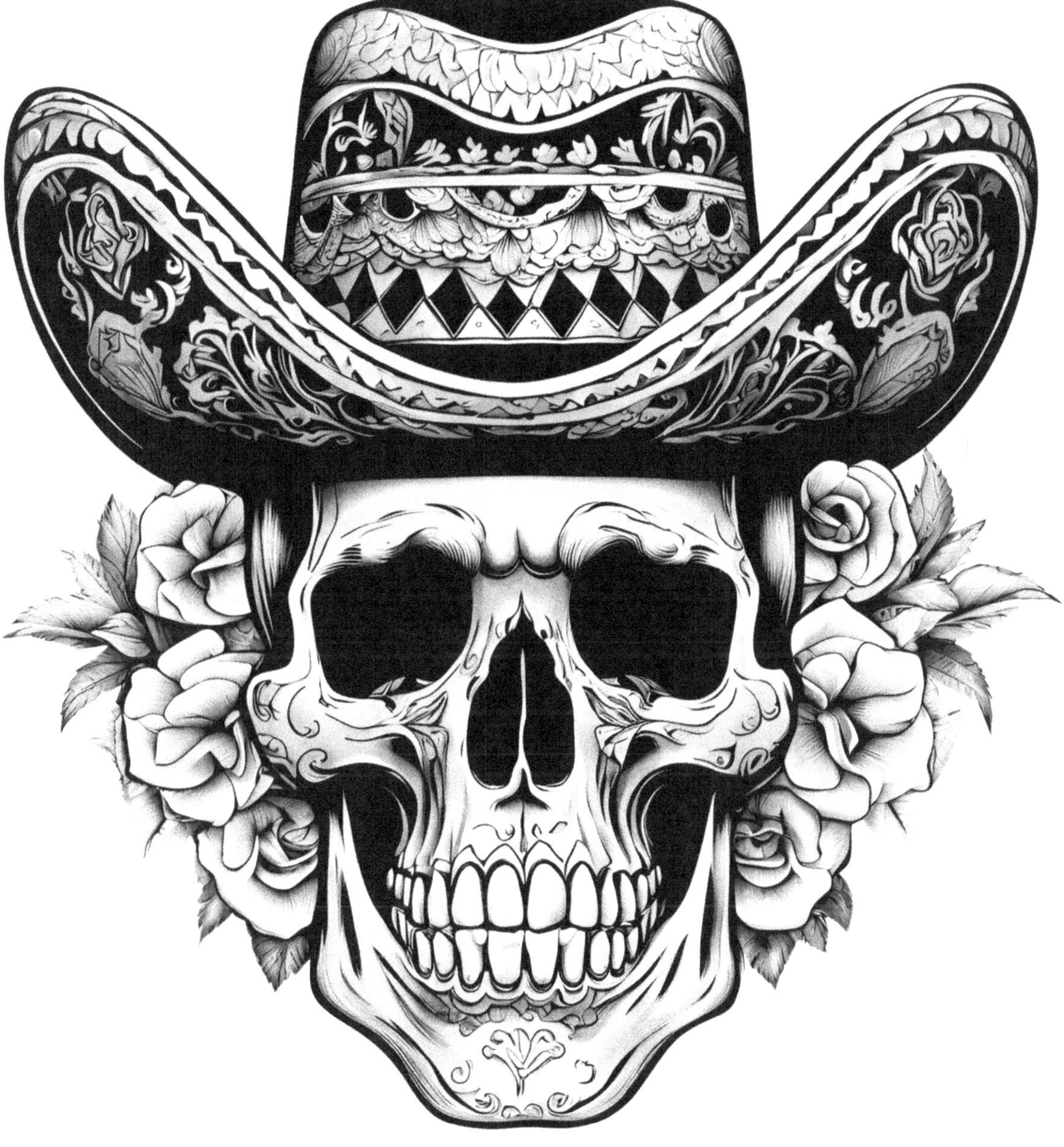

TRADITIONAL SKULL TATTOOS

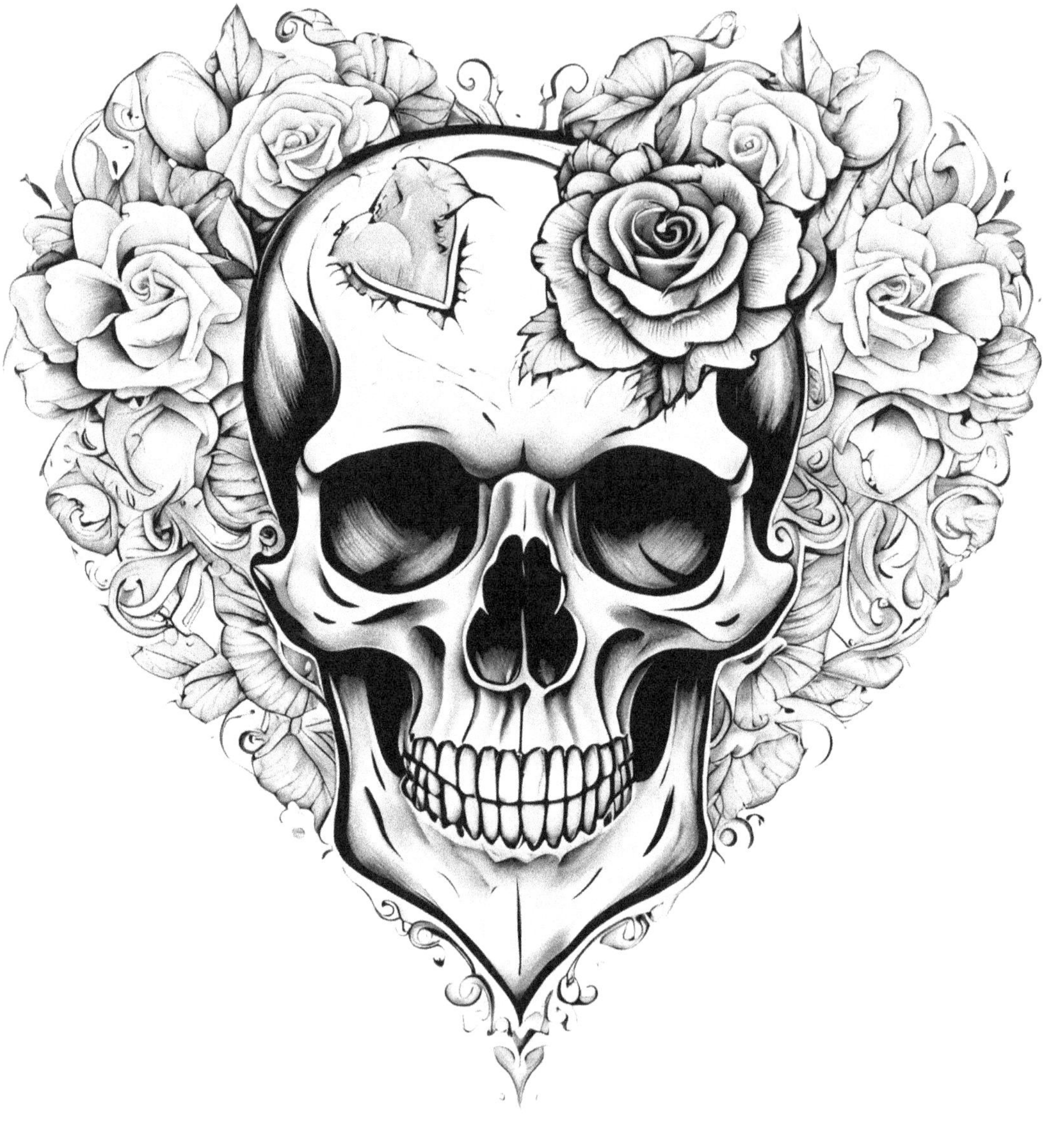

TRADITIONAL SKULL TATTOOS

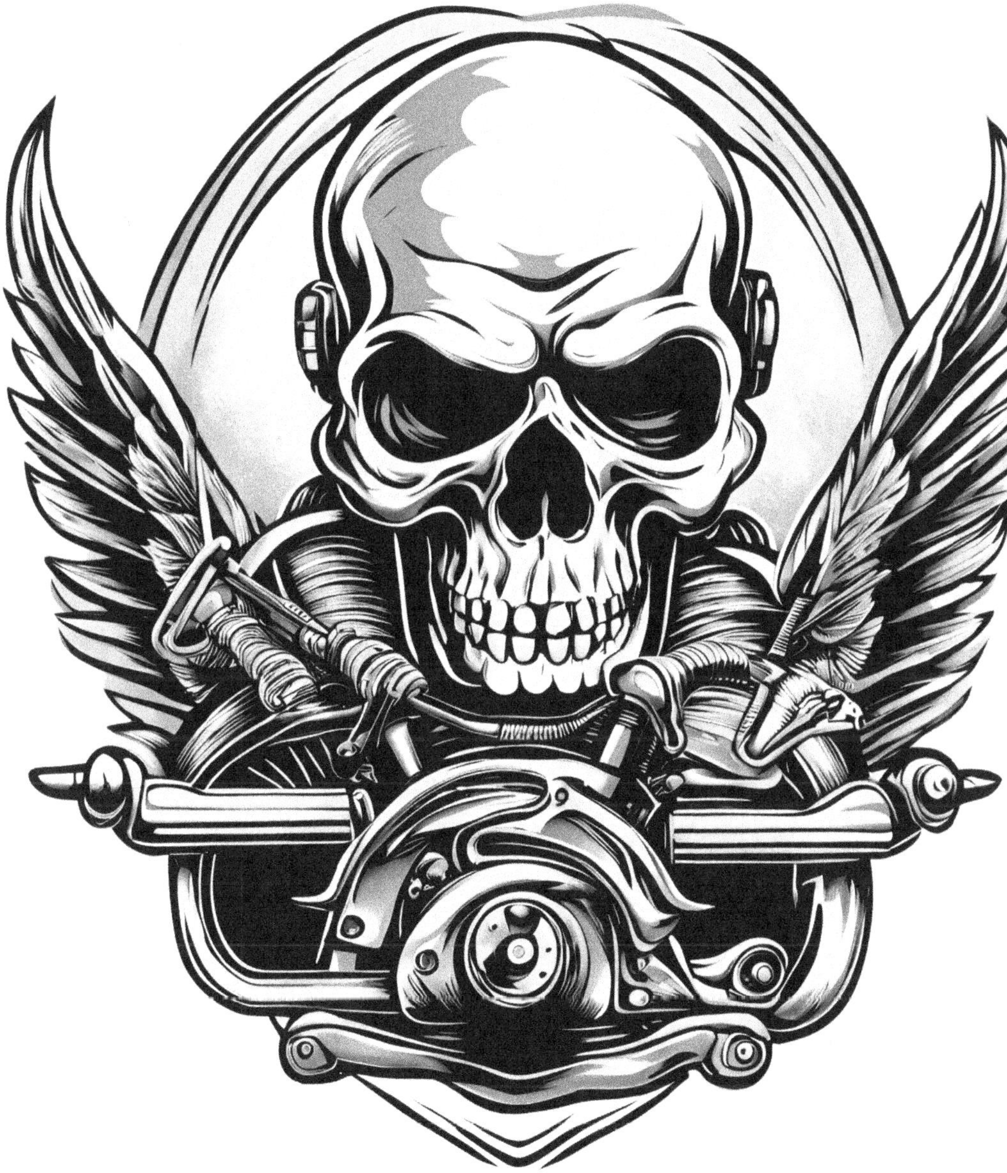

TRADITIONAL SKULL TATTOOS

TRADITIONAL SKULL TATTOOS

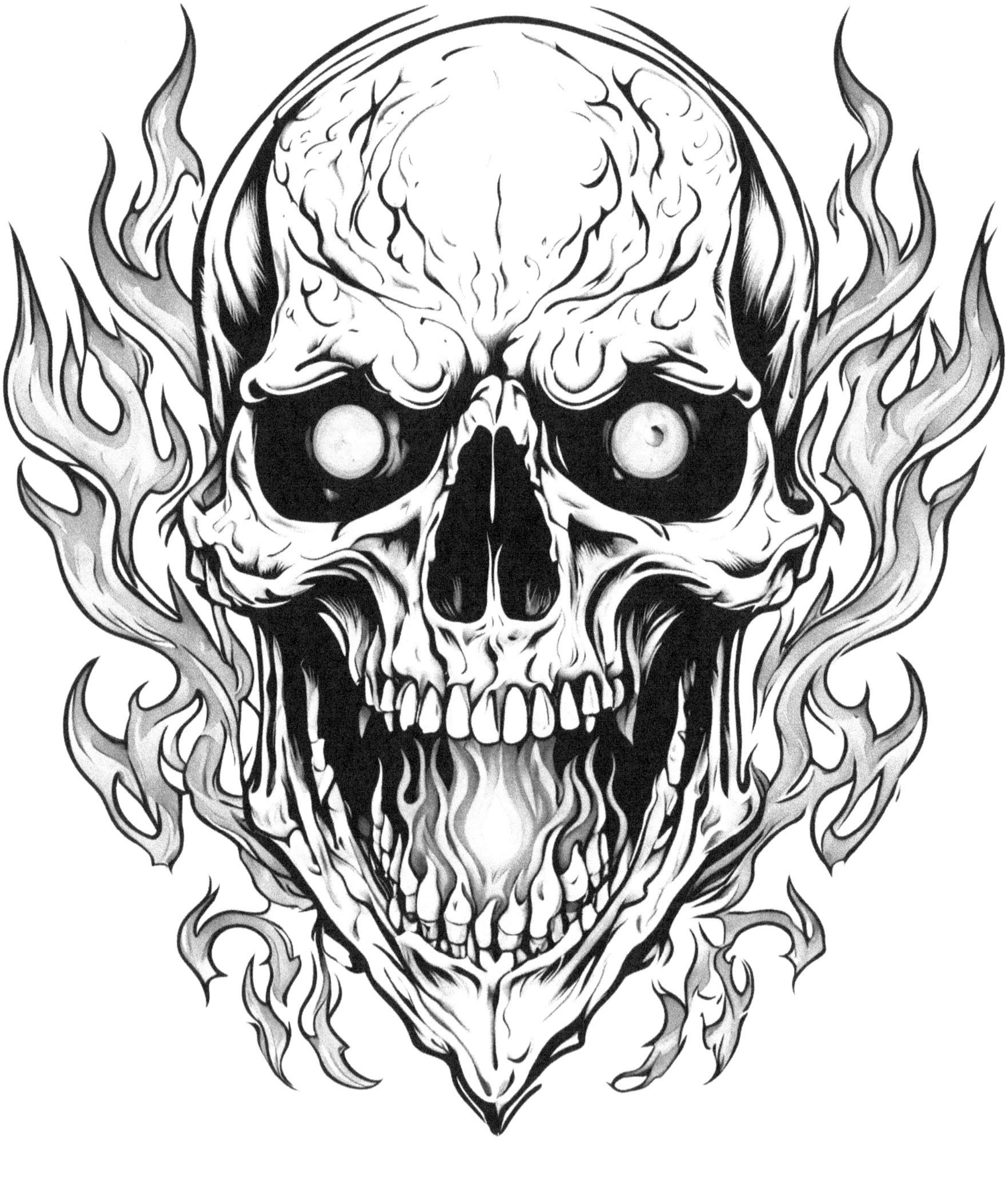

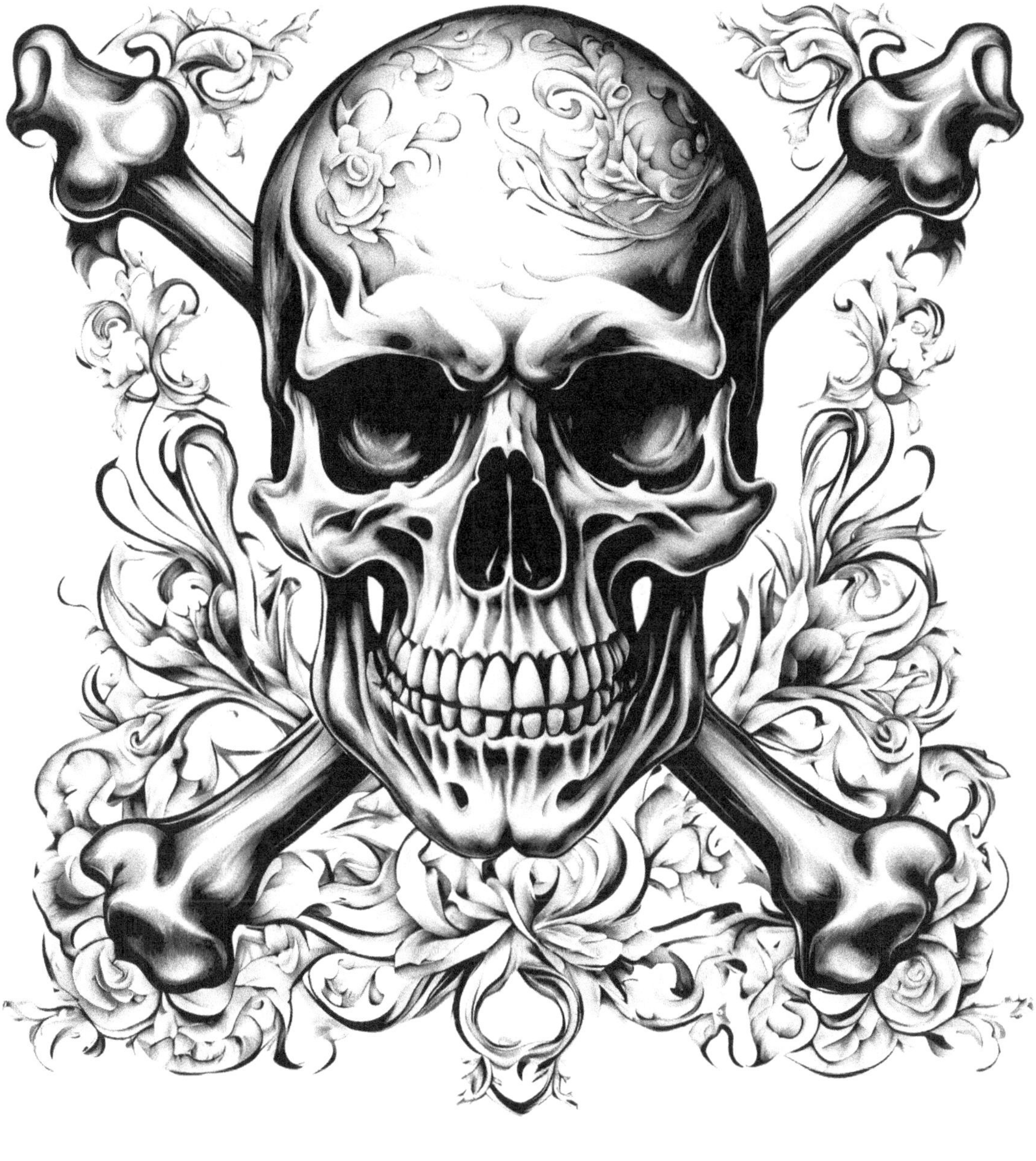

TRADITIONAL SKULL TATTOOS

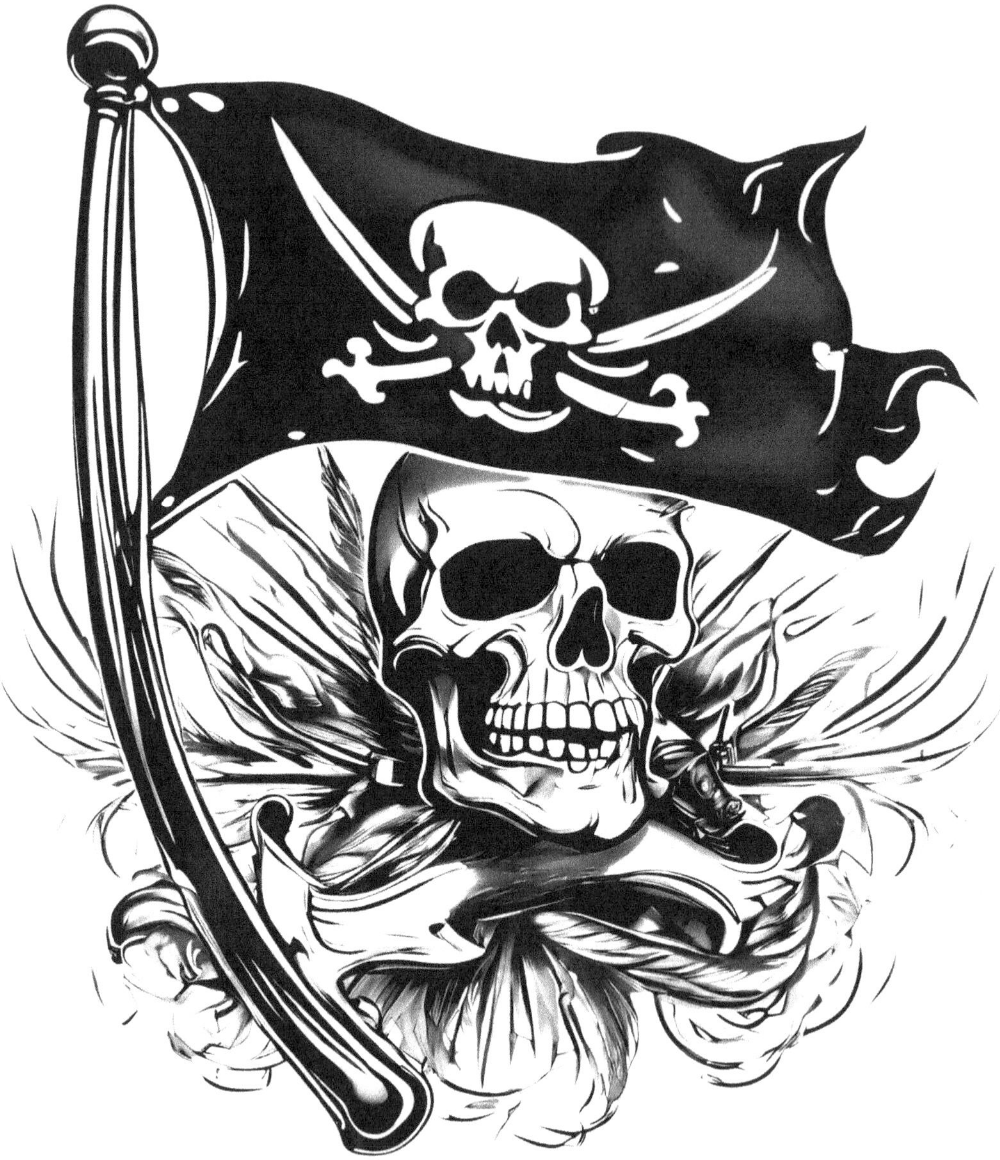

TRADITIONAL SKULL TATTOOS

SCARY SKULL TATTOOS

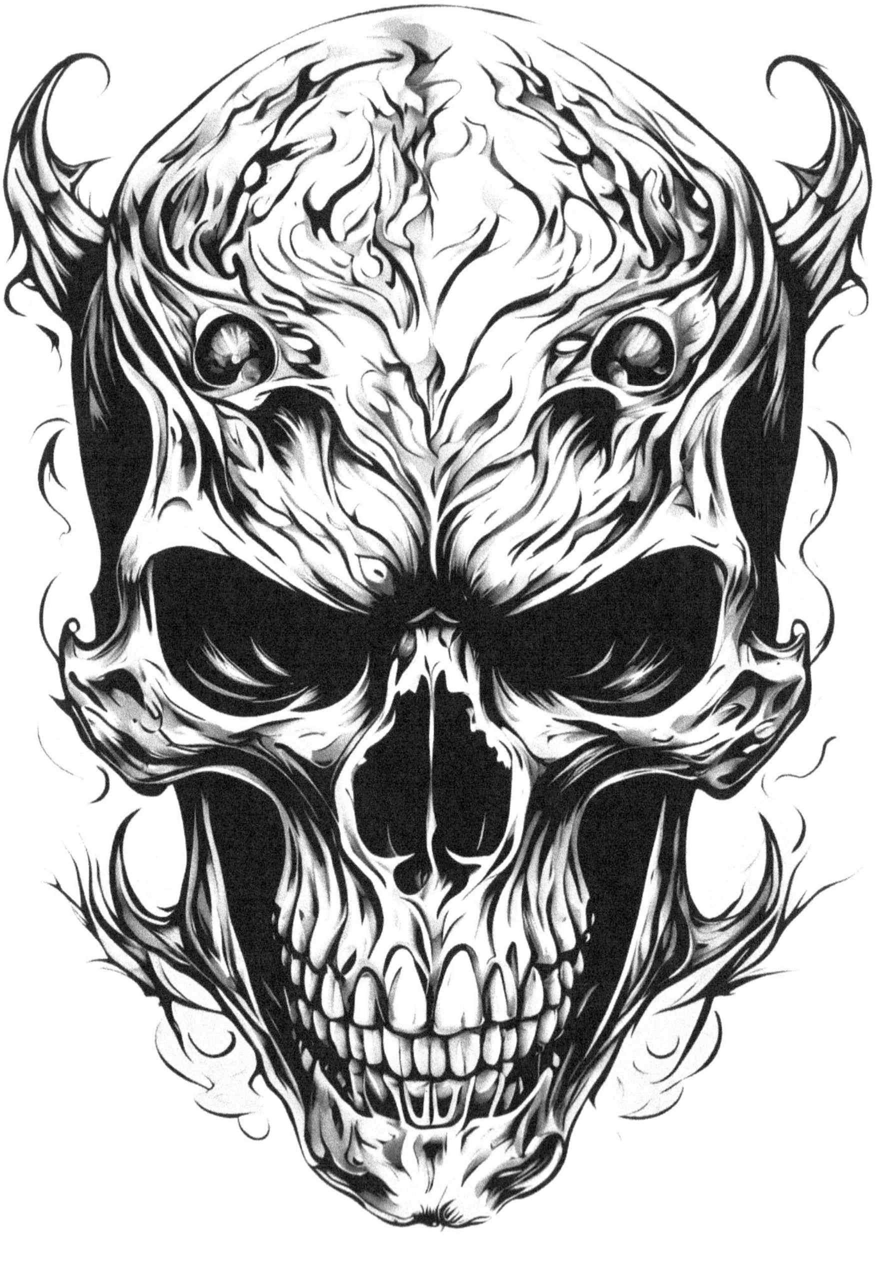

SCARY SKULL TATTOOS

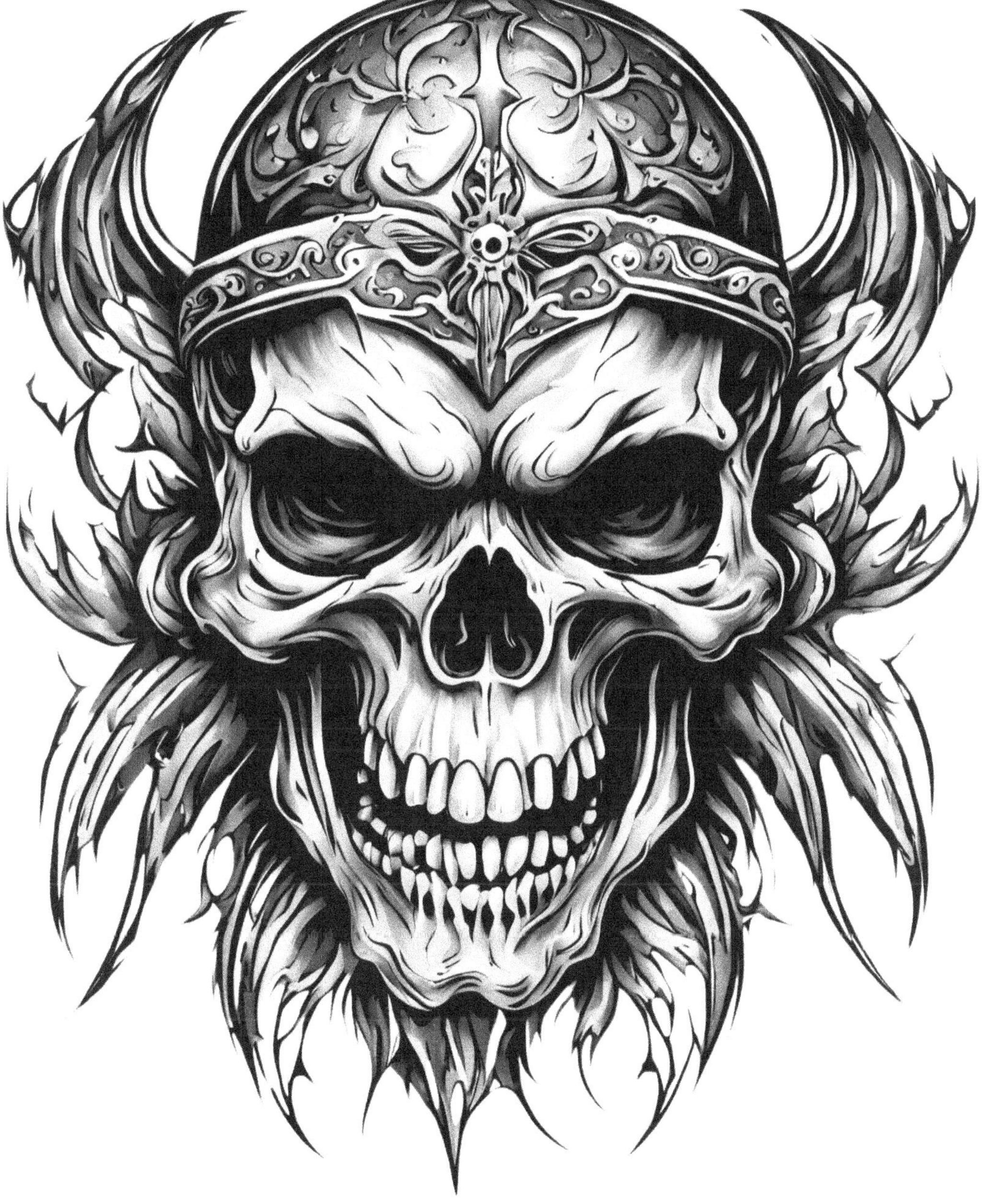

SCARY SKULL TATTOOS

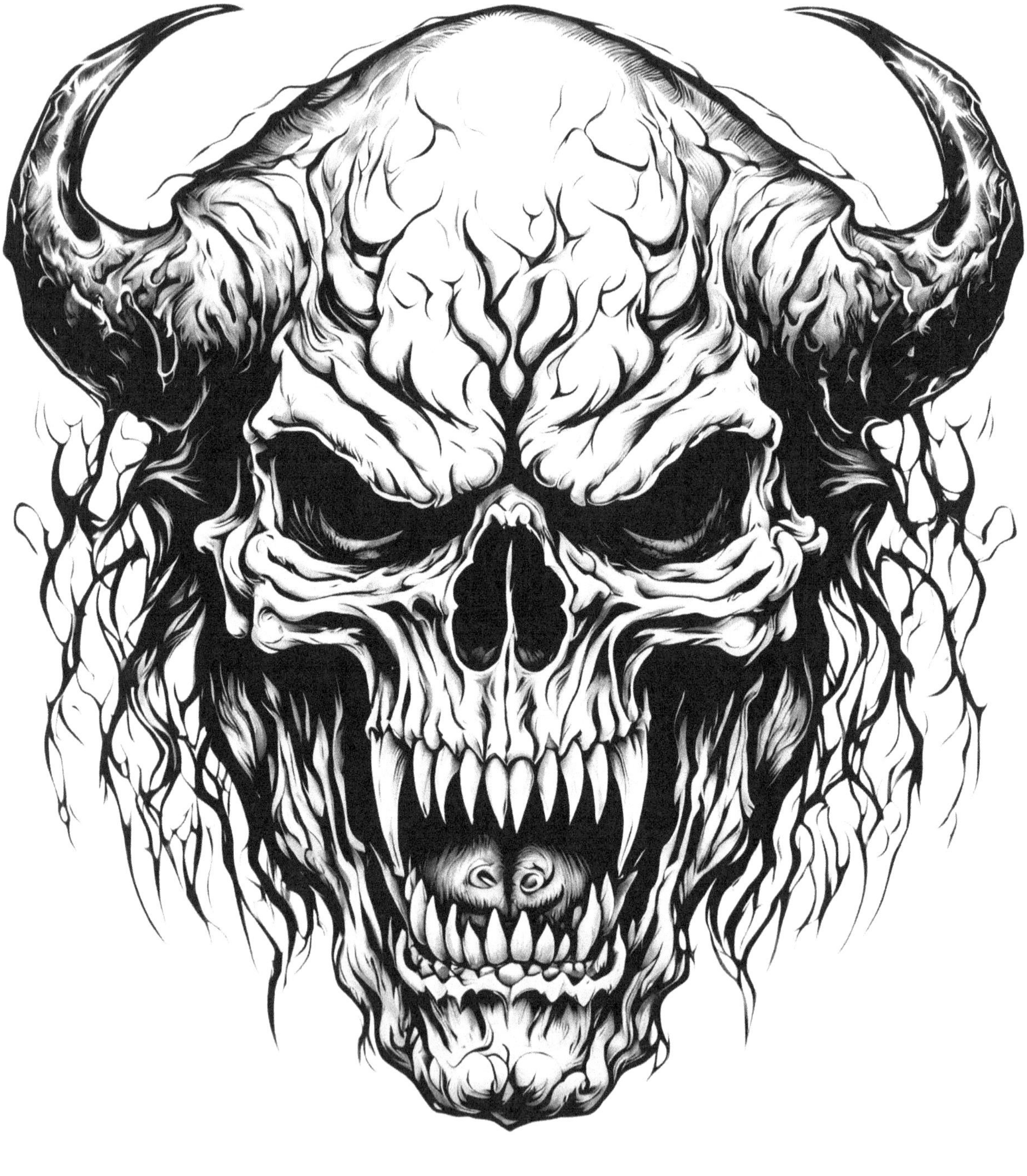

SCARY SKULL TATTOOS

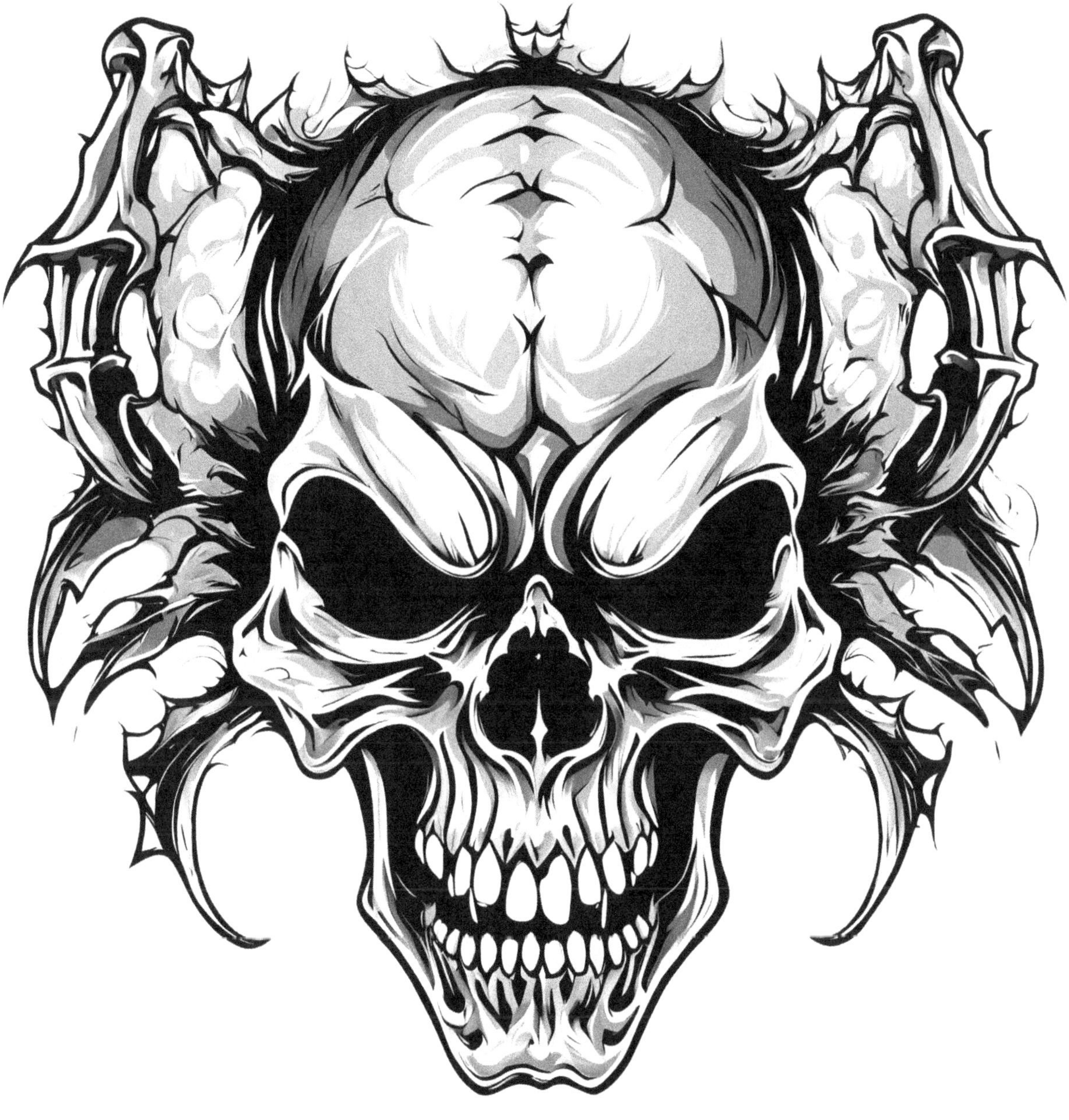

SCARY SKULL TATTOOS

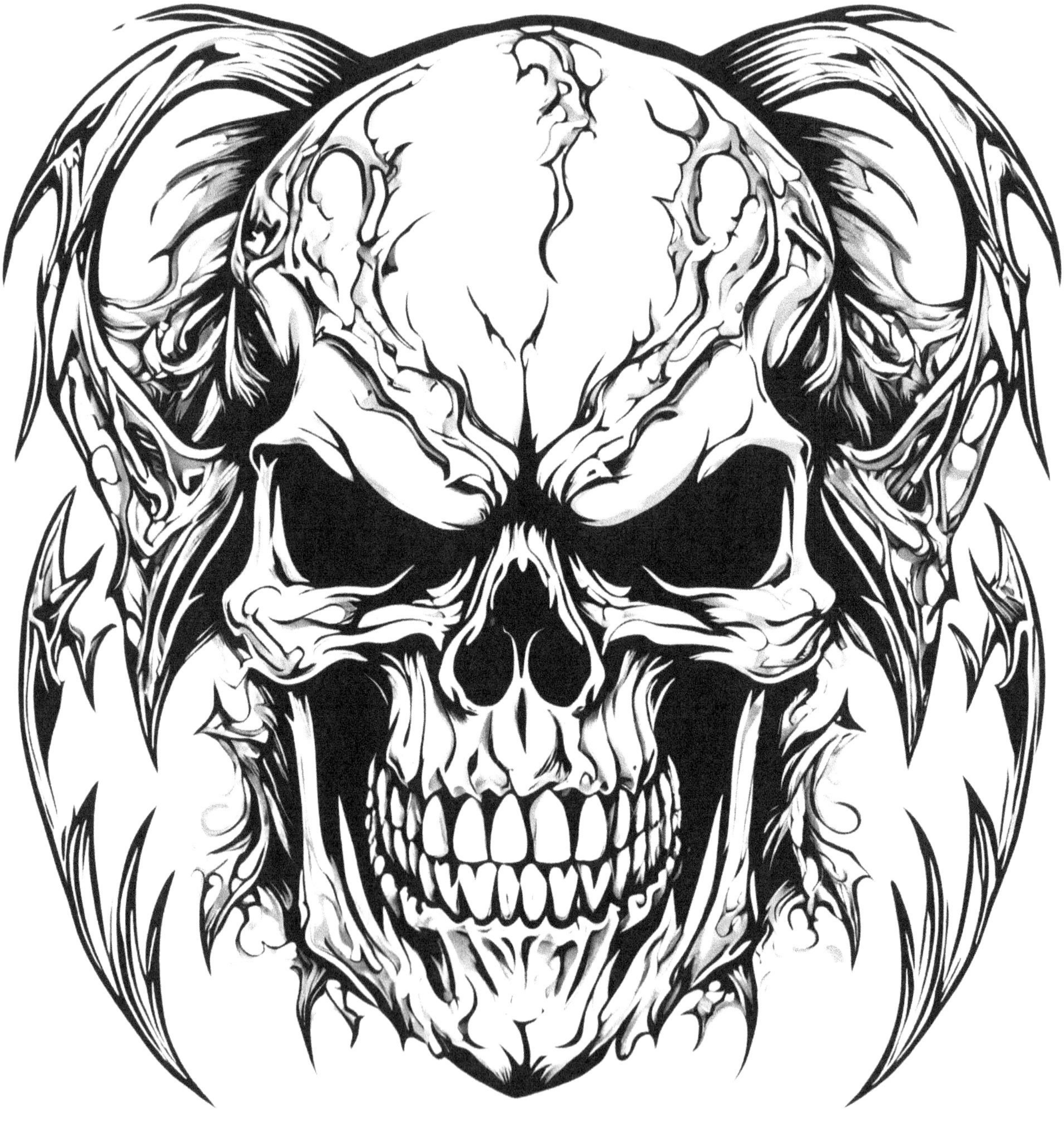

SCARY SKULL TATTOOS

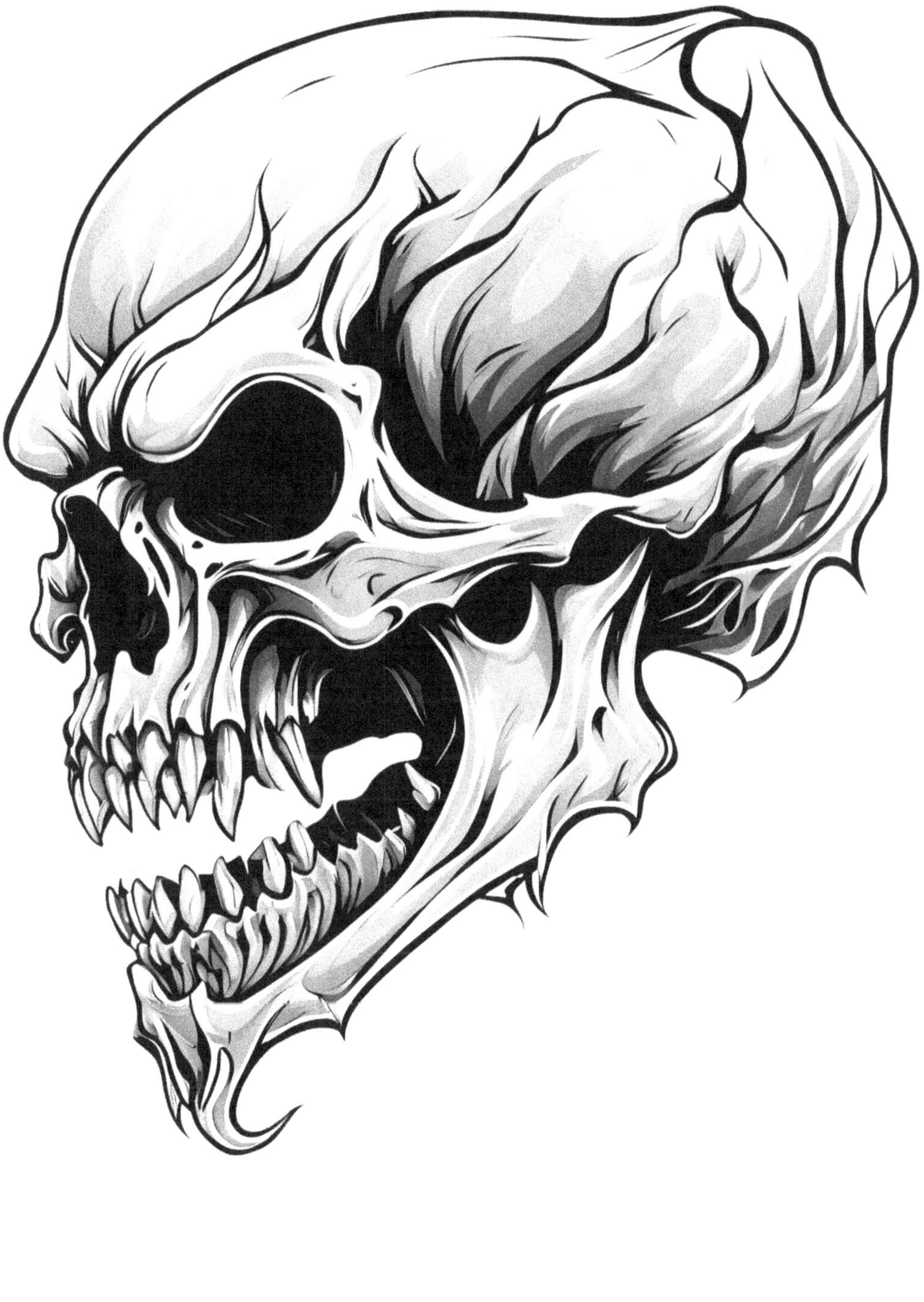

SCARY SKULL TATTOOS

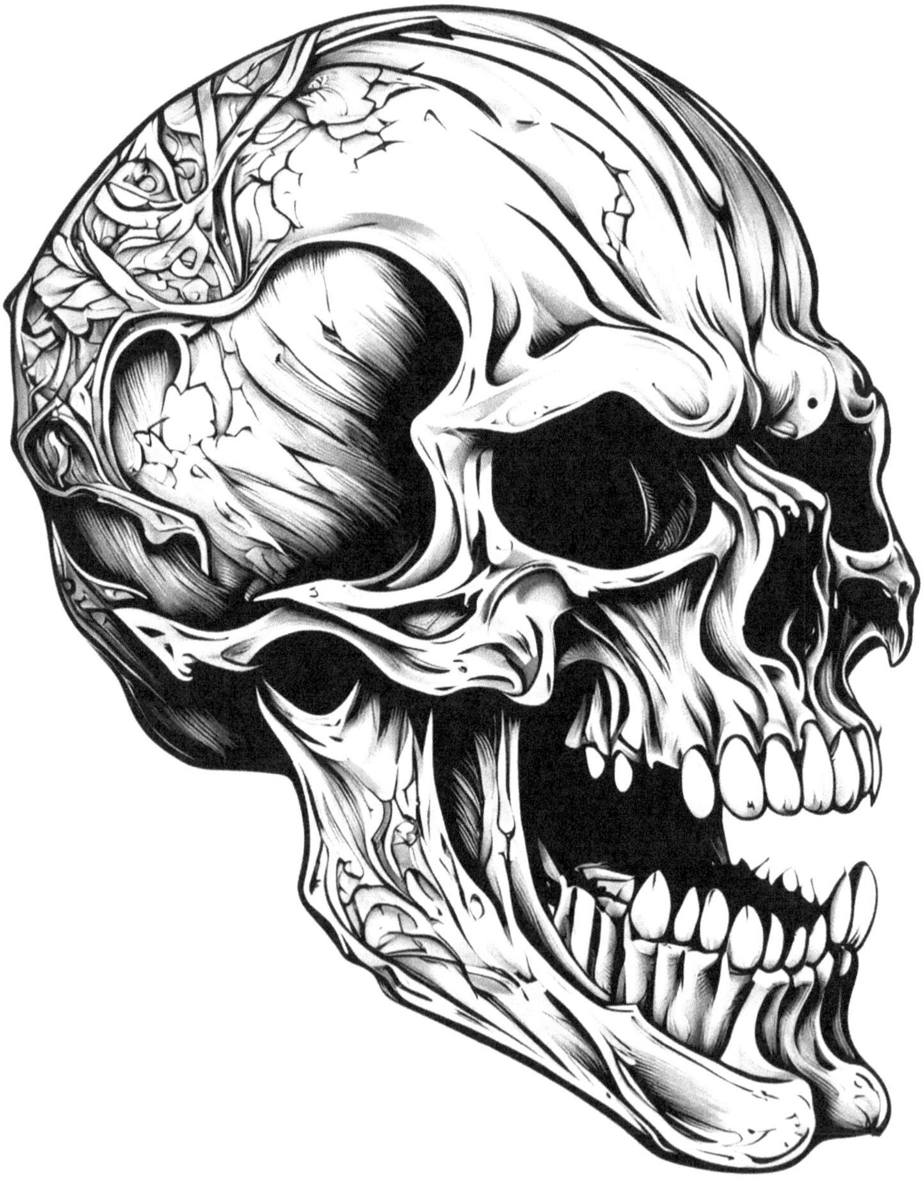

SCARY SKULL TATTOOS

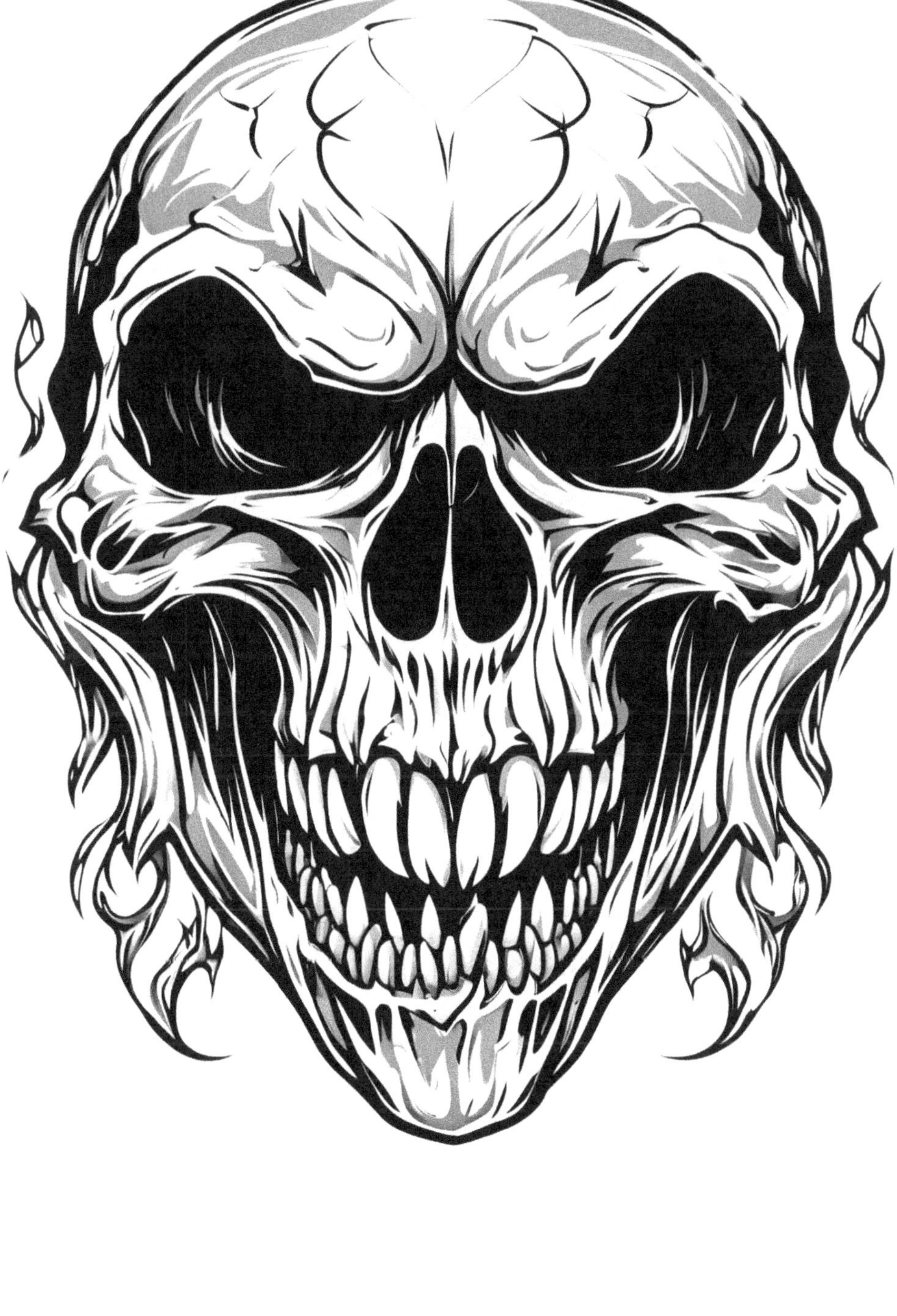

SCARY SKULL TATTOOS

SCARY SKULL TATTOOS

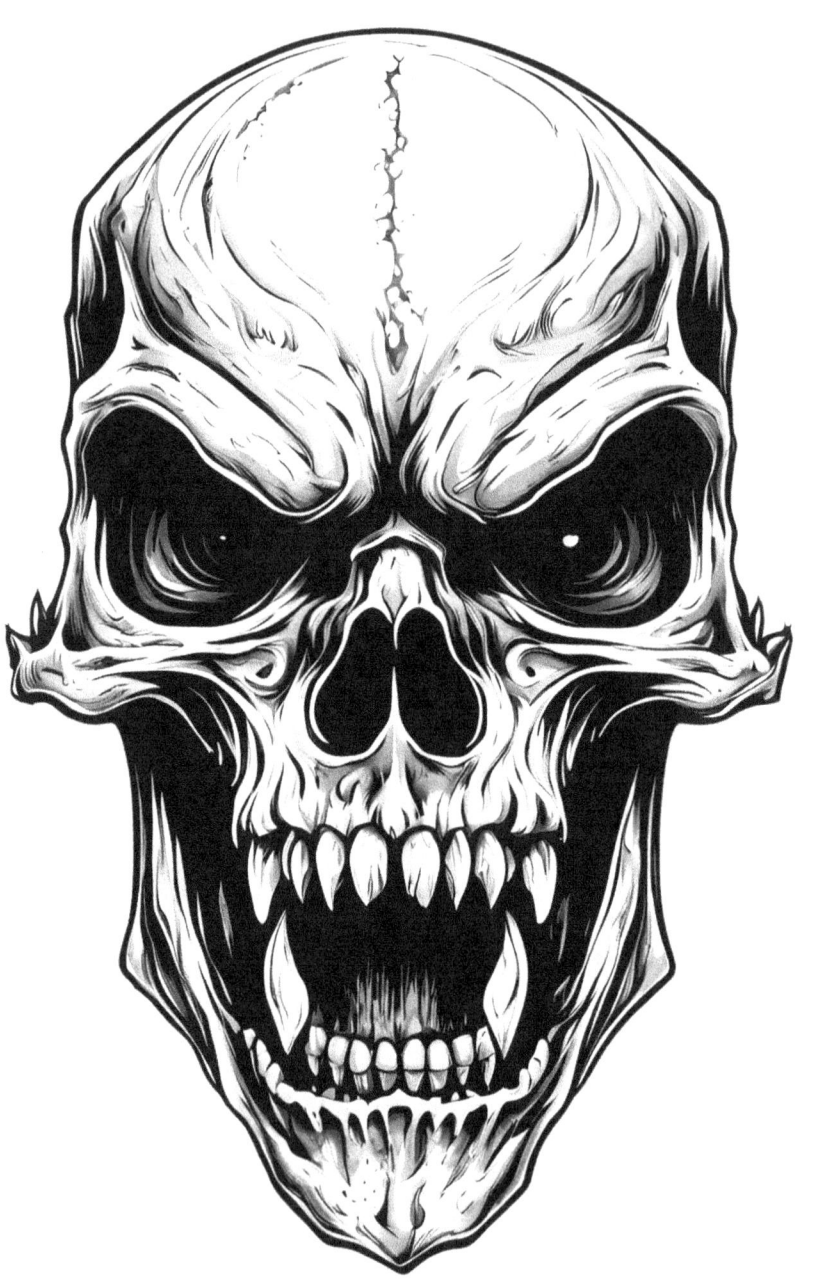

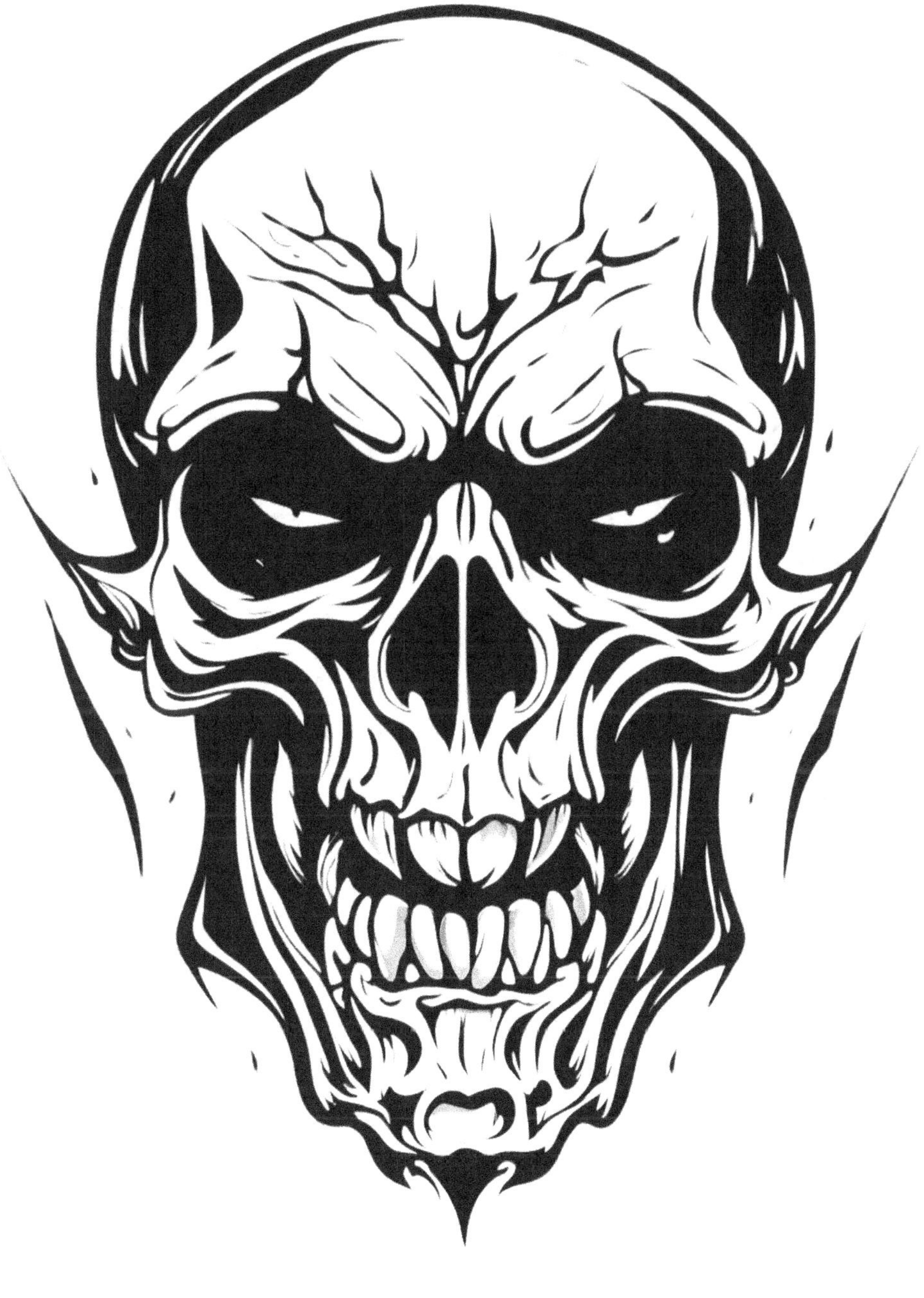

SCARY SKULL TATTOOS

SCARY SKULL TATTOOS

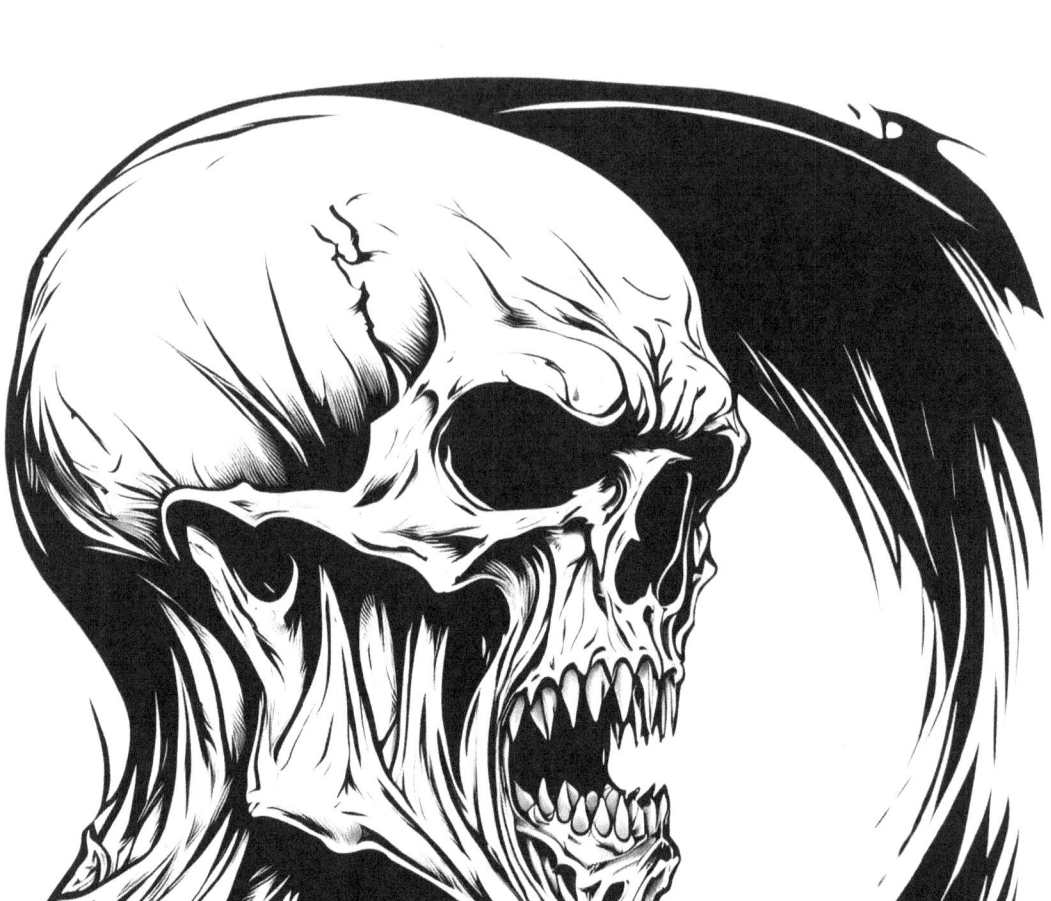

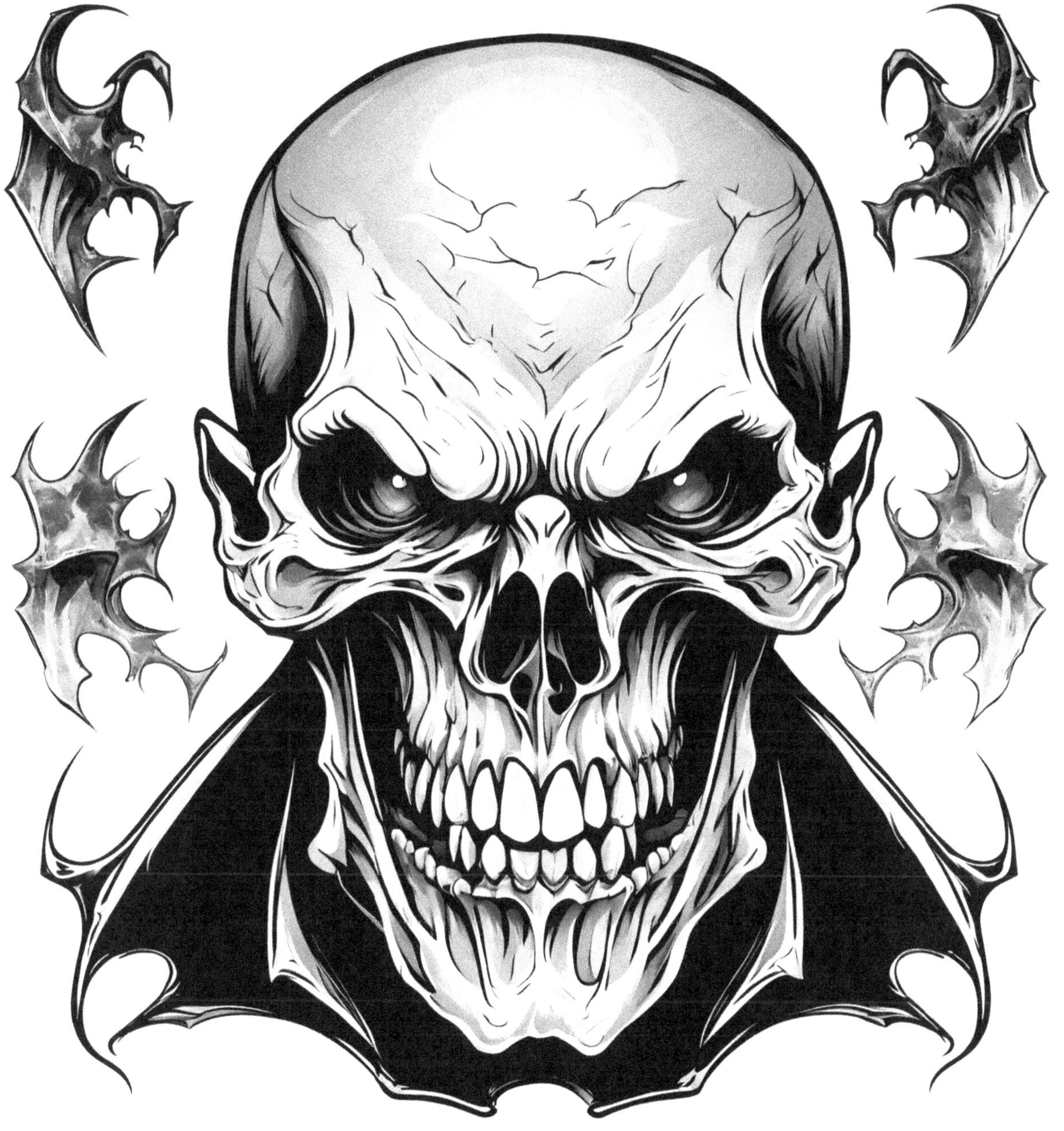

SCARY SKULL TATTOOS

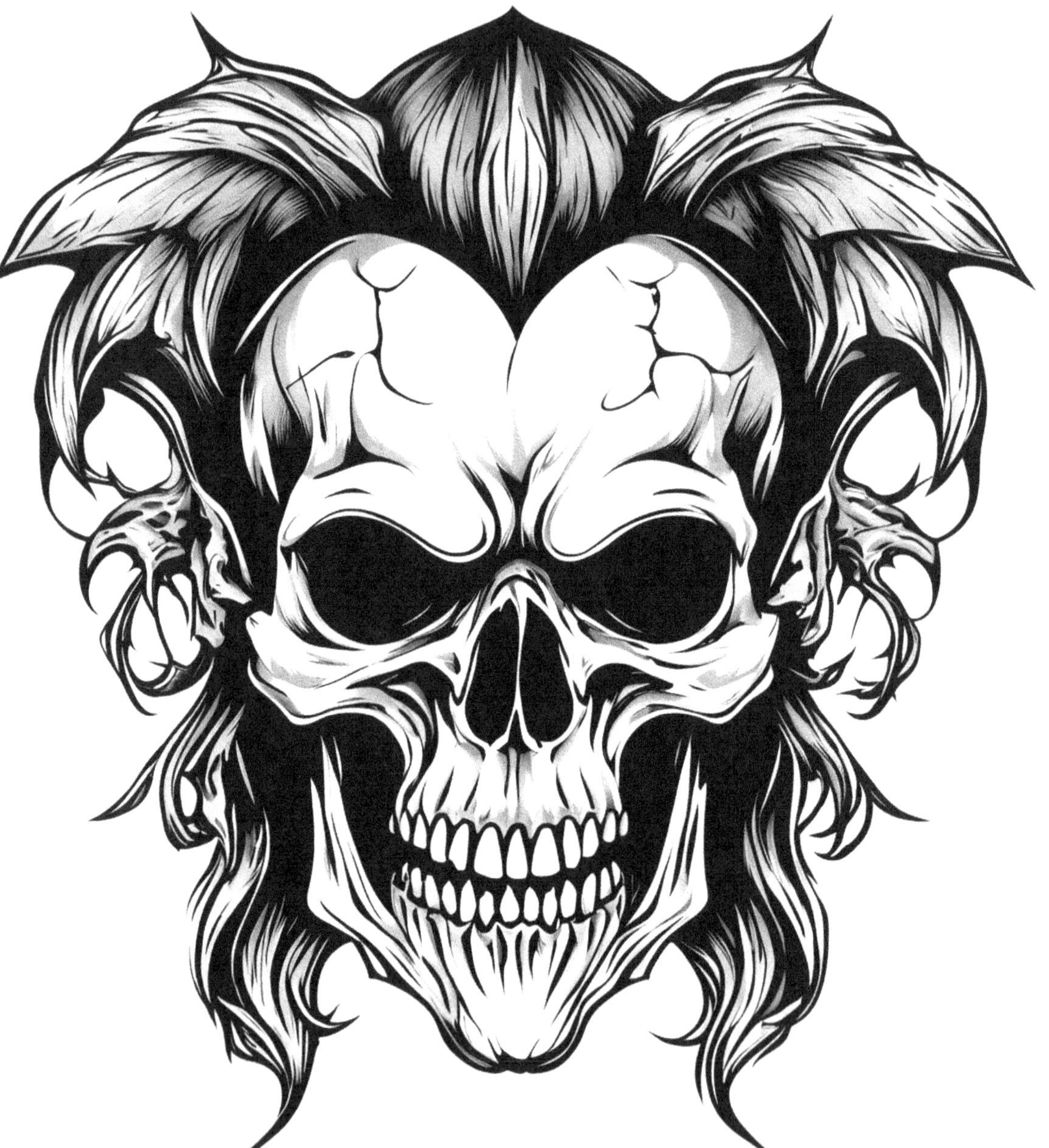

SCARY SKULL TATTOOS

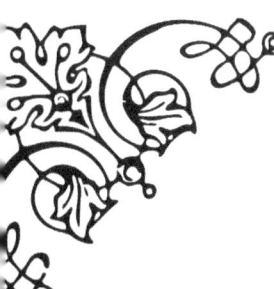

UNUSUAL SKULL TATTOOS

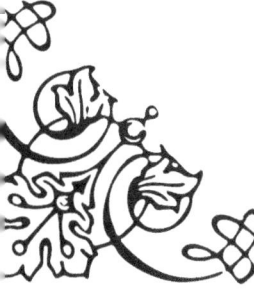

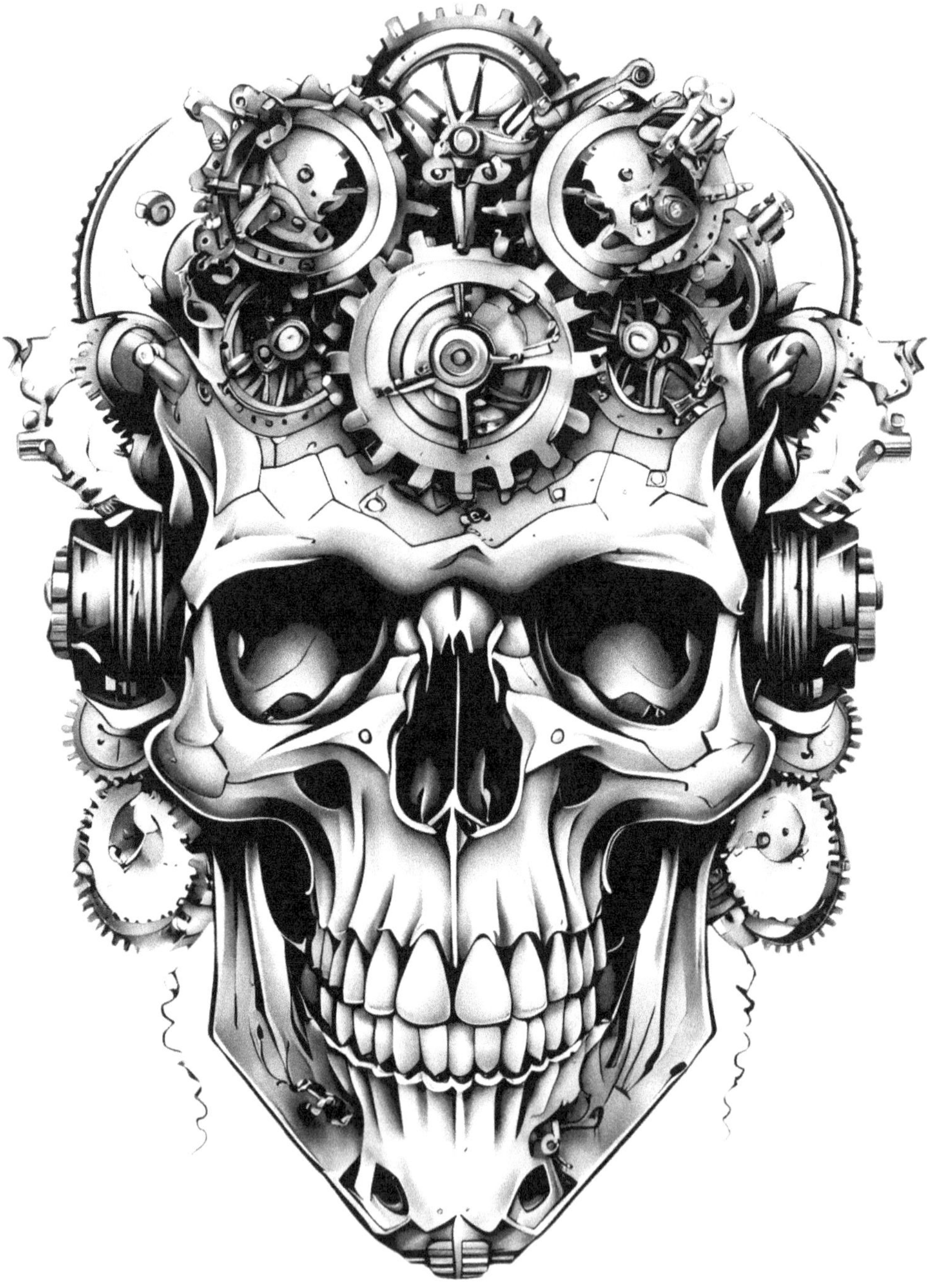

UNUSUAL SKULL TATTOOS

UNUSUAL SKULL TATTOOS

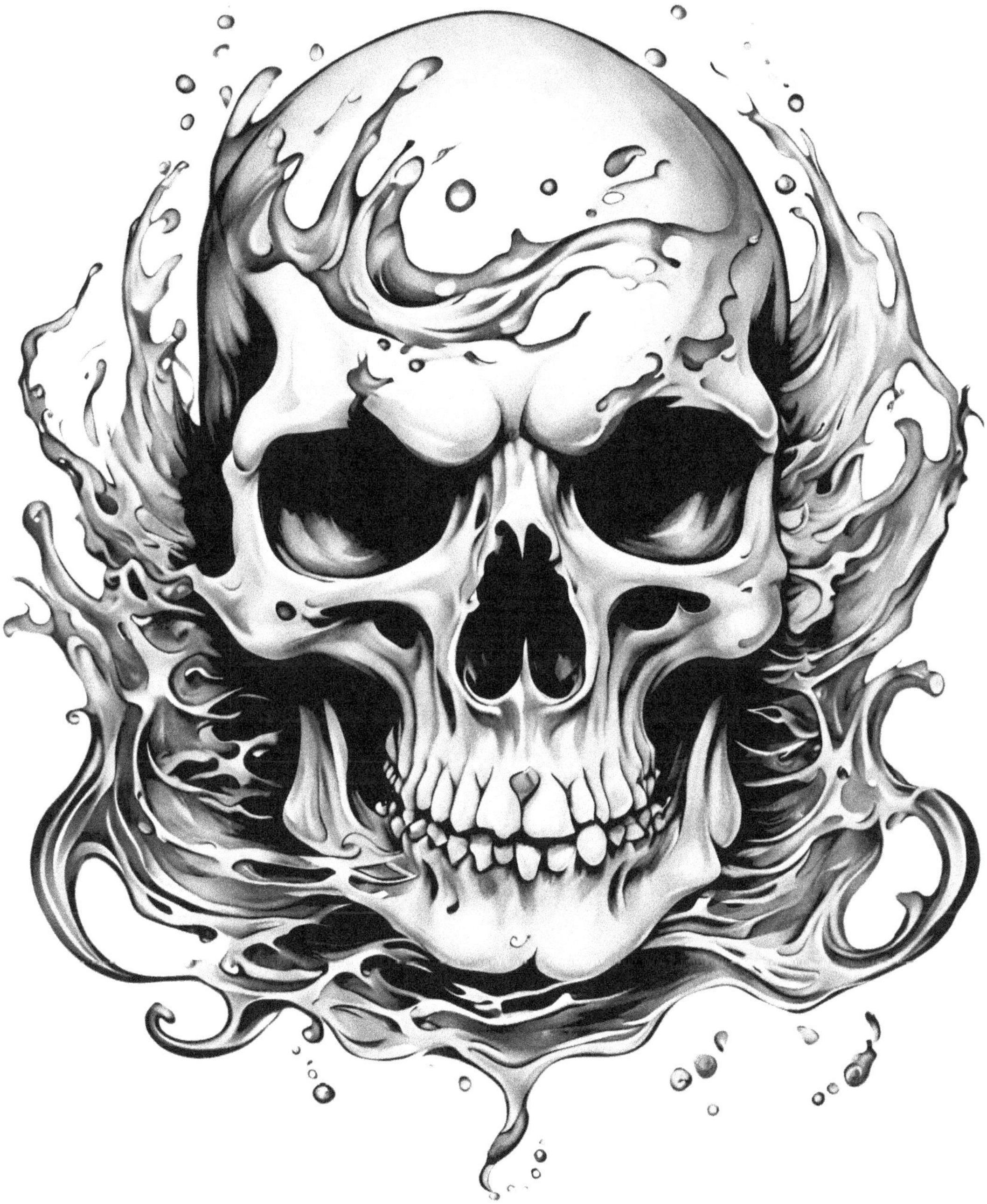

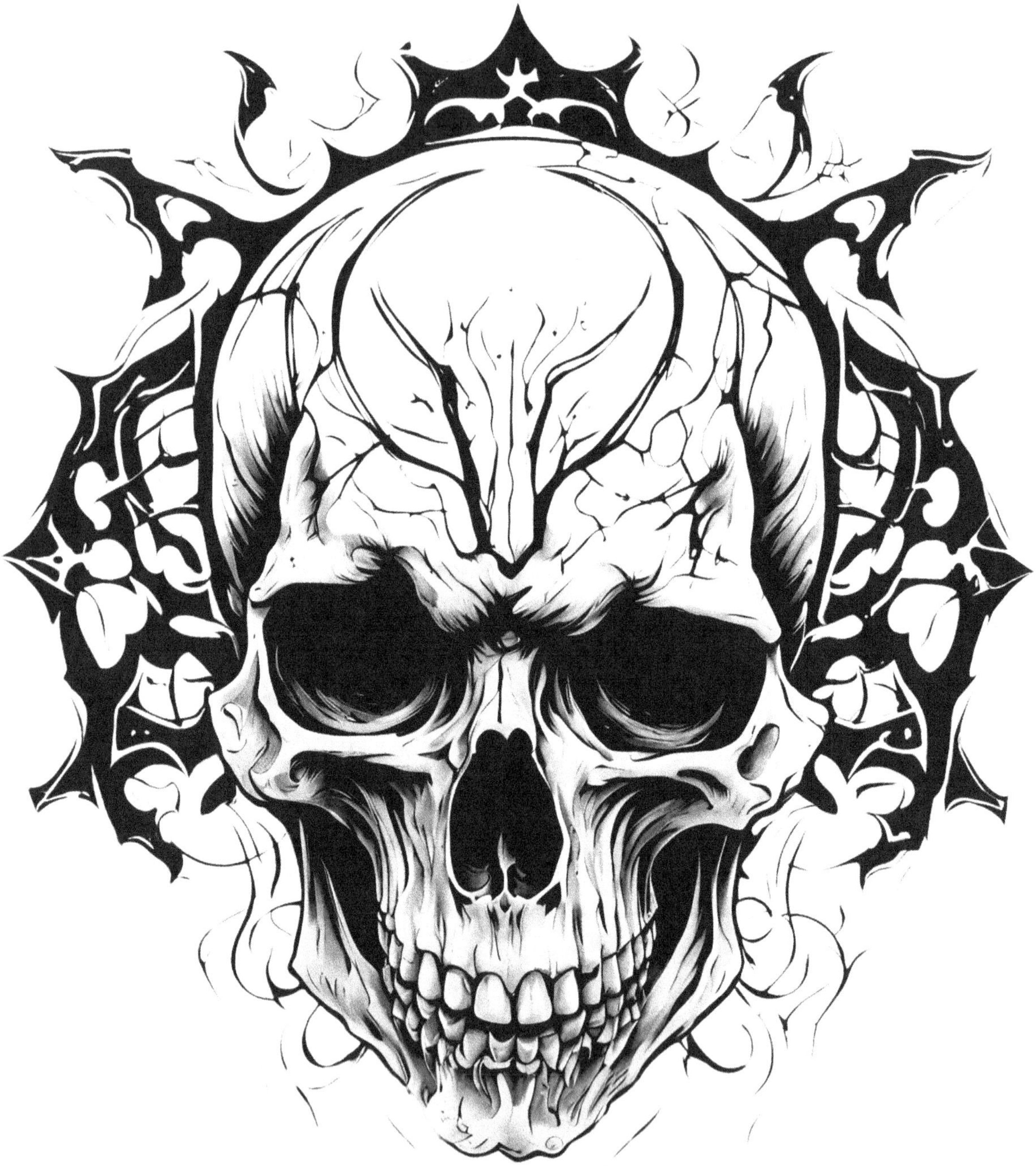

UNUSUAL SKULL TATTOOS

UNUSUAL SKULL TATTOOS

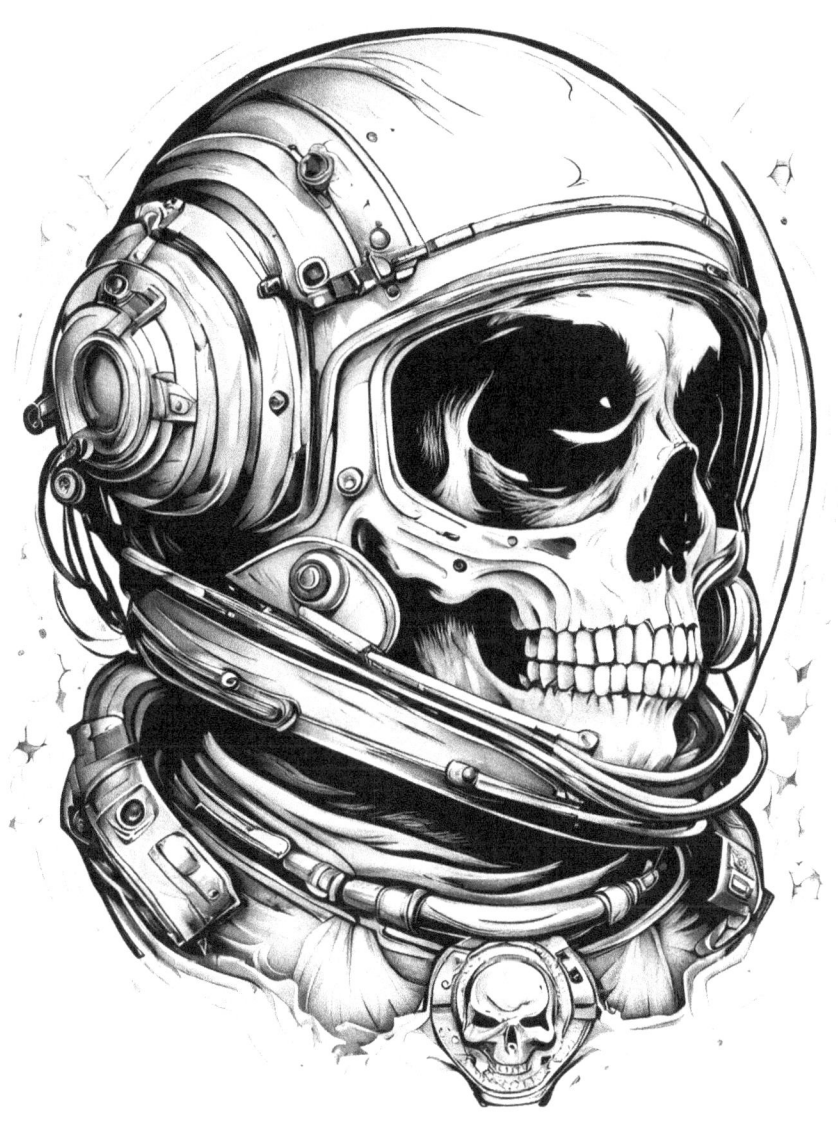

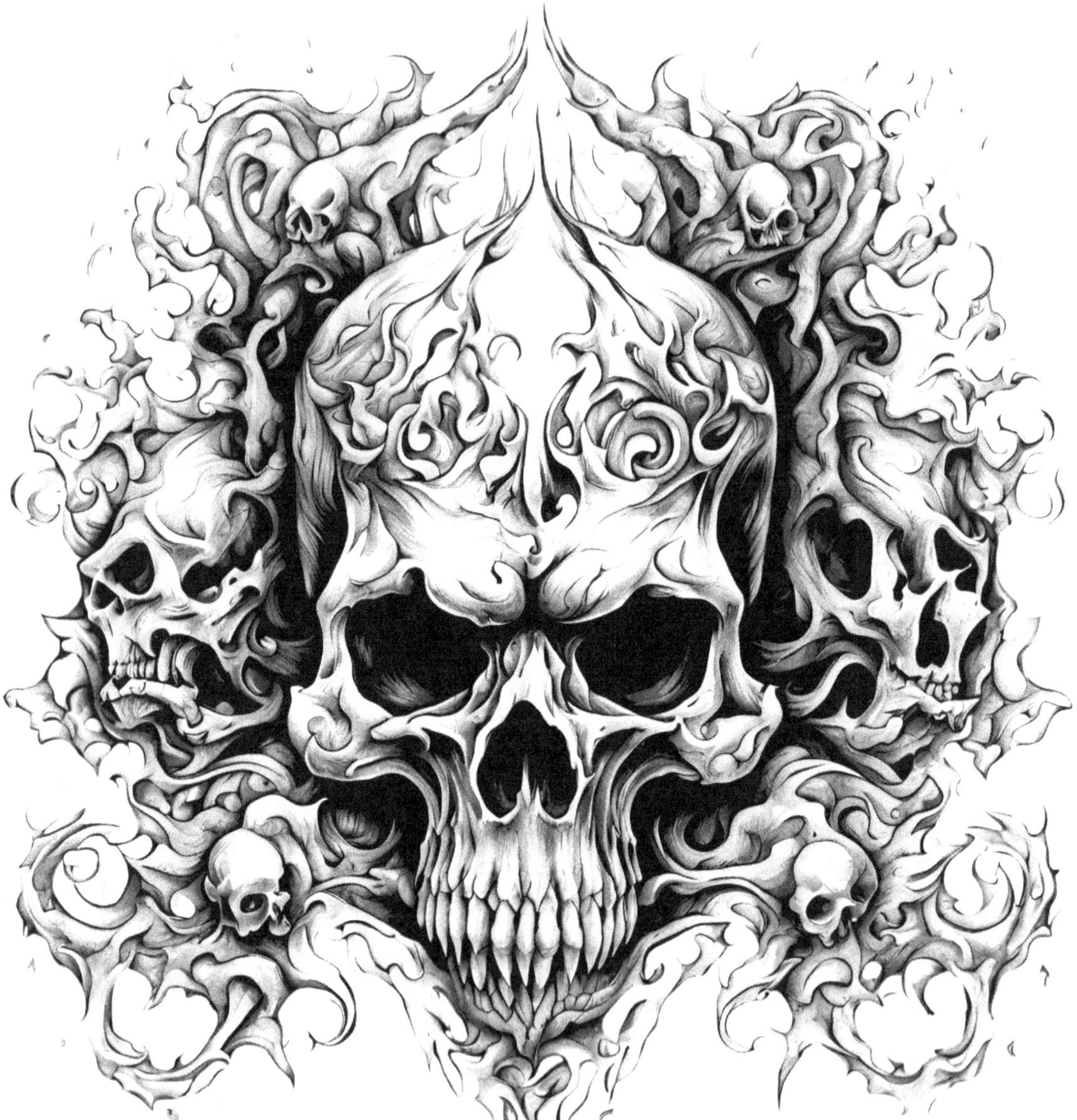

UNUSUAL SKULL TATTOOS

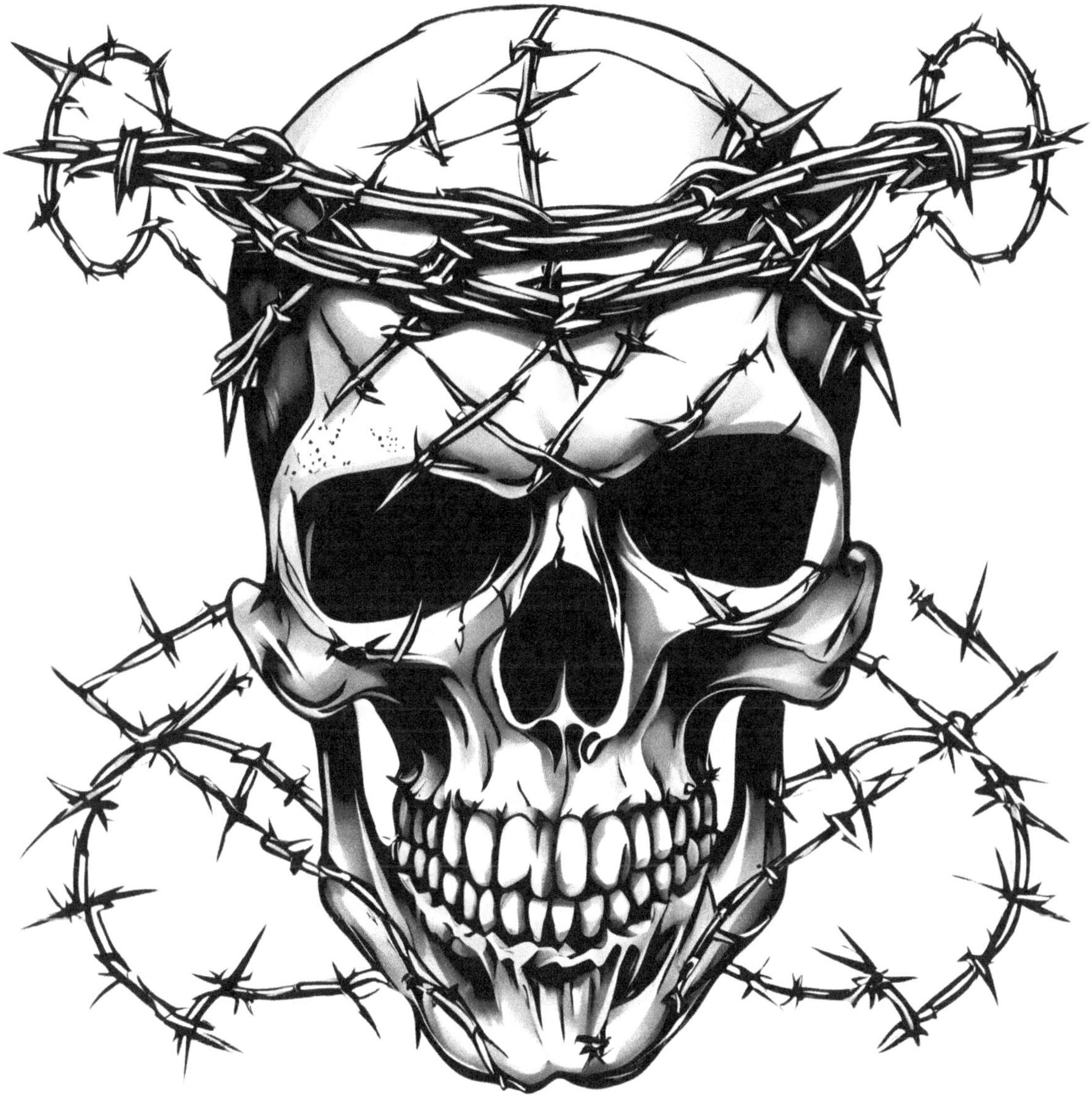

UNUSUAL SKULL TATTOOS

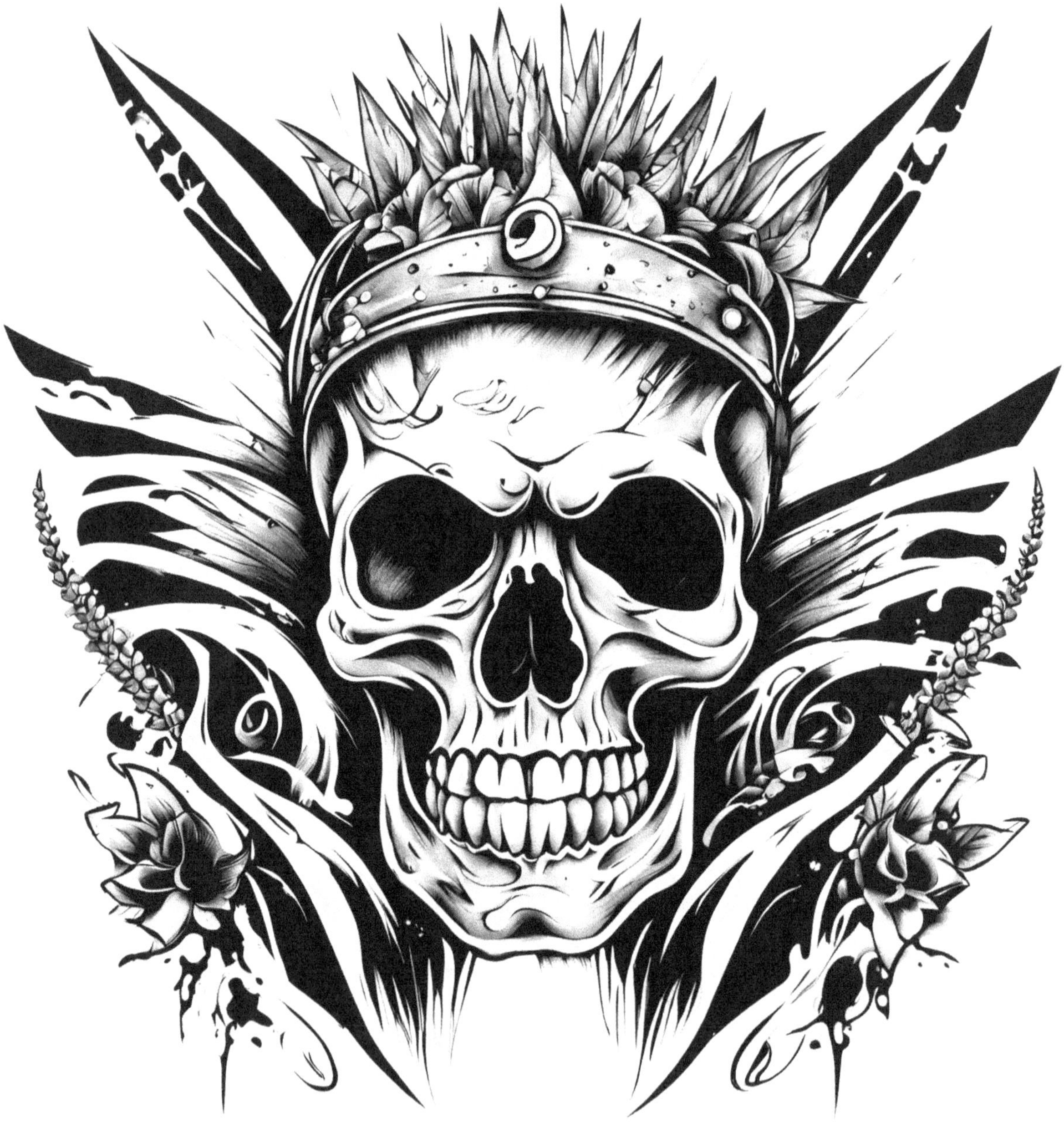

UNUSUAL SKULL TATTOOS

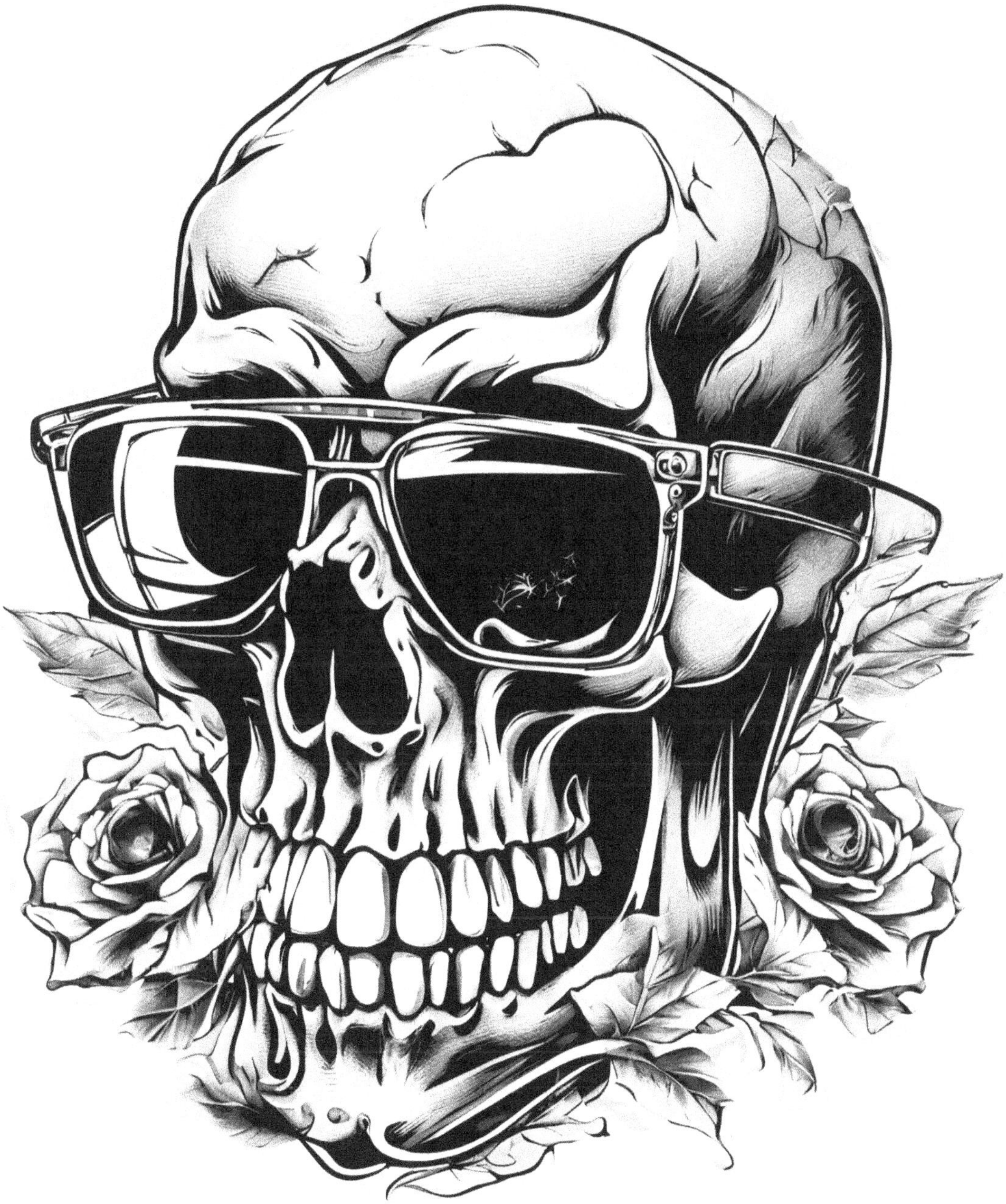

UNUSUAL SKULL TATTOOS

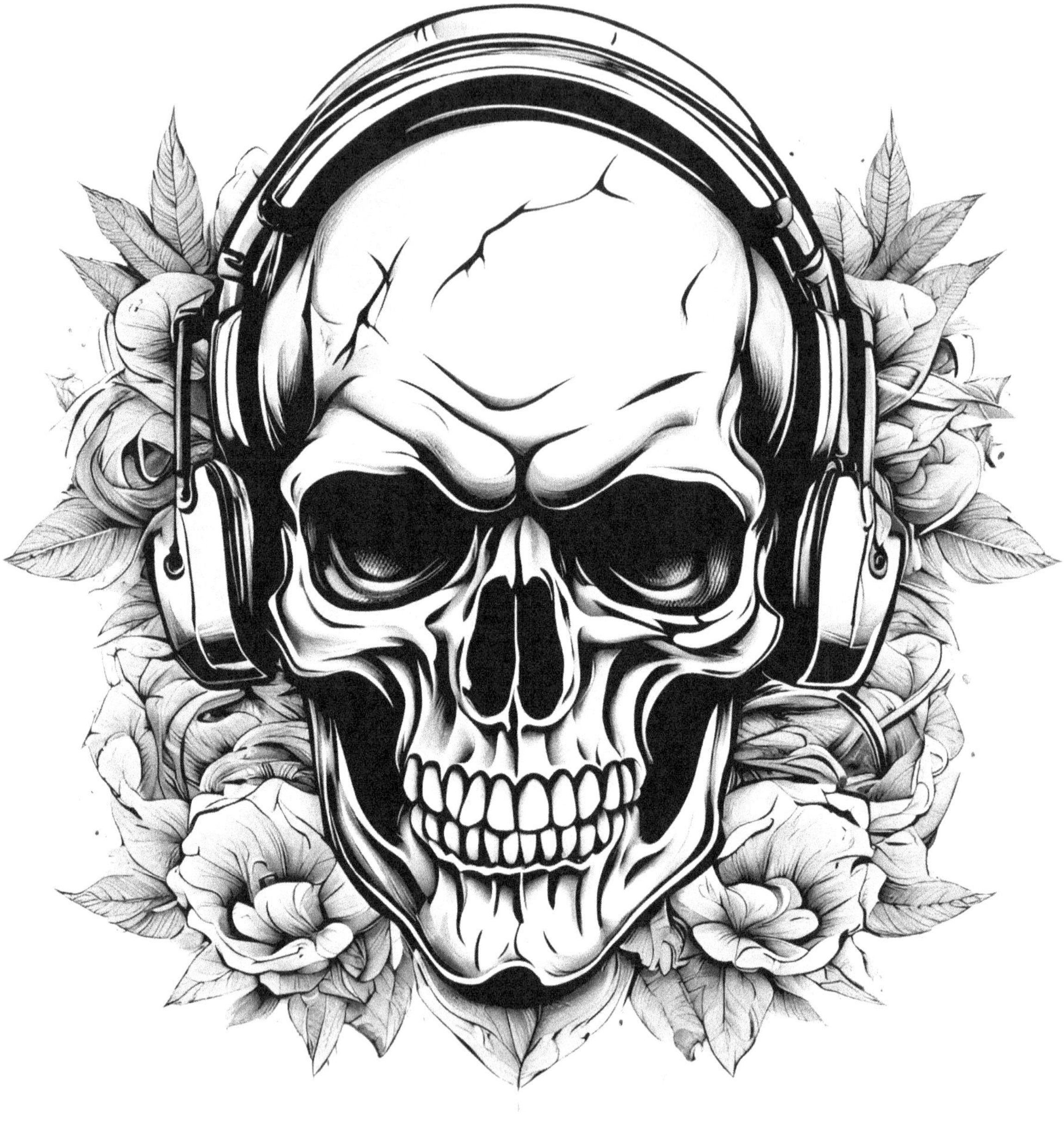

UNUSUAL SKULL TATTOOS

UNUSUAL SKULL TATTOOS

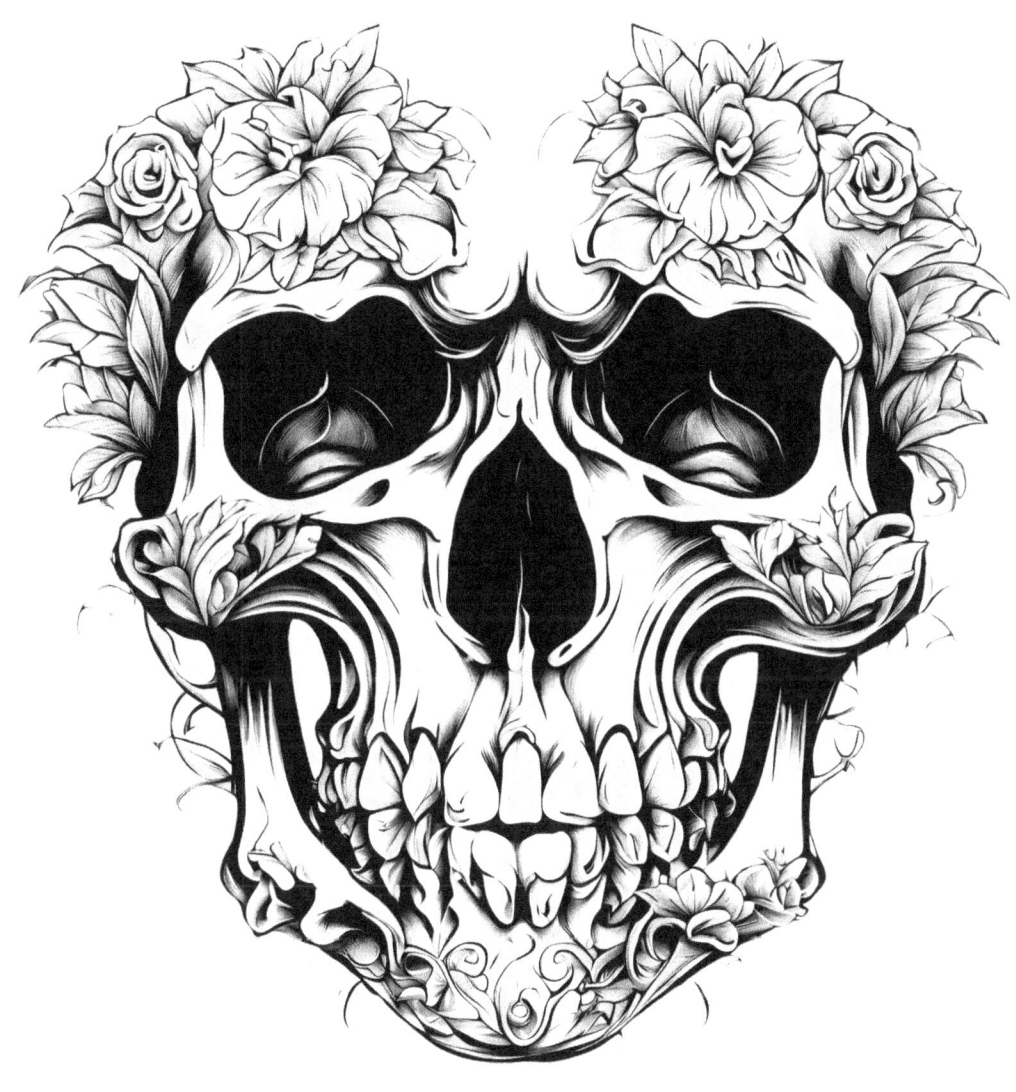

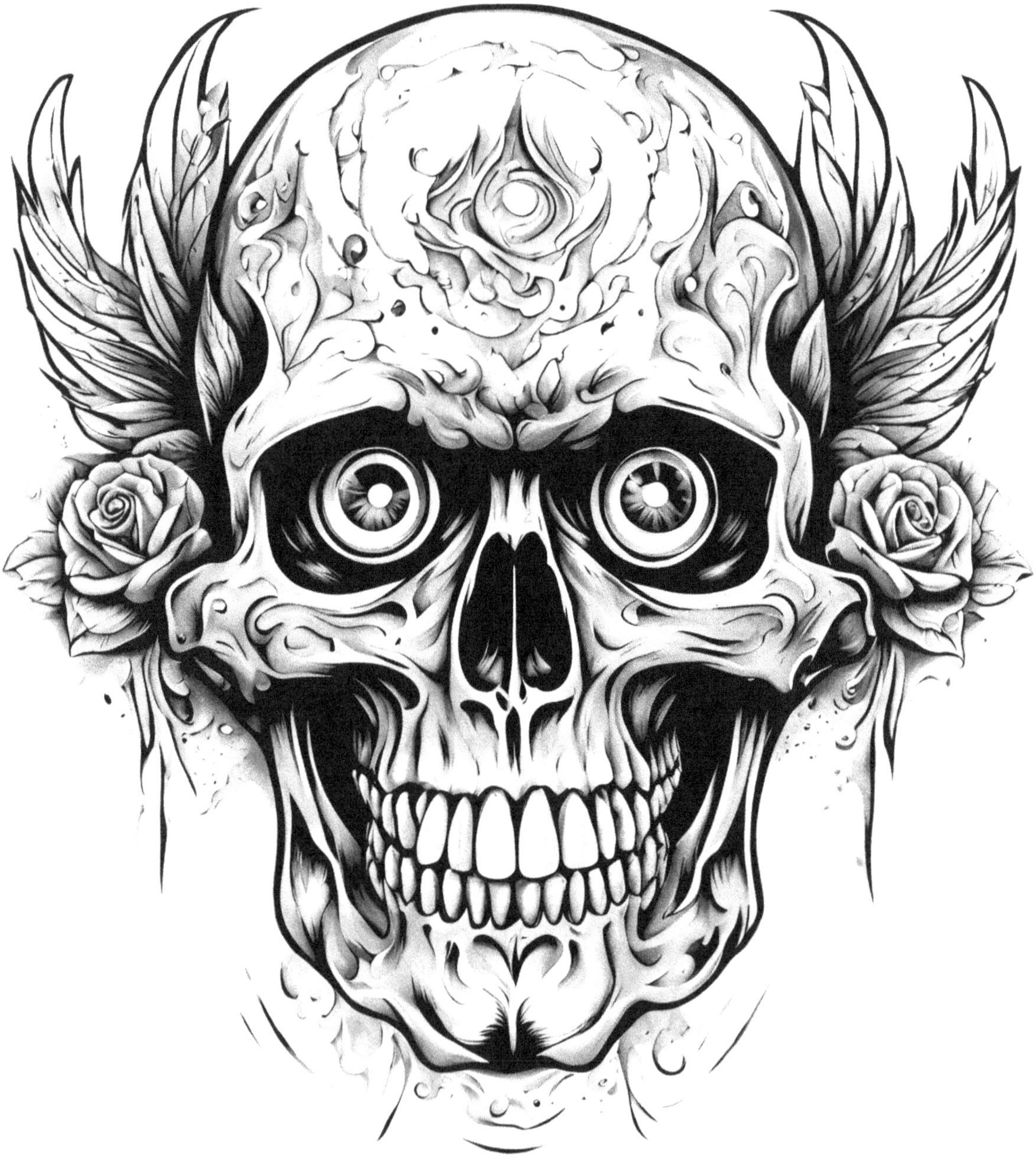

UNUSUAL SKULL TATTOOS

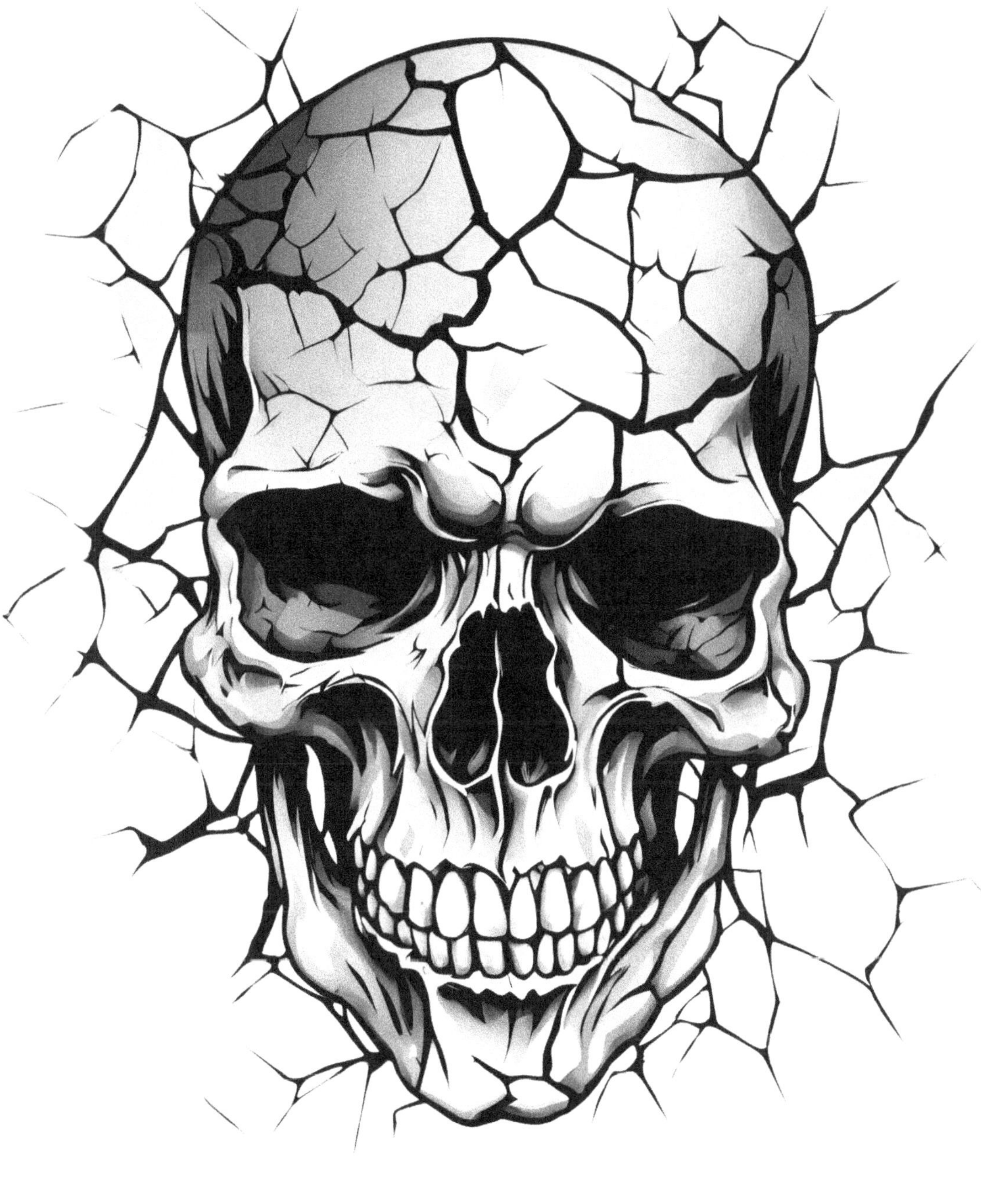

UNUSUAL SKULL TATTOOS

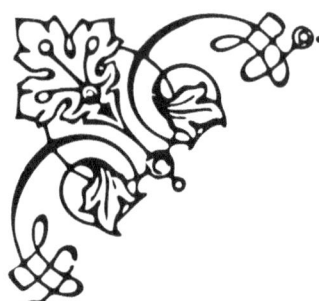
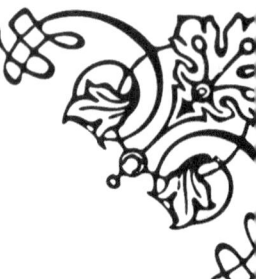

FUNNY SKULL TATTOOS

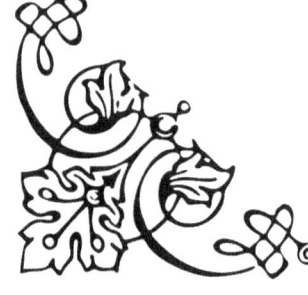

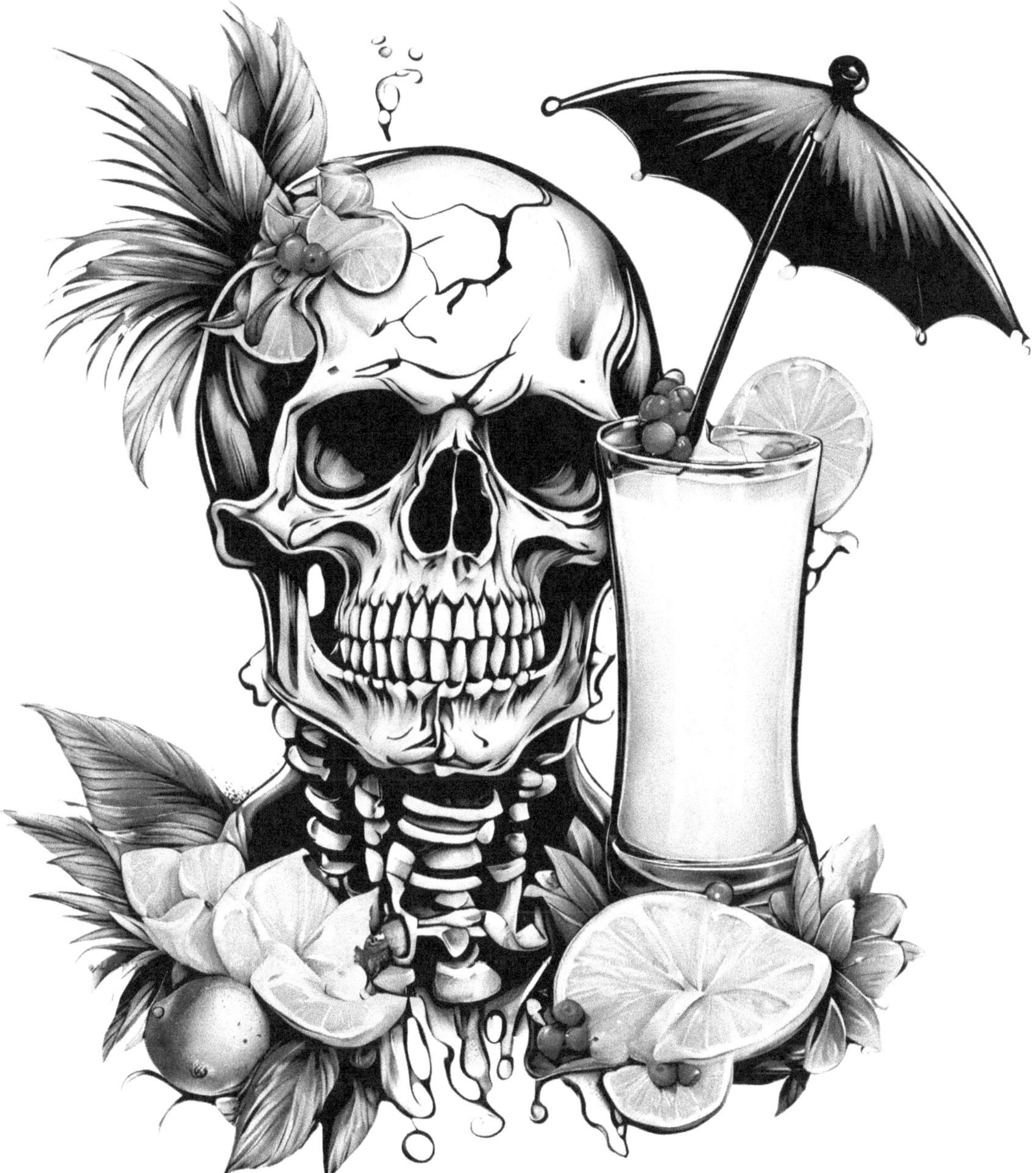

FUNNY SKULL TATTOOS

FUNNY SKULL TATTOOS

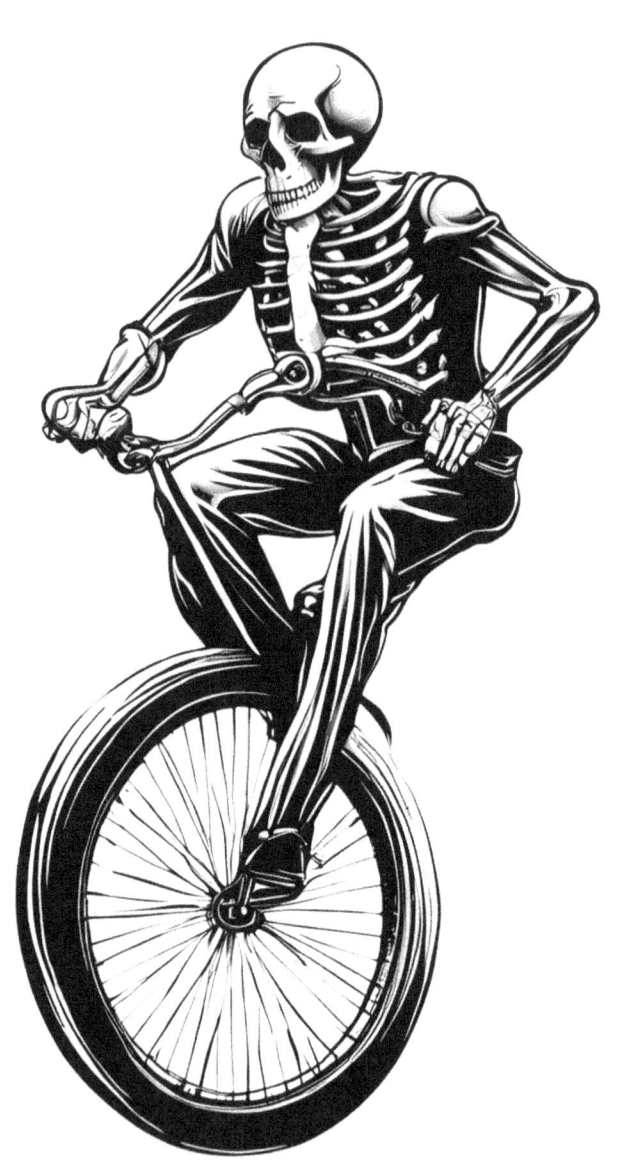

FUNNY SKULL TATTOOS

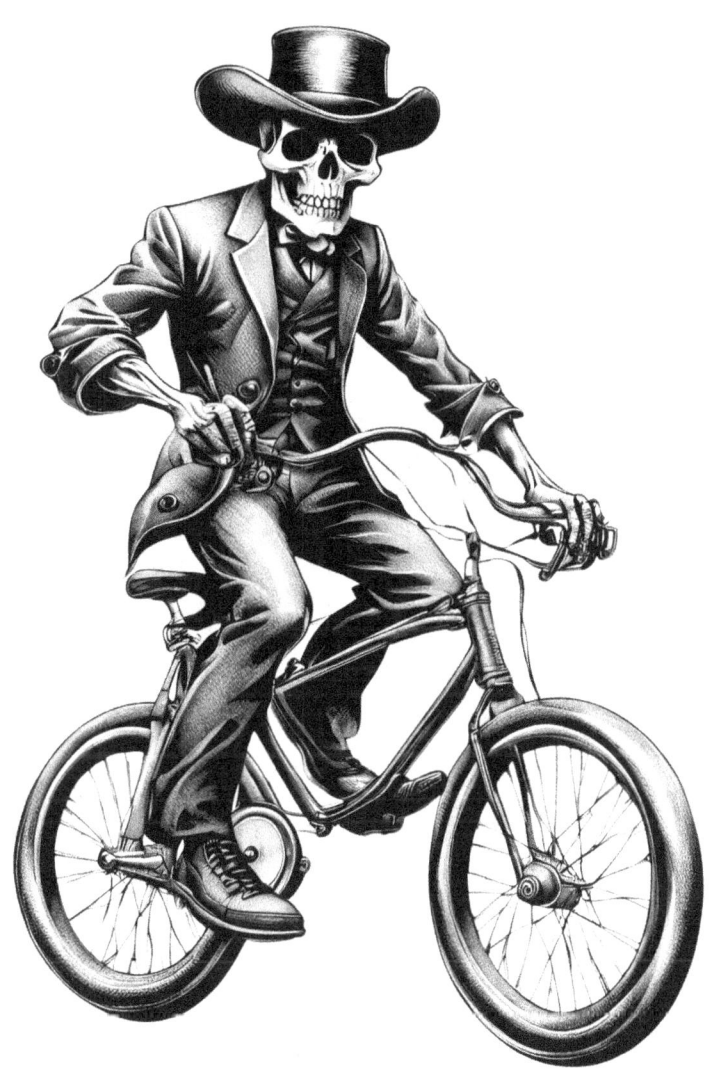

FUNNY SKULL TATTOOS

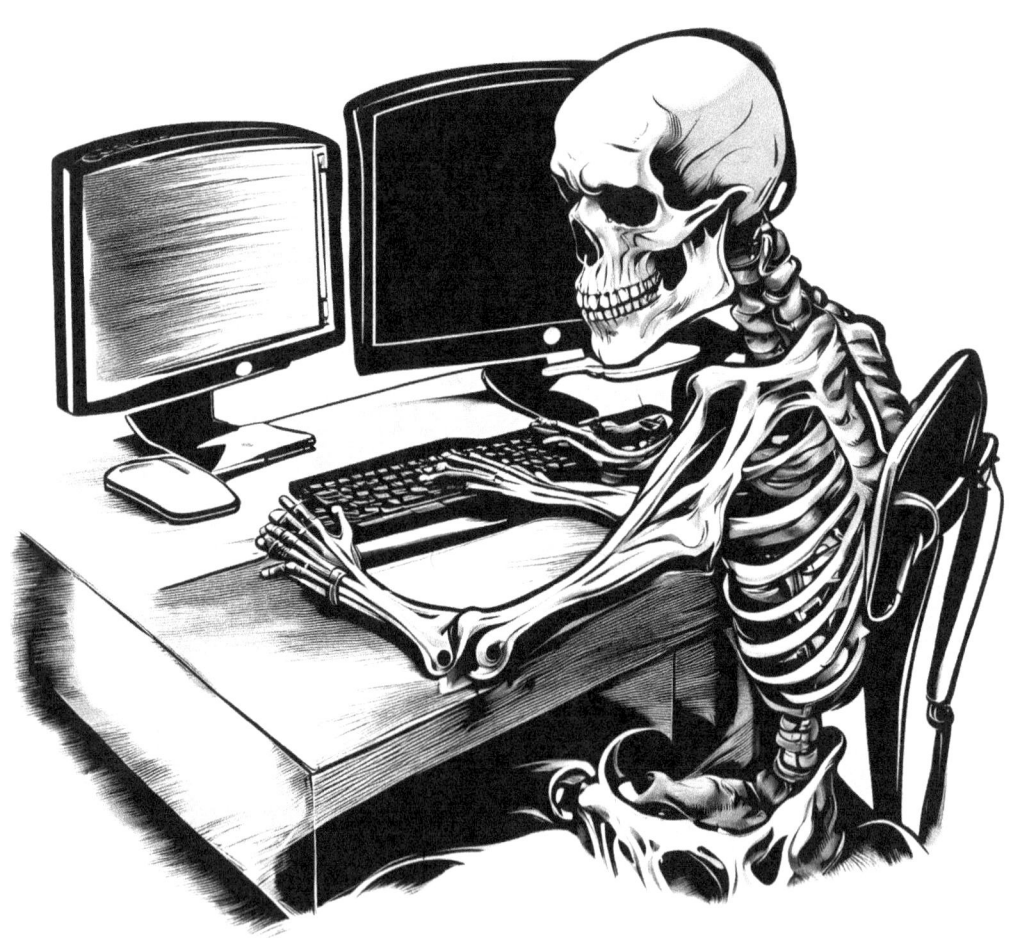

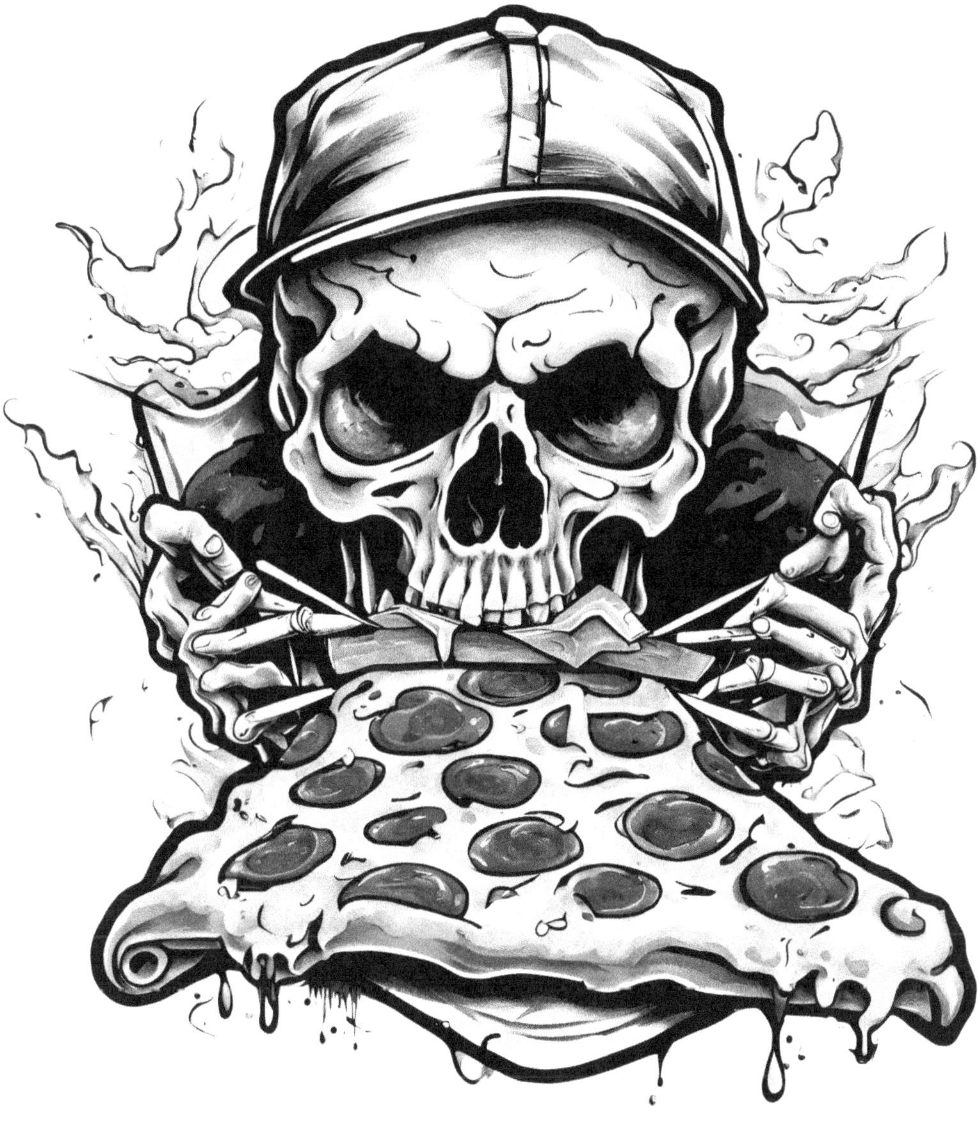

FUNNY SKULL TATTOOS

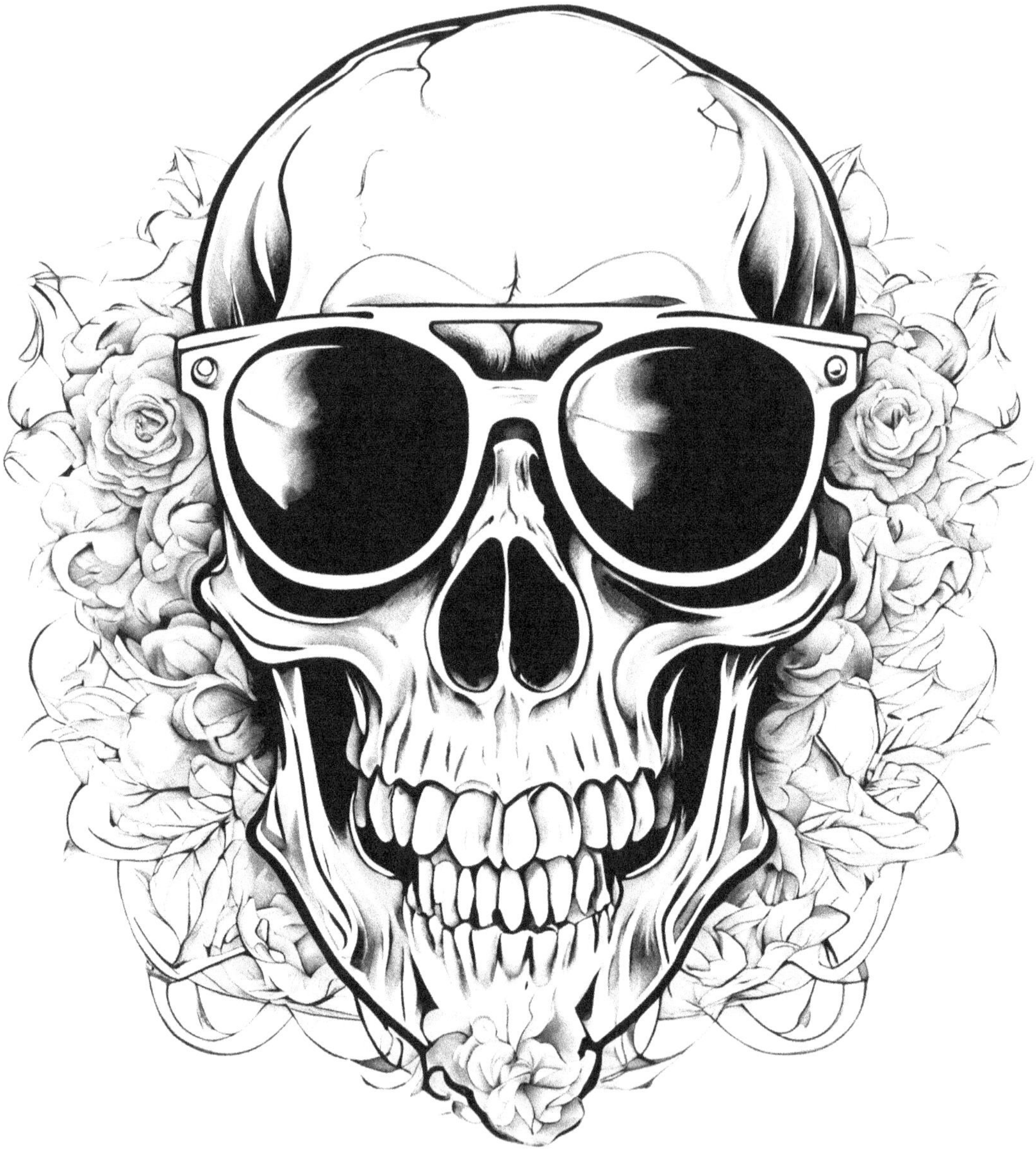

FUNNY SKULL TATTOOS

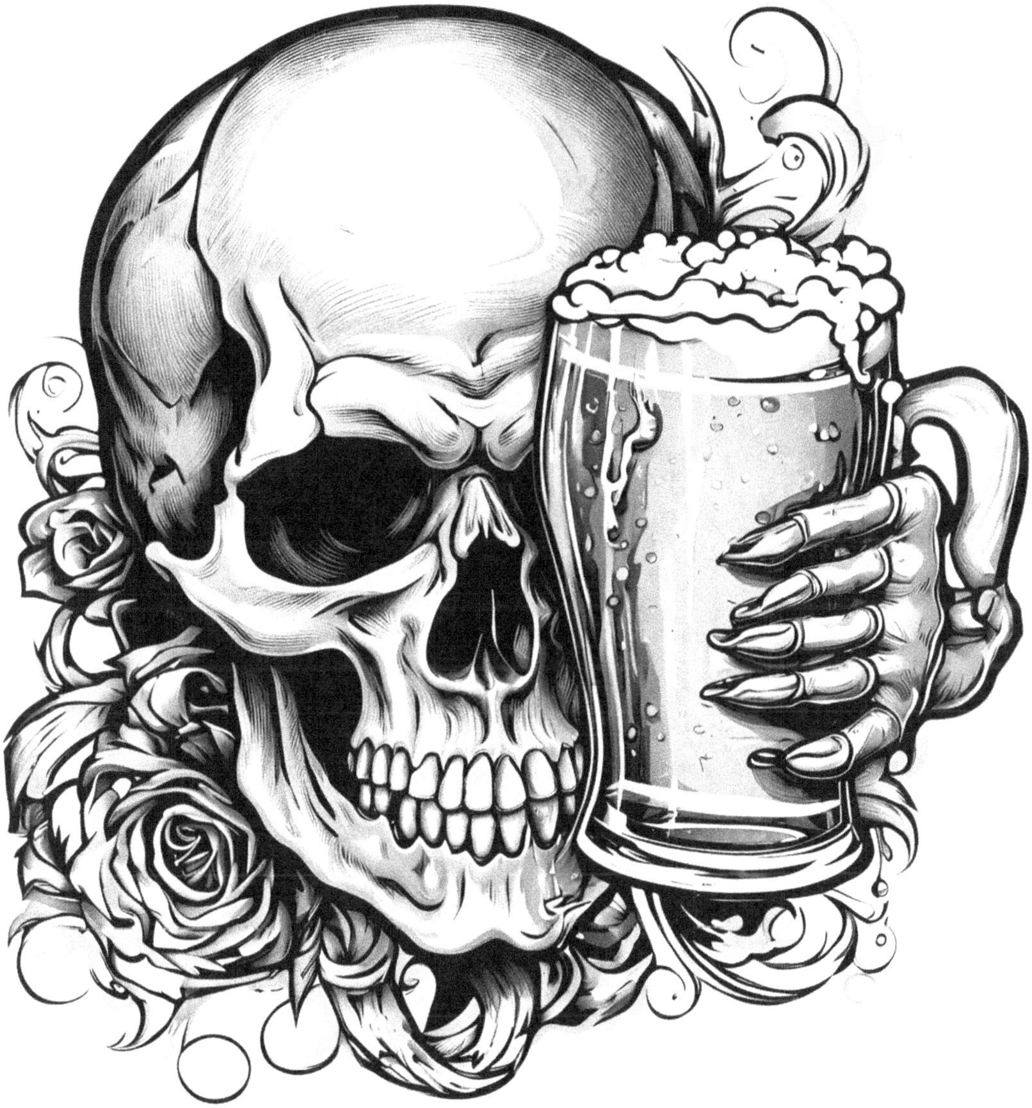

FUNNY SKULL TATTOOS

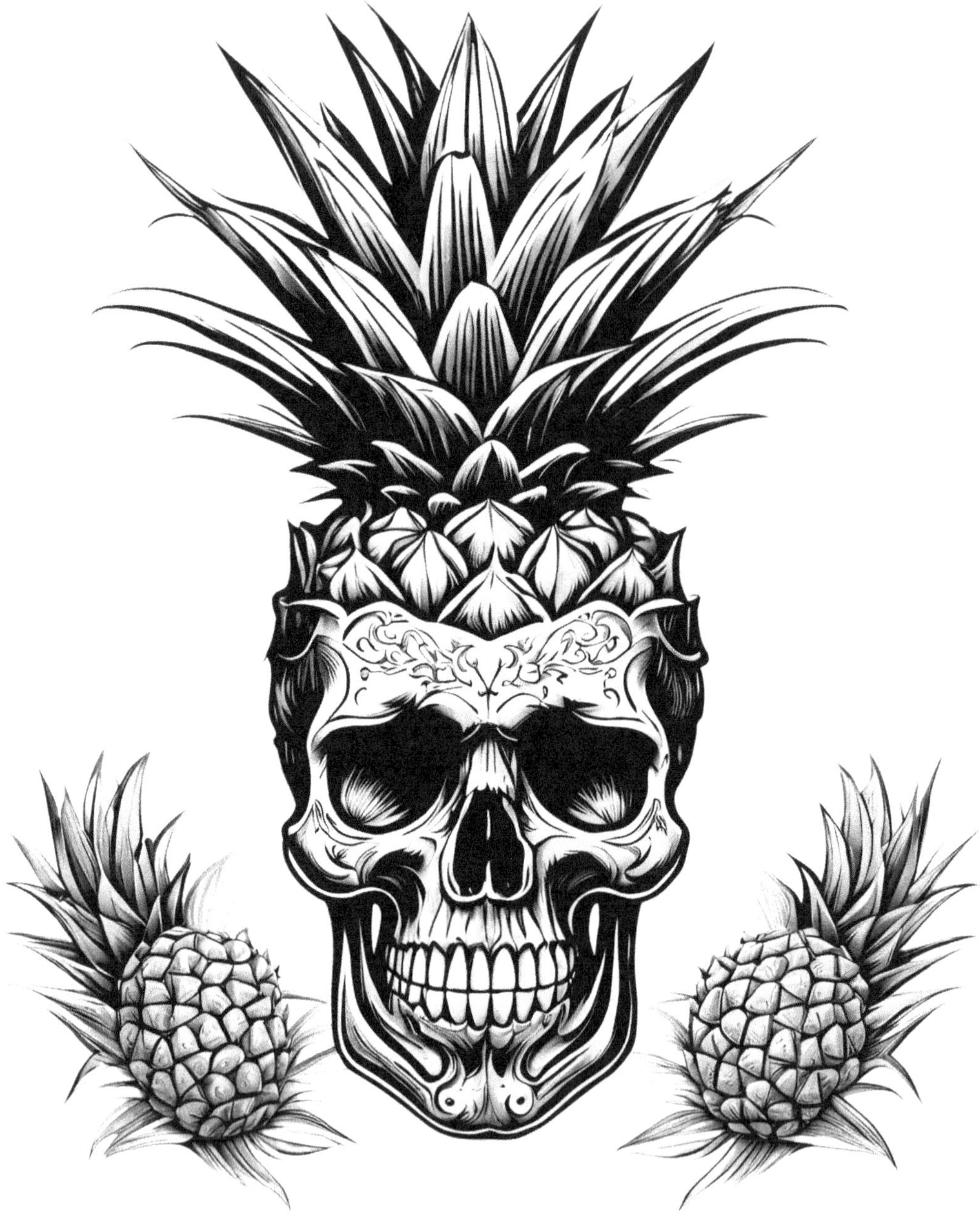

FUNNY SKULL TATTOOS

FUNNY SKULL TATTOOS

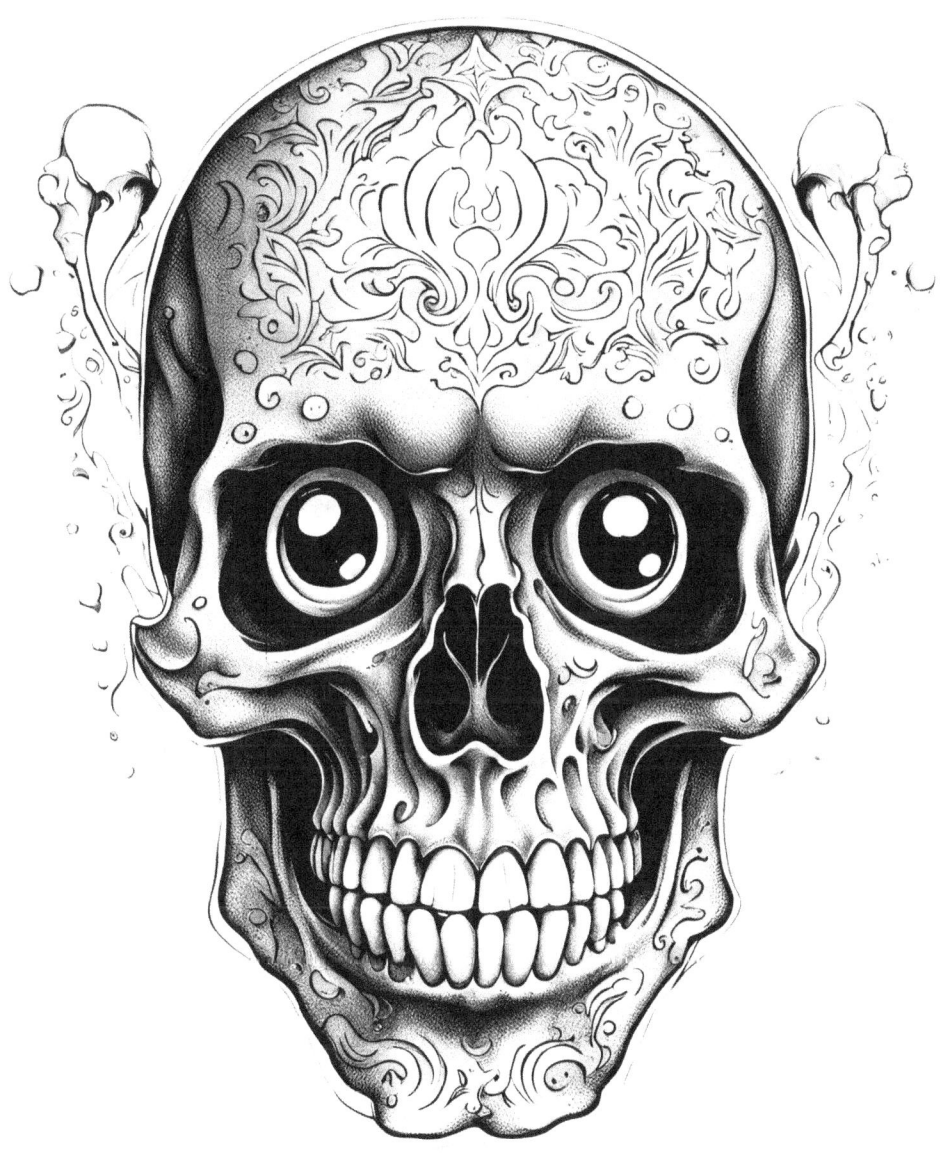

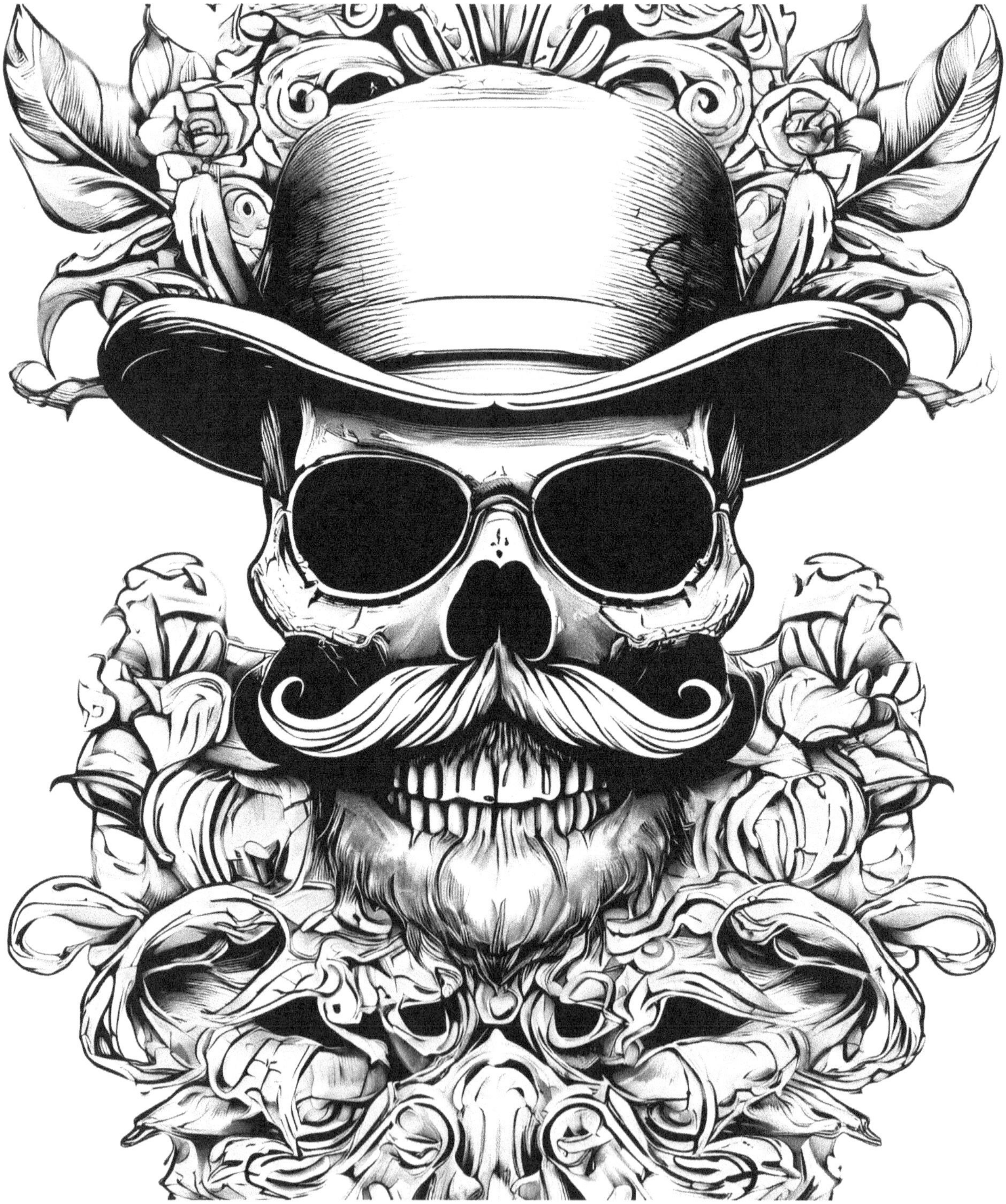

FUNNY SKULL TATTOOS

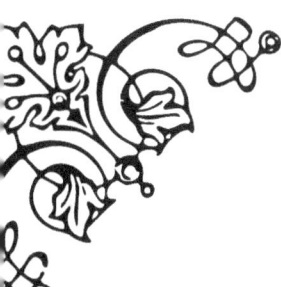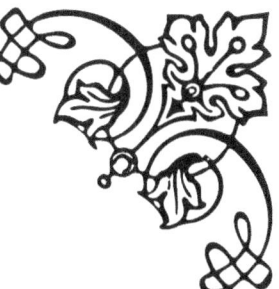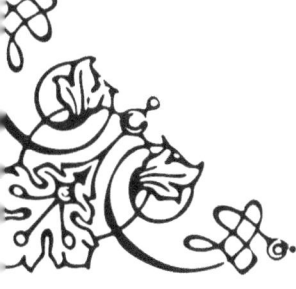

SUGAR SKULL TATTOOS

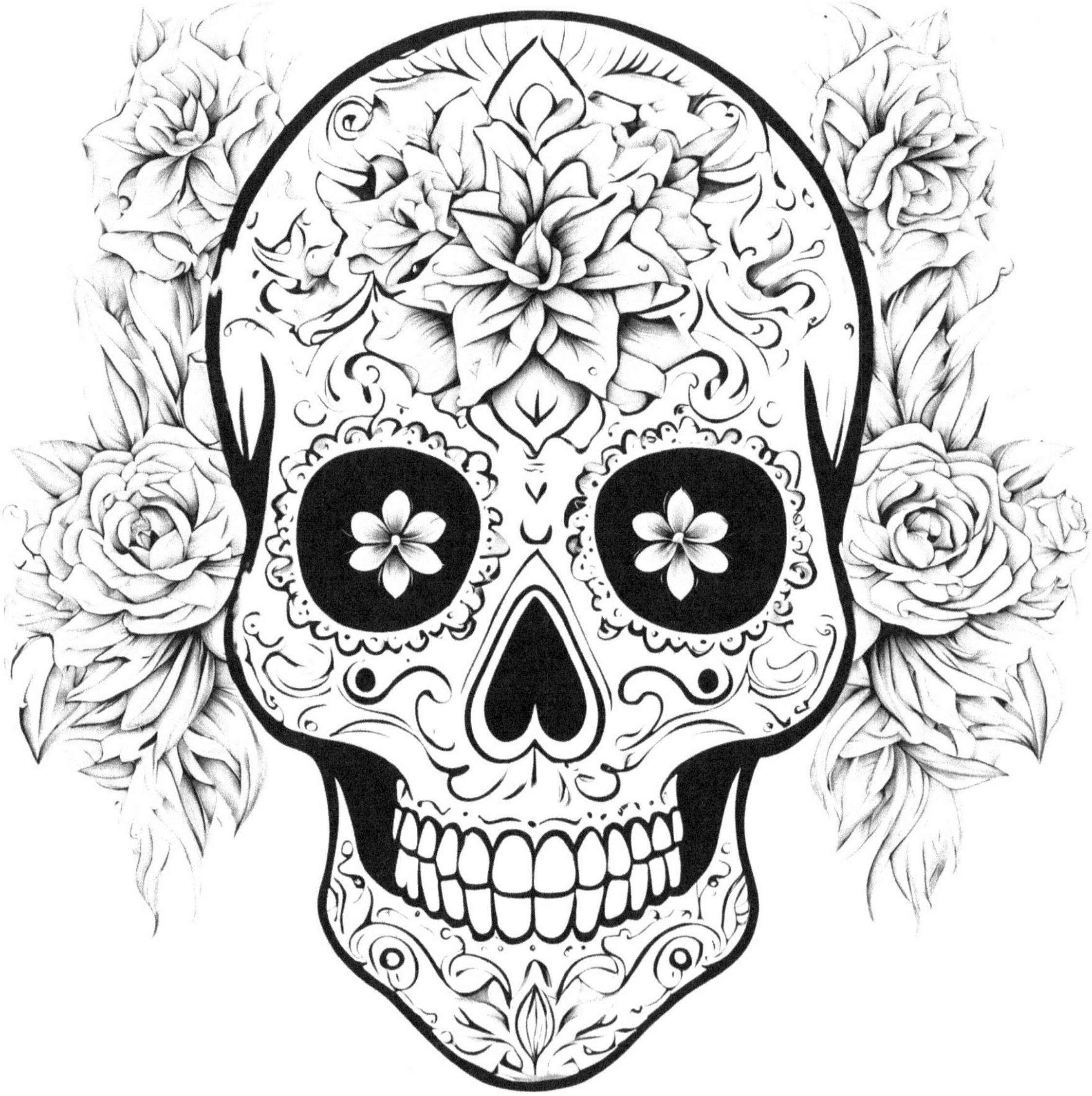

SUGAR SKULL TATTOOS

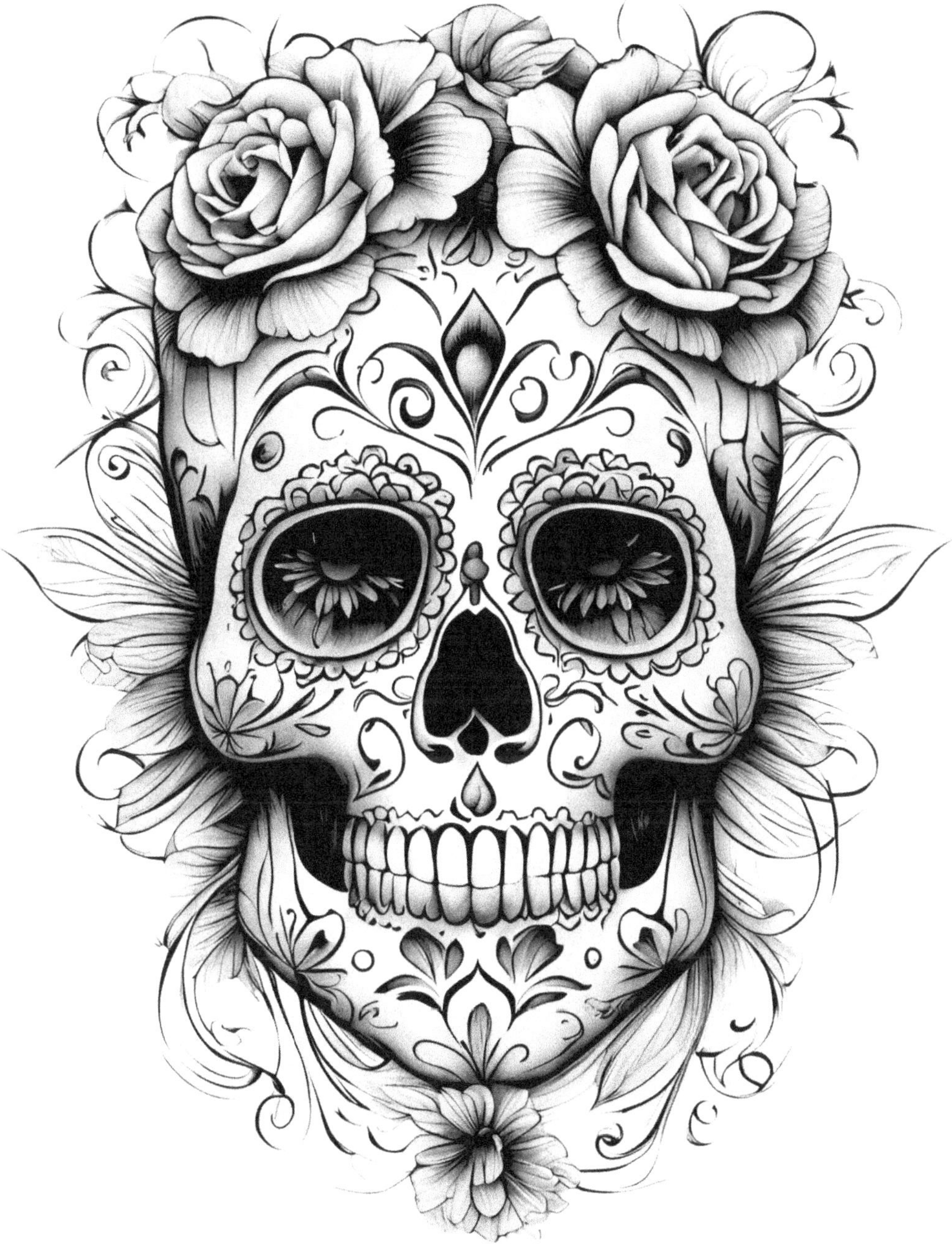

SUGAR SKULL TATTOOS

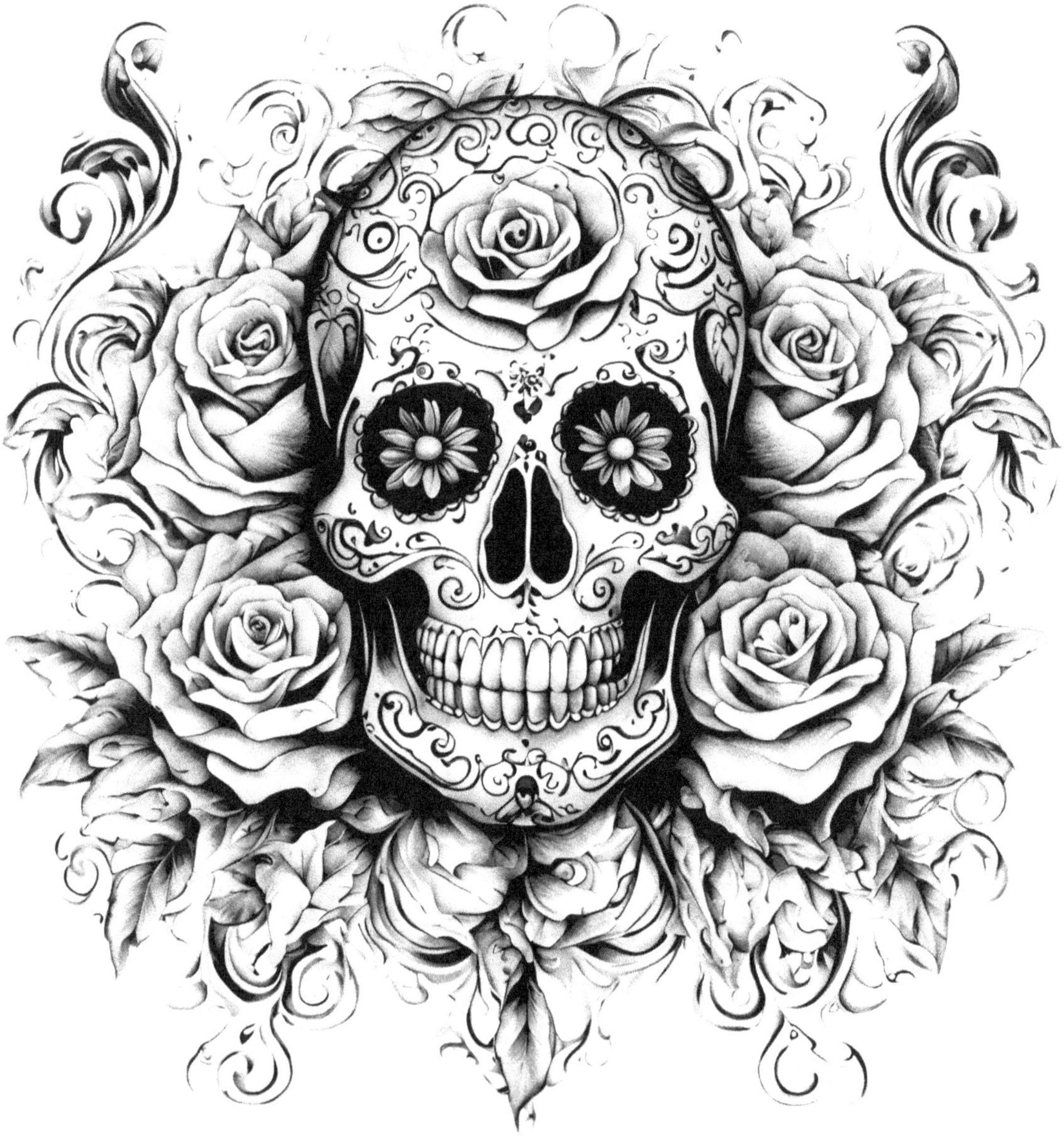

SUGAR SKULL TATTOOS

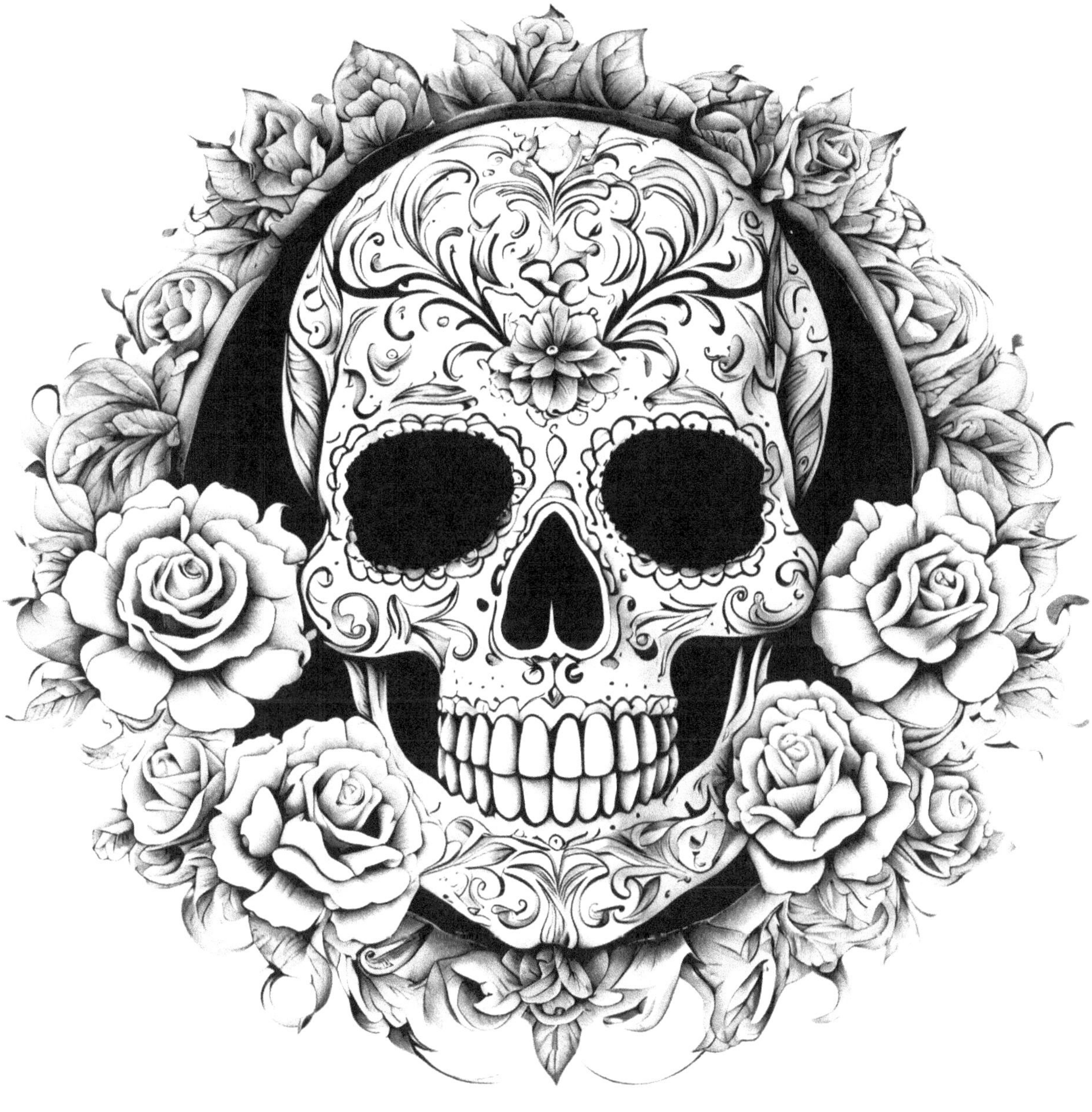

SUGAR SKULL TATTOOS

SUGAR SKULL TATTOOS

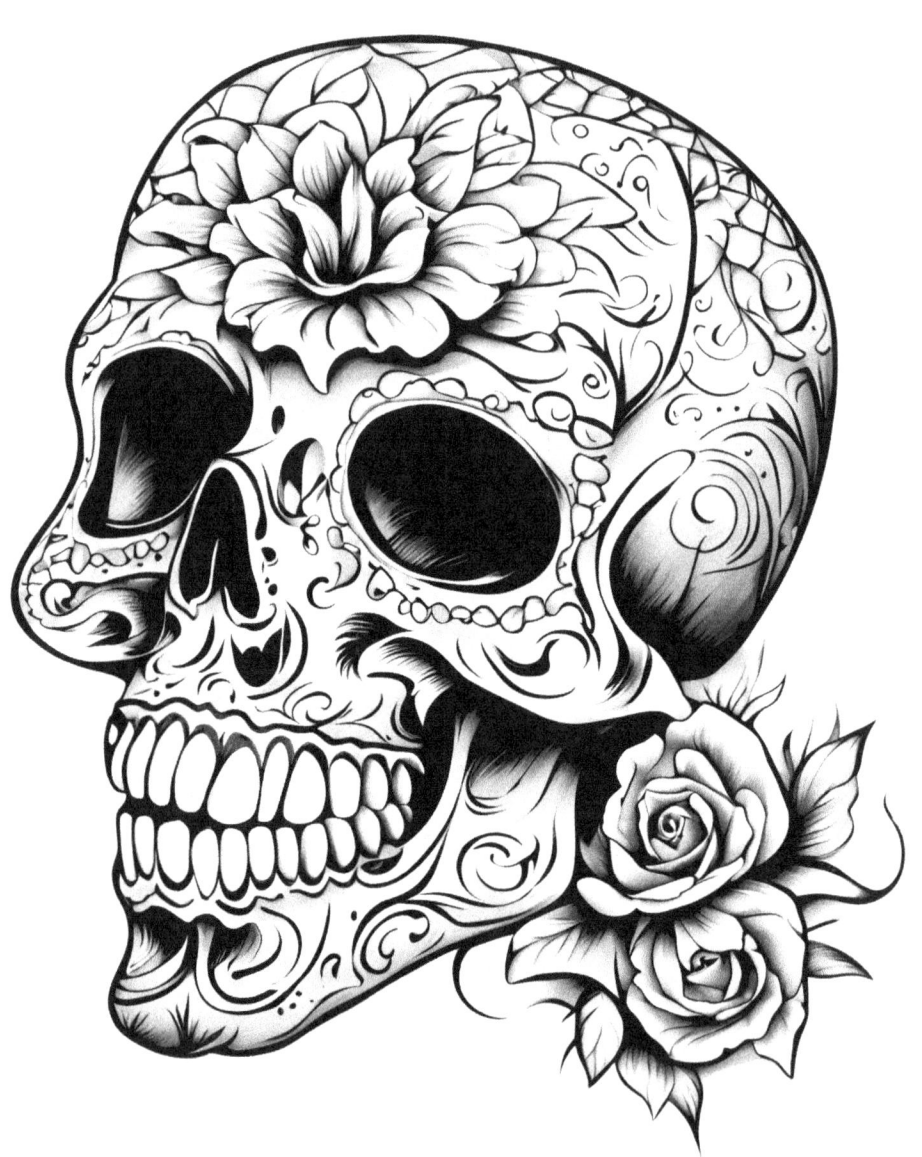

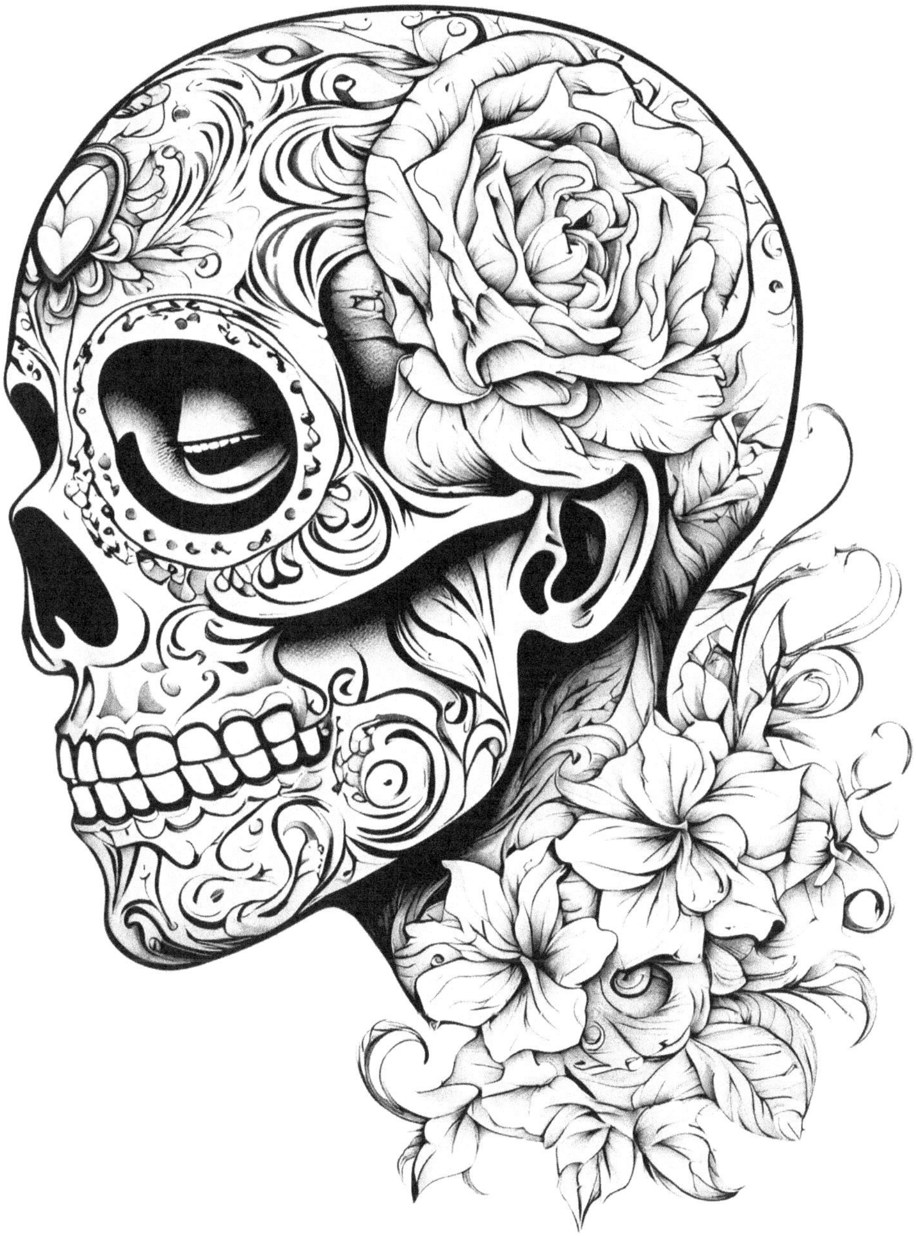

SUGAR SKULL TATTOOS

SUGAR SKULL TATTOOS

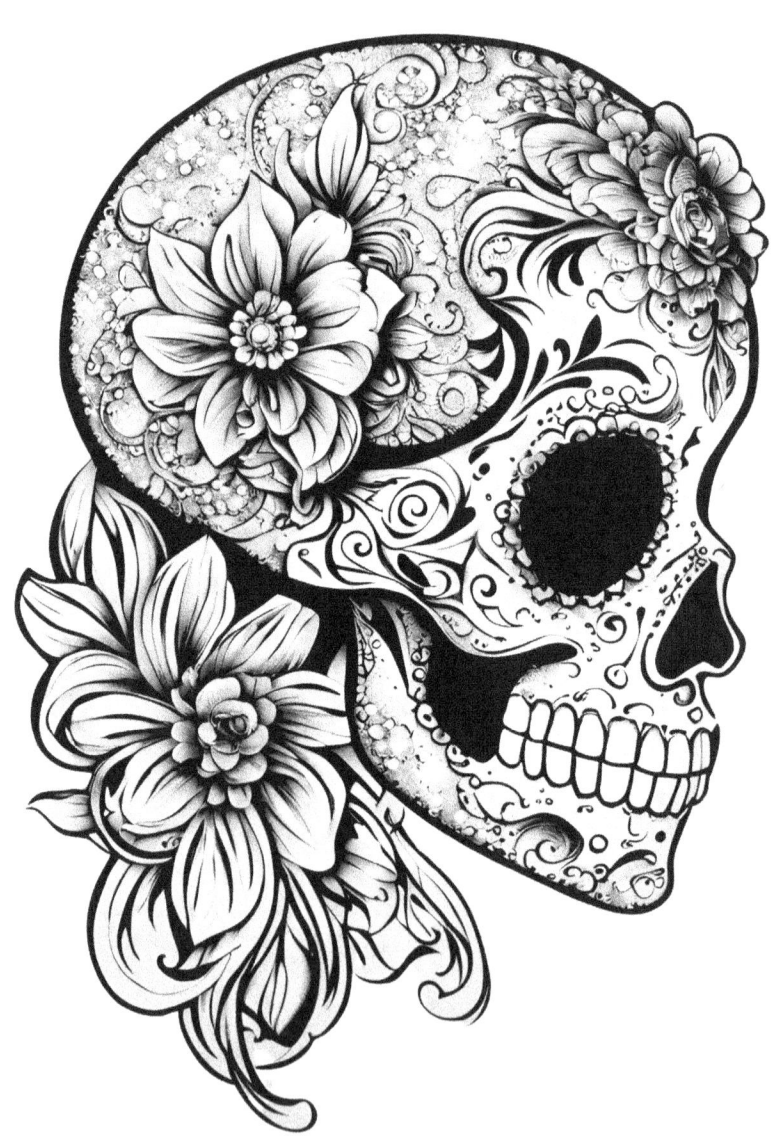

SUGAR SKULL TATTOOS

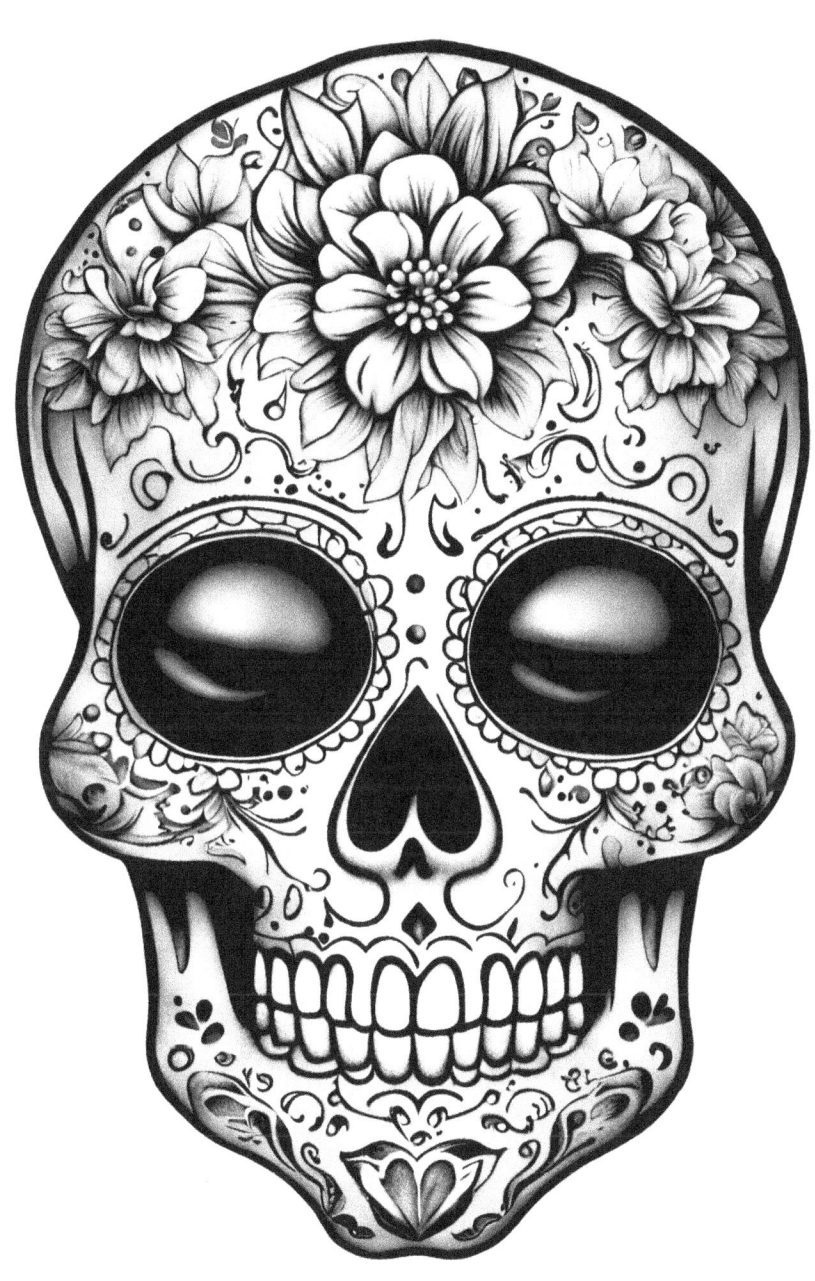

SUGAR SKULL TATTOOS

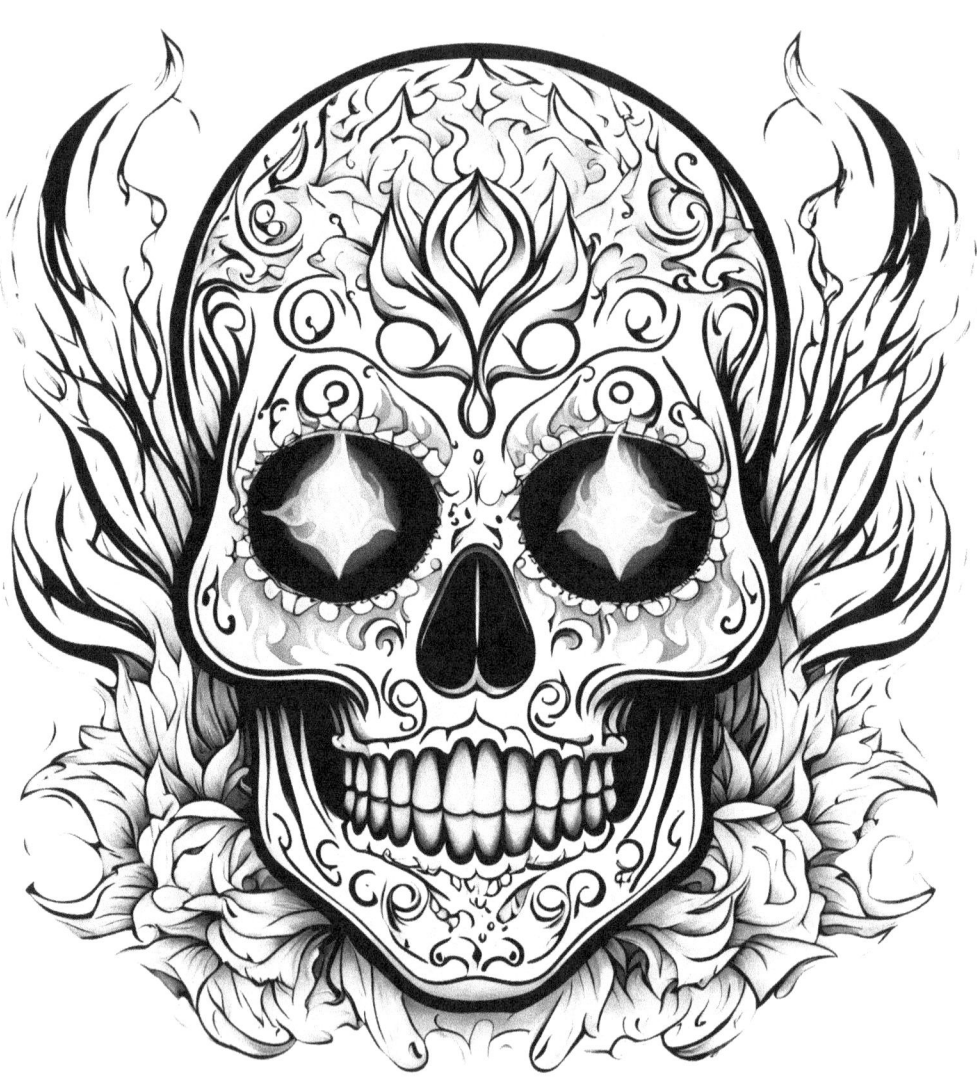

SUGAR SKULL TATTOOS

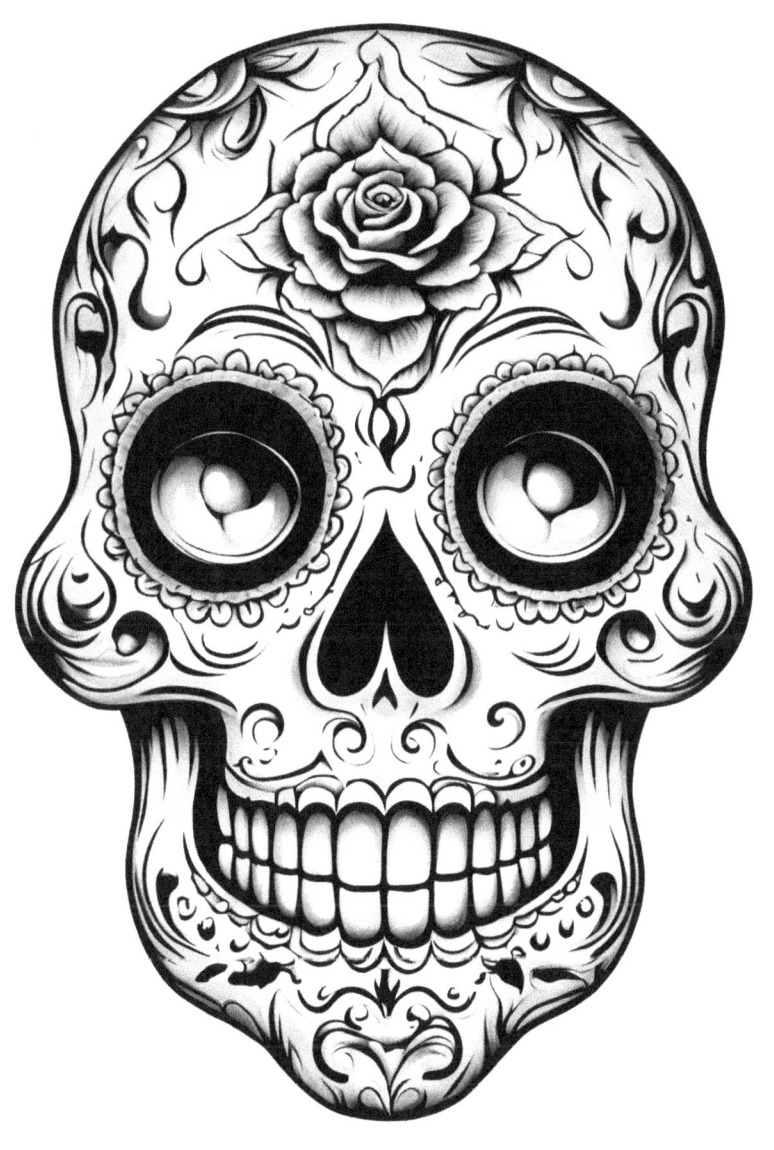

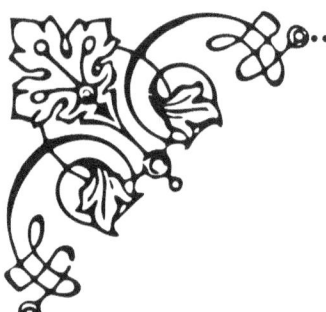
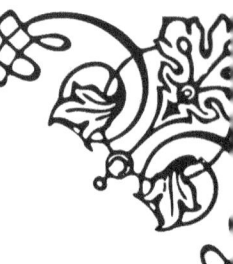

TRIBAL SKULL TATTOOS

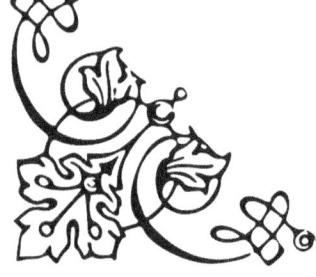

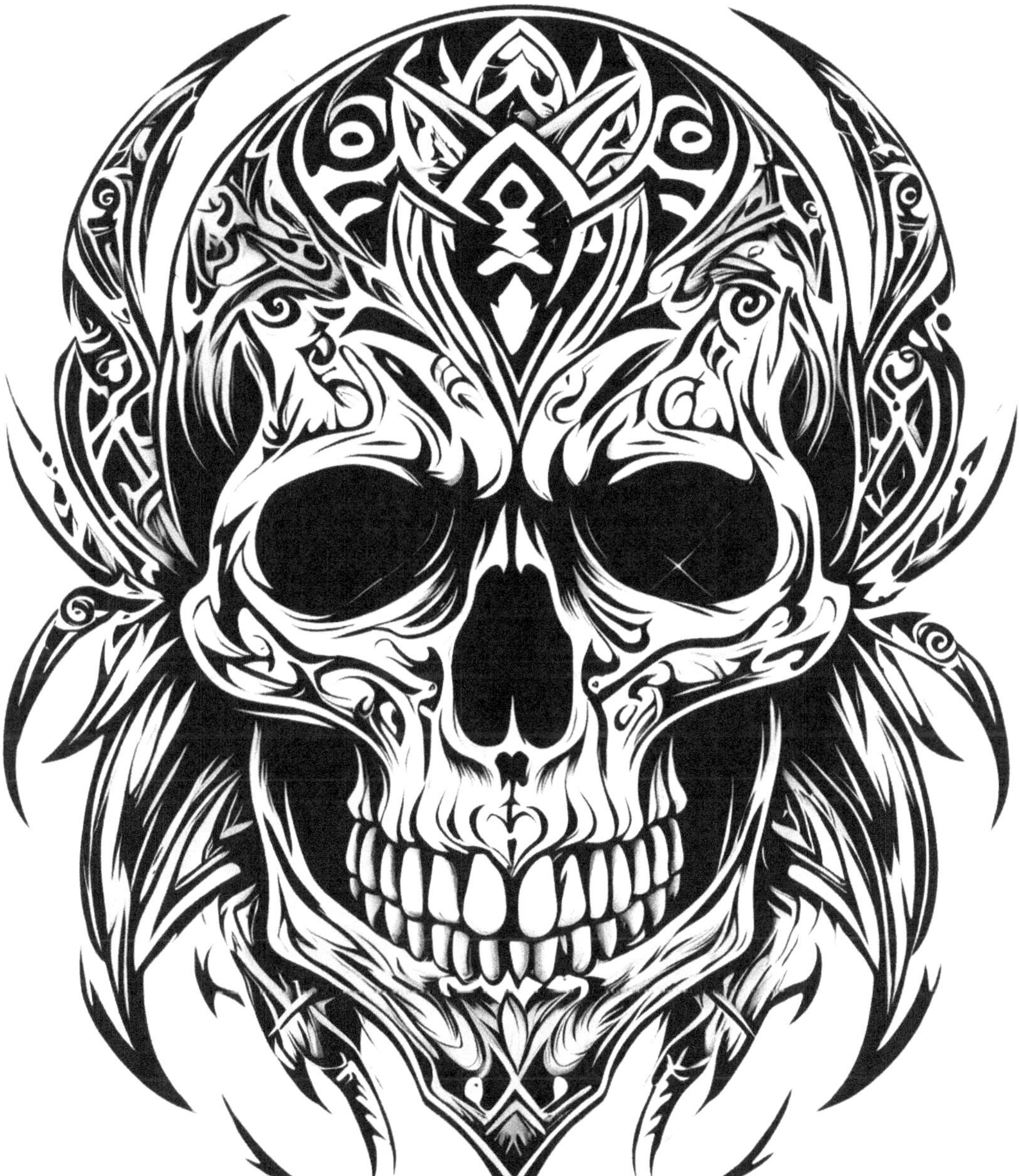

TRIBAL SKULL TATTOOS

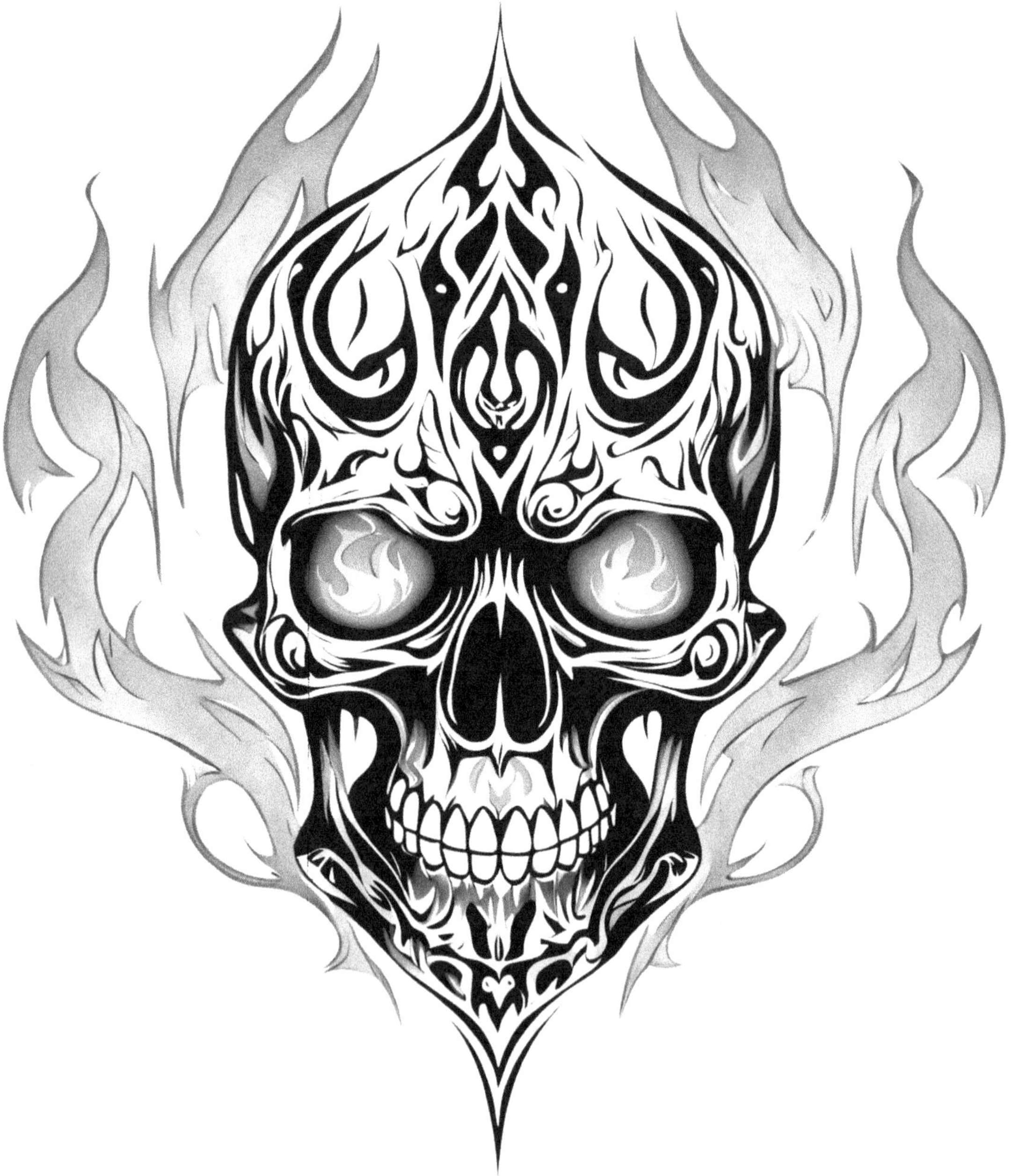

TRIBAL SKULL TATTOOS

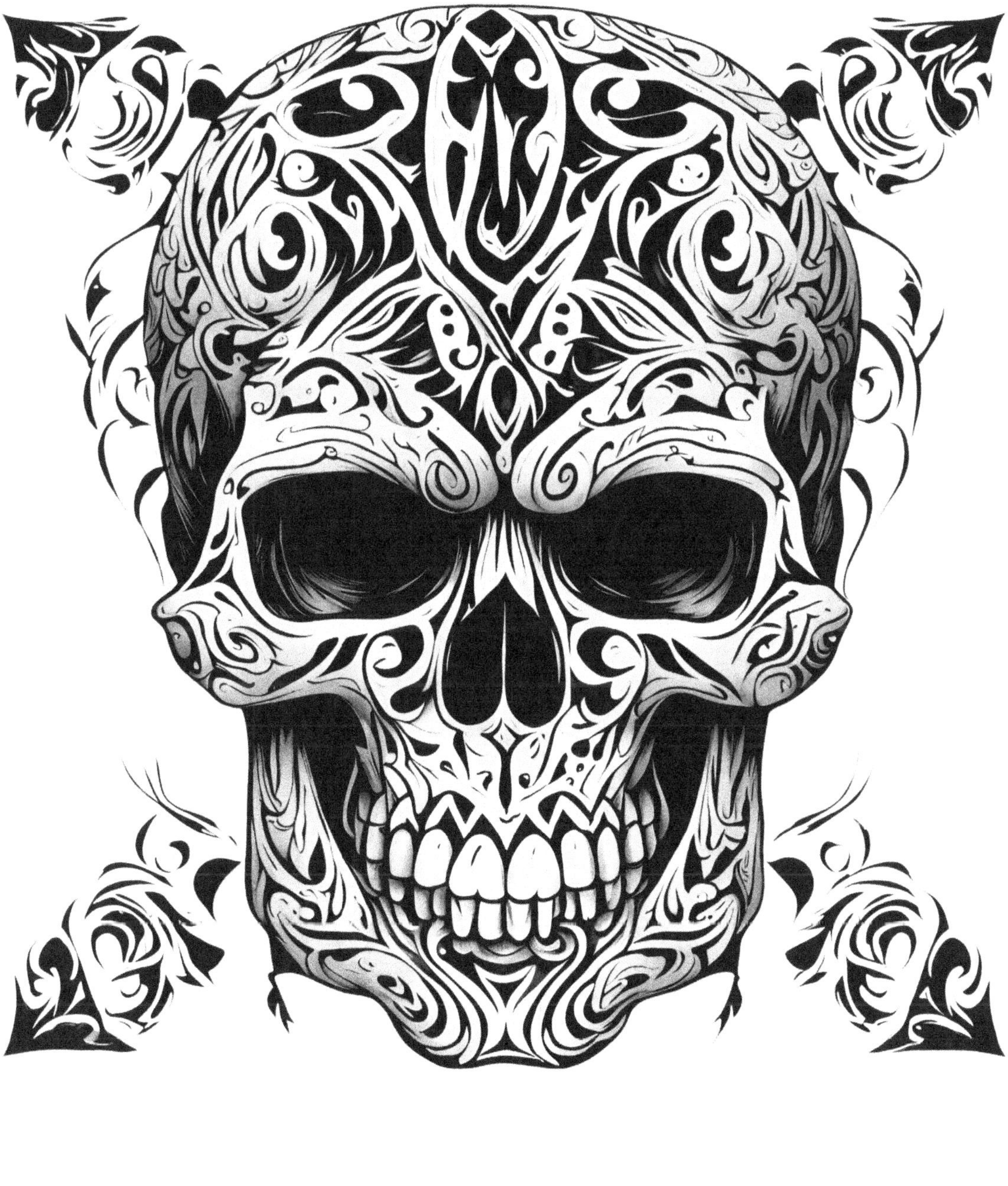

TRIBAL SKULL TATTOOS

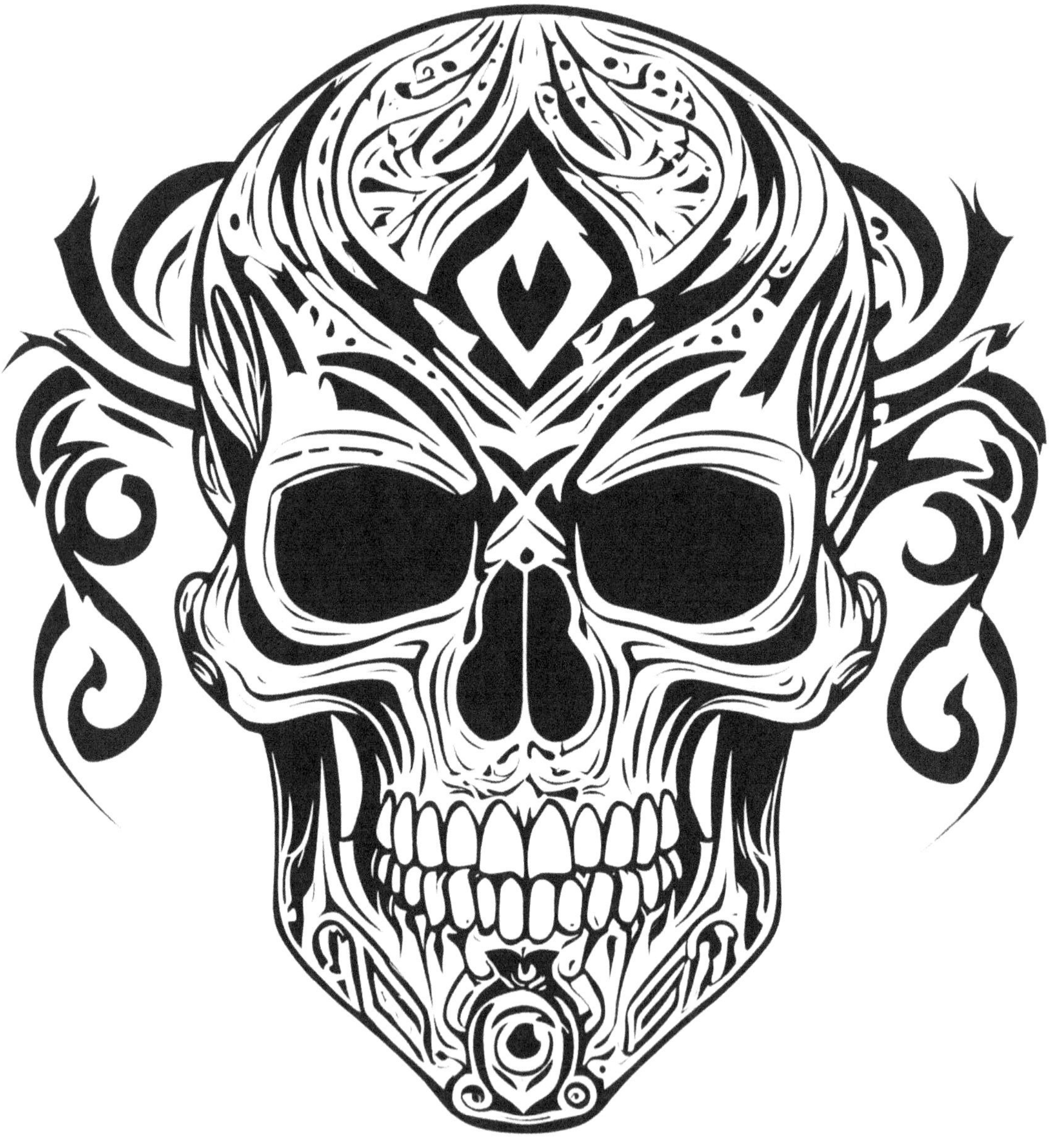

TRIBAL SKULL TATTOOS

TRIBAL SKULL TATTOOS

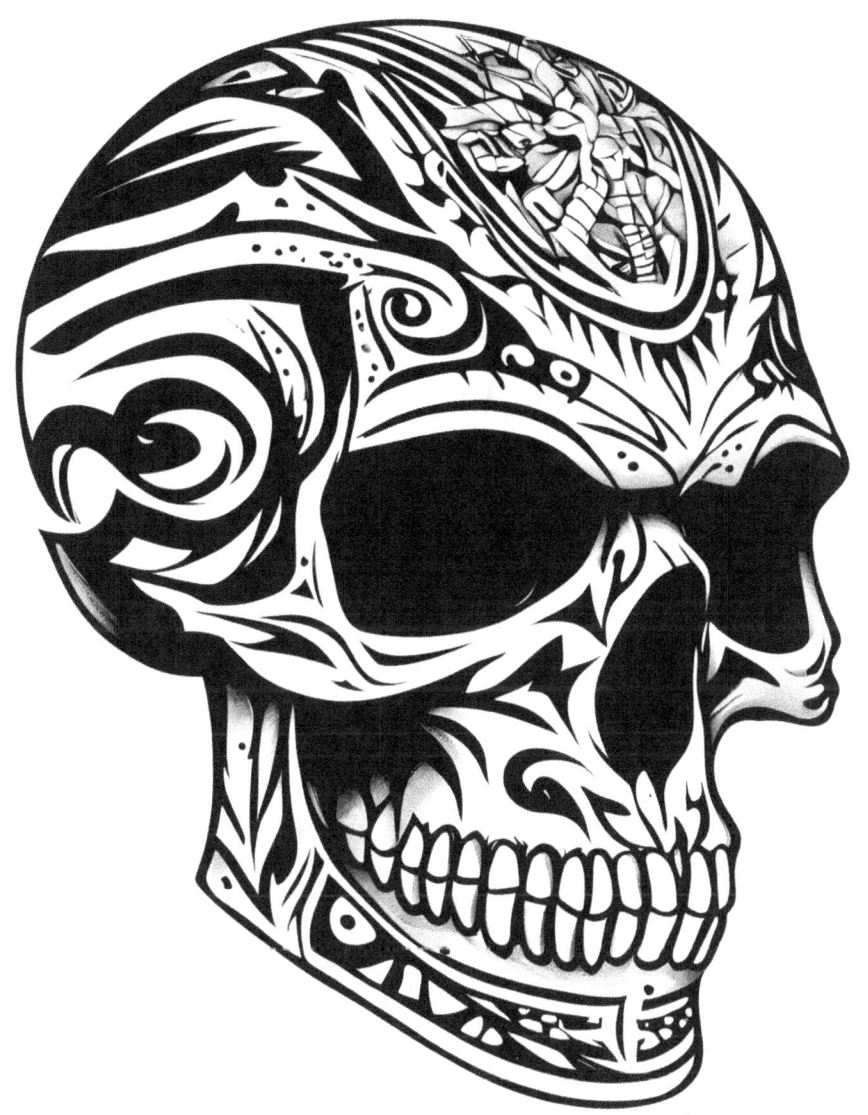

TRIBAL SKULL TATTOOS

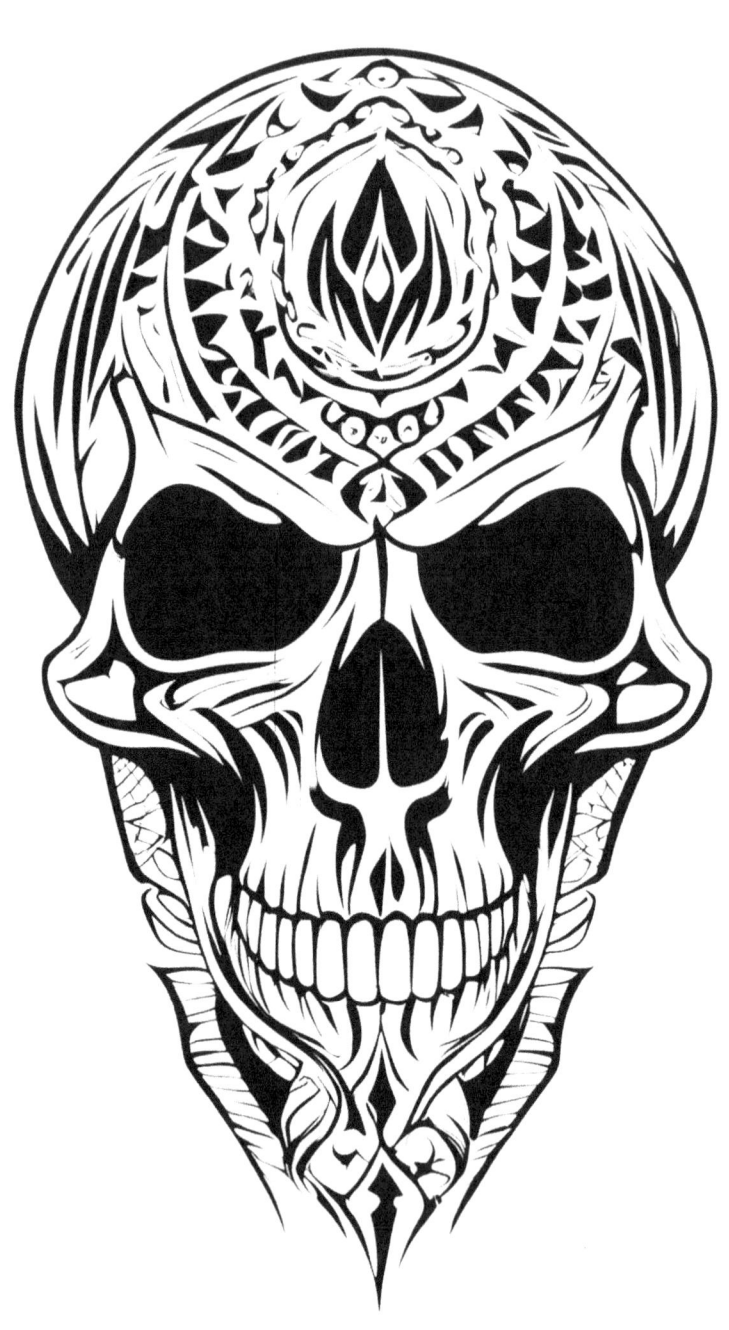

TRIBAL SKULL TATTOOS

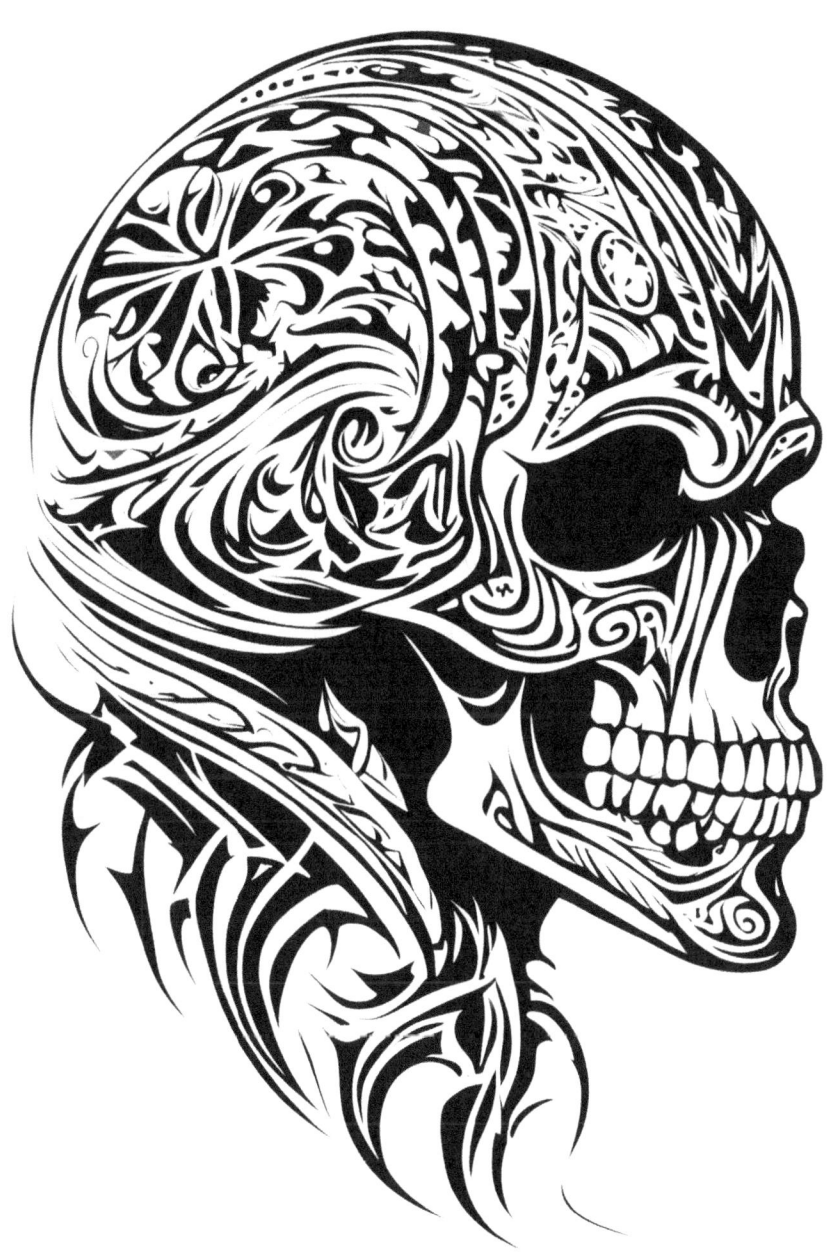

TRIBAL SKULL TATTOOS

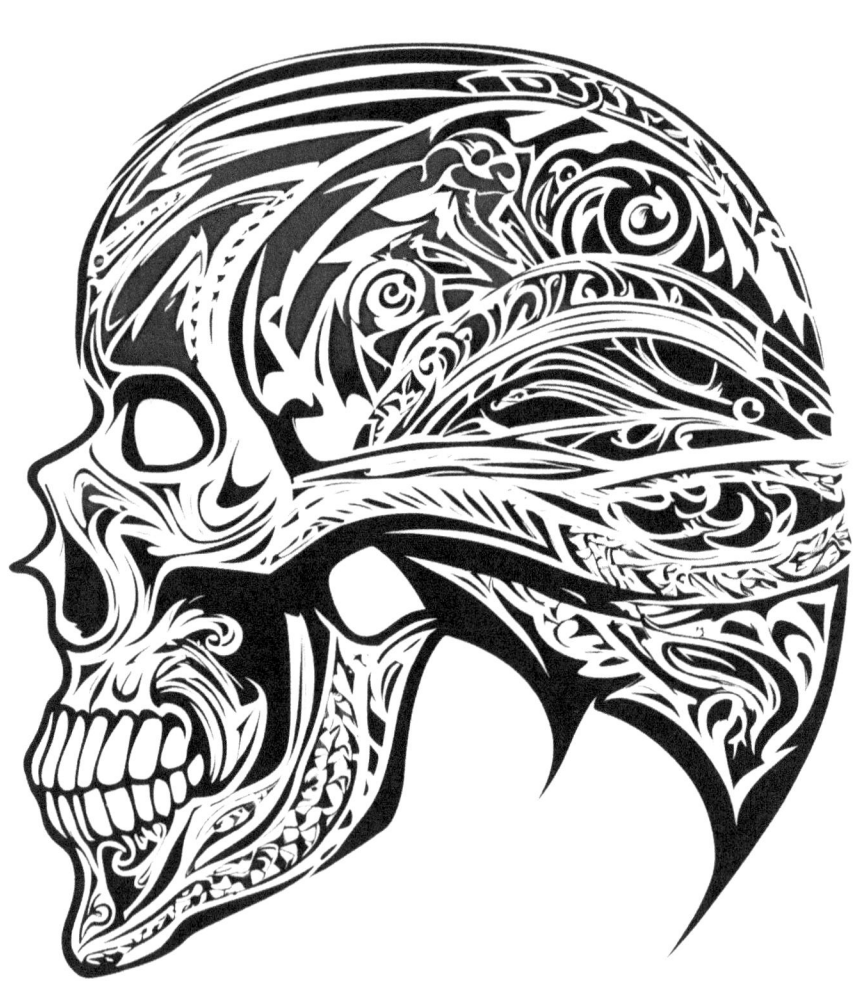

TRIBAL SKULL TATTOOS

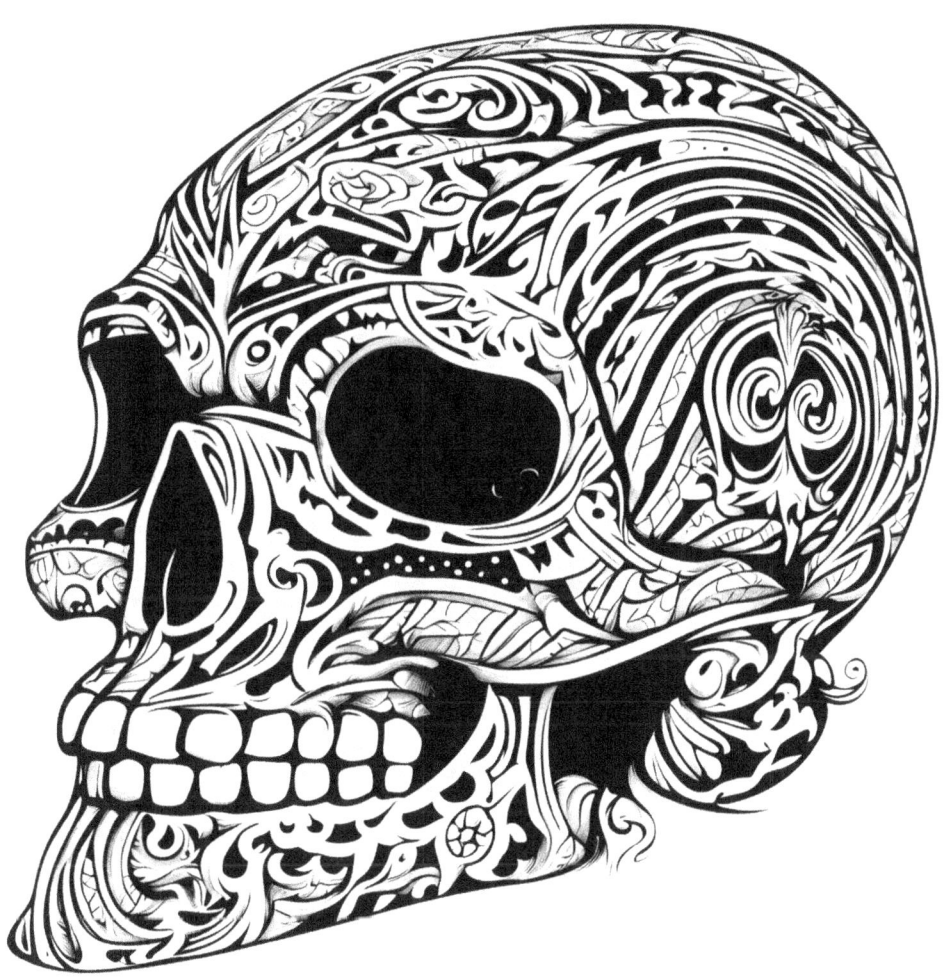

TRIBAL SKULL TATTOOS

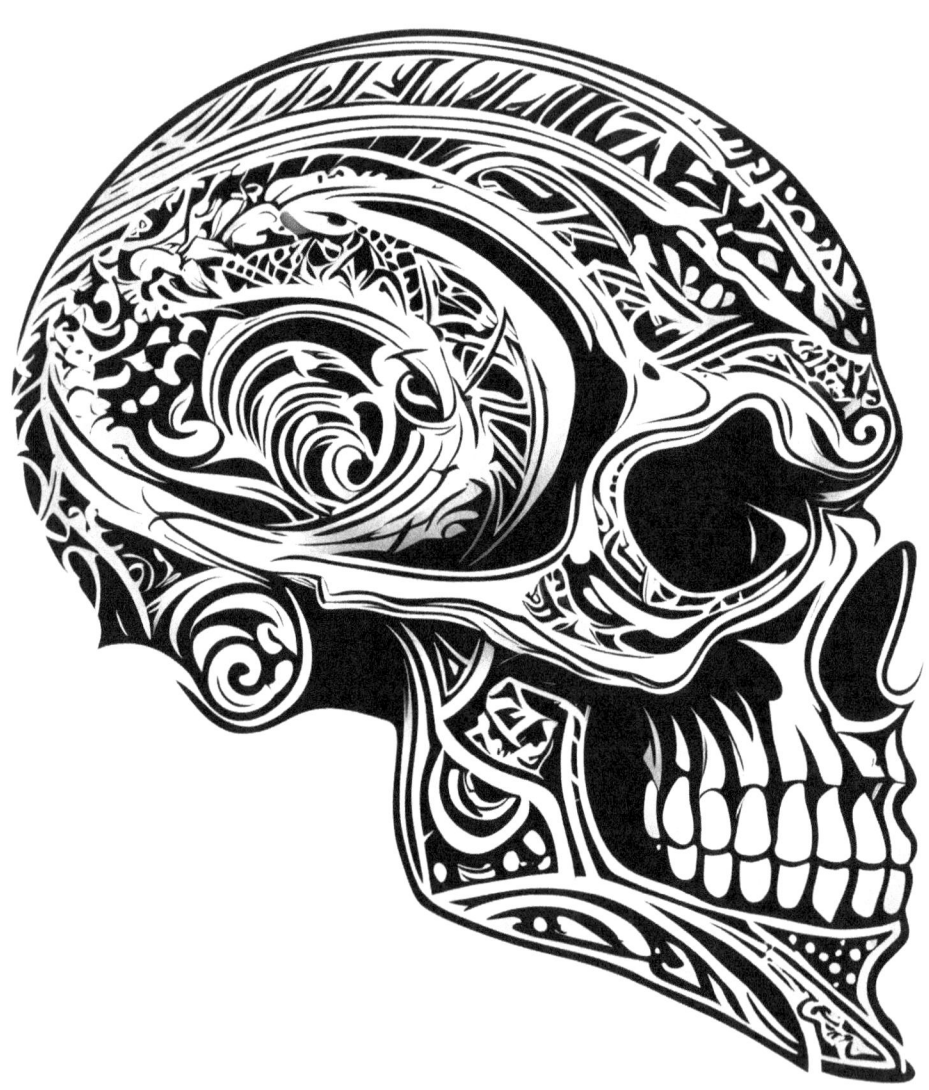

TRIBAL SKULL TATTOOS

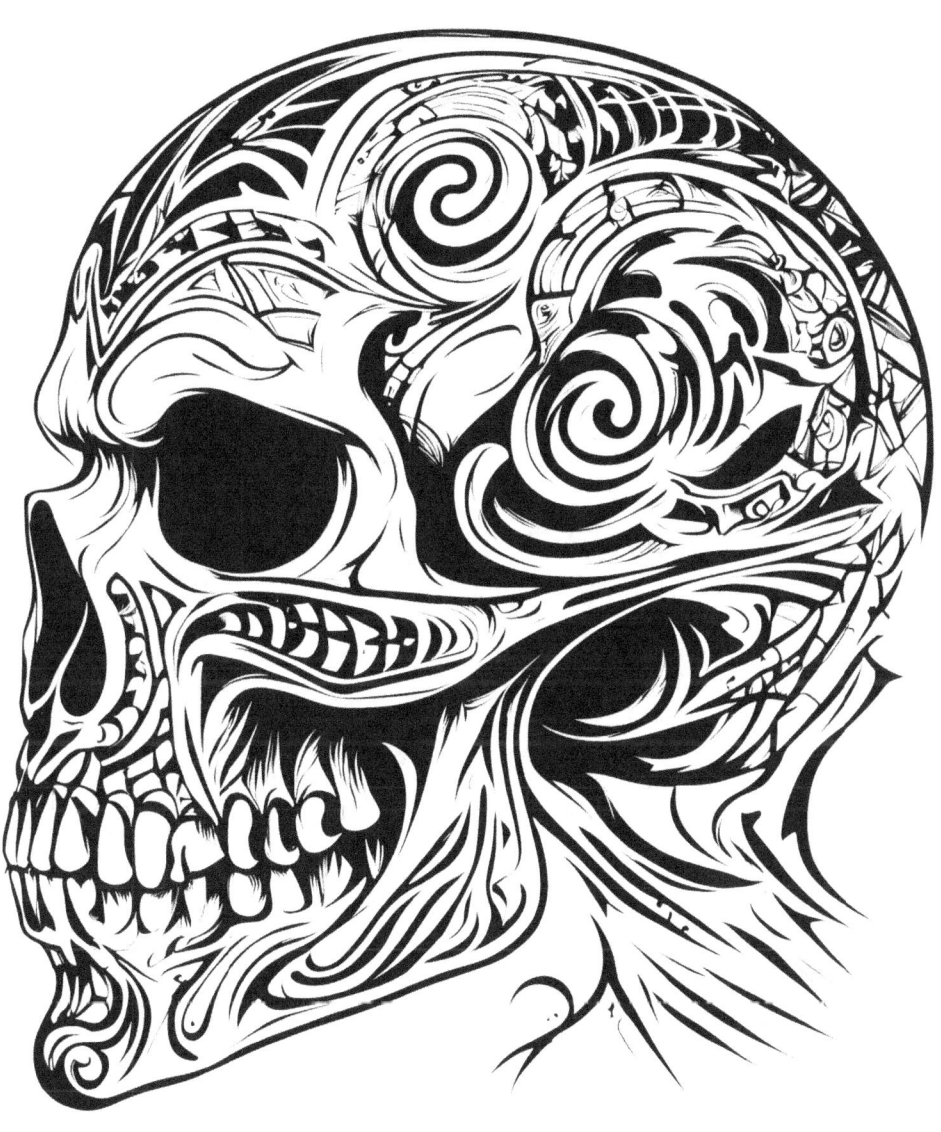

TRIBAL SKULL TATTOOS

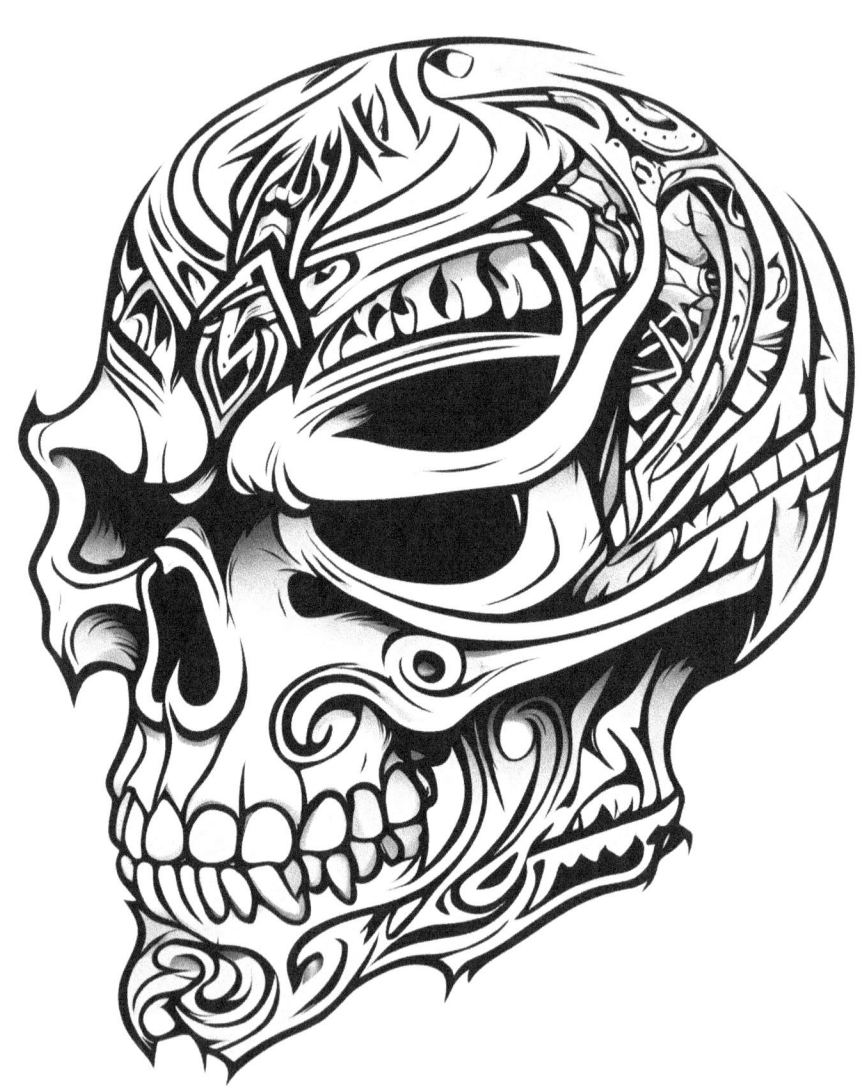

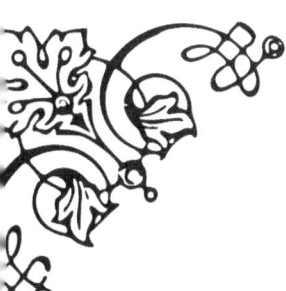
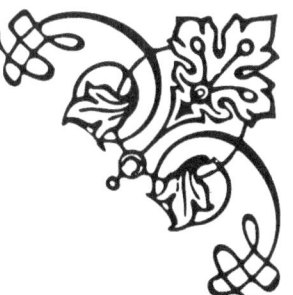

GRIM REAPER SKULL TATTOOS

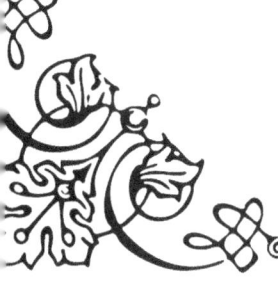
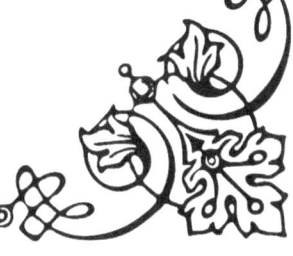

GRIM REAPER SKULL TATTOOS

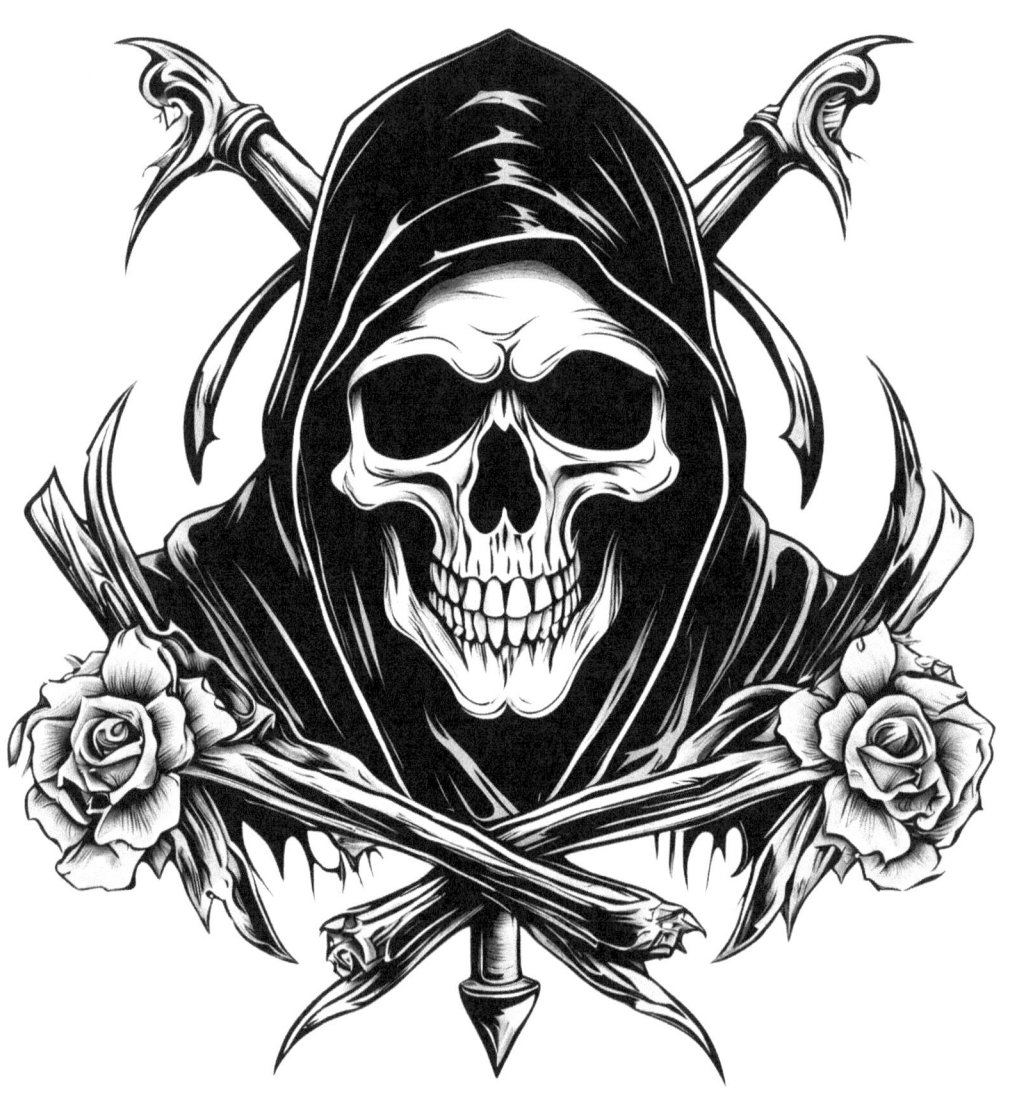

GRIM REAPER SKULL TATTOOS

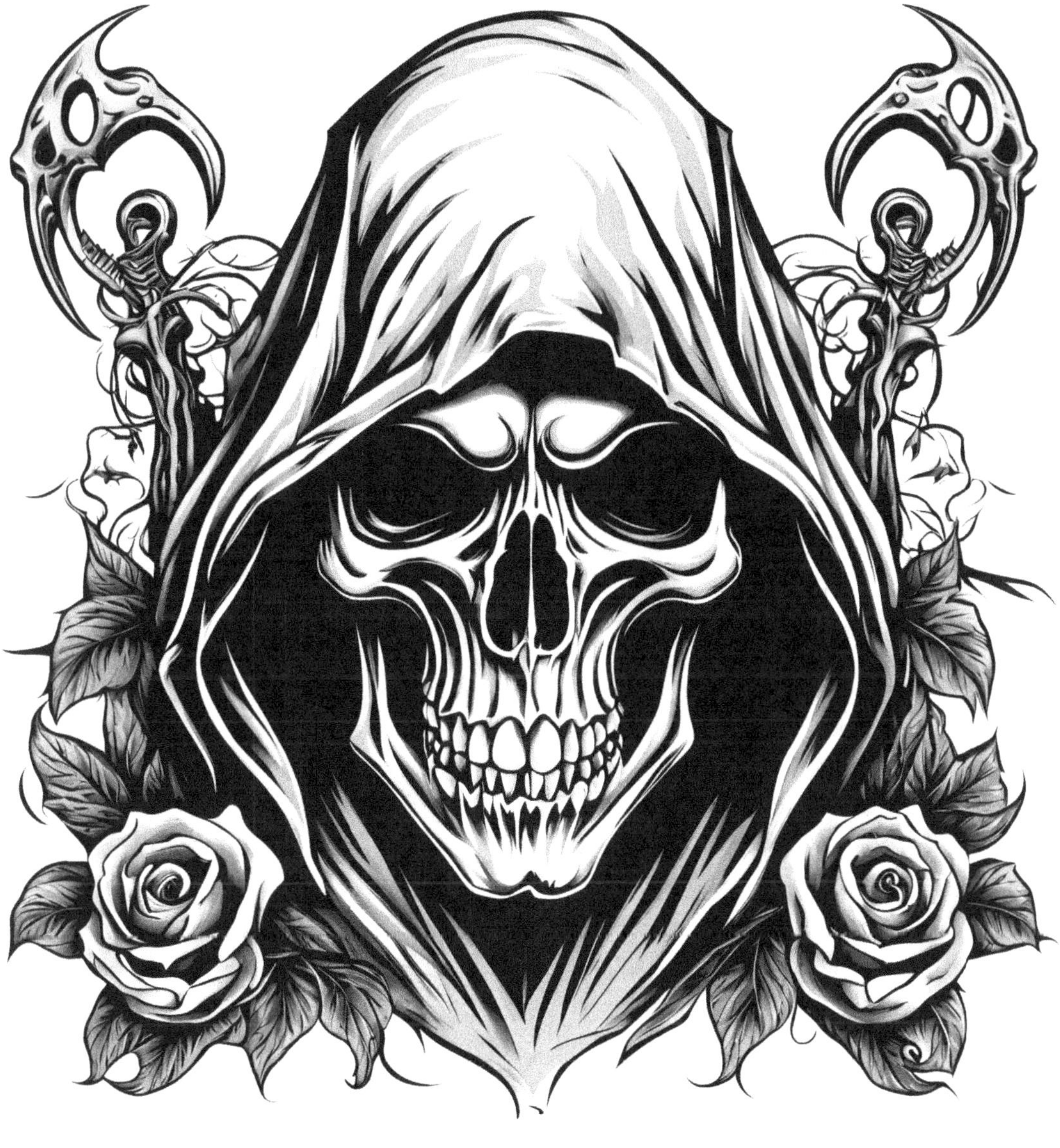

GRIM REAPER SKULL TATTOOS

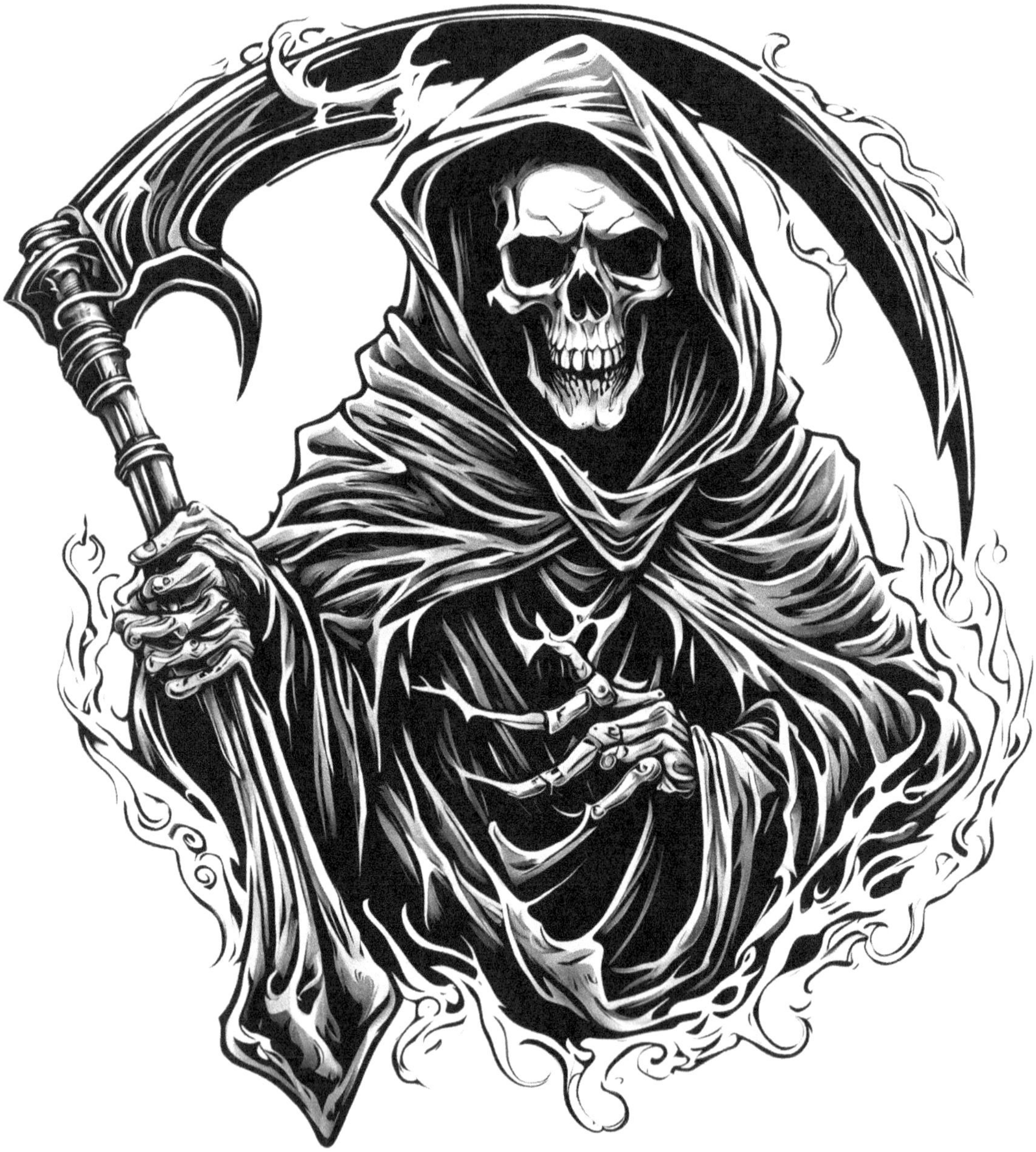

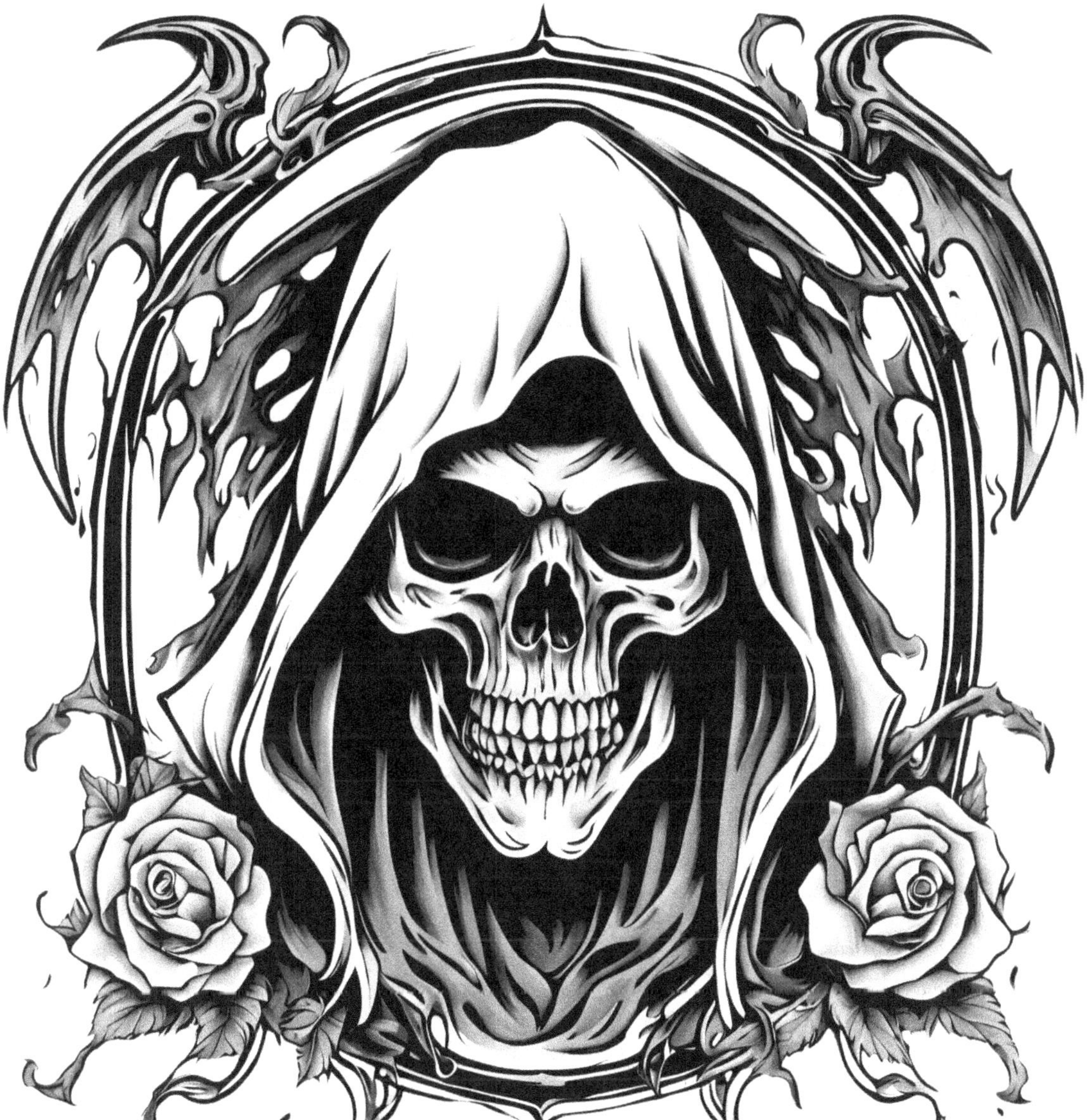

GRIM REAPER SKULL TATTOOS

GRIM REAPER SKULL TATTOOS

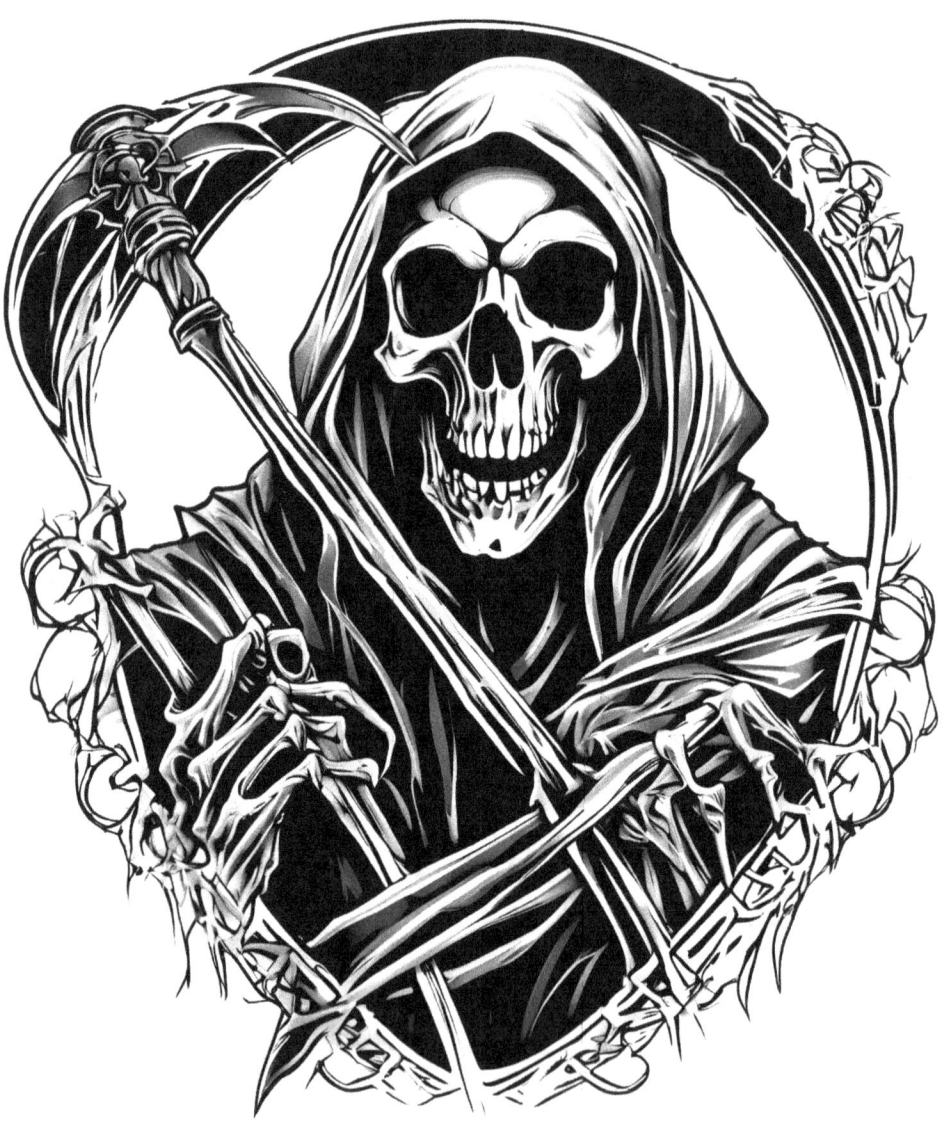

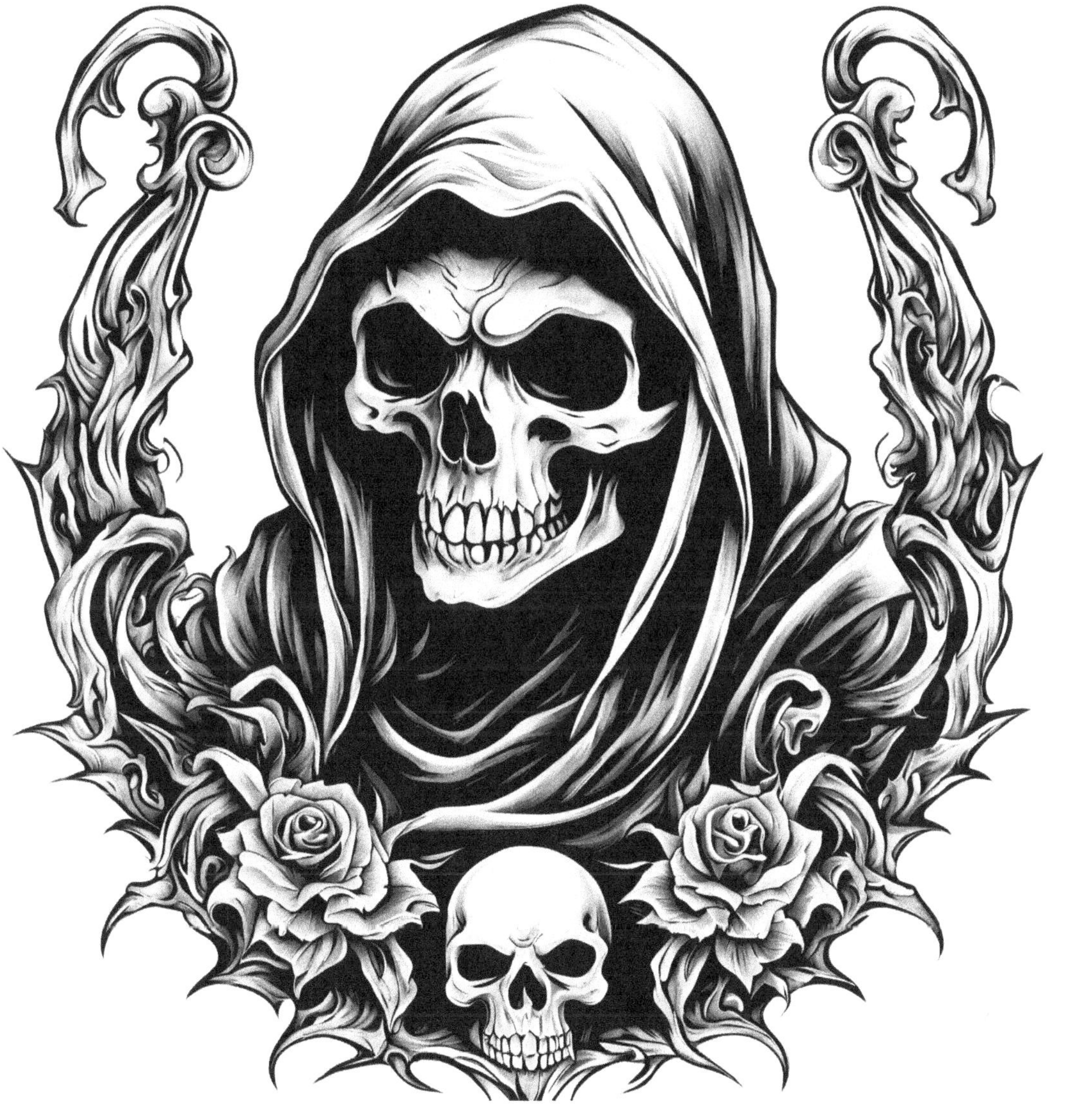

GRIM REAPER SKULL TATTOOS

GRIM REAPER SKULL TATTOOS

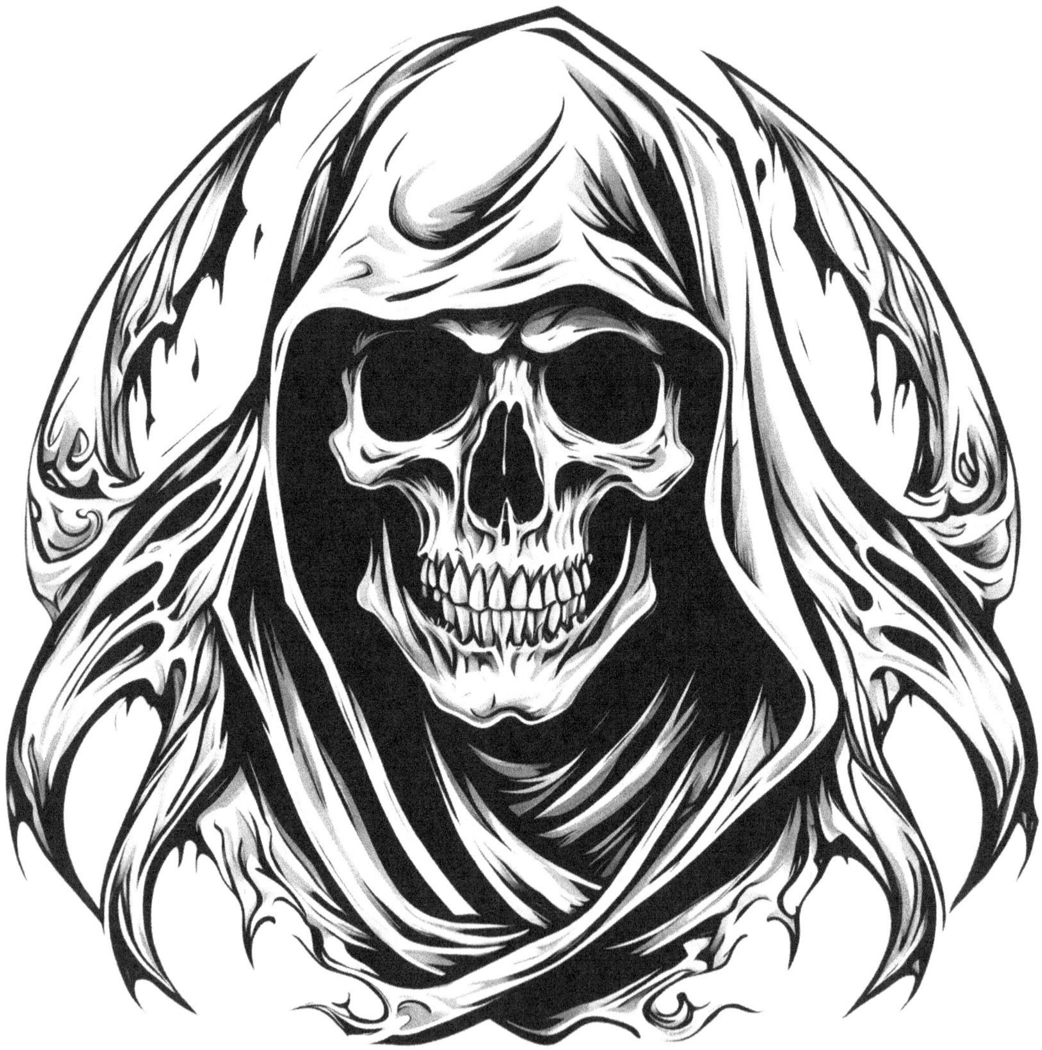

GRIM REAPER SKULL TATTOOS

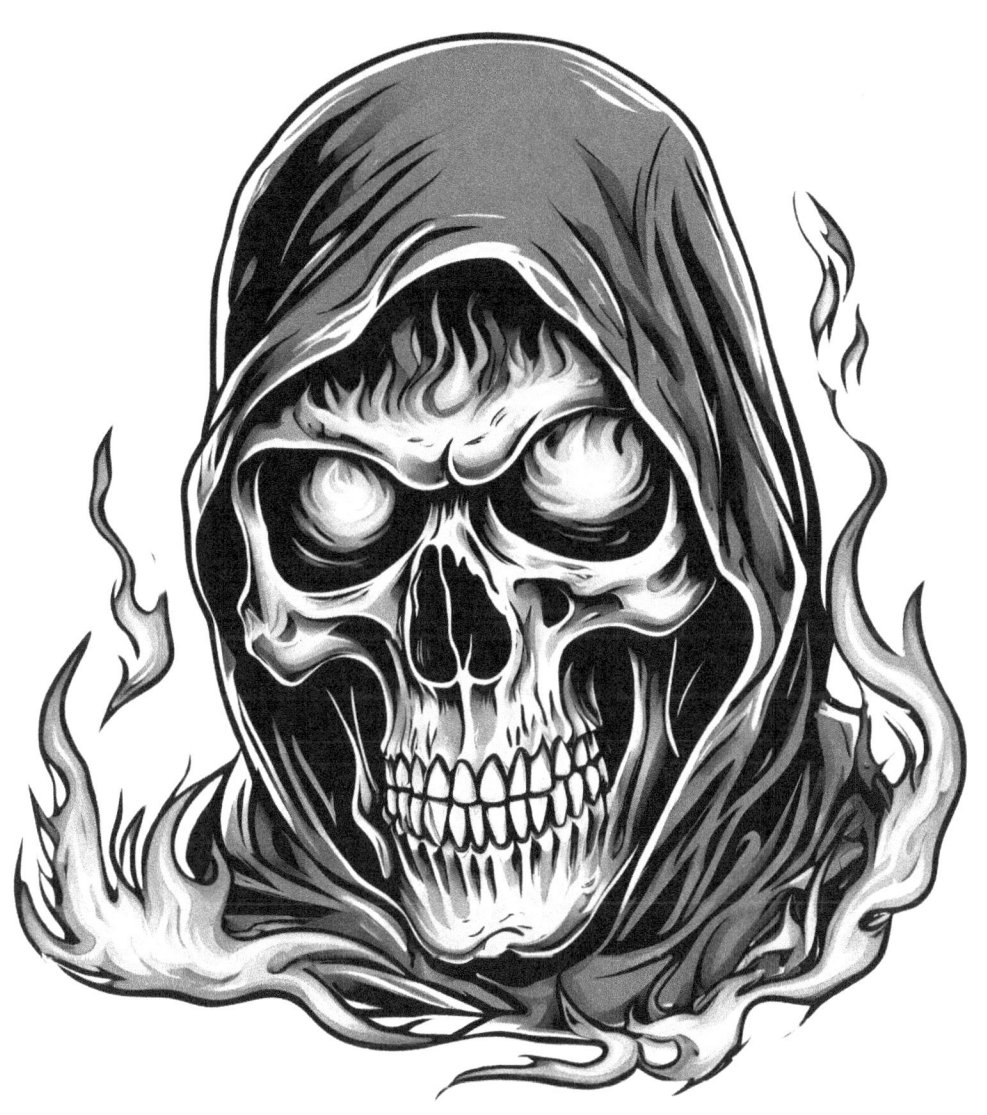

GRIM REAPER SKULL TATTOOS

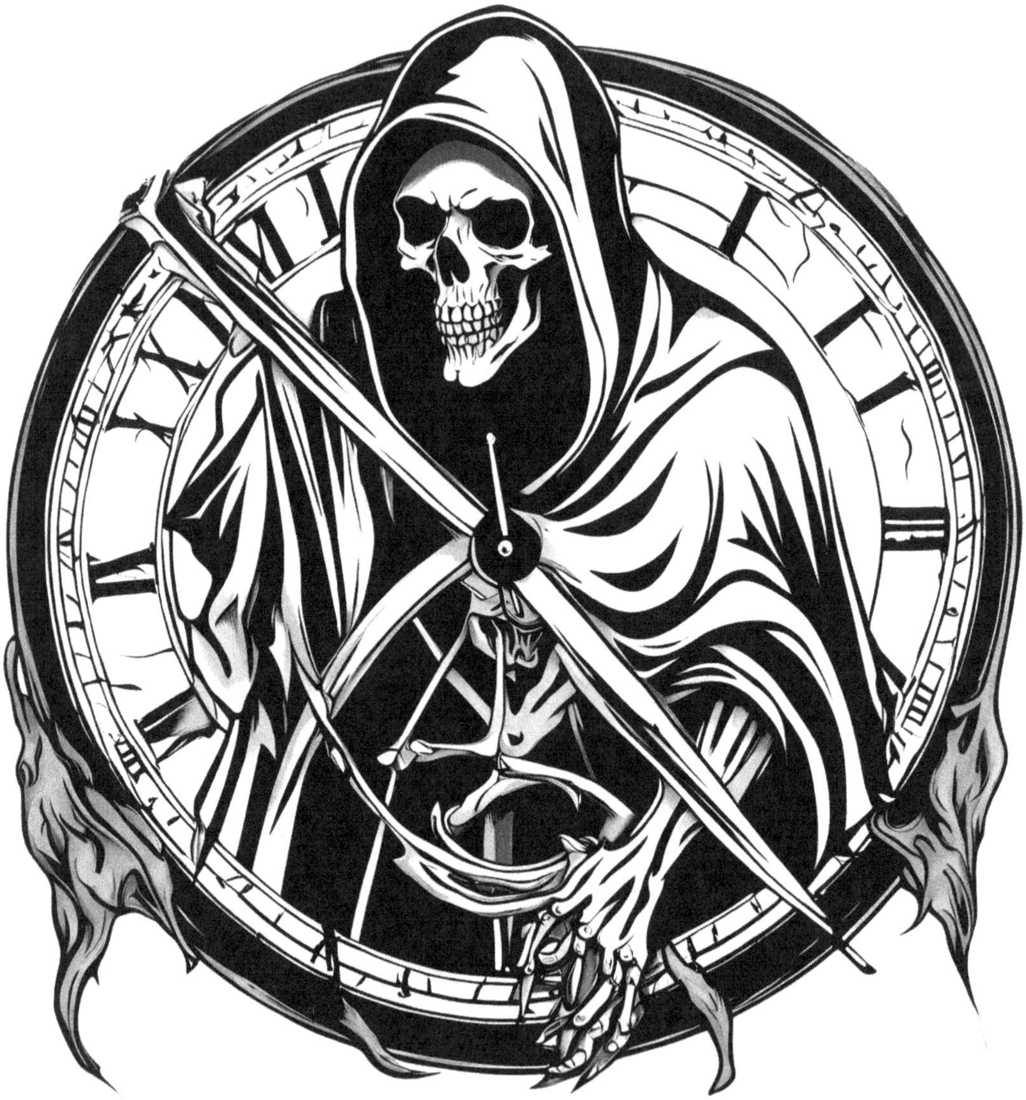

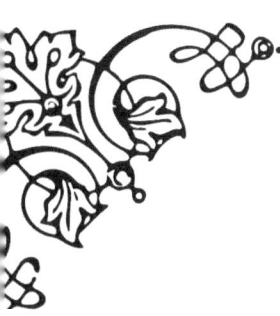
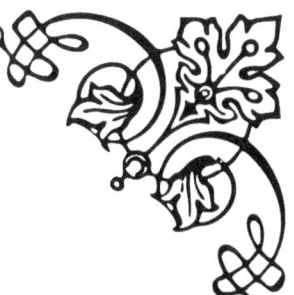

SERPENT SKULL TATTOOS

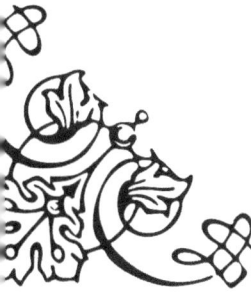

SERPENT SKULL TATTOOS

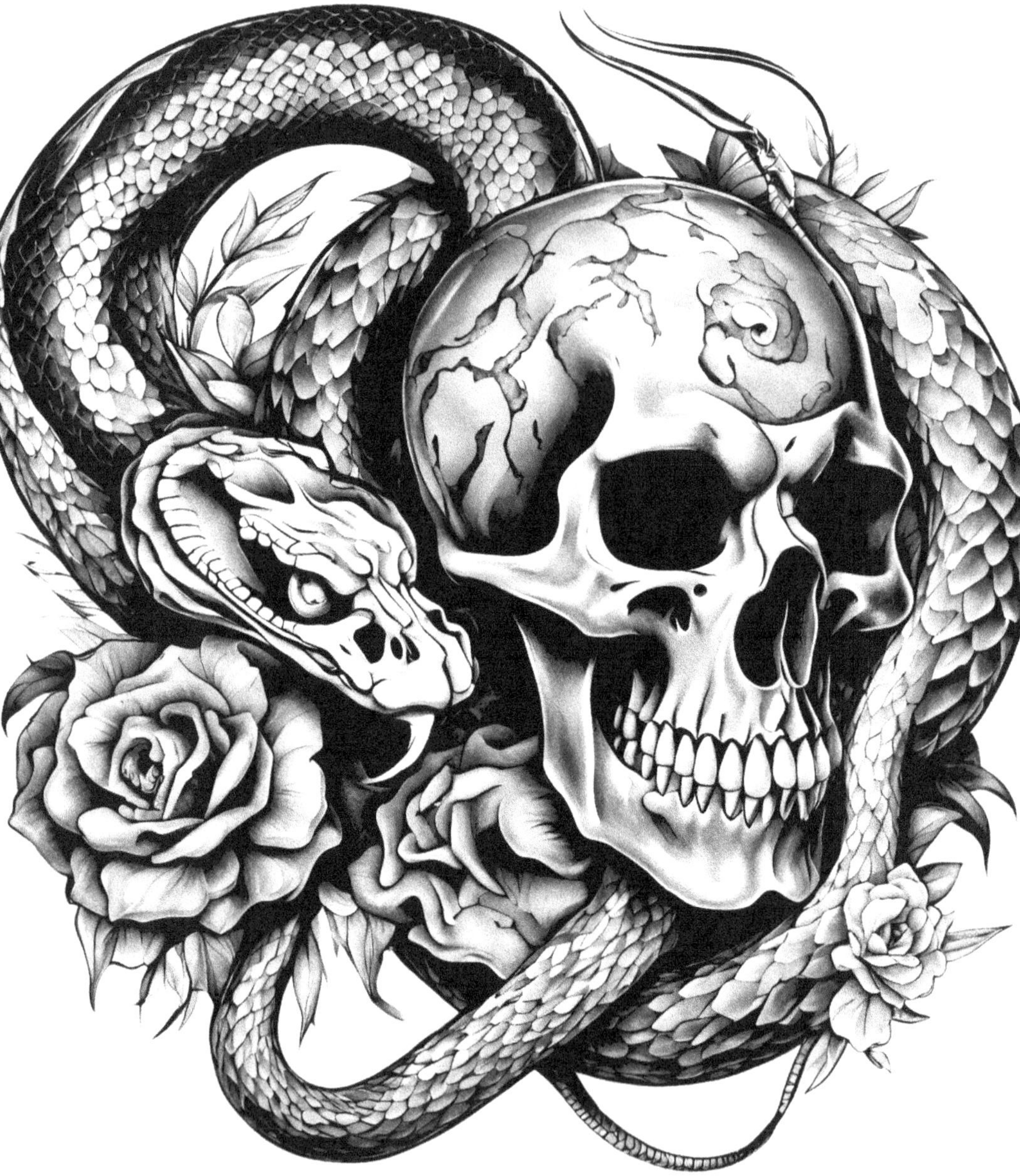

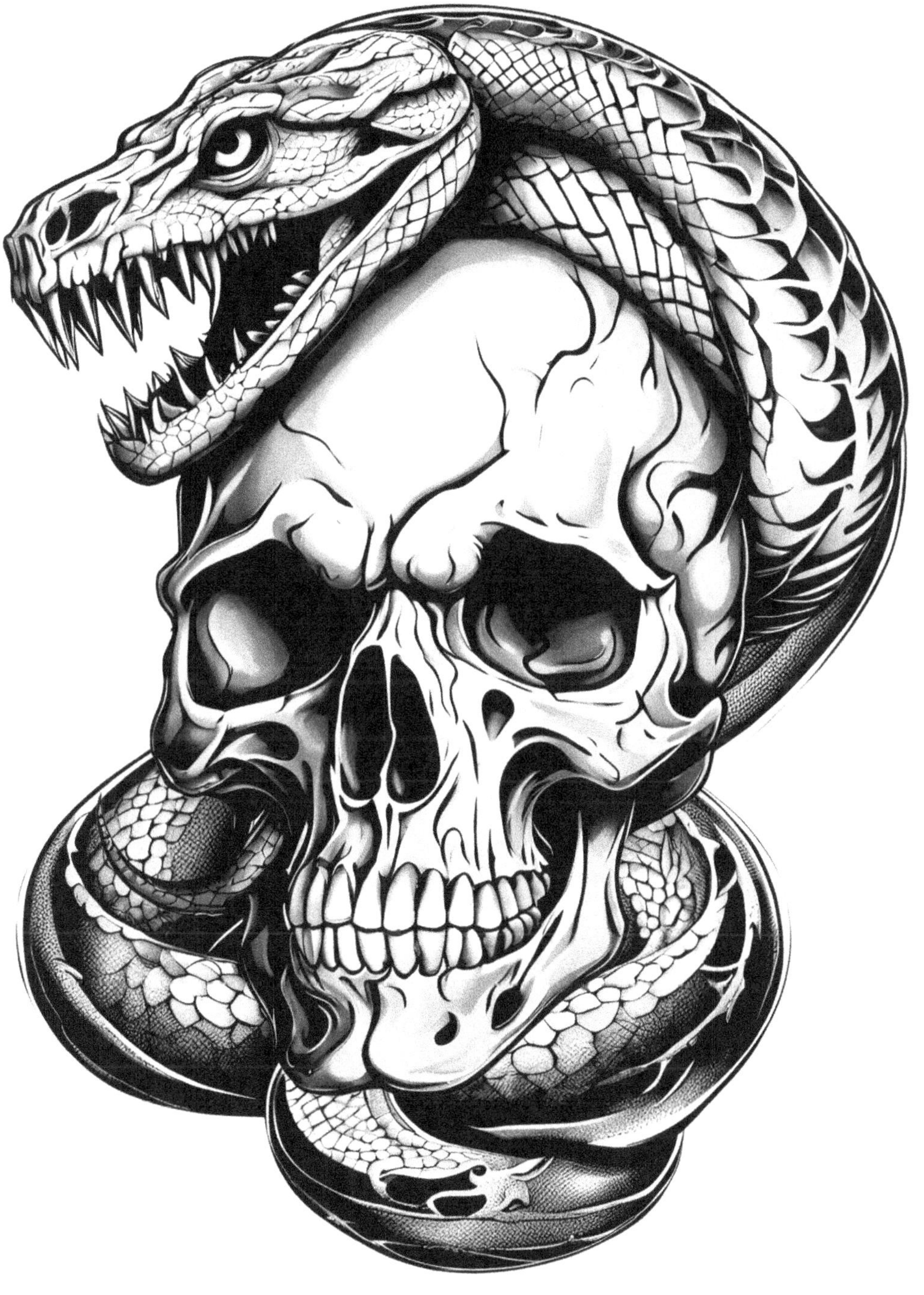

SERPENT SKULL TATTOOS

SERPENT SKULL TATTOOS

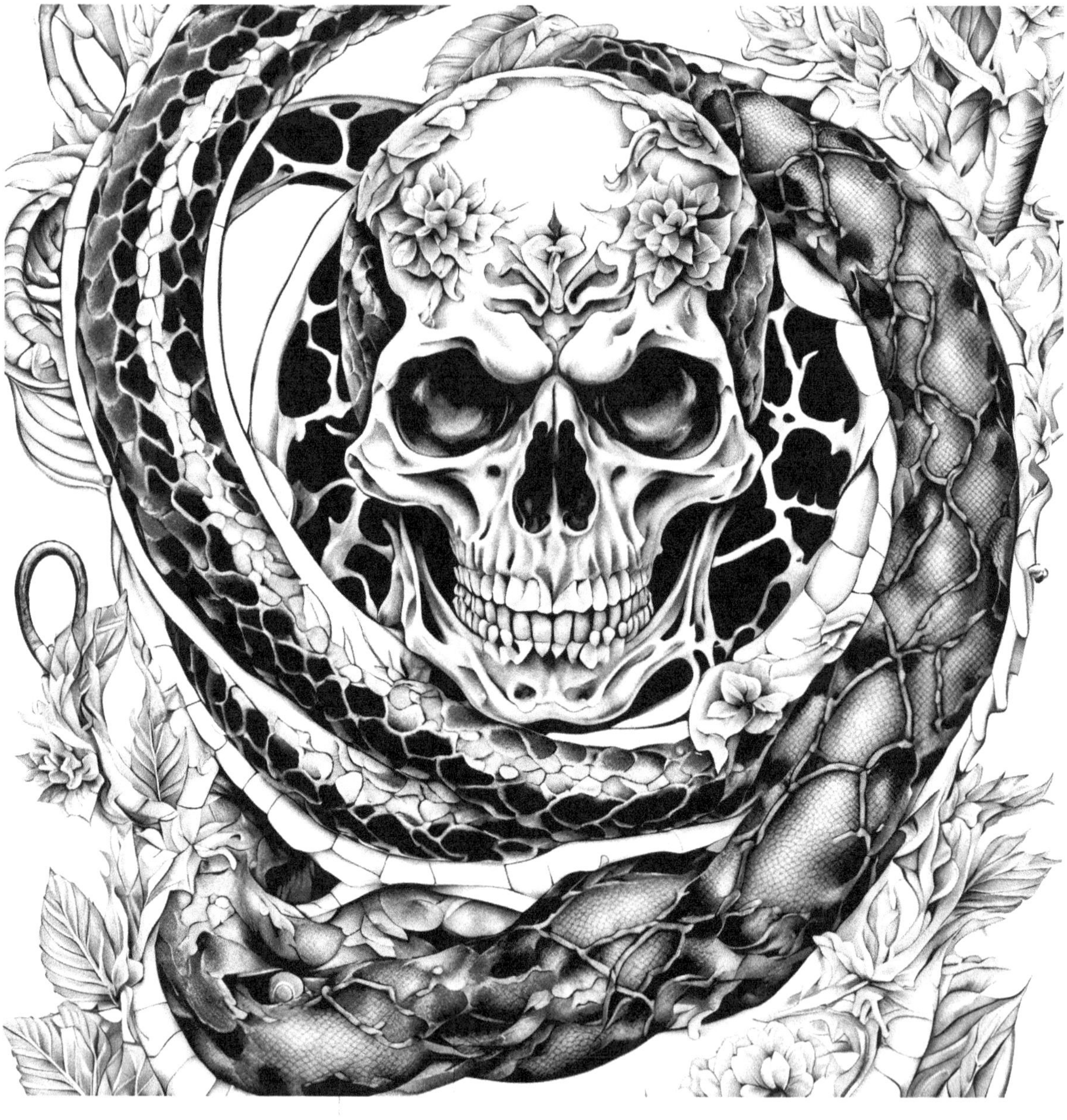

SERPENT SKULL TATTOOS

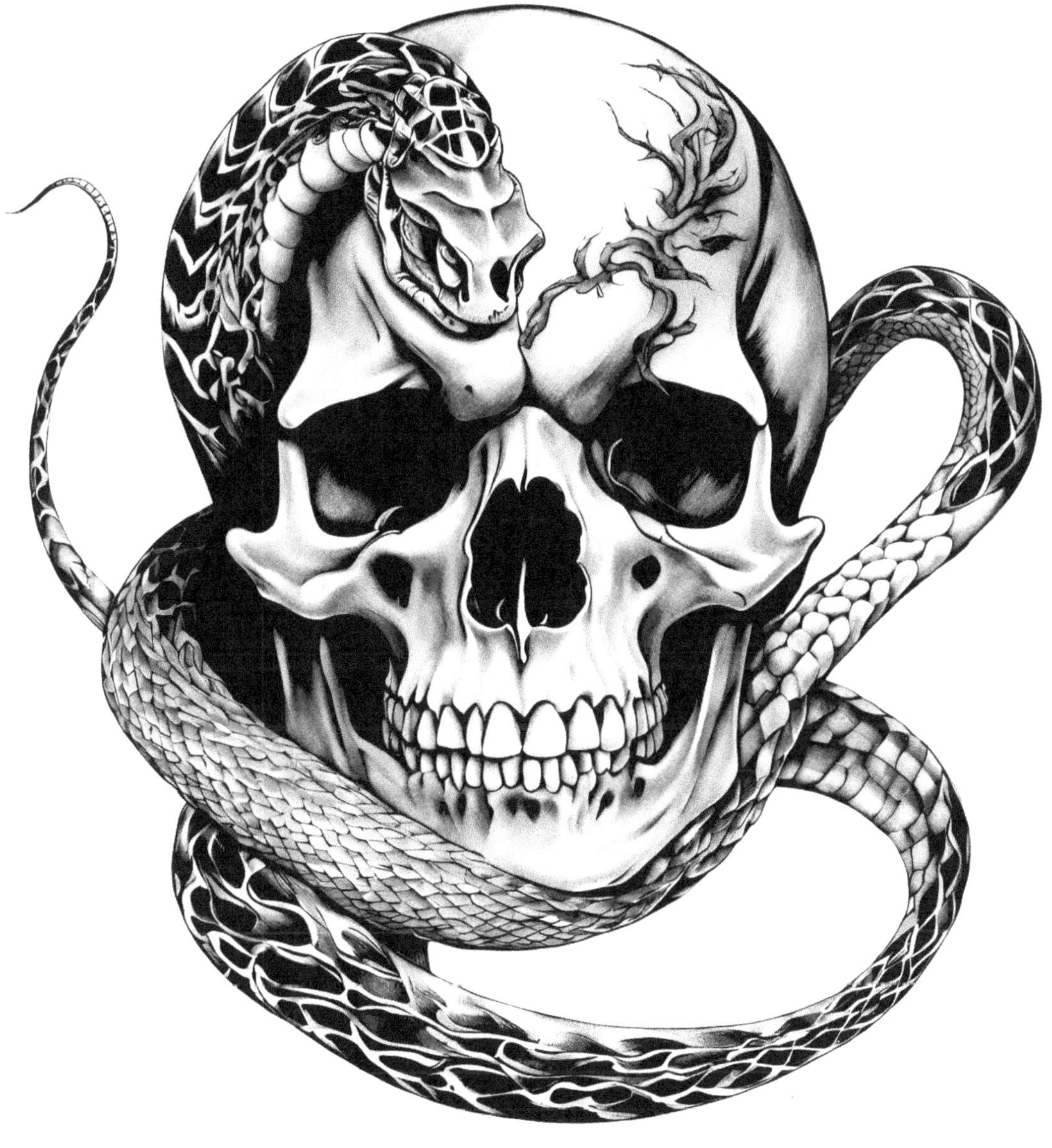

PAGE 129

SERPENT SKULL TATTOOS

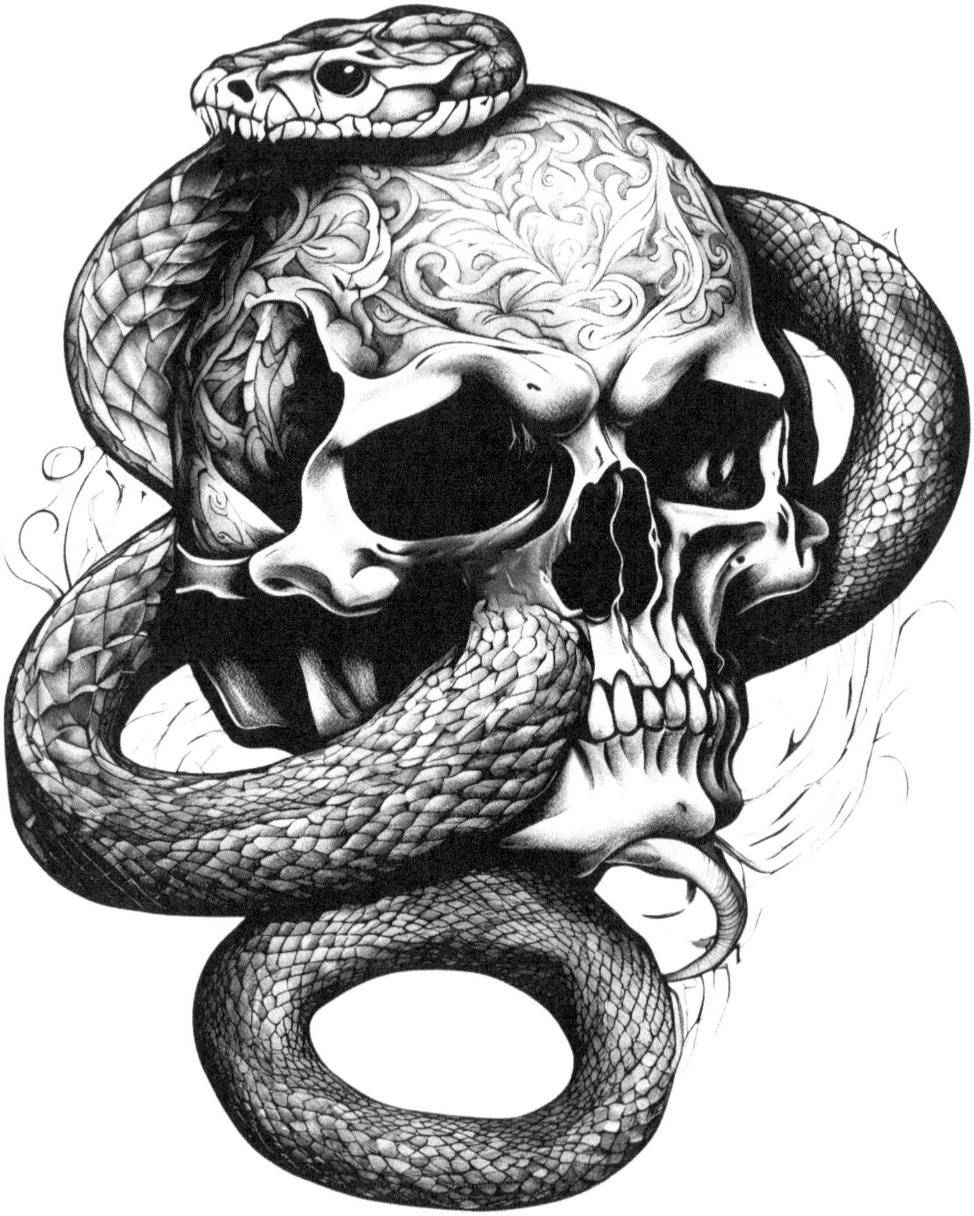

SERPENT SKULL TATTOOS

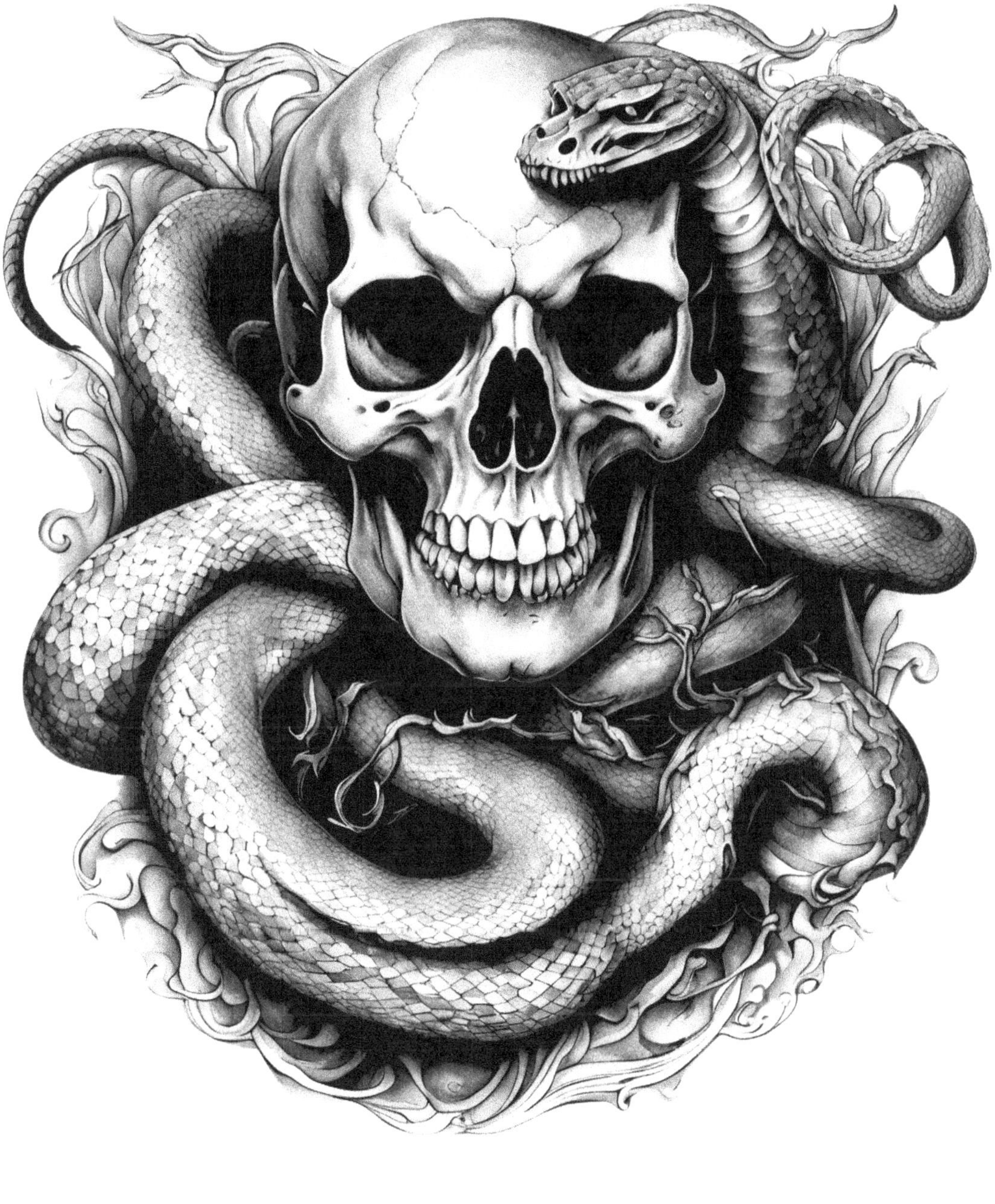

SERPENT SKULL TATTOOS

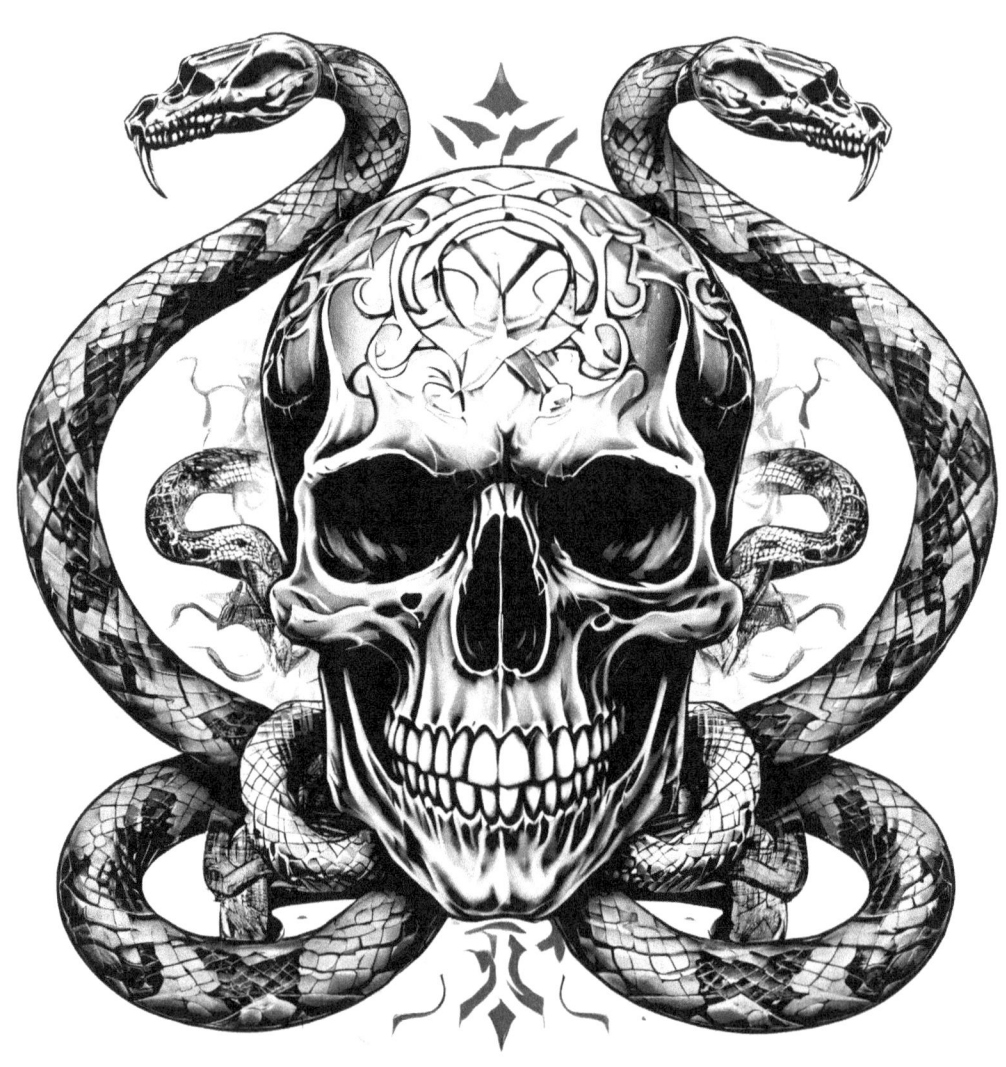

SERPENT SKULL TATTOOS

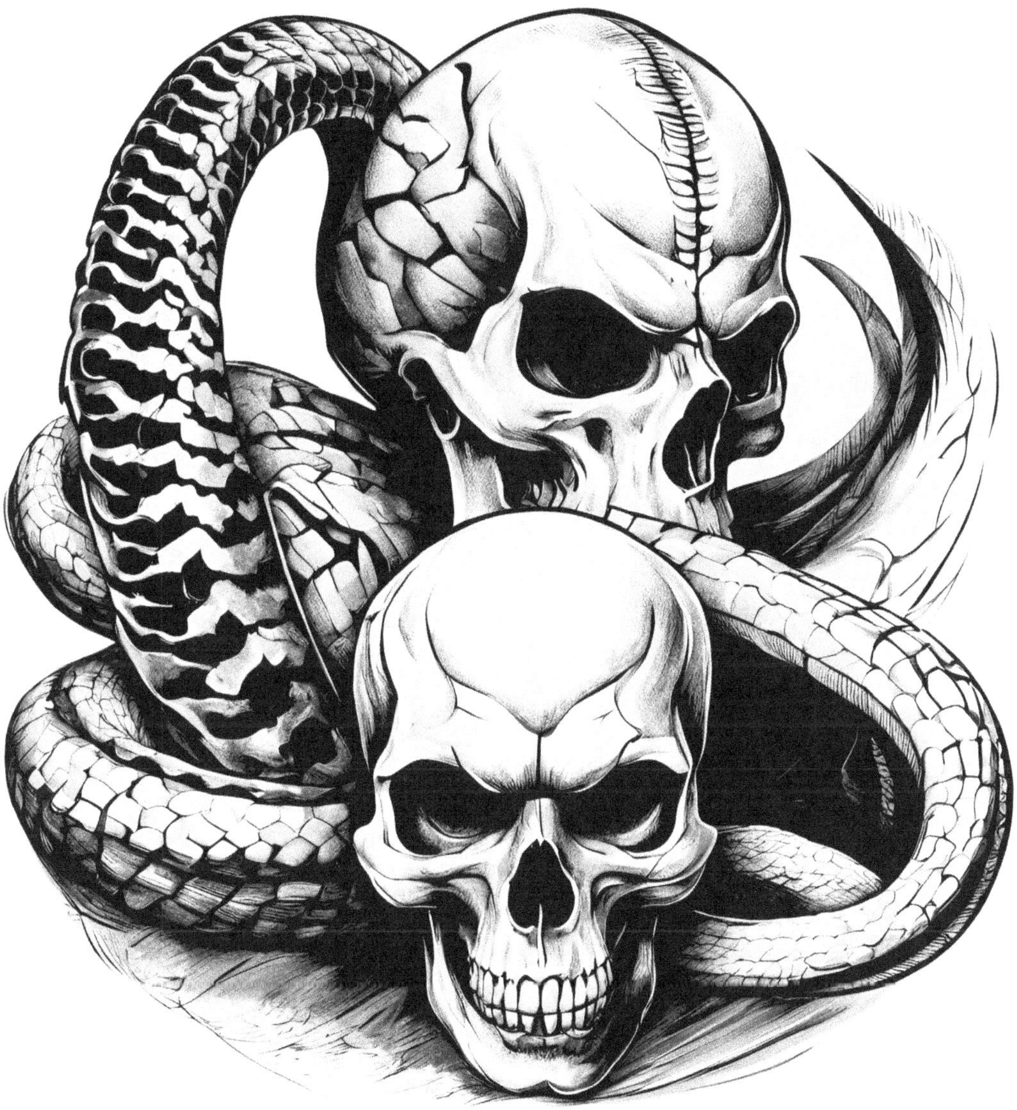

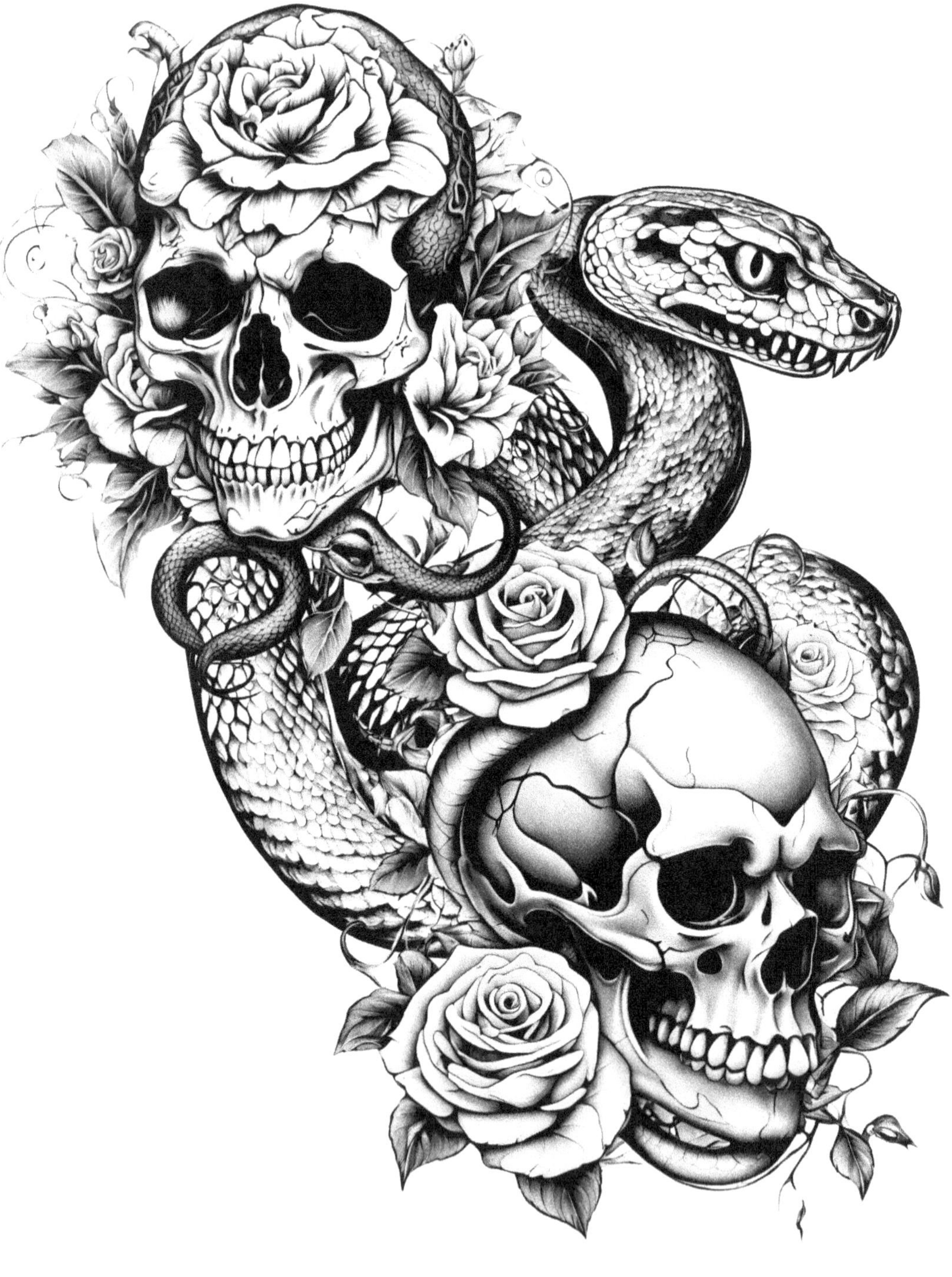

SERPENT SKULL TATTOOS

SERPENT SKULL TATTOOS

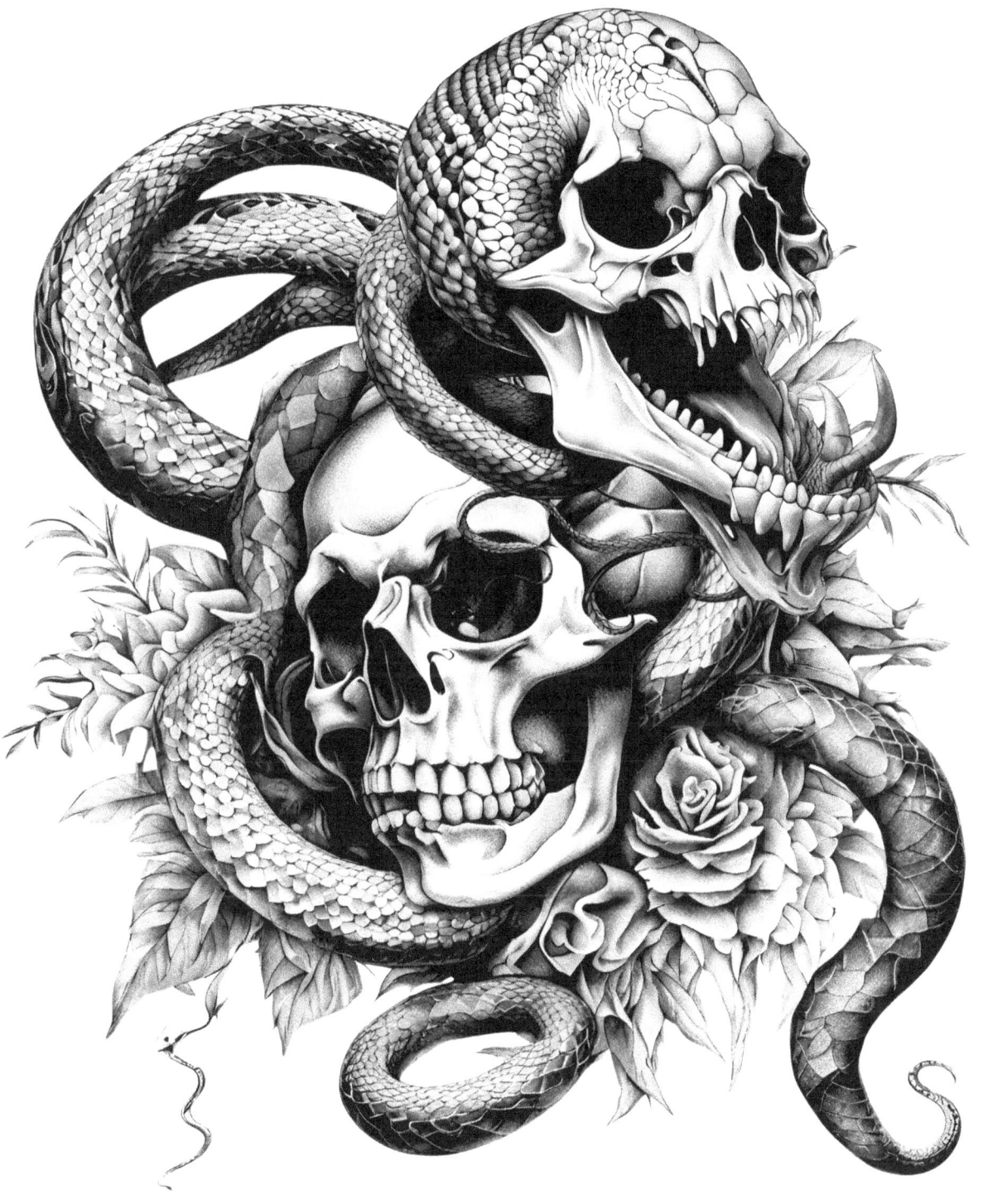

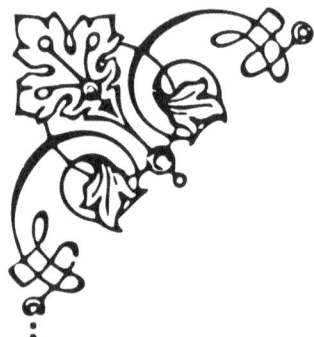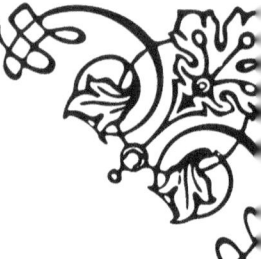

SKULL WITH WINGS TATTOOS

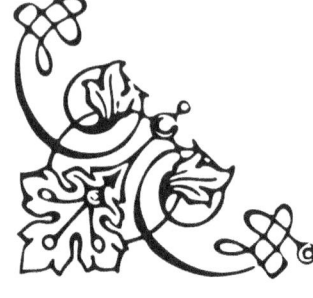

SKULL WITH WINGS TATTOOS

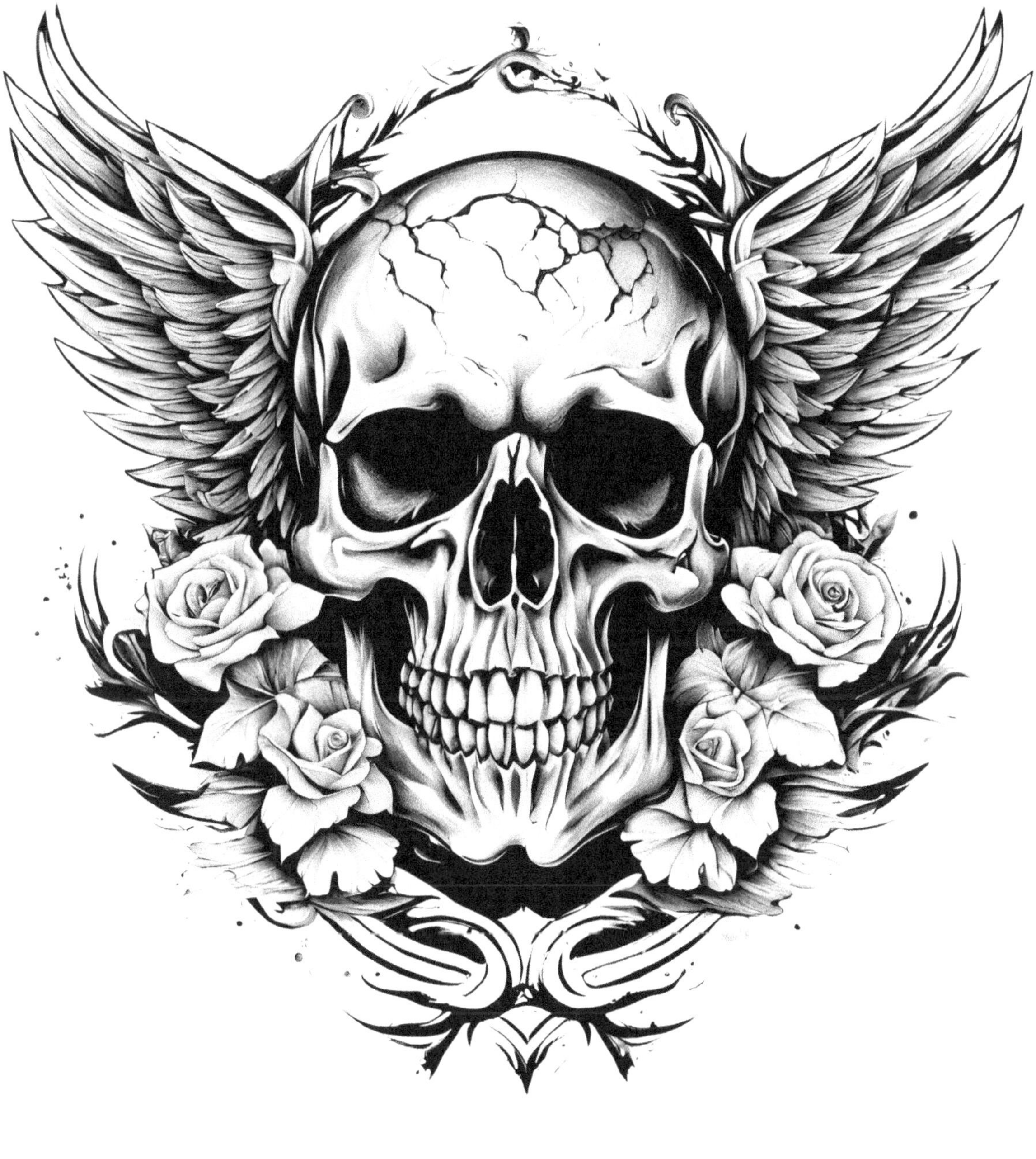

SKULL WITH WINGS TATTOOS

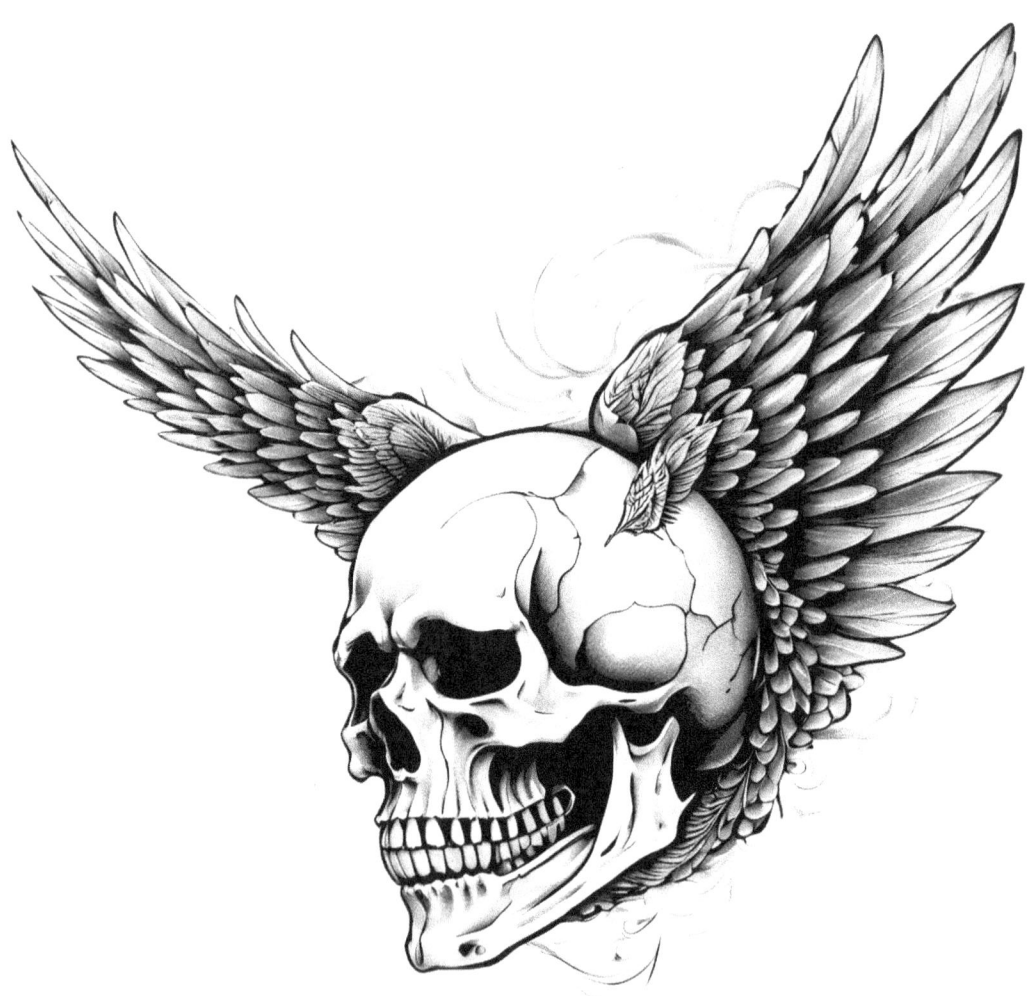

SKULL WITH WINGS TATTOOS

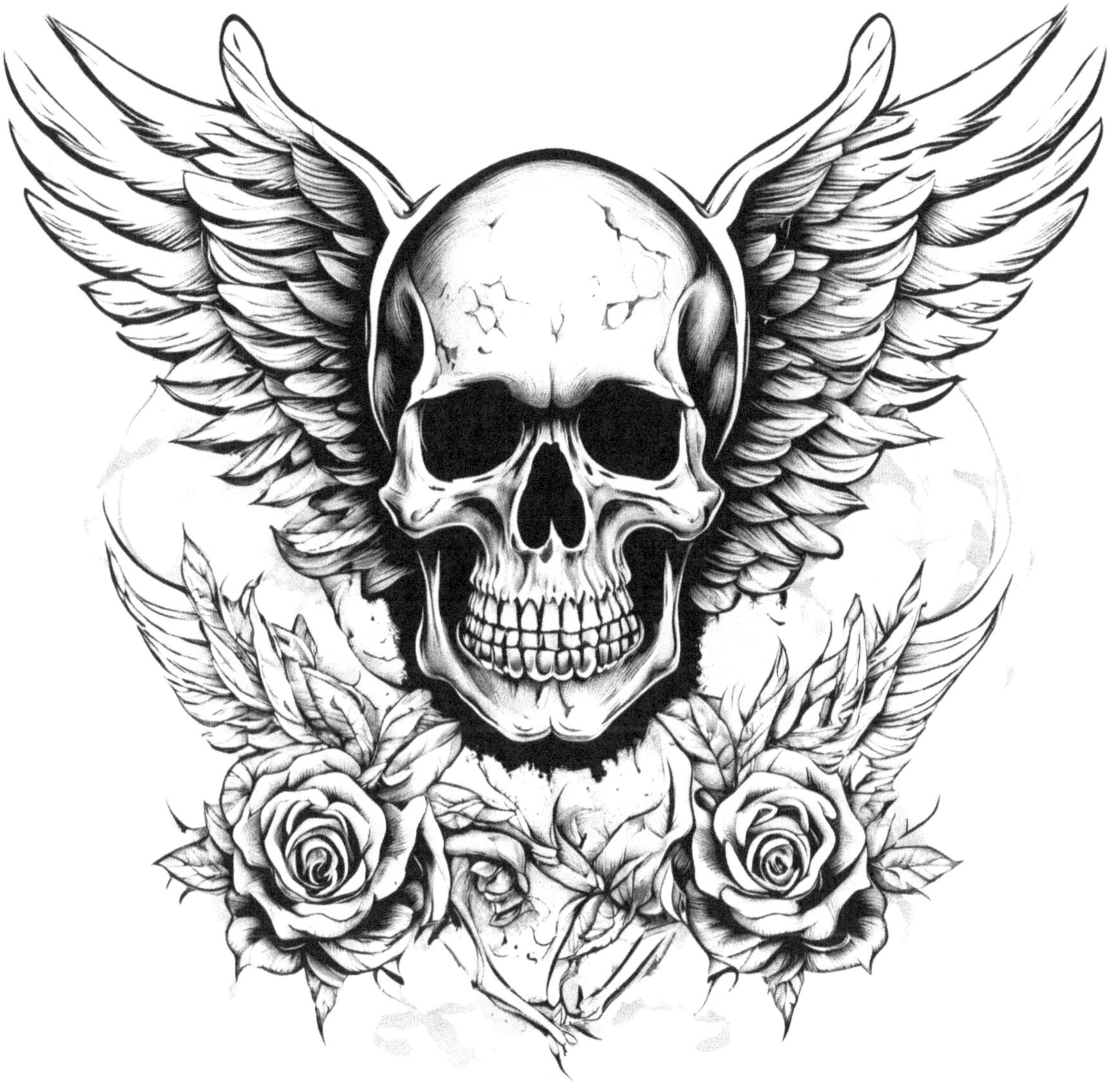

SKULL WITH WINGS TATTOOS

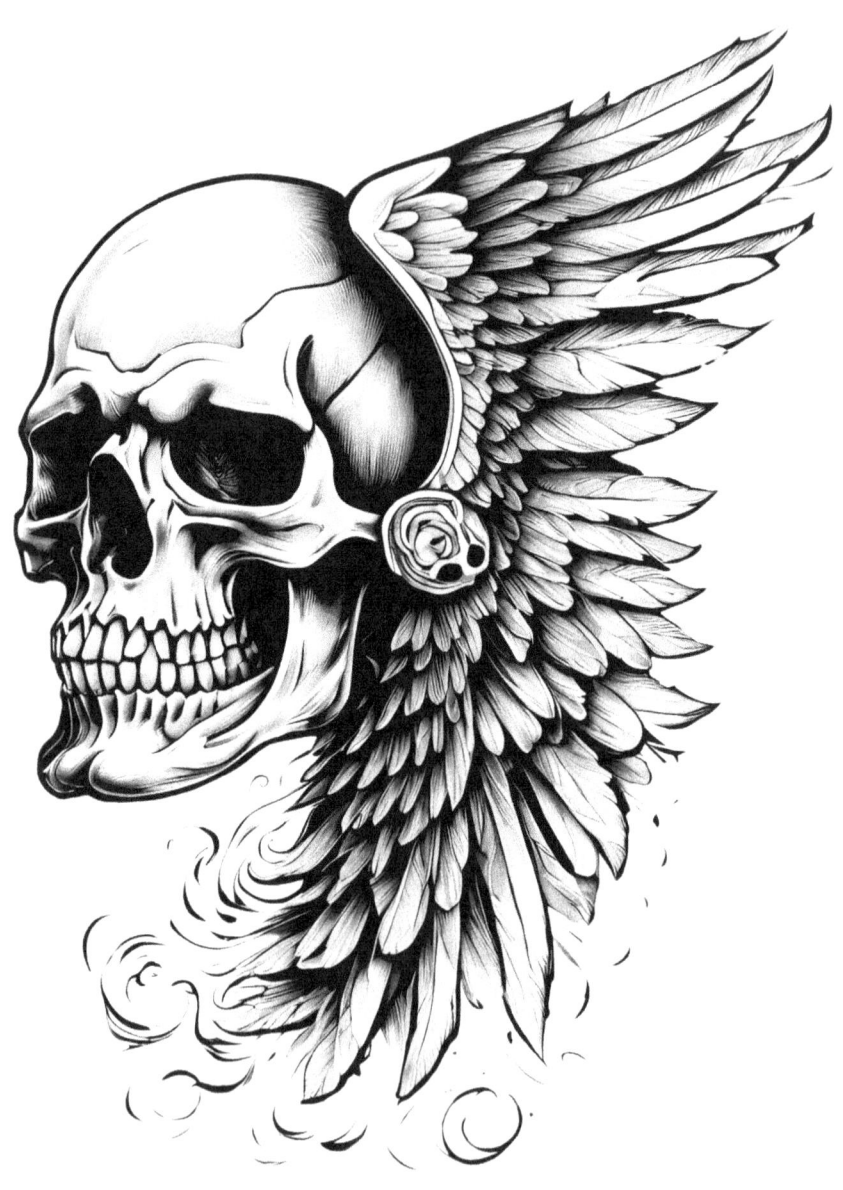

SKULL WITH WINGS TATTOOS

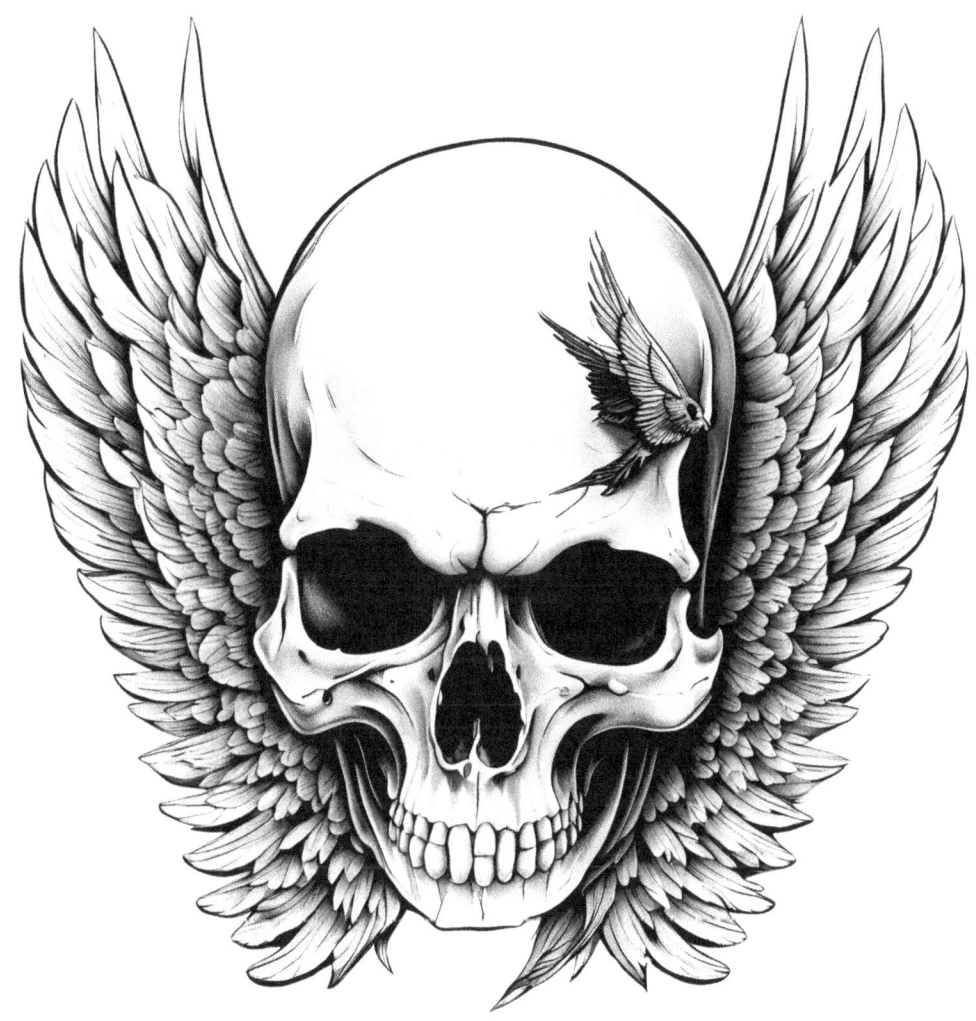

SKULL WITH WINGS TATTOOS

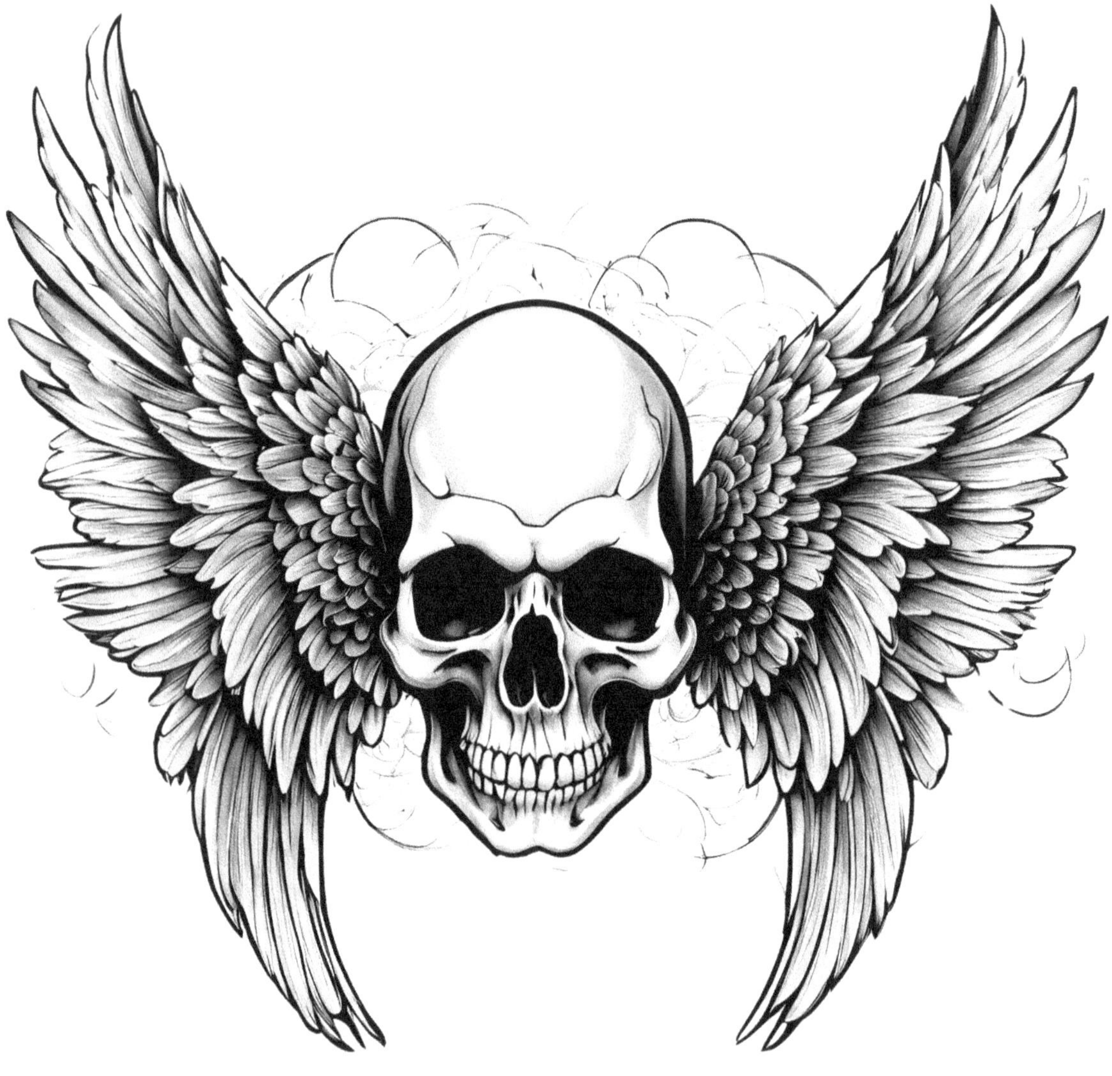

SKULL WITH WINGS TATTOOS

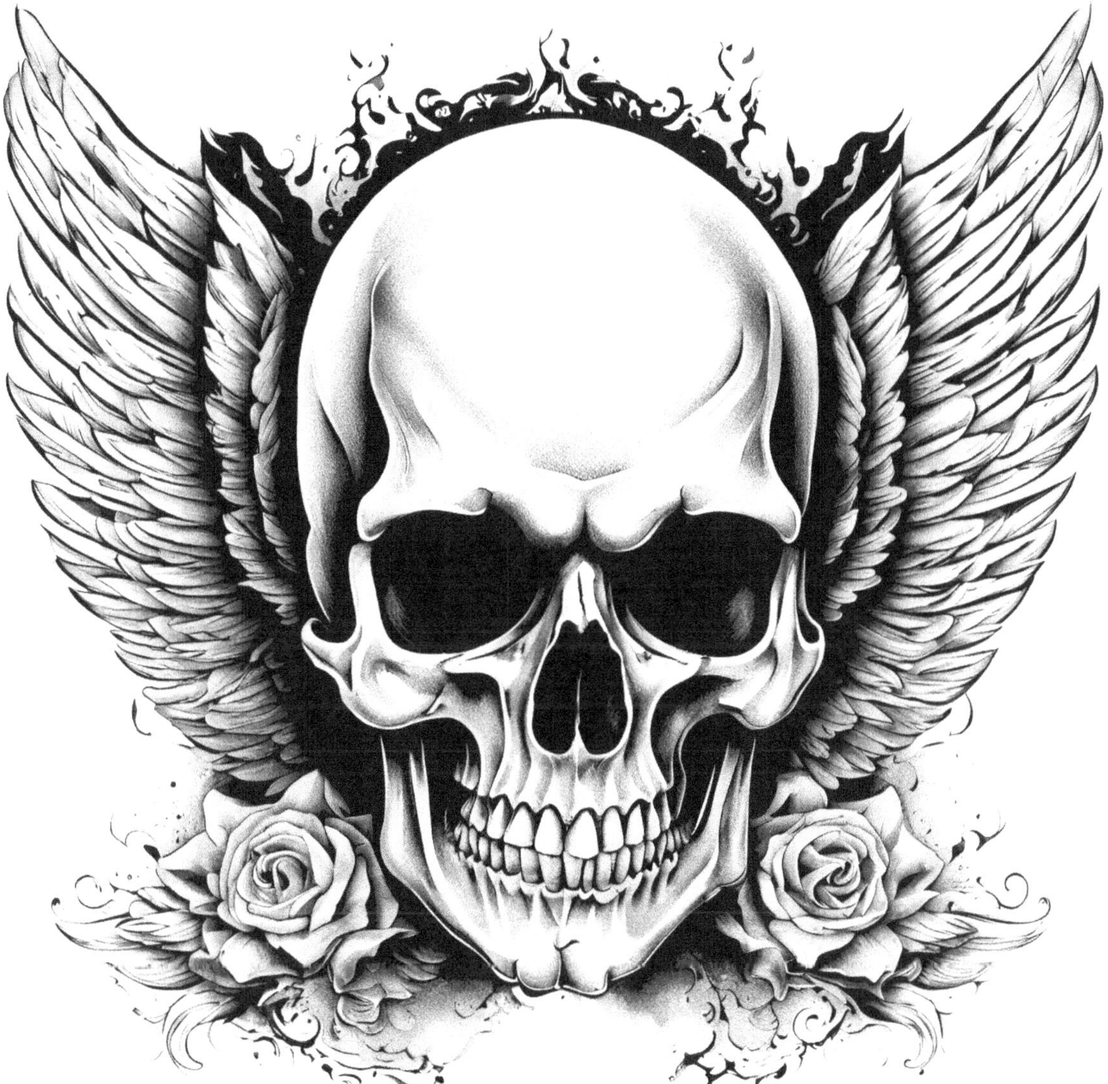

SKULL WITH WINGS TATTOOS

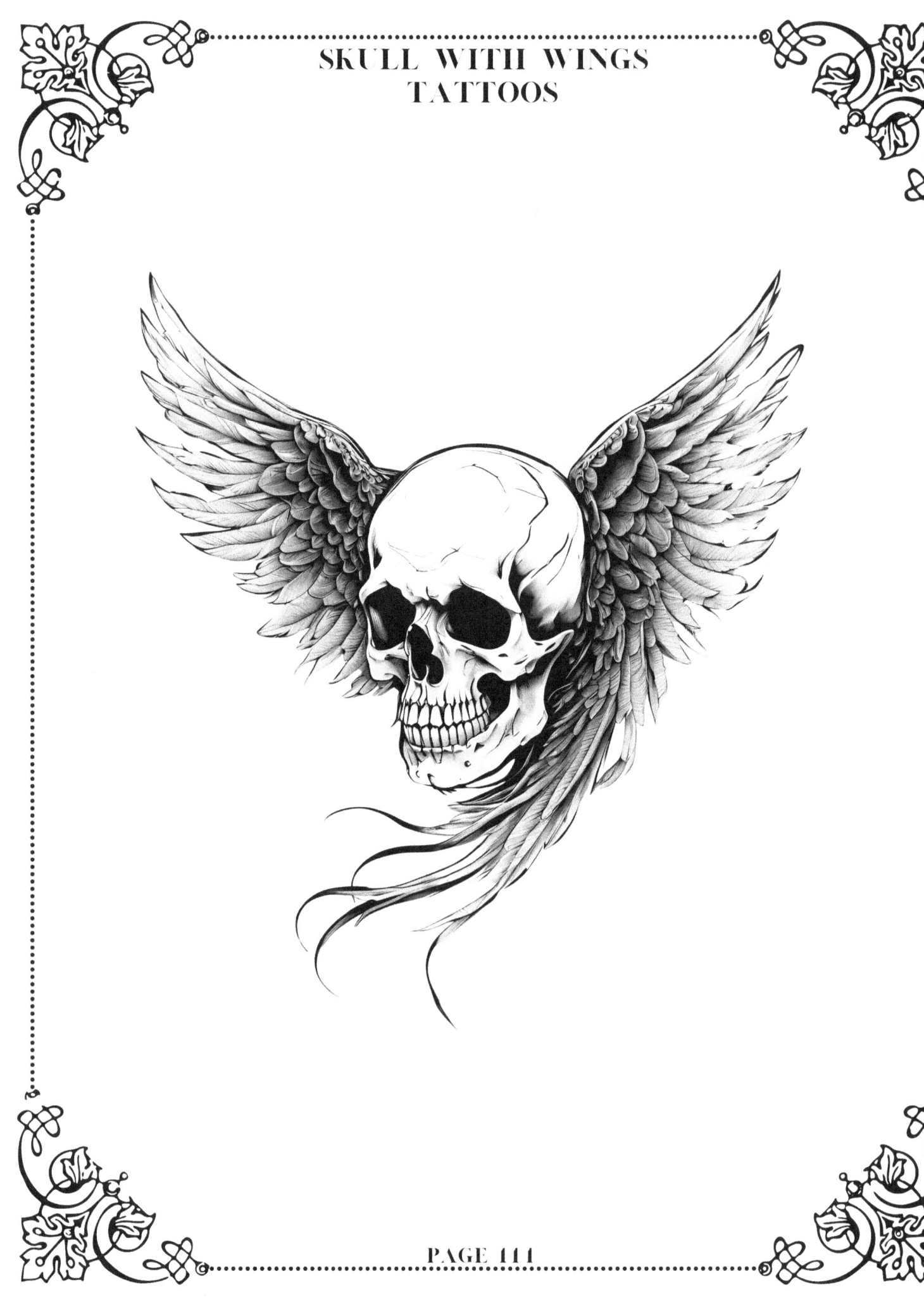

SKULL WITH WINGS TATTOOS

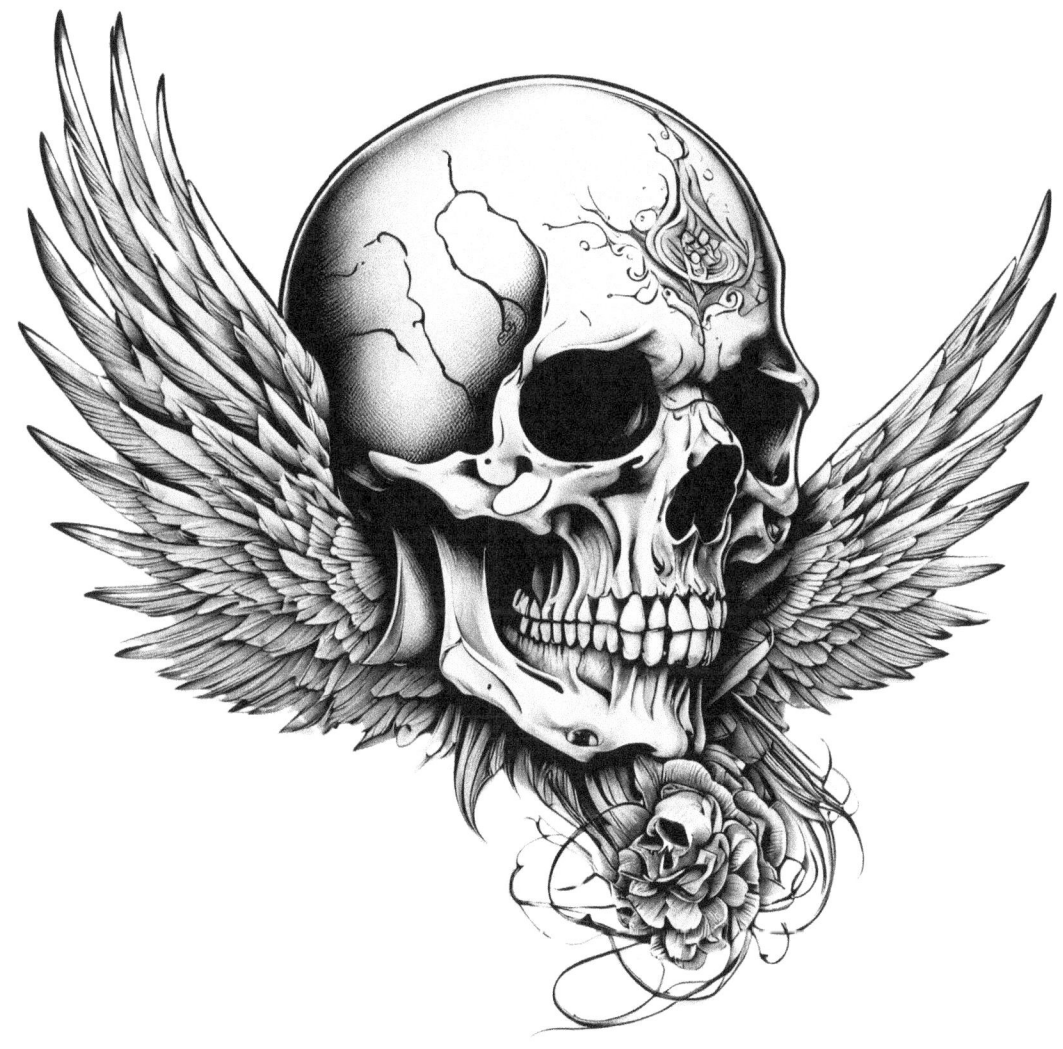

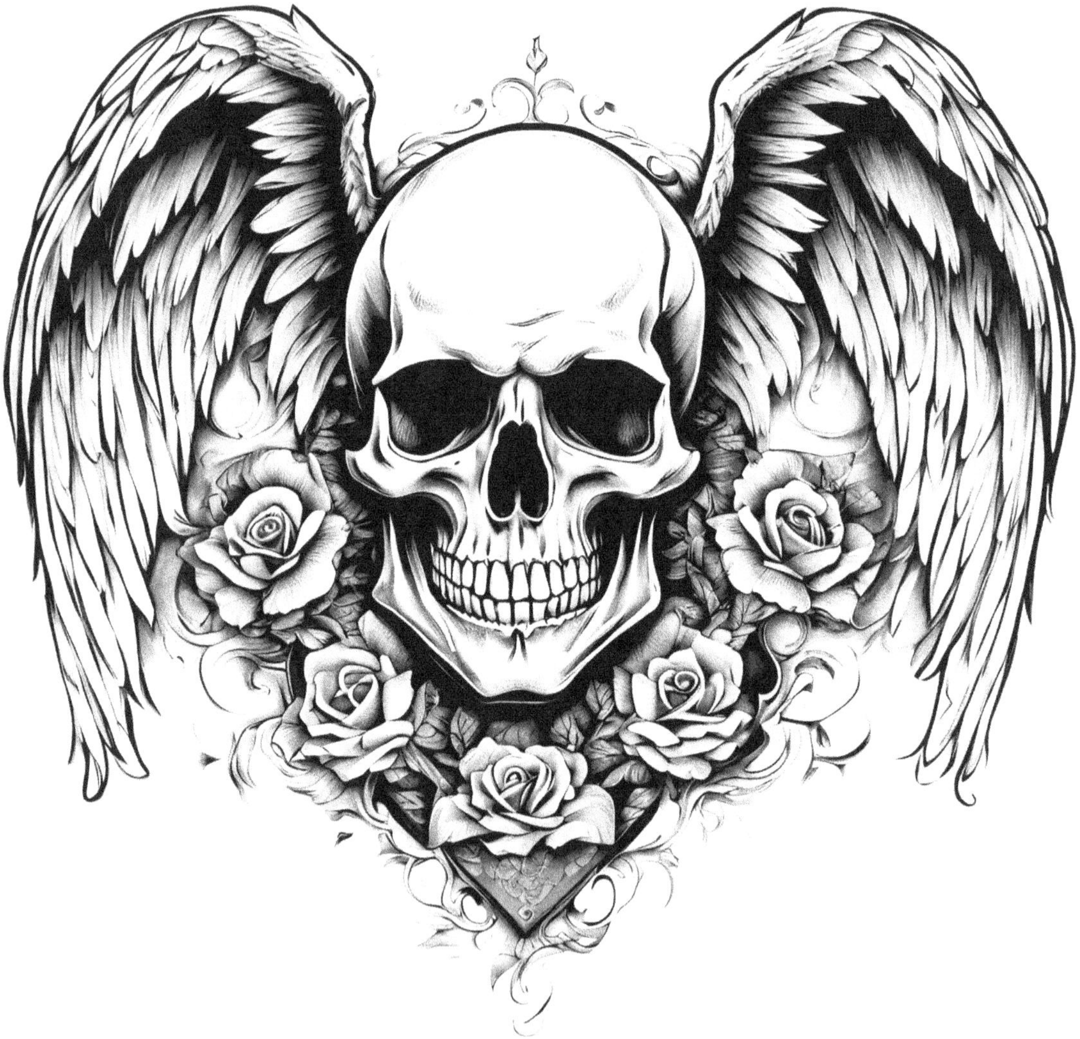

SKULL WITH WINGS TATTOOS

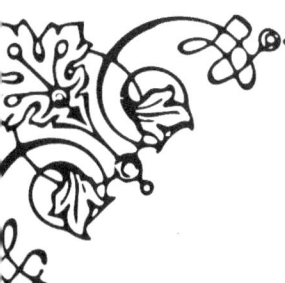
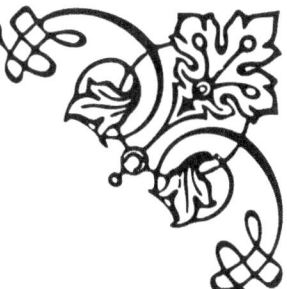

CELTIC SKULL TATTOOS

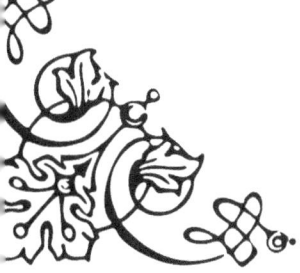
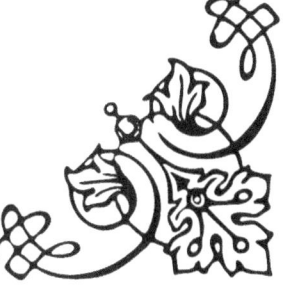

CELTIC SKULL TATTOOS

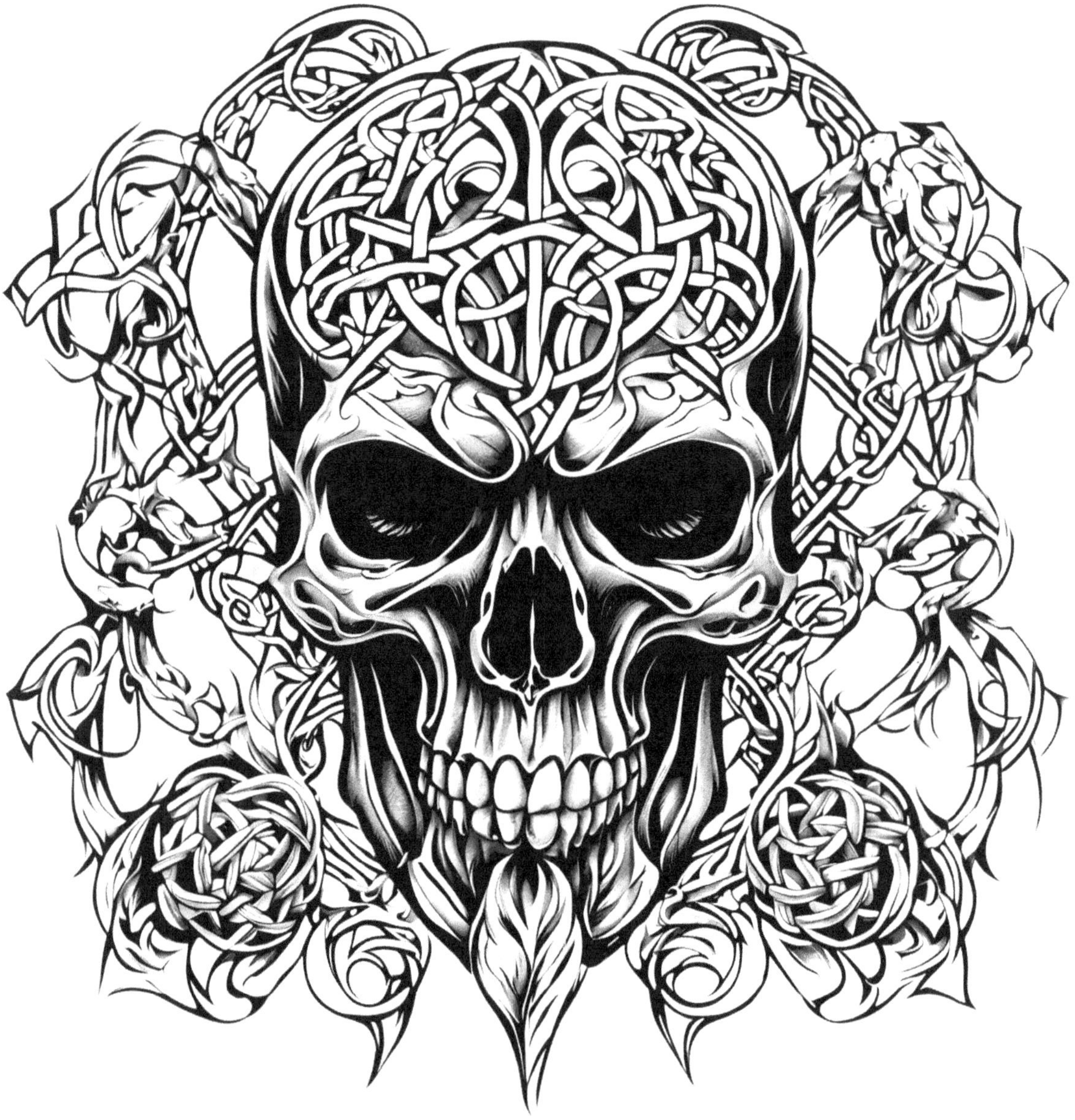

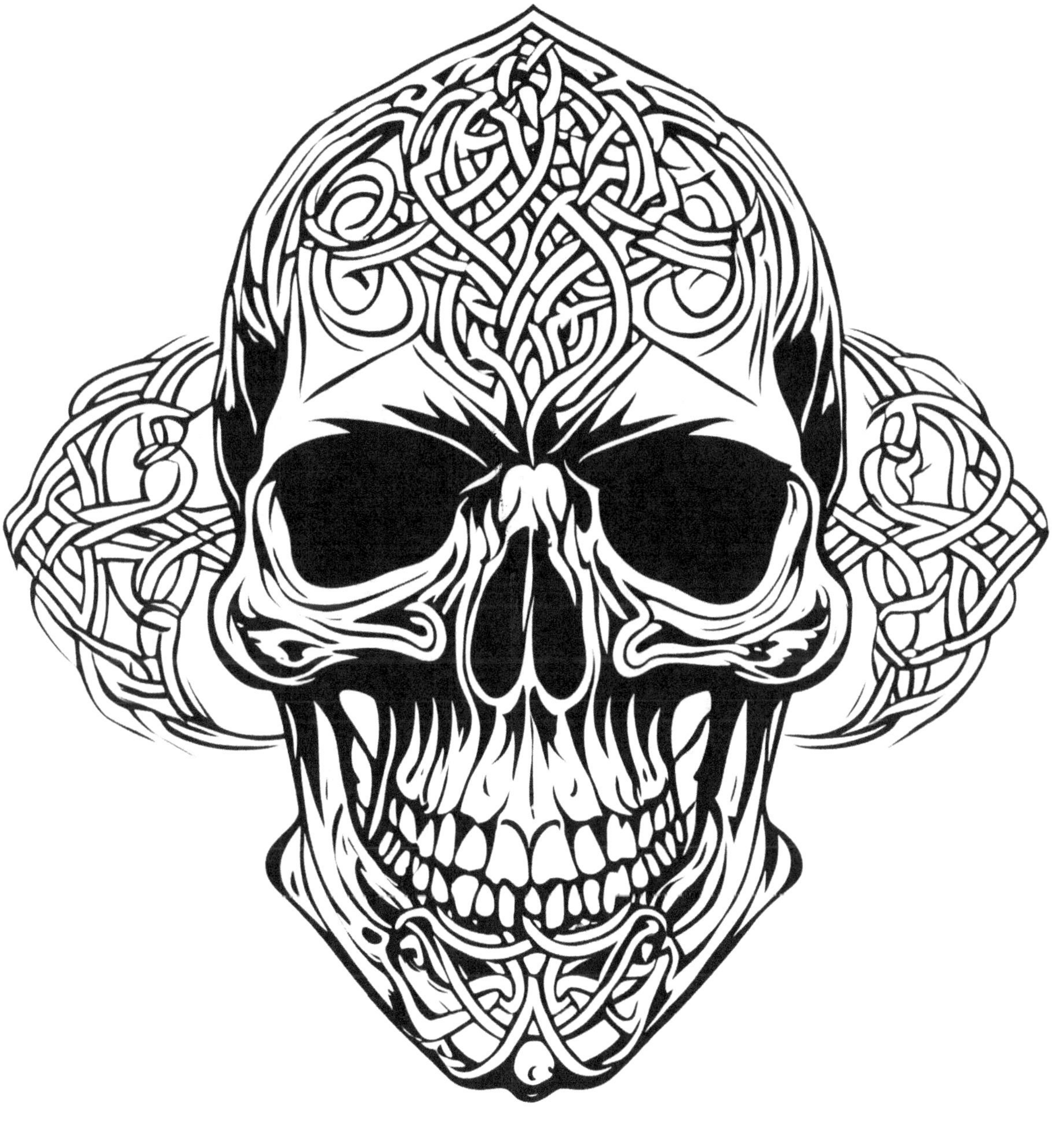

CELTIC SKULL TATTOOS

CELTIC SKULL TATTOOS

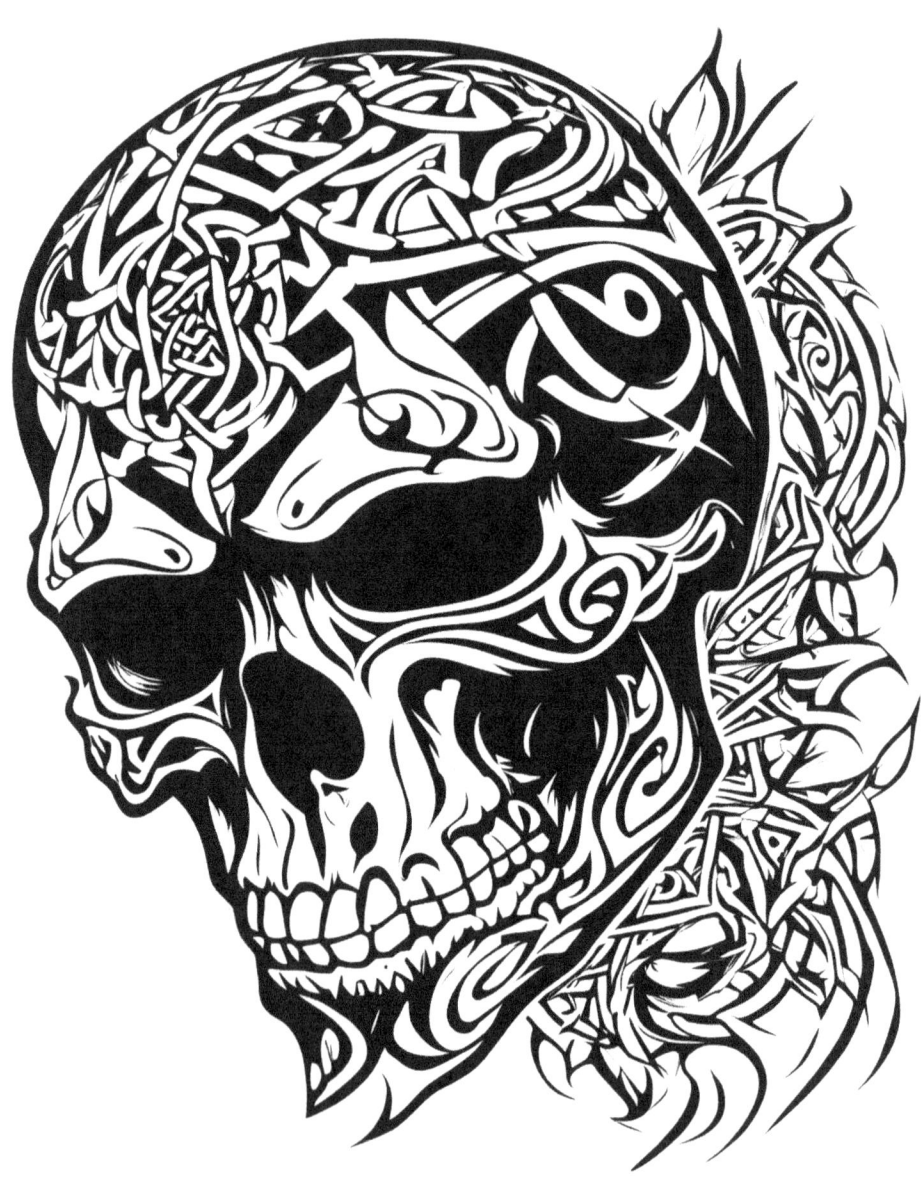

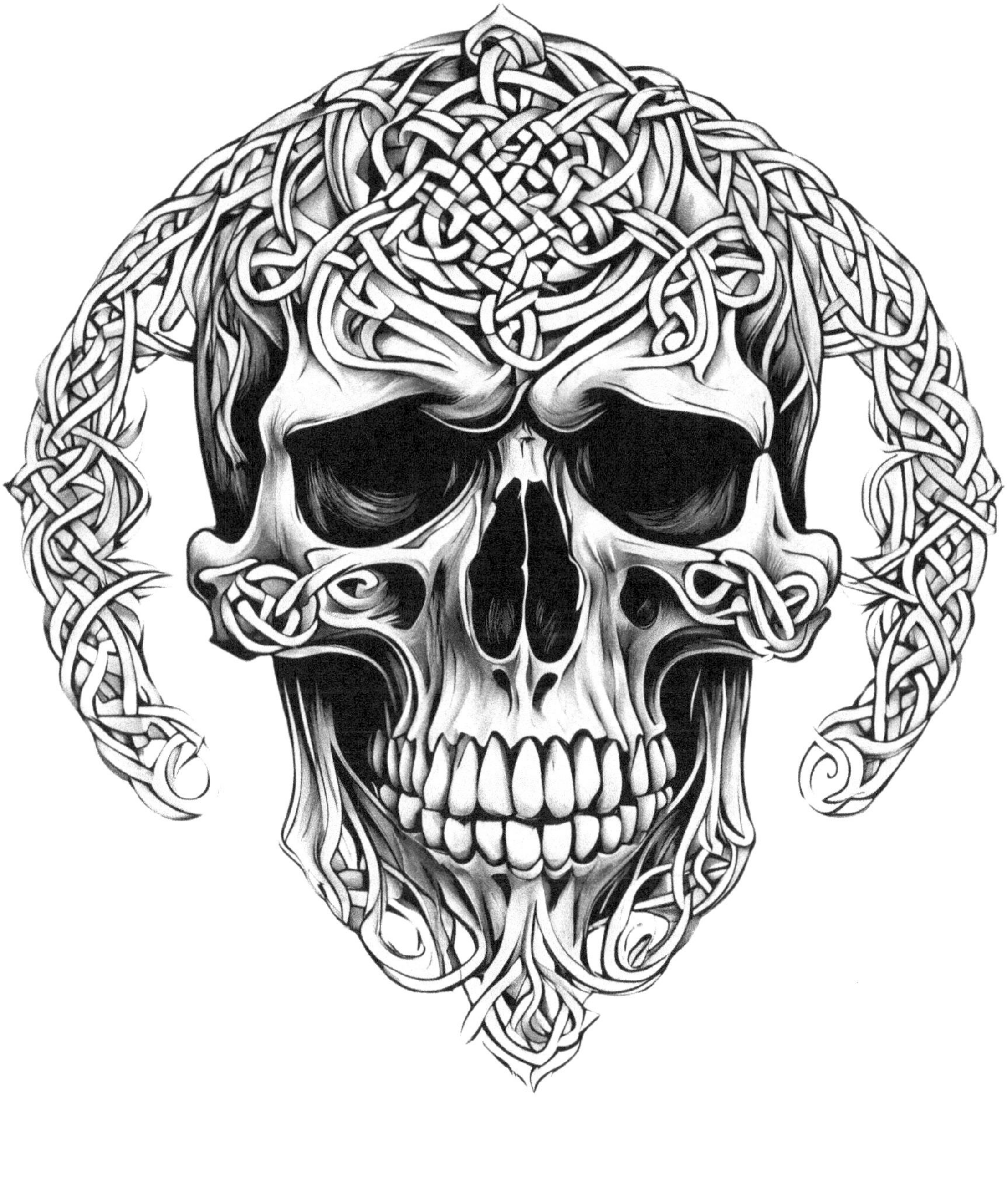

CELTIC SKULL TATTOOS

CELTIC SKULL TATTOOS

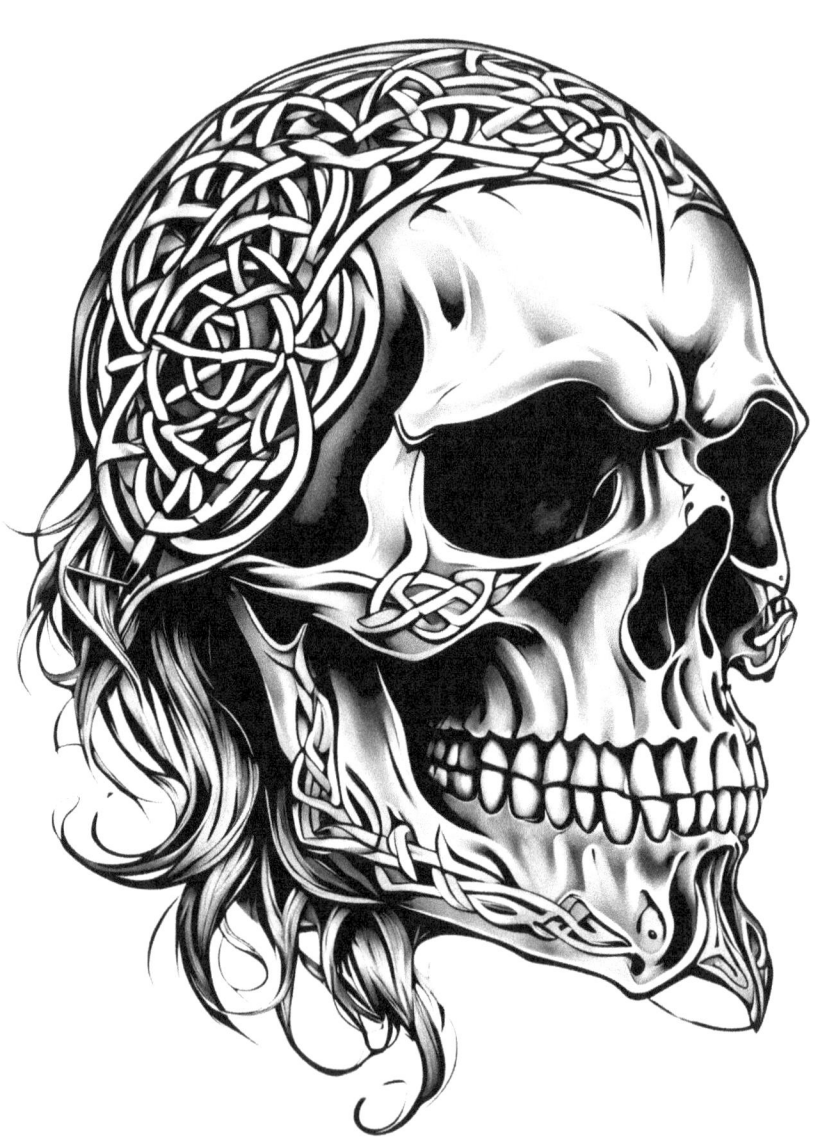

CELTIC SKULL TATTOOS

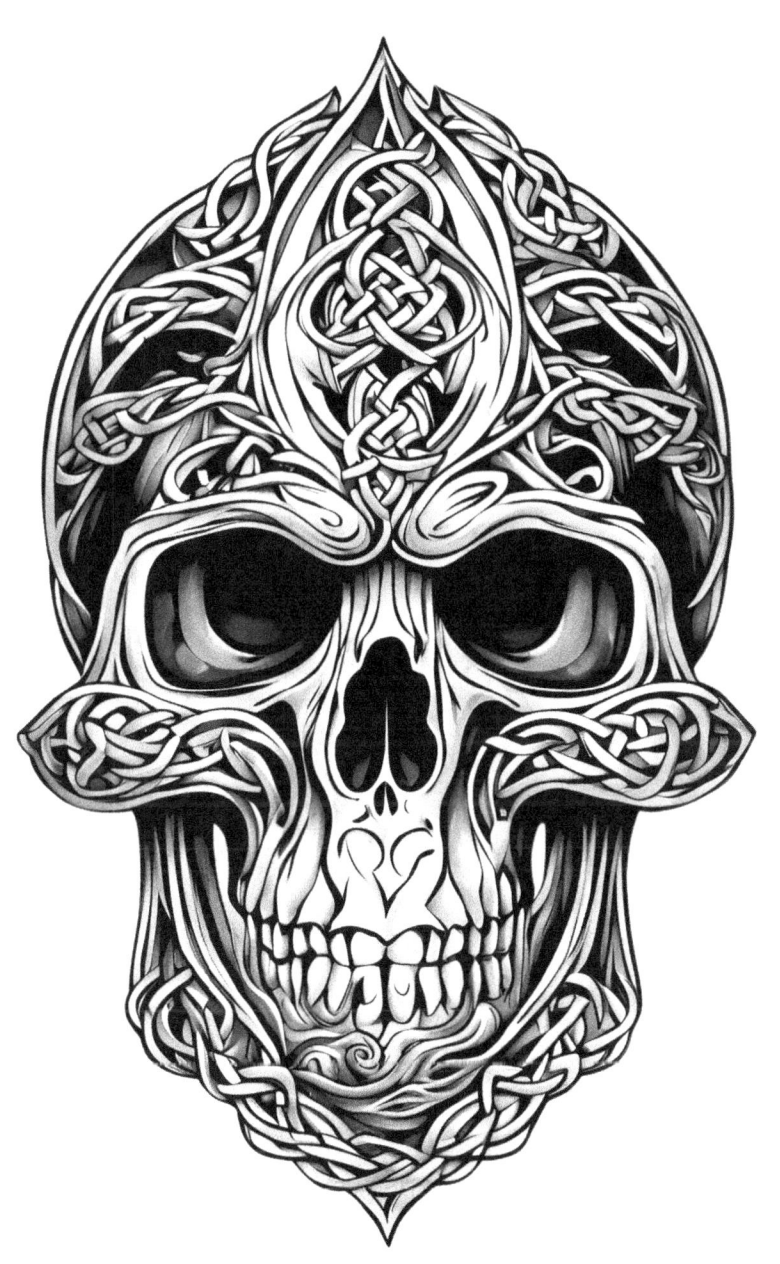

CELTIC SKULL TATTOOS

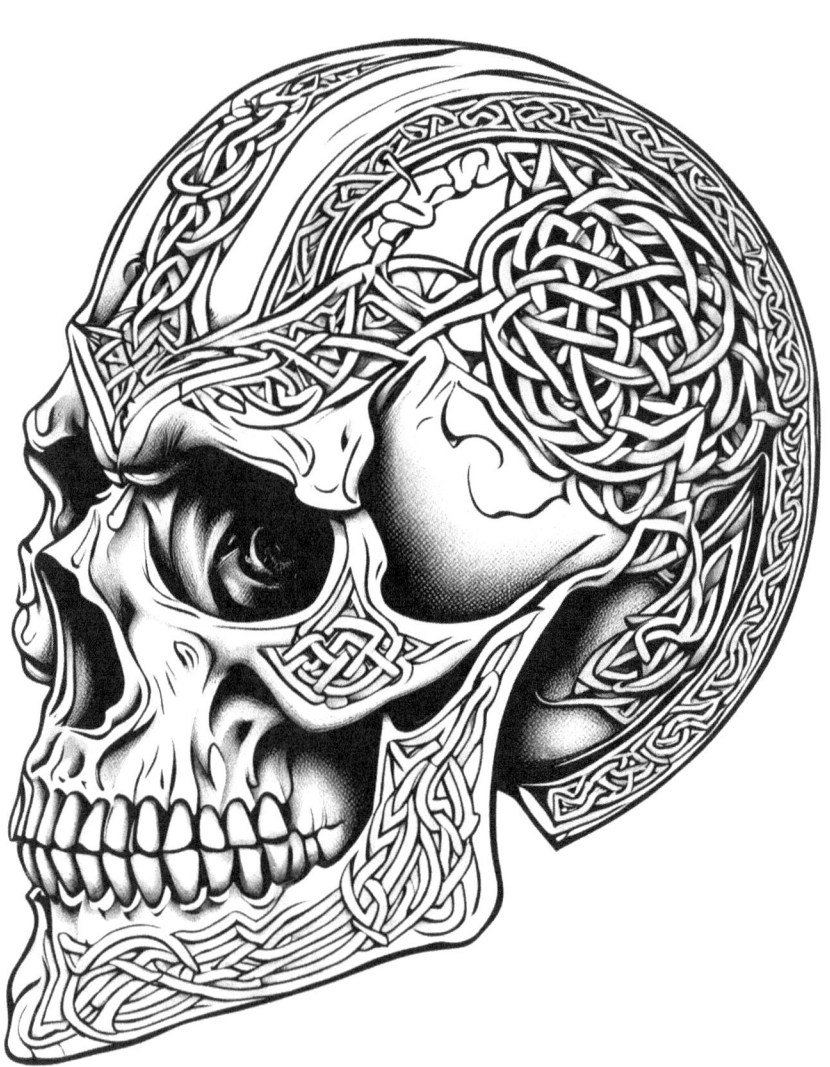

CELTIC SKULL TATTOOS

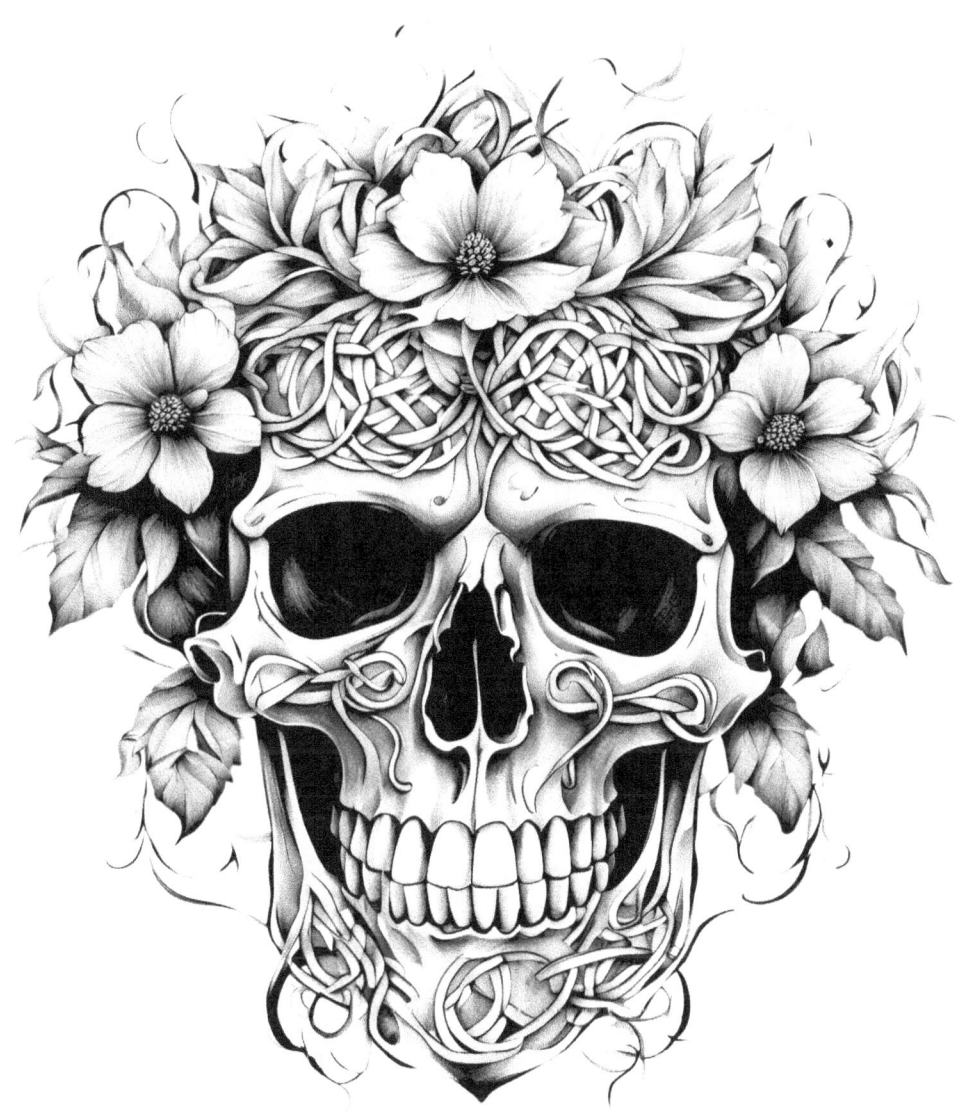

CELTIC SKULL TATTOOS

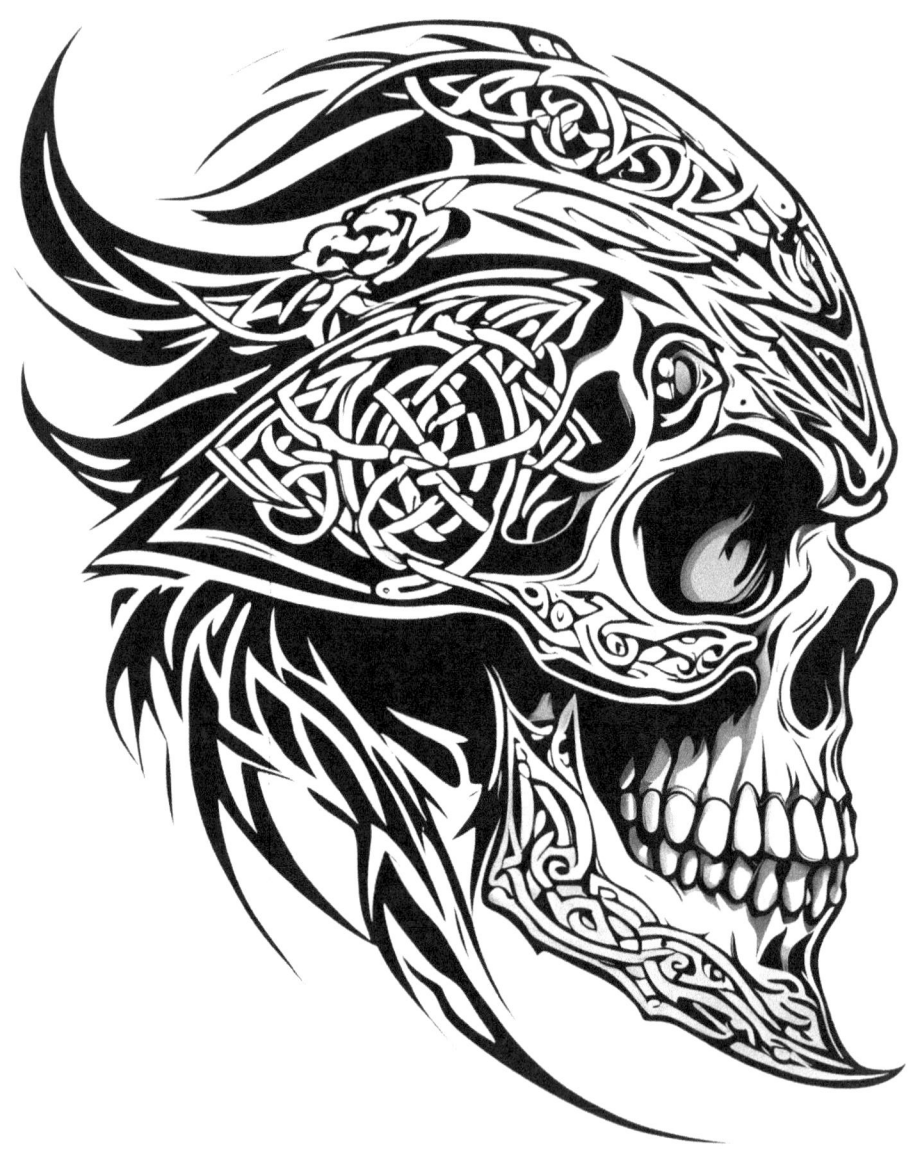

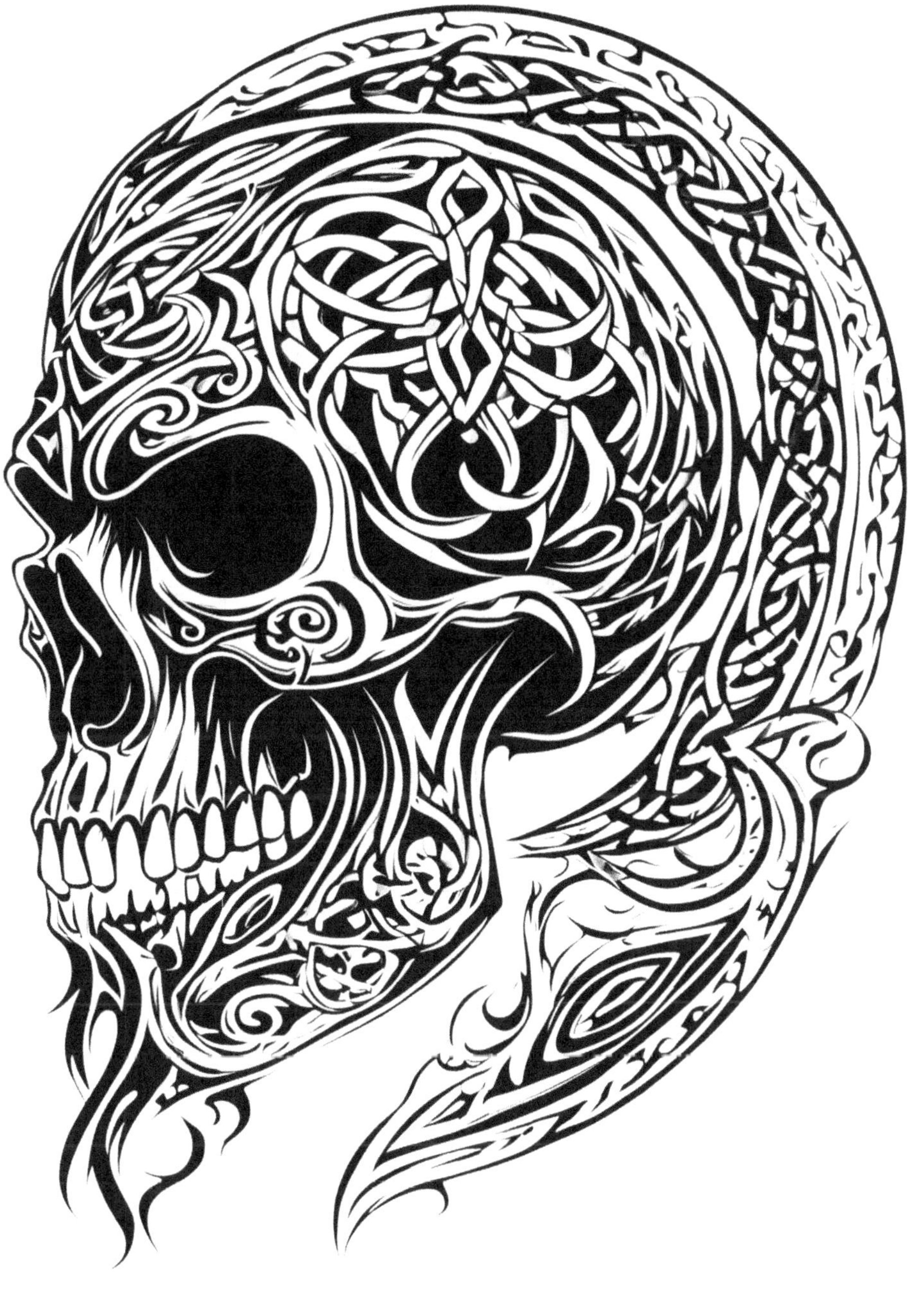

CELTIC SKULL TATTOOS

CELTIC SKULL TATTOOS

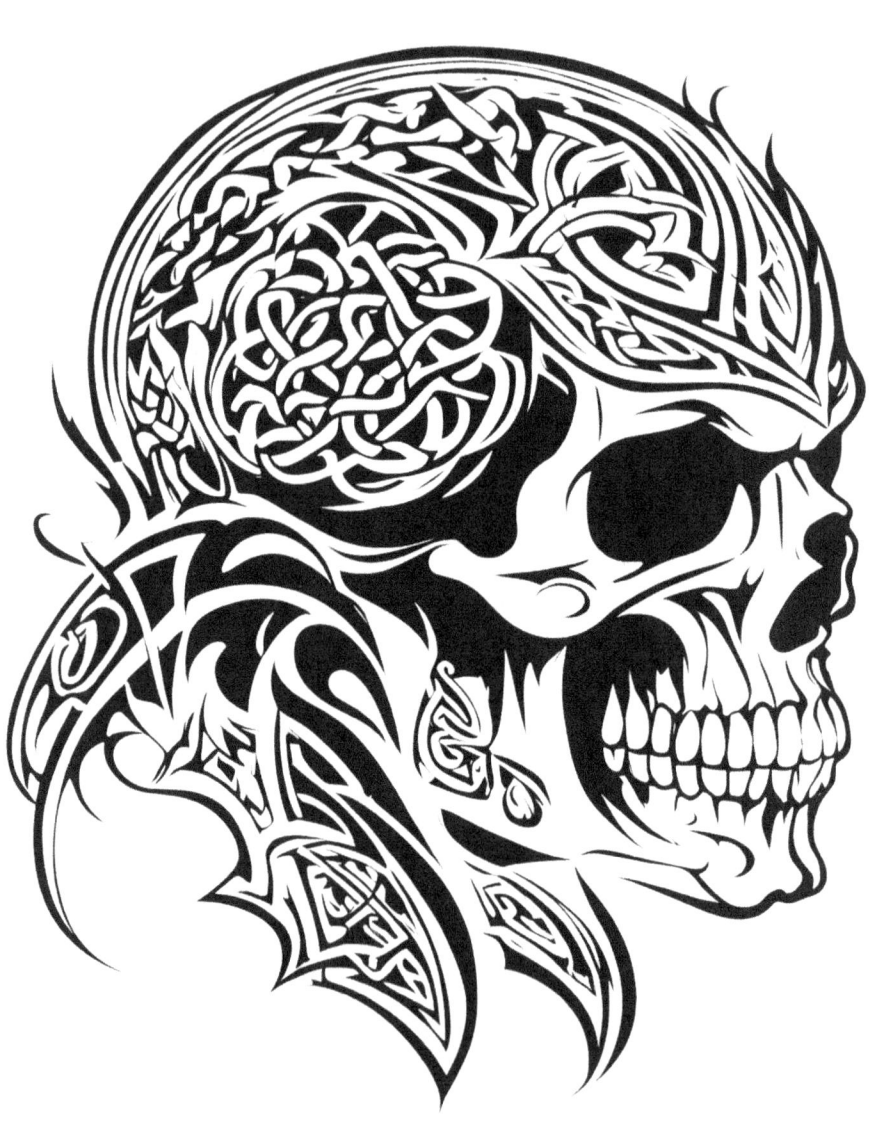

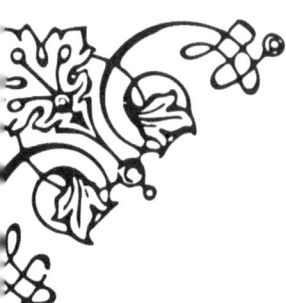

NATURE SKULL TATTOOS

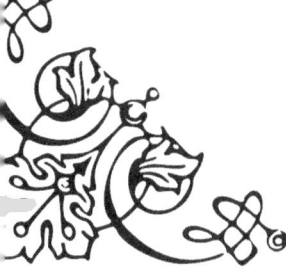

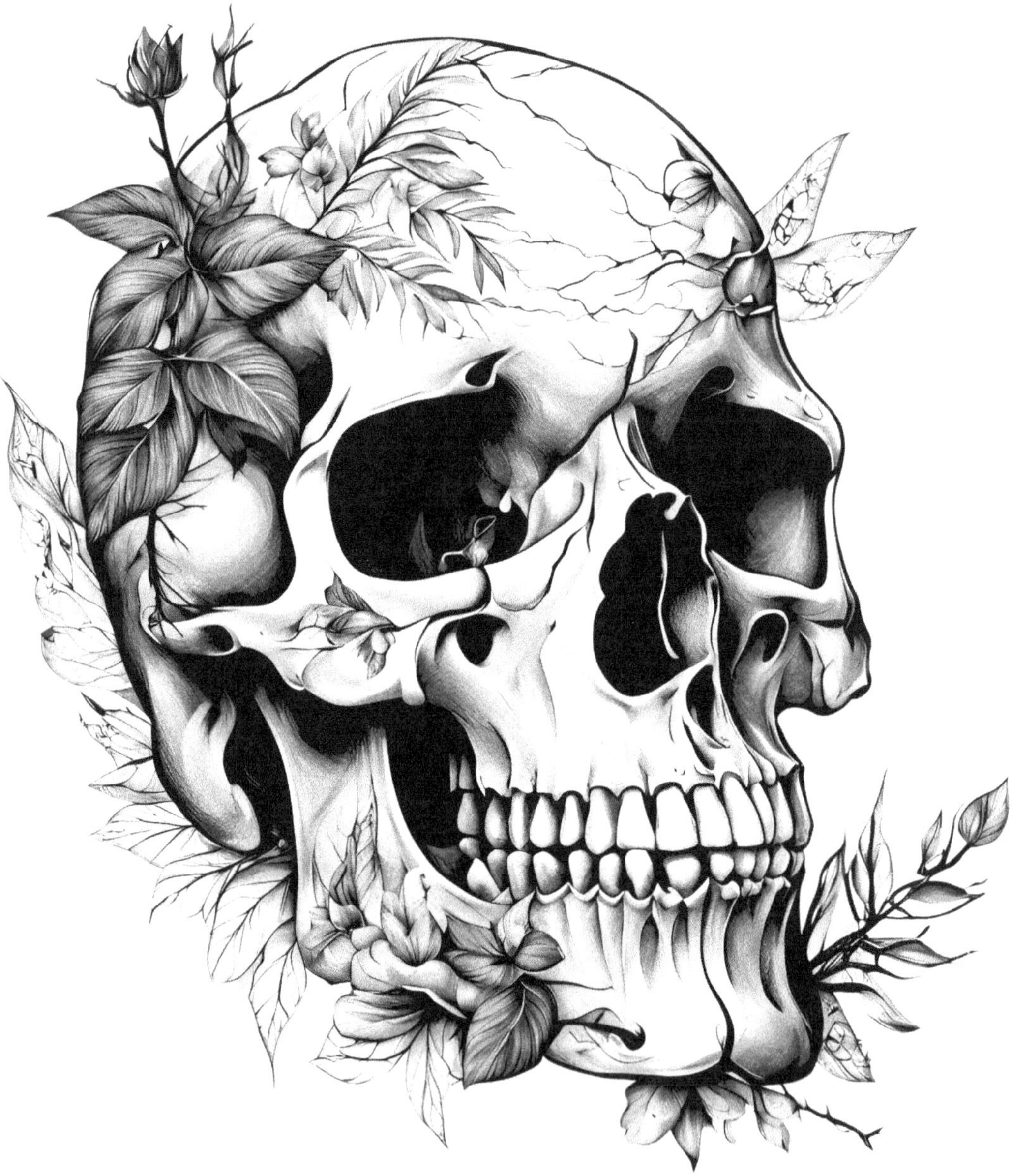

NATURE SKULL TATTOOS

NATURE SKULL TATTOOS

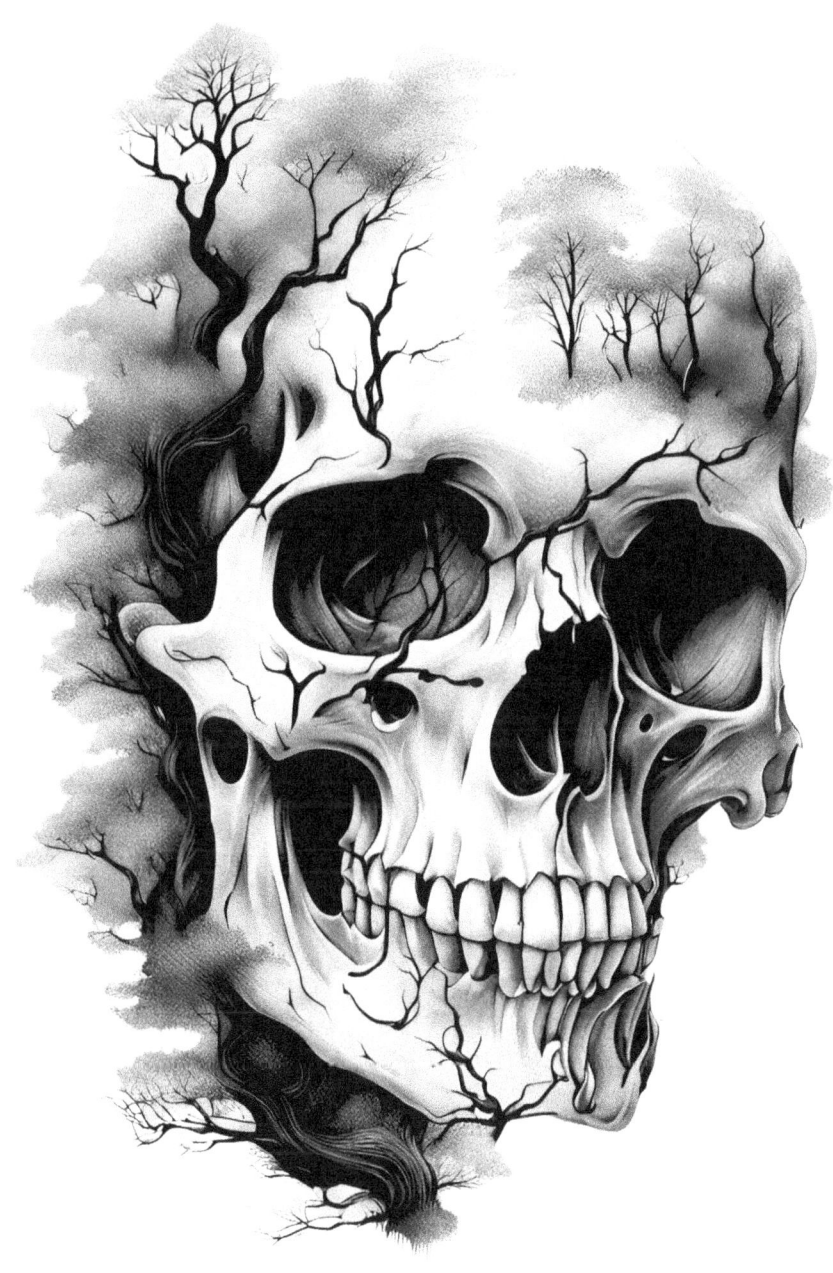

NATURE SKULL TATTOOS

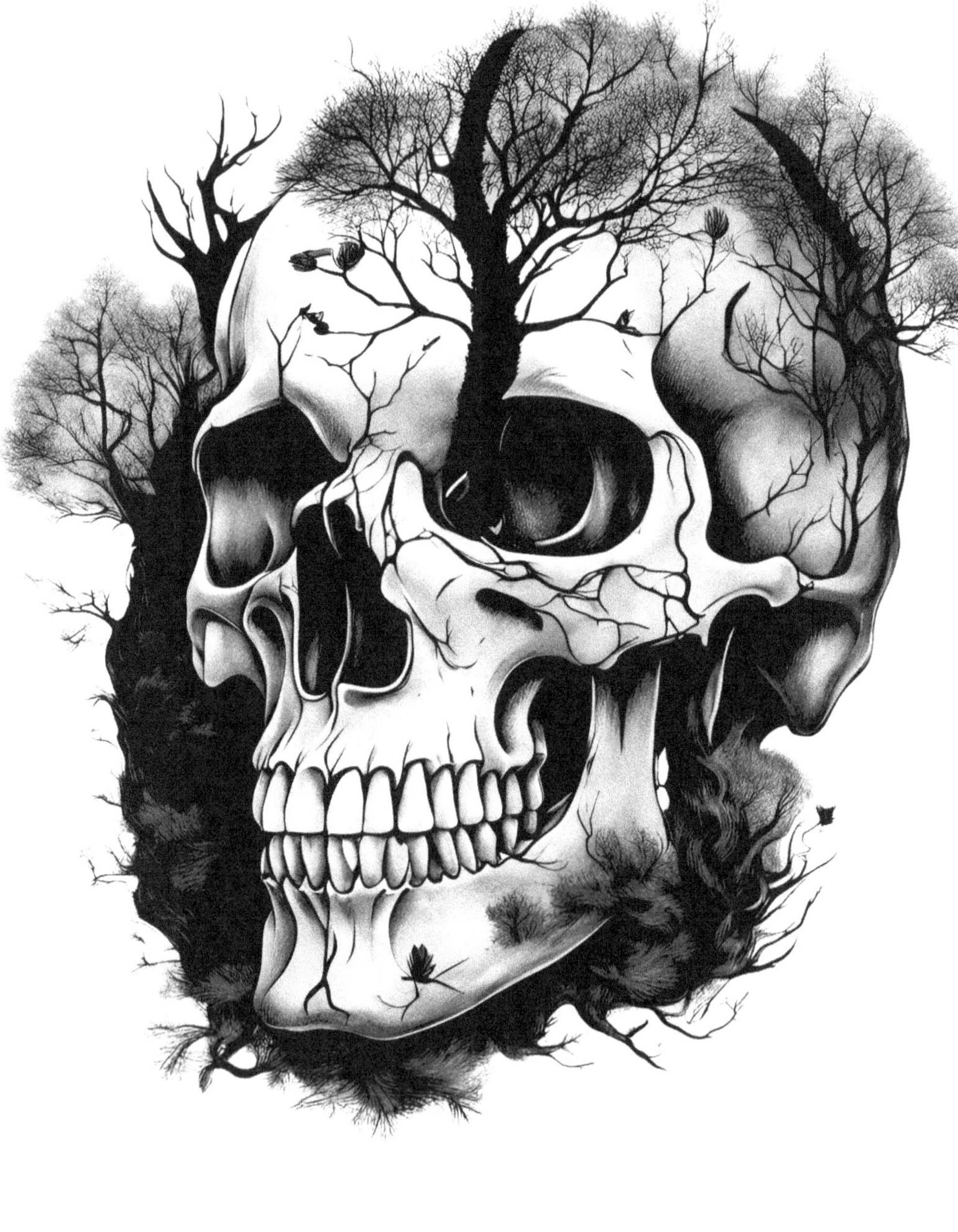

NATURE SKULL TATTOOS

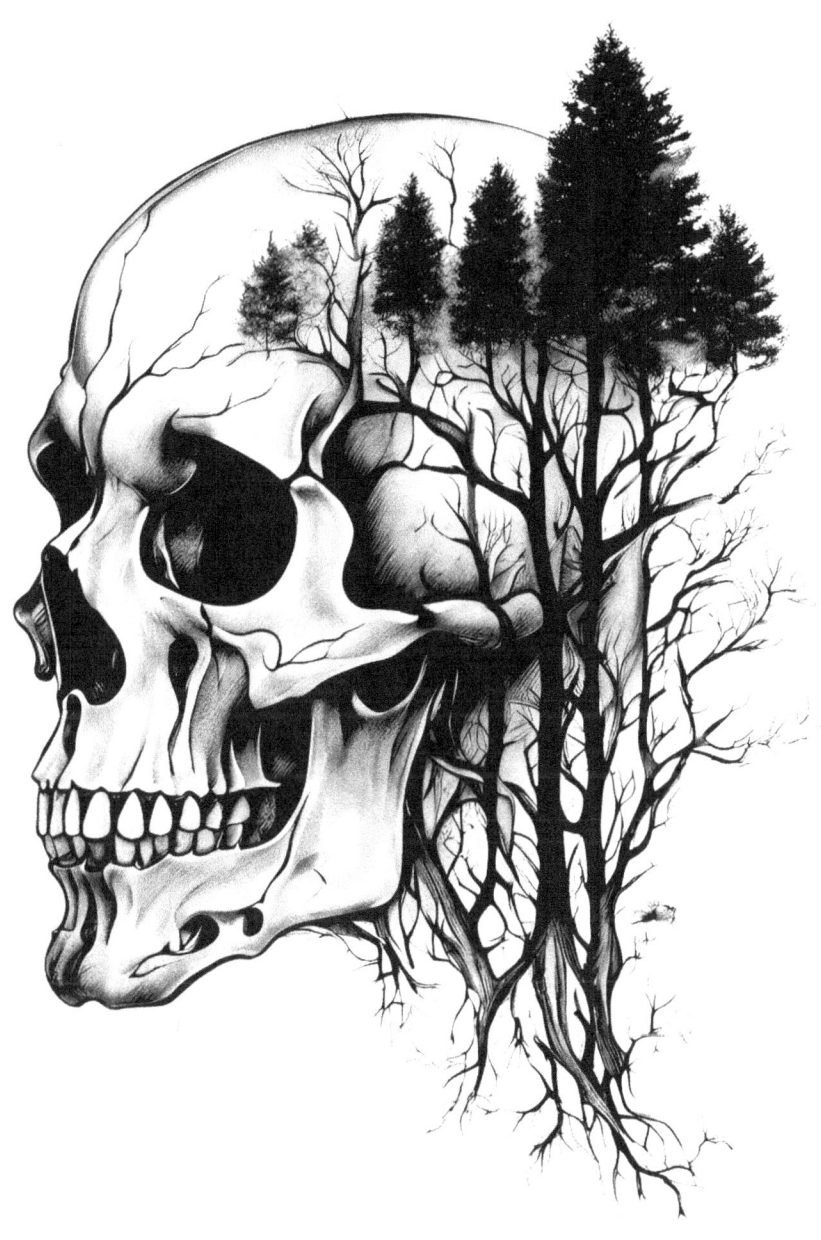

NATURE SKULL TATTOOS

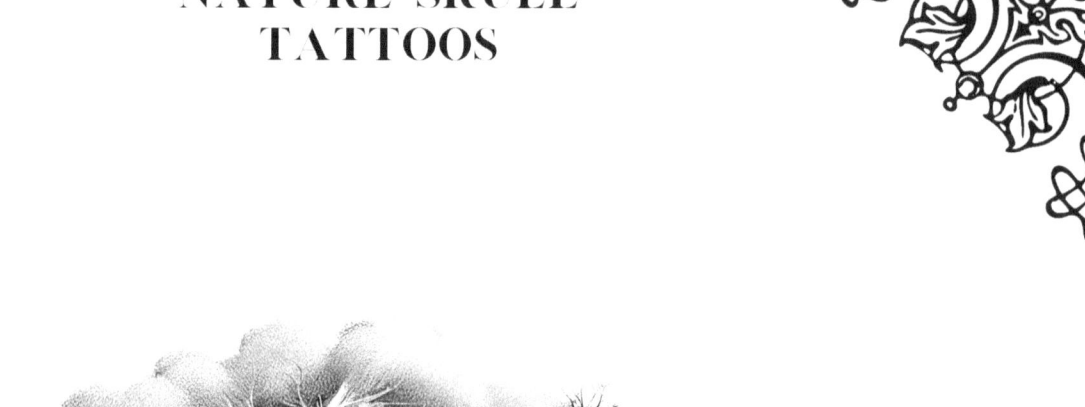

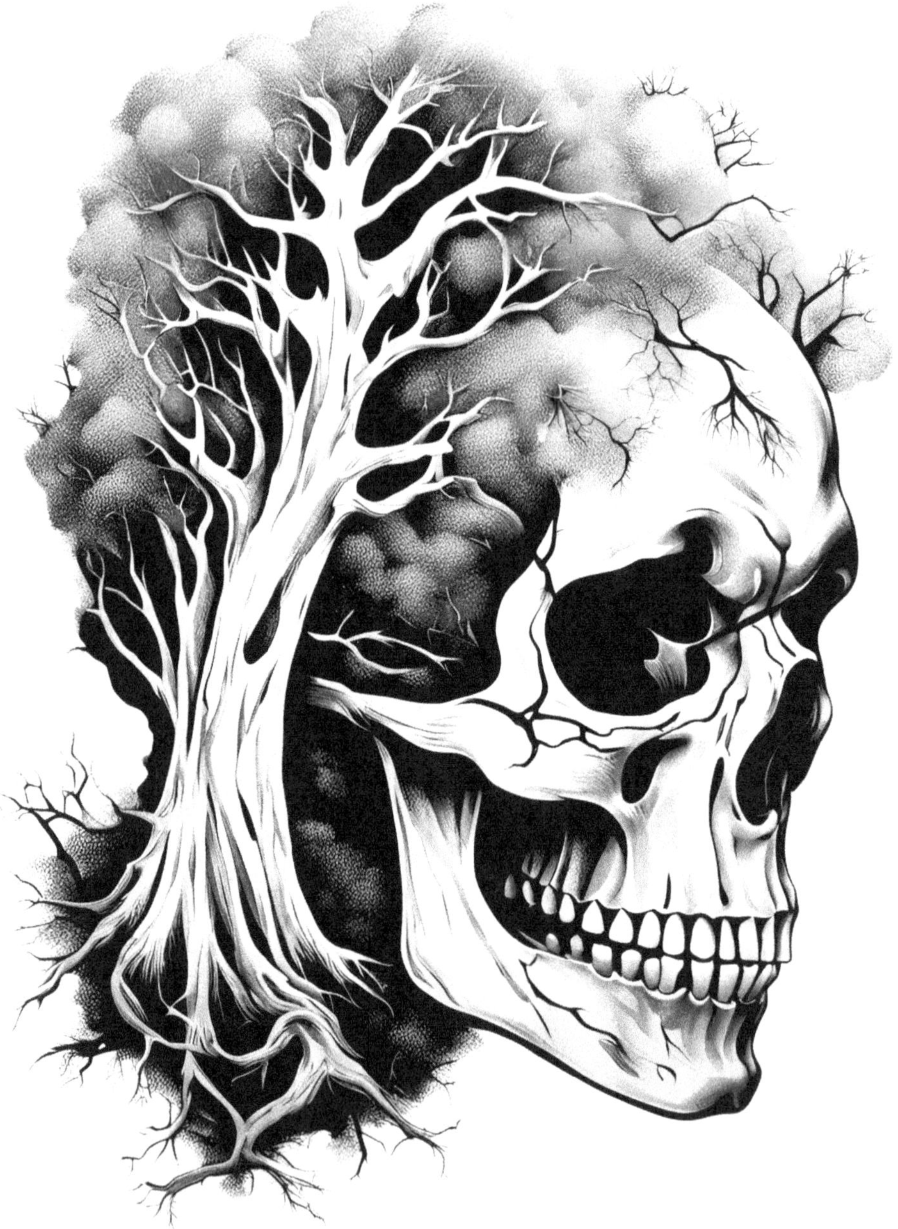

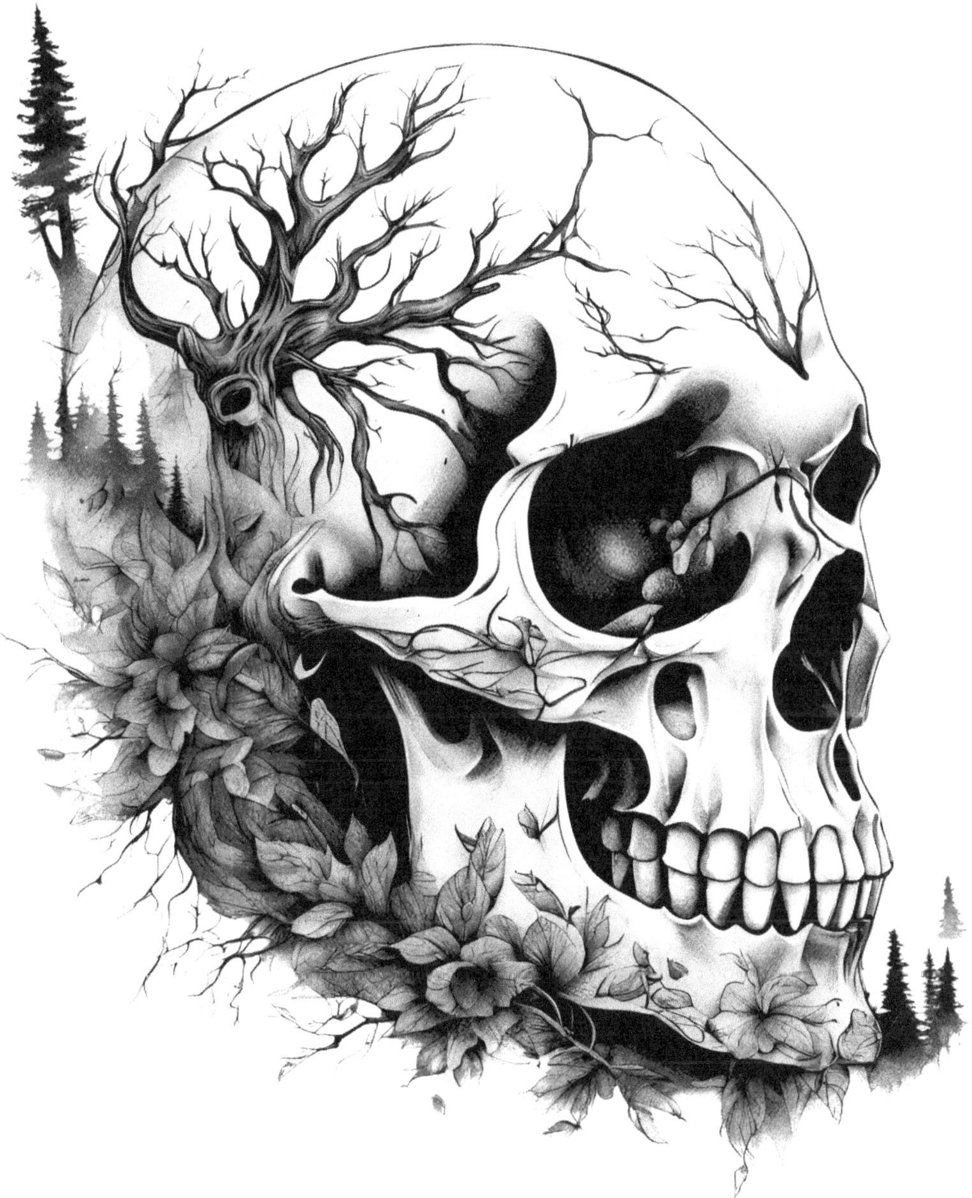

NATURE SKULL TATTOOS

NATURE SKULL TATTOOS

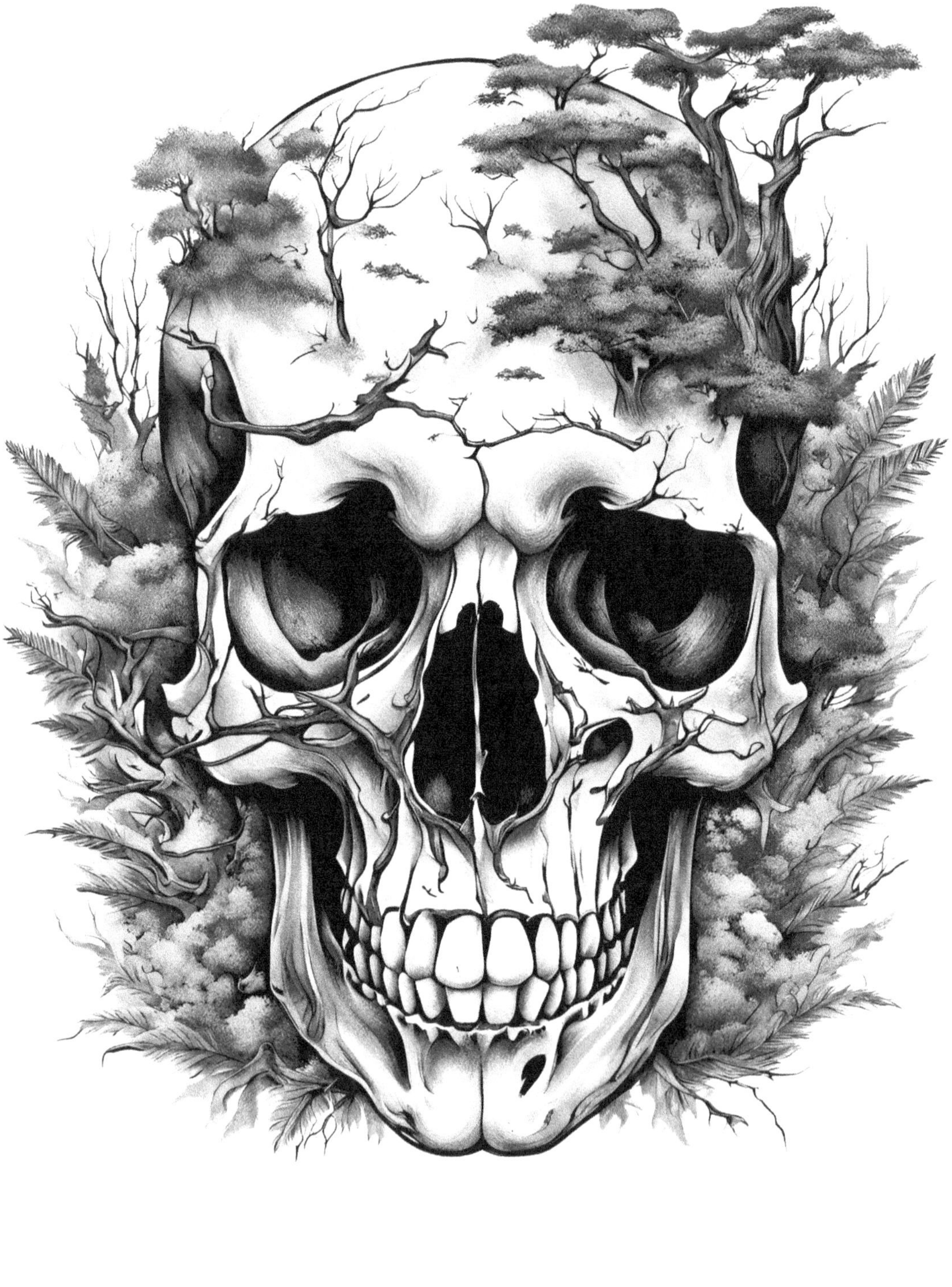

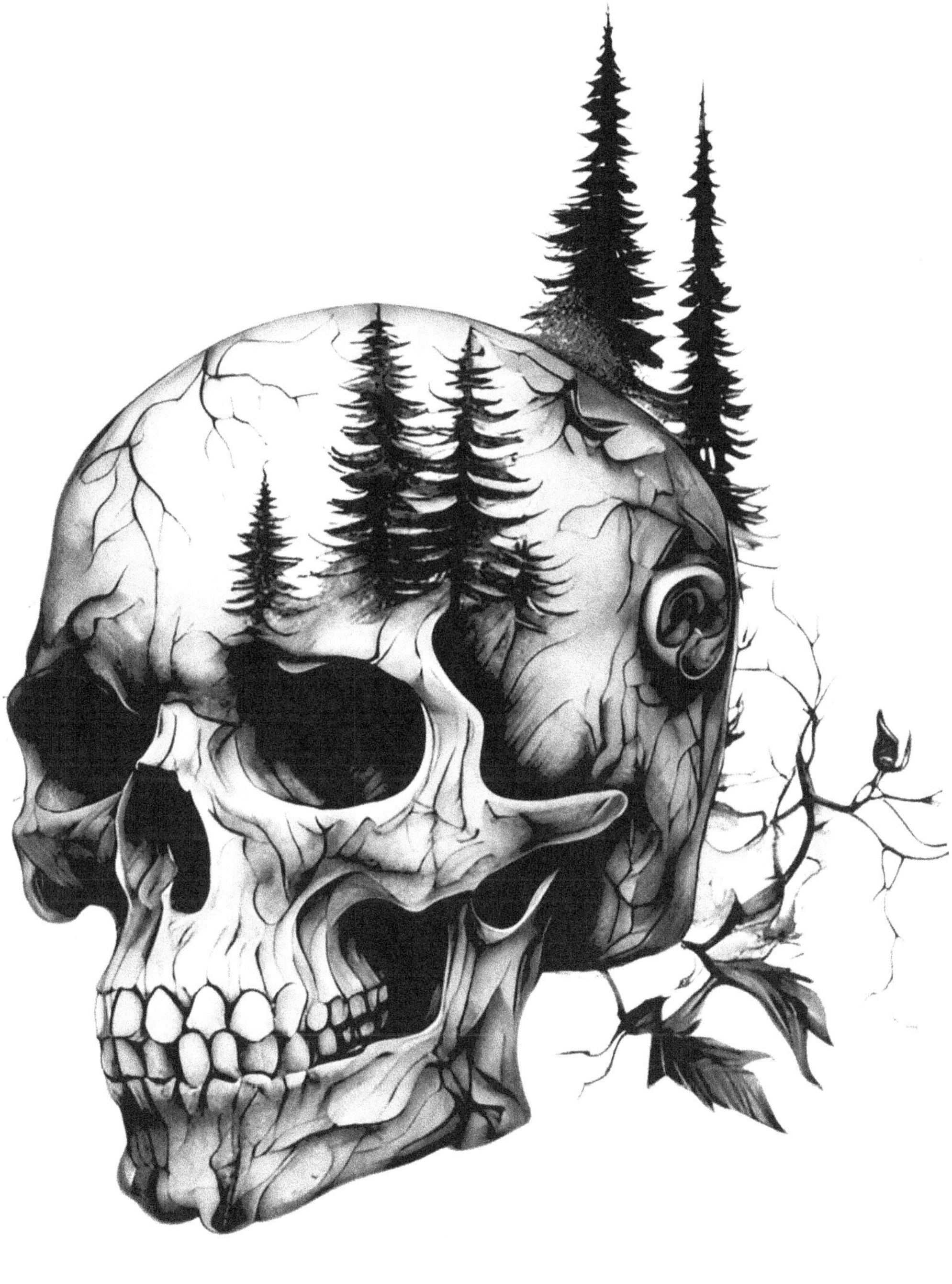

NATURE SKULL TATTOOS

NATURE SKULL TATTOOS

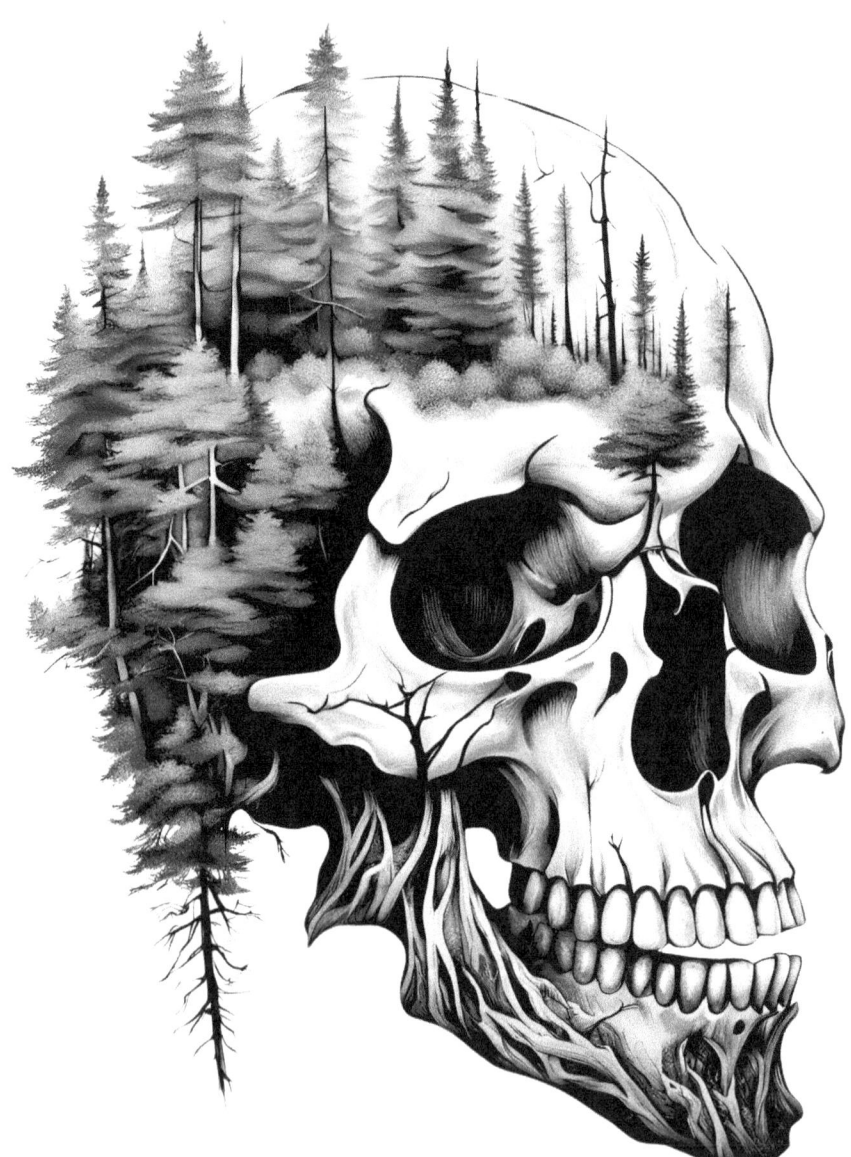

NATURE SKULL TATTOOS

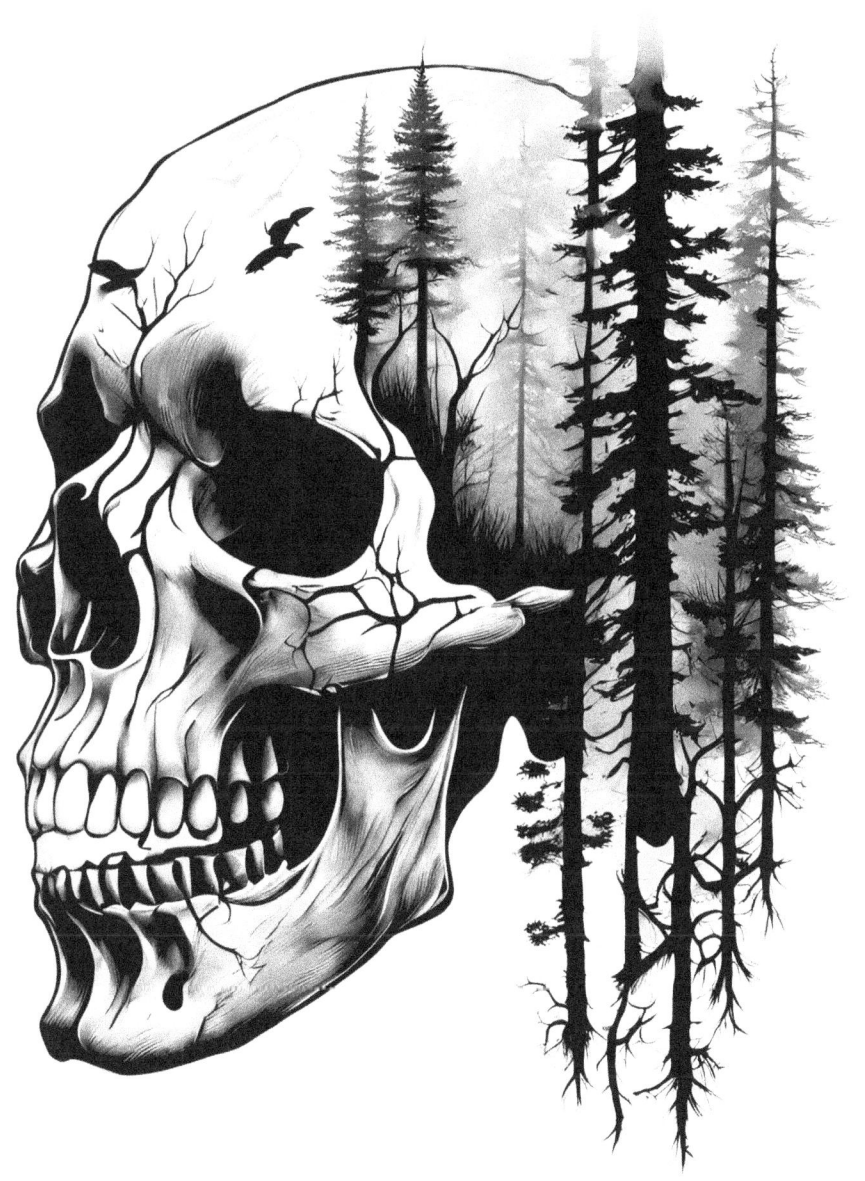

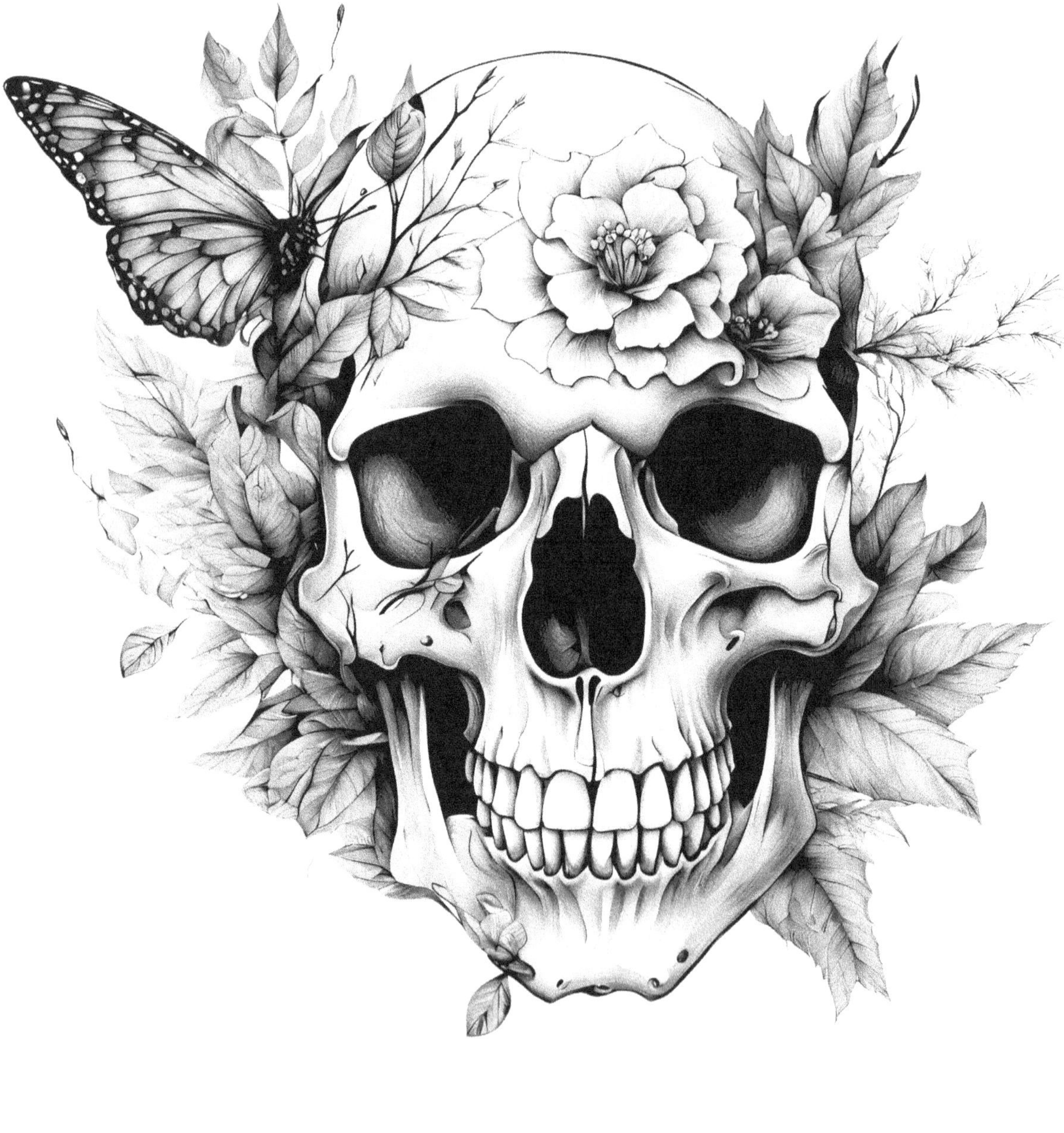

NATURE SKULL TATTOOS

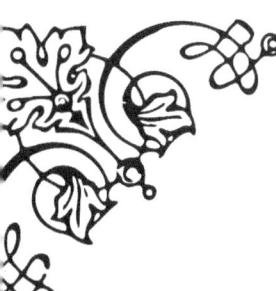
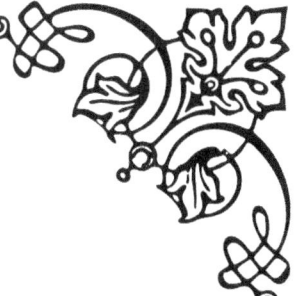

GEOMETRIC SKULL TATTOOS

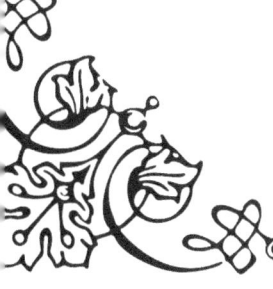

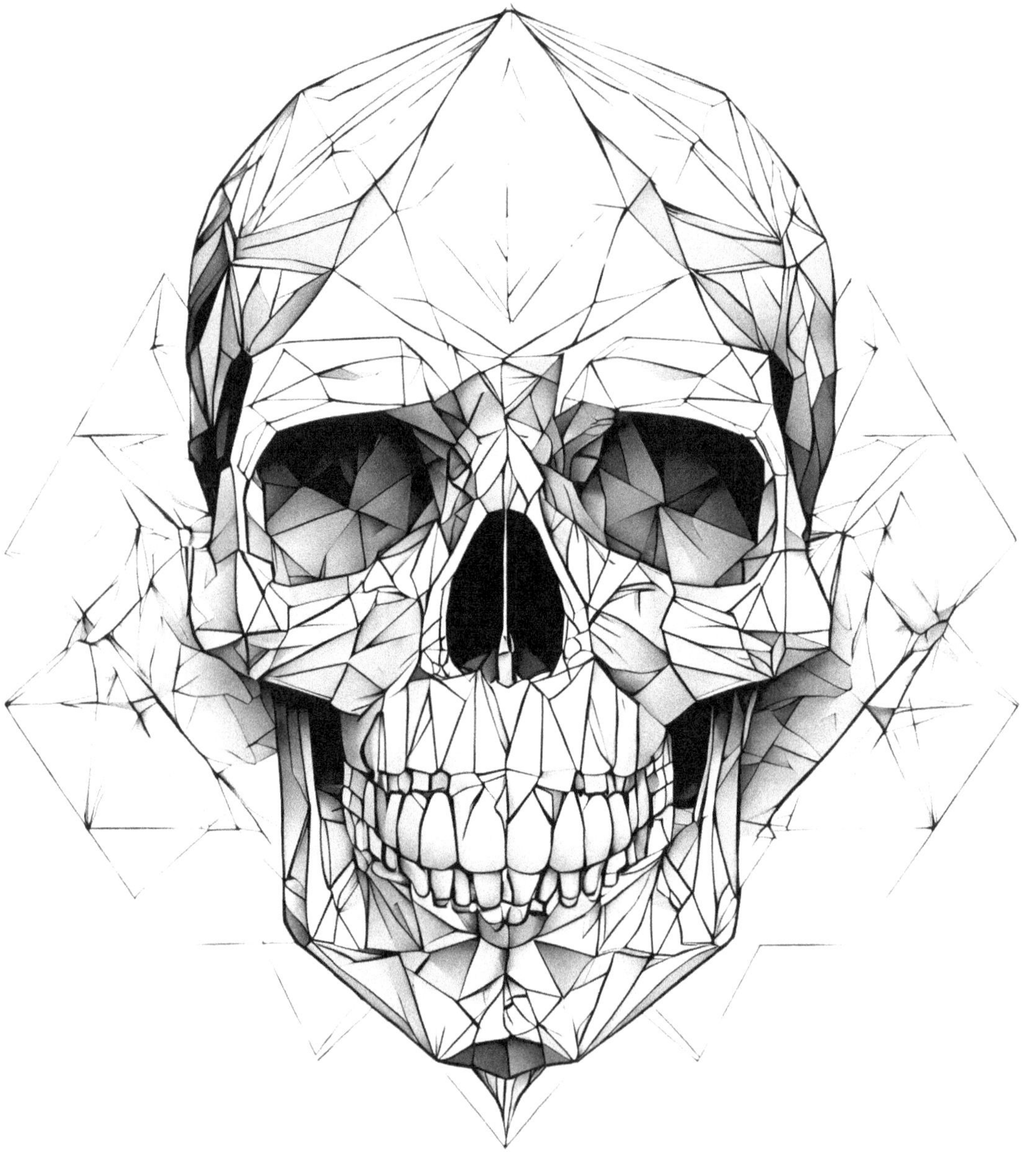

GEOMETRIC SKULL TATTOOS

GEOMETRIC SKULL TATTOOS

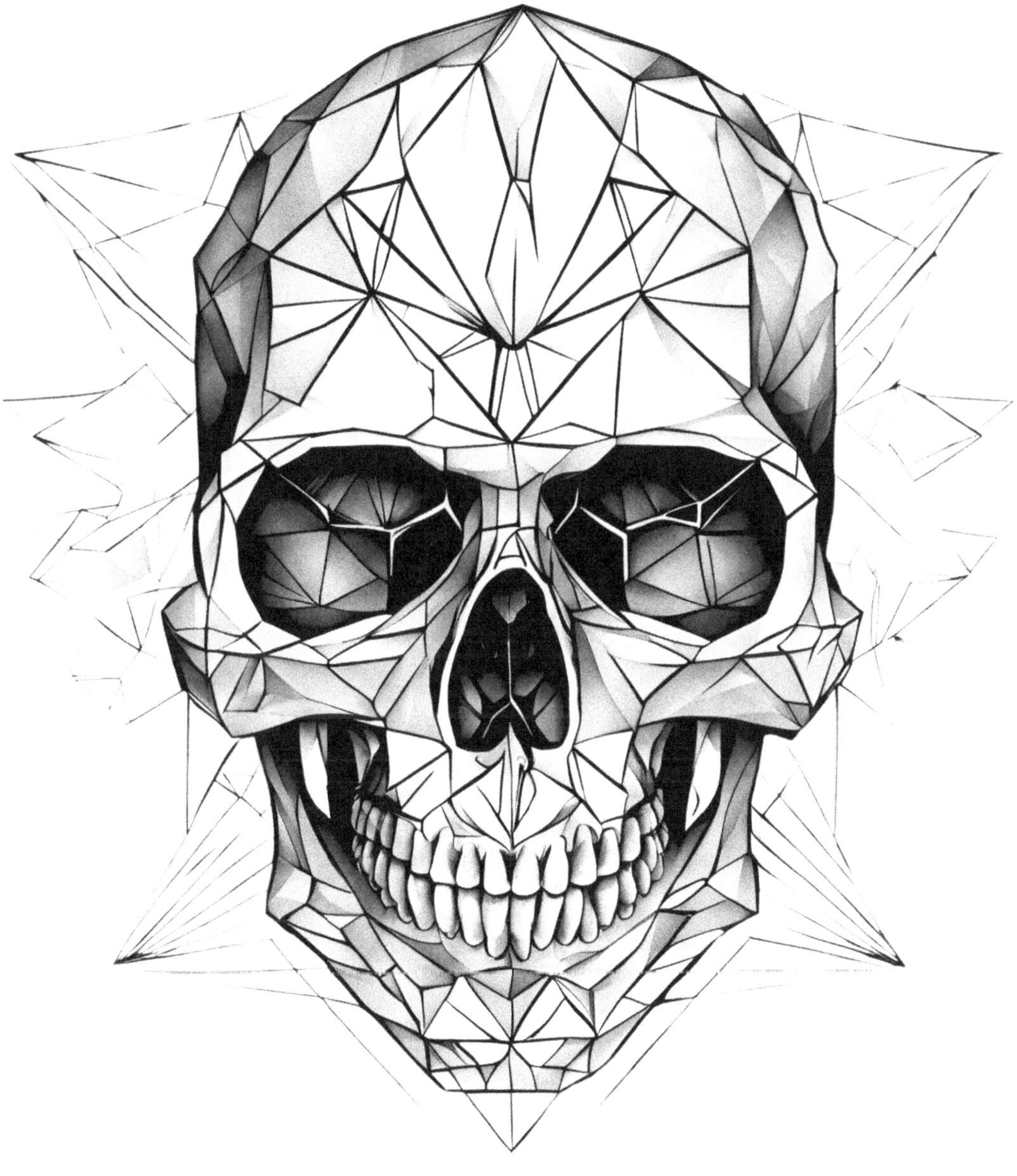

GEOMETRIC SKULL TATTOOS

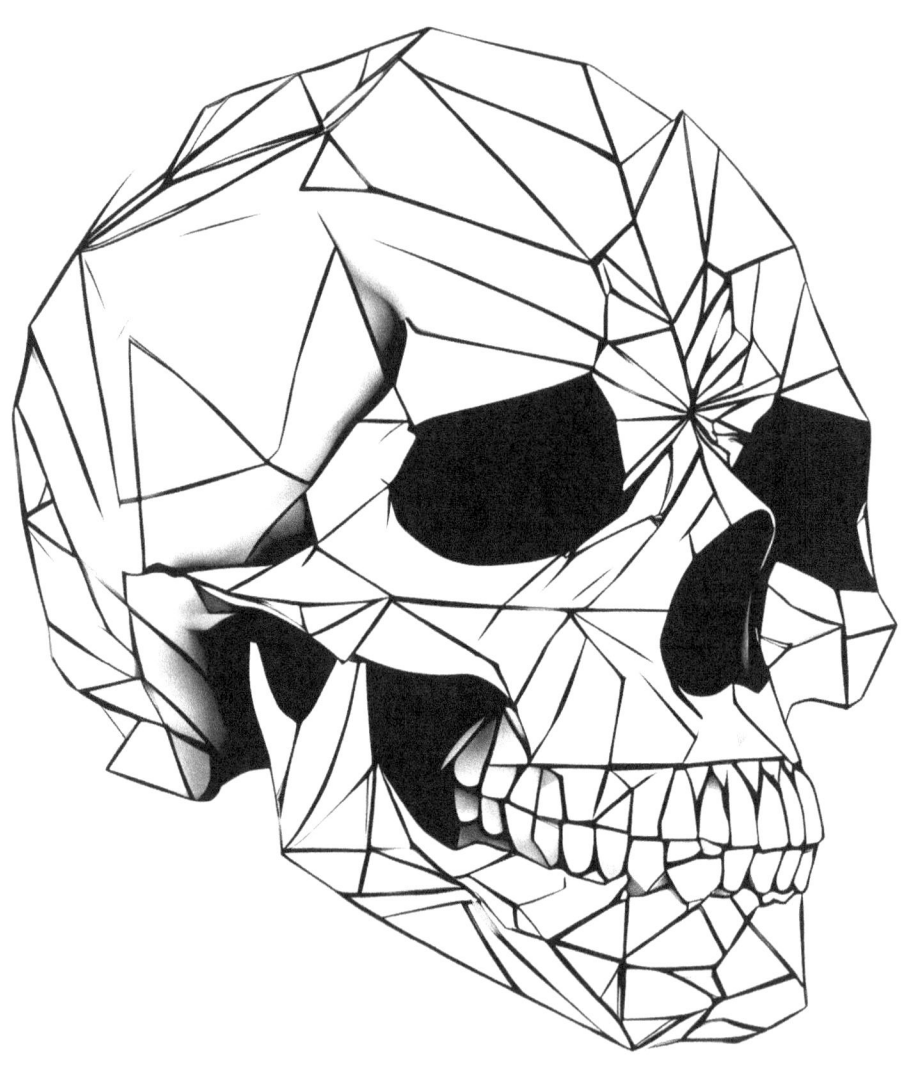

GEOMETRIC SKULL TATTOOS

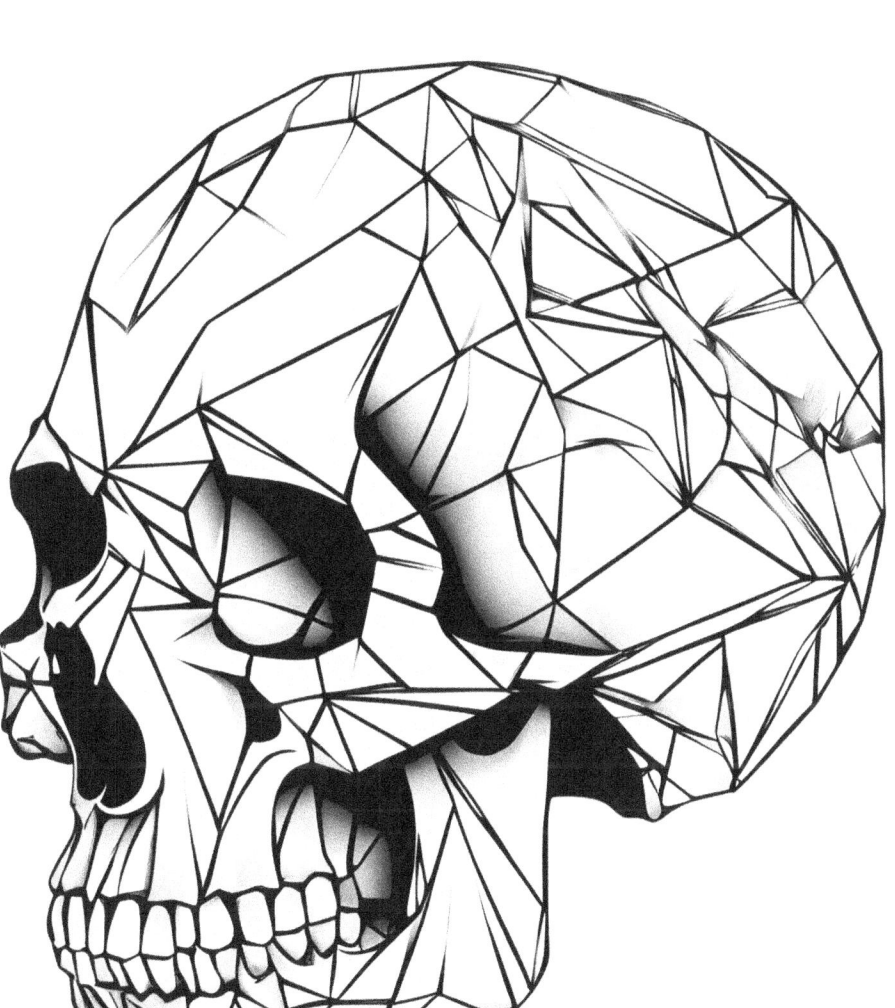

GEOMETRIC SKULL TATTOOS

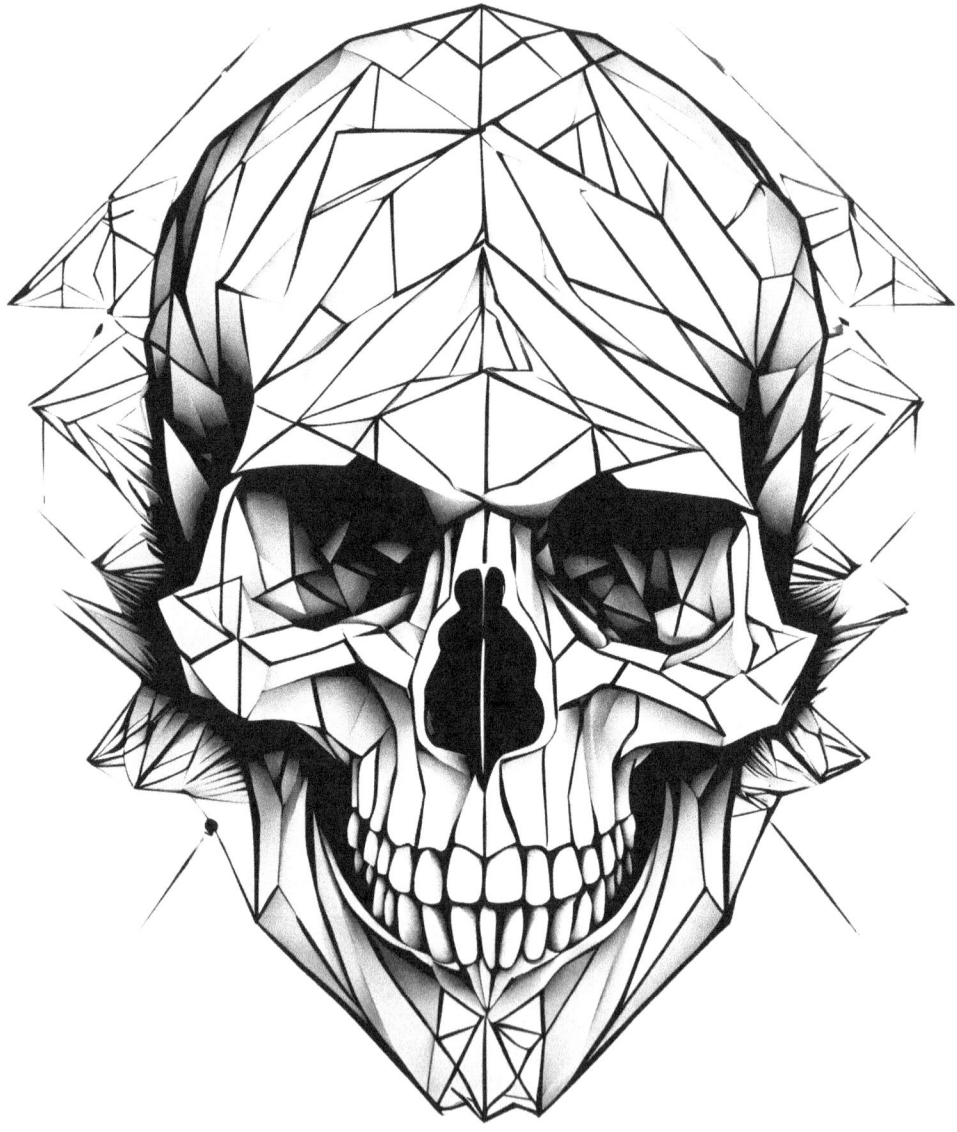

GEOMETRIC SKULL TATTOOS

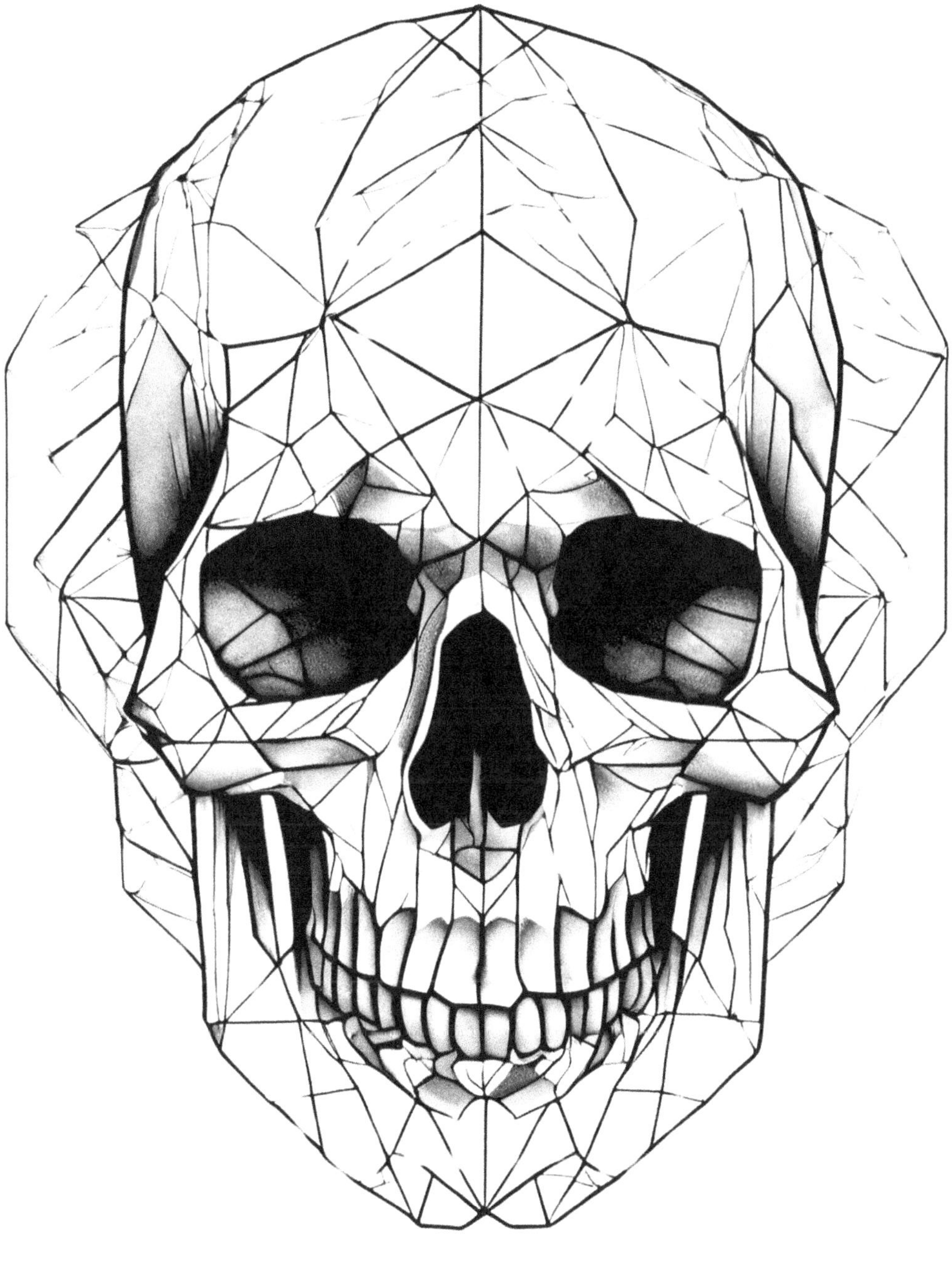

GEOMETRIC SKULL TATTOOS

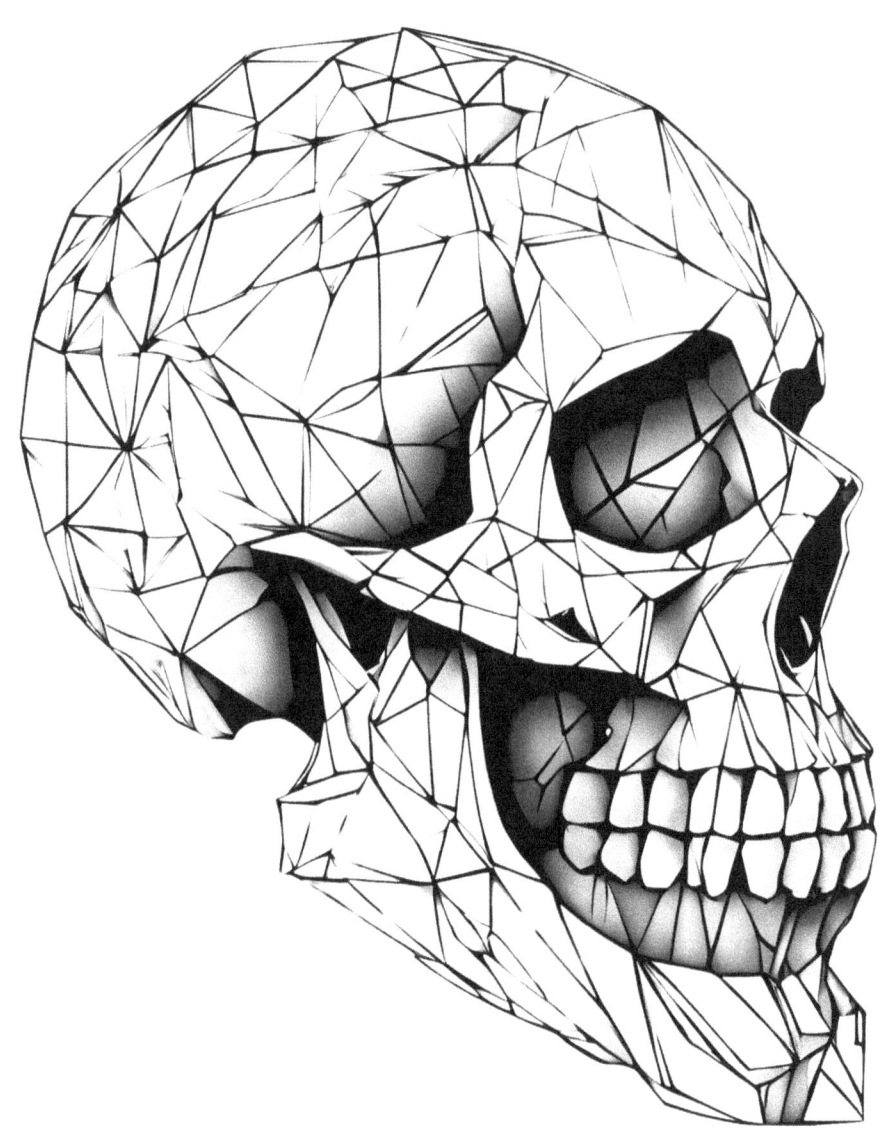

GEOMETRIC SKULL TATTOOS

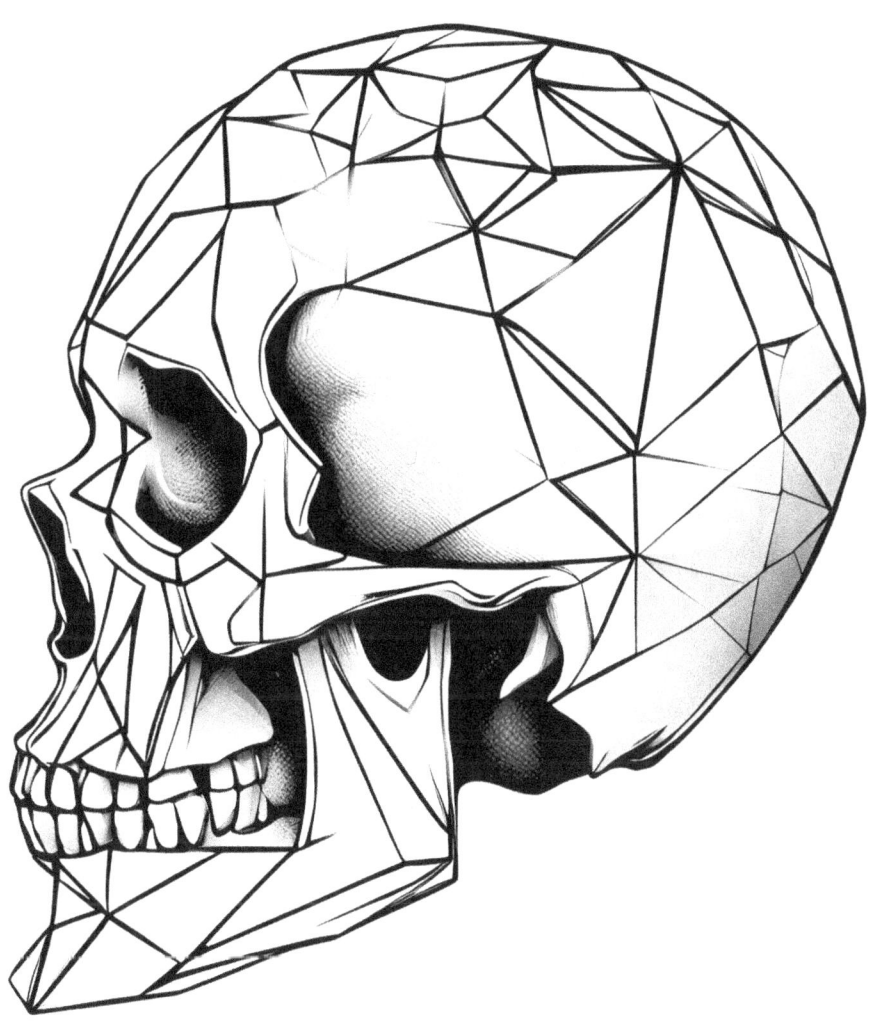

ANIMAL SKULL TATTOOS

ANIMAL SKULL TATTOOS

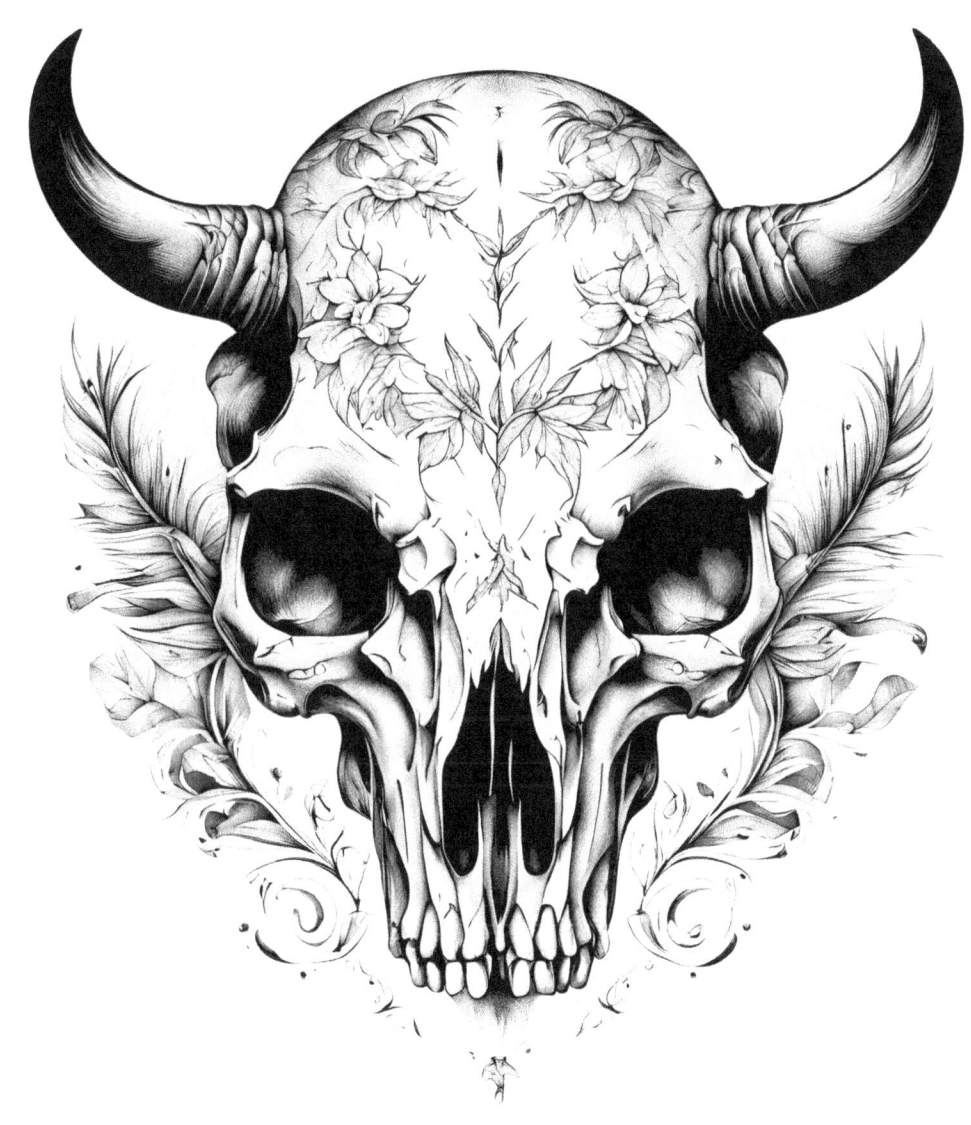

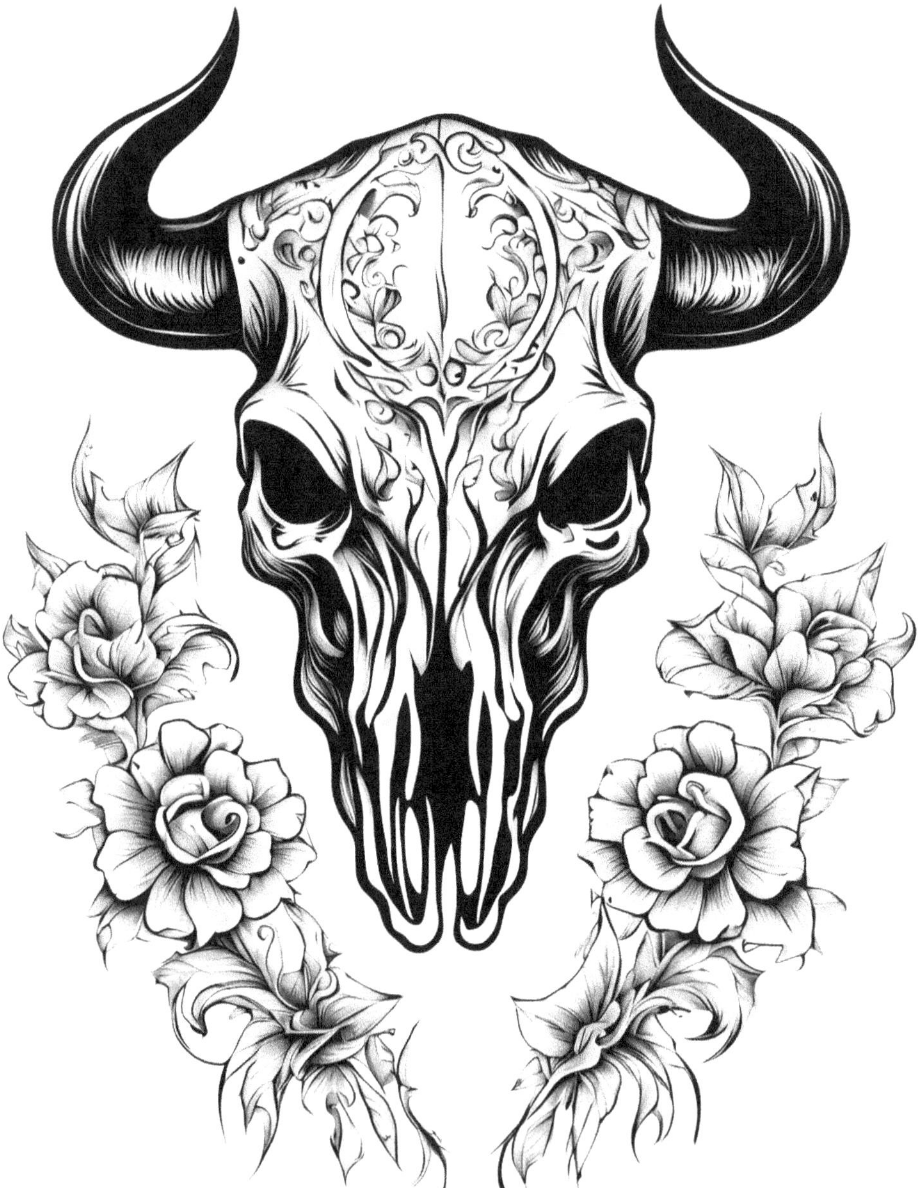

ANIMAL SKULL TATTOOS

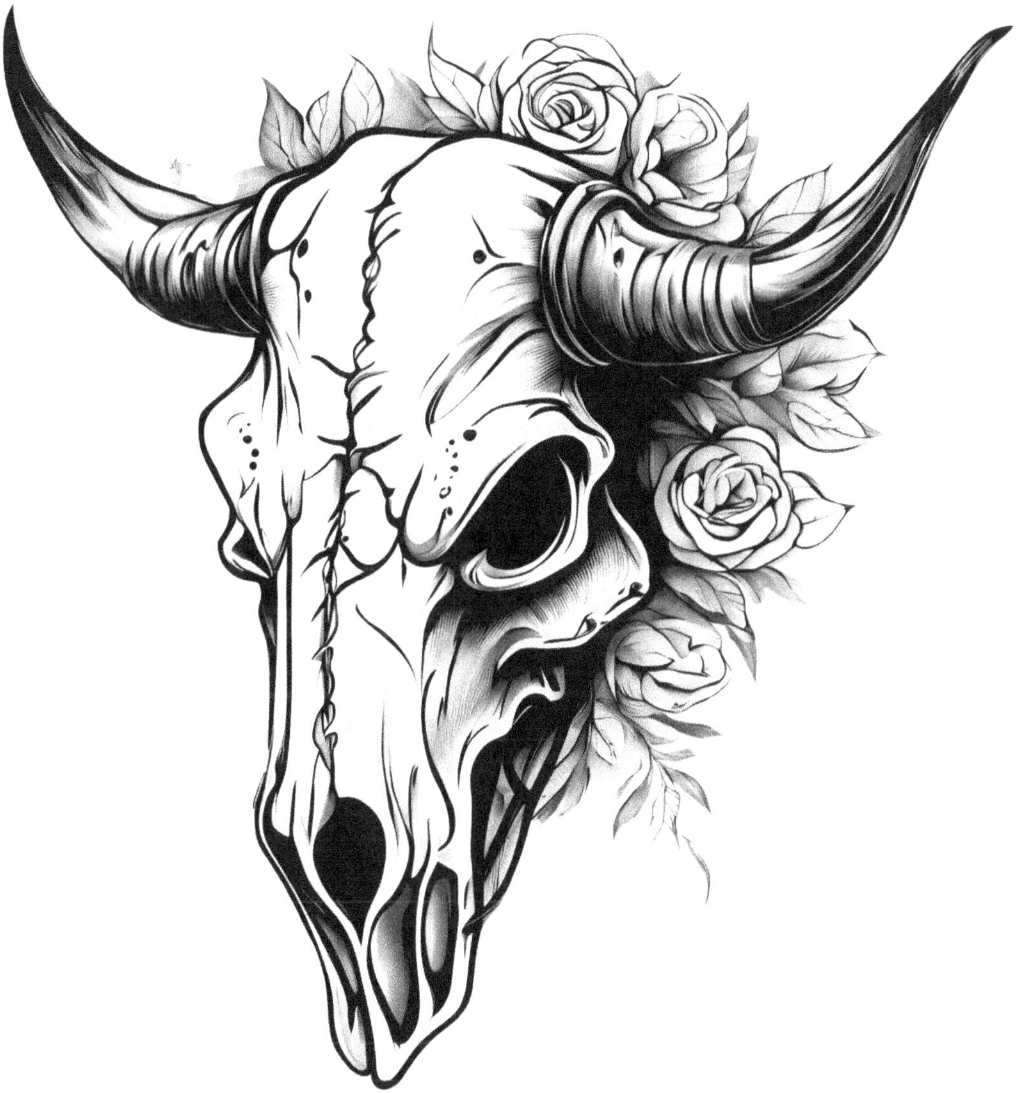

ANIMAL SKULL TATTOOS

ANIMAL SKULL TATTOOS

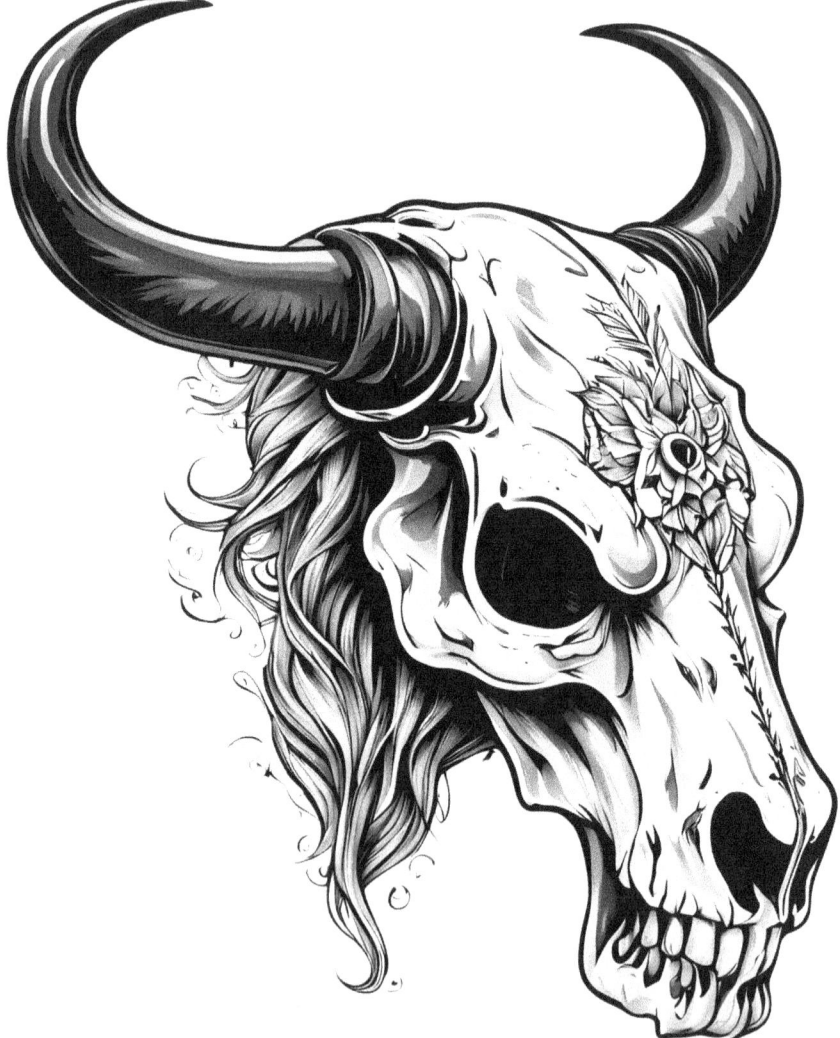

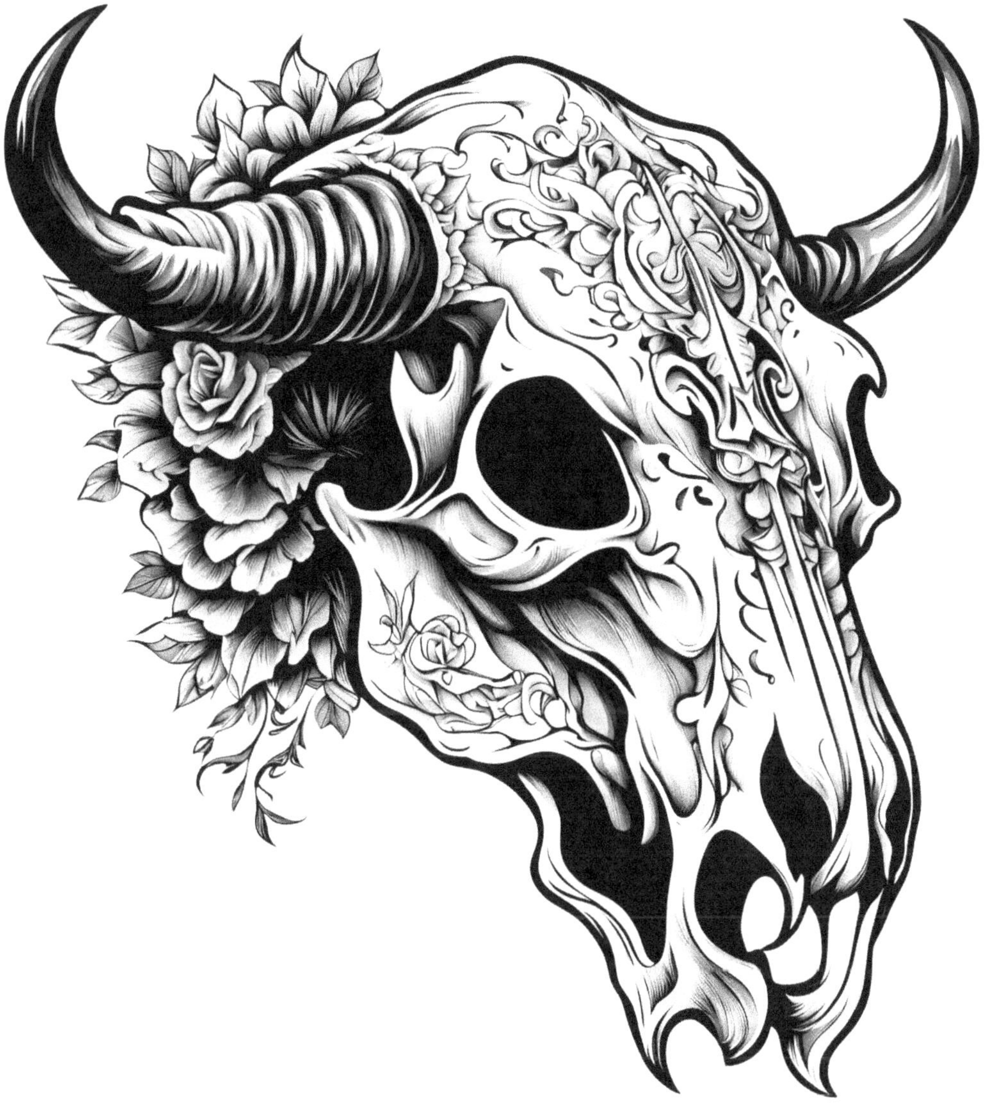

ANIMAL SKULL TATTOOS

ANIMAL SKULL TATTOOS

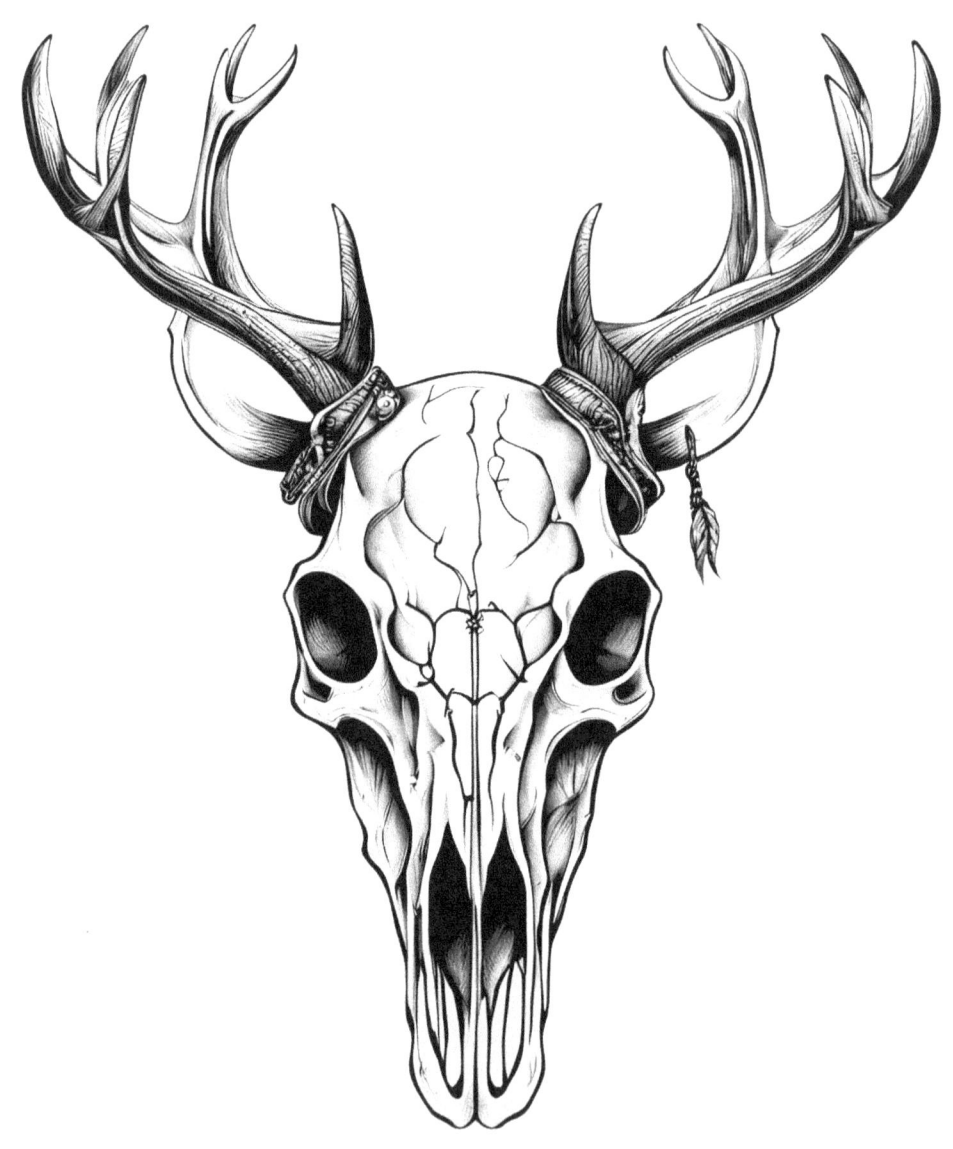

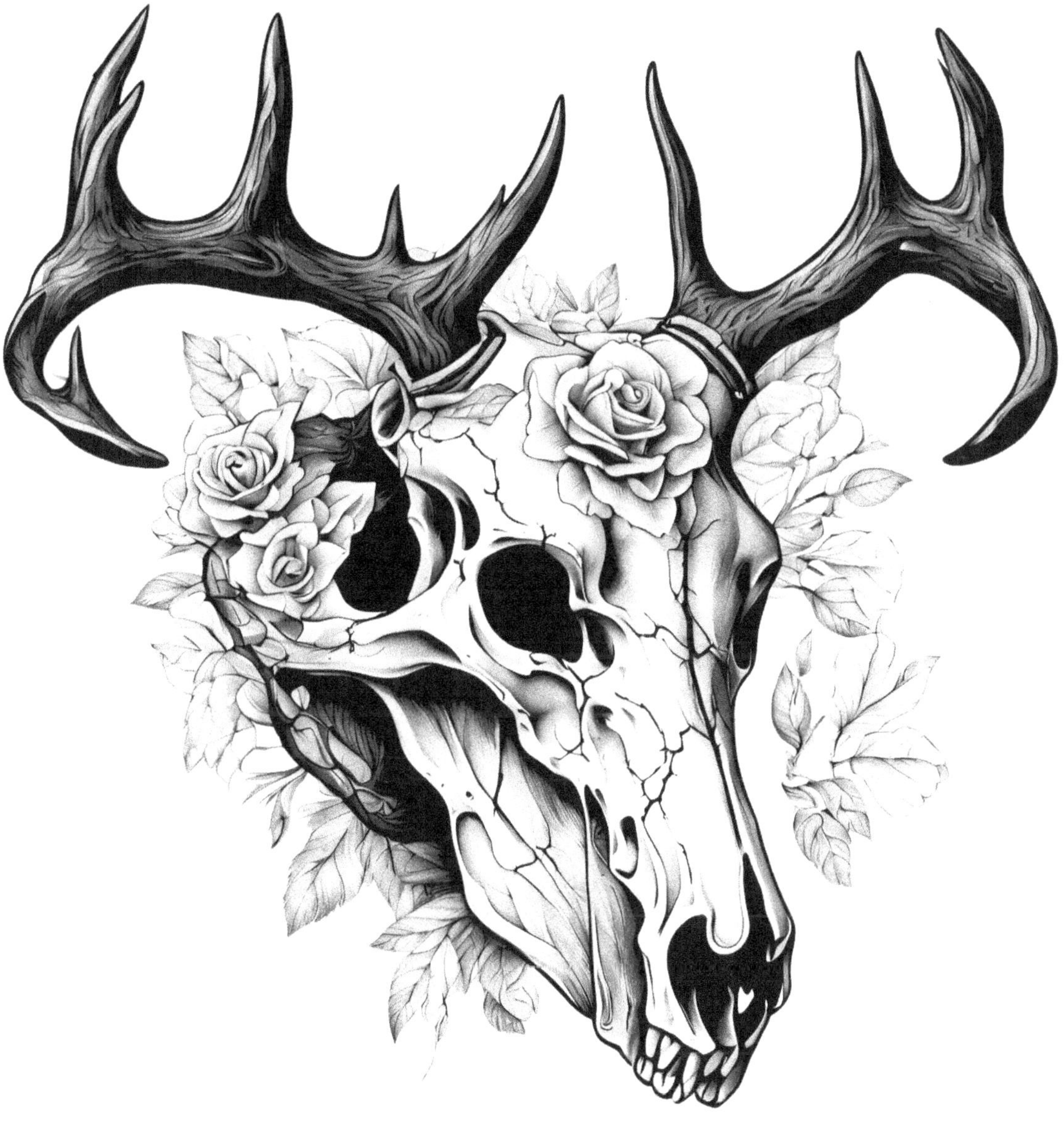

ANIMAL SKULL TATTOOS

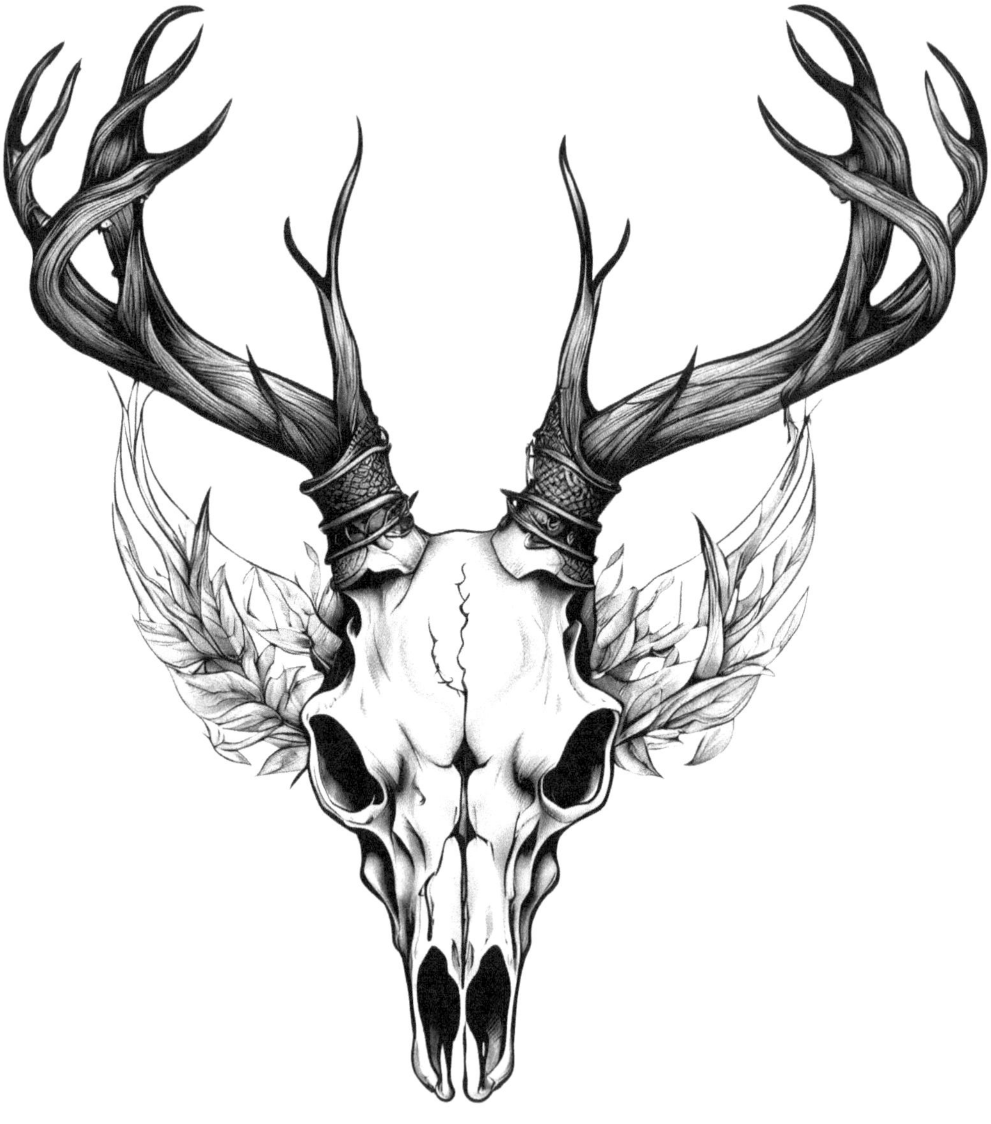

ANIMAL SKULL TATTOOS

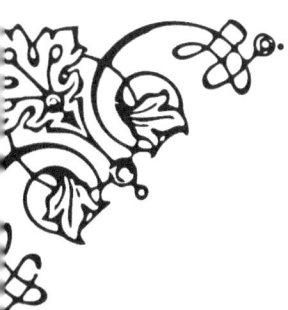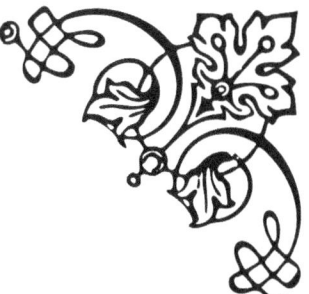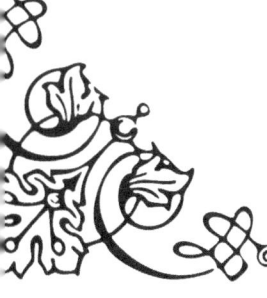

ALIEN SKULL TATTOOS

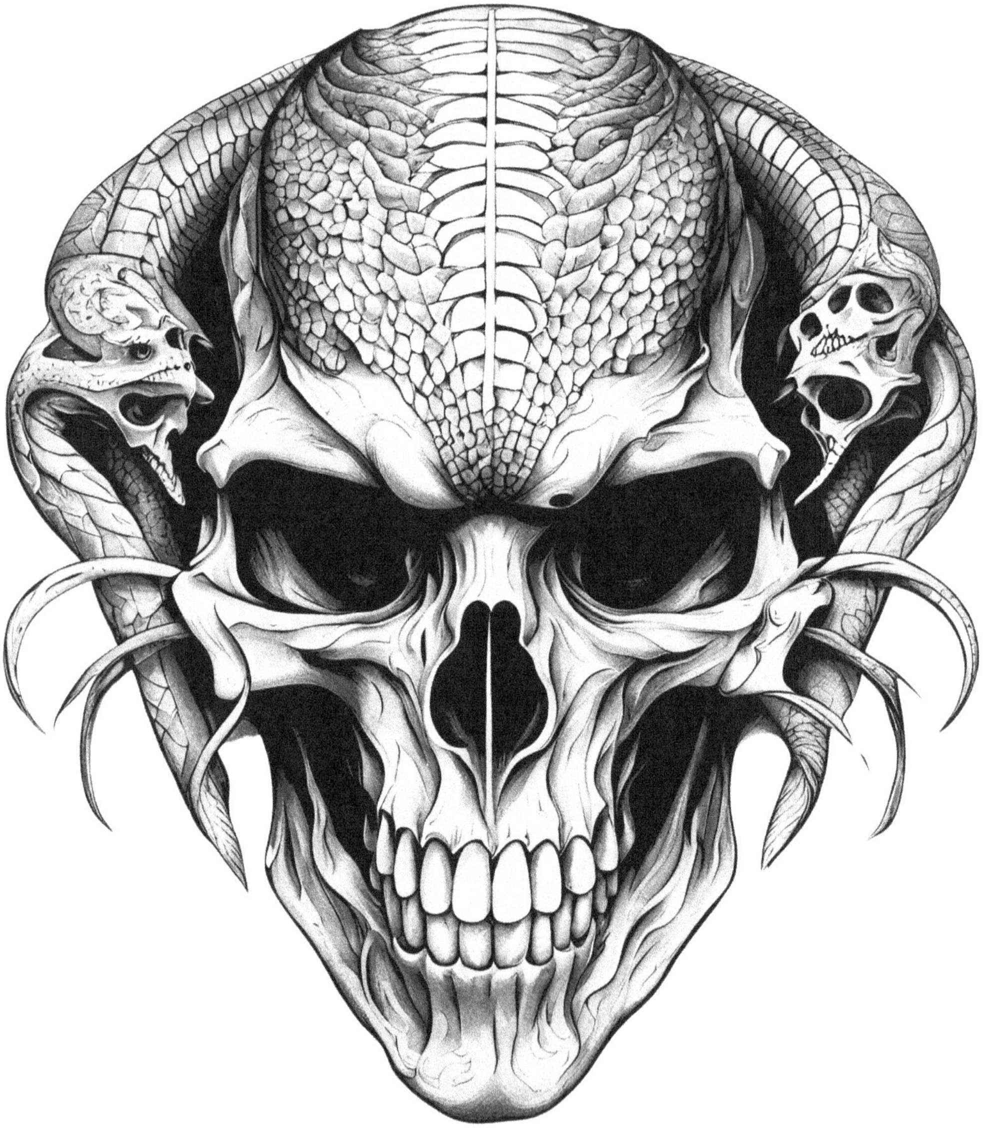

ALIEN SKULL TATTOOS

ALIEN SKULL TATTOOS

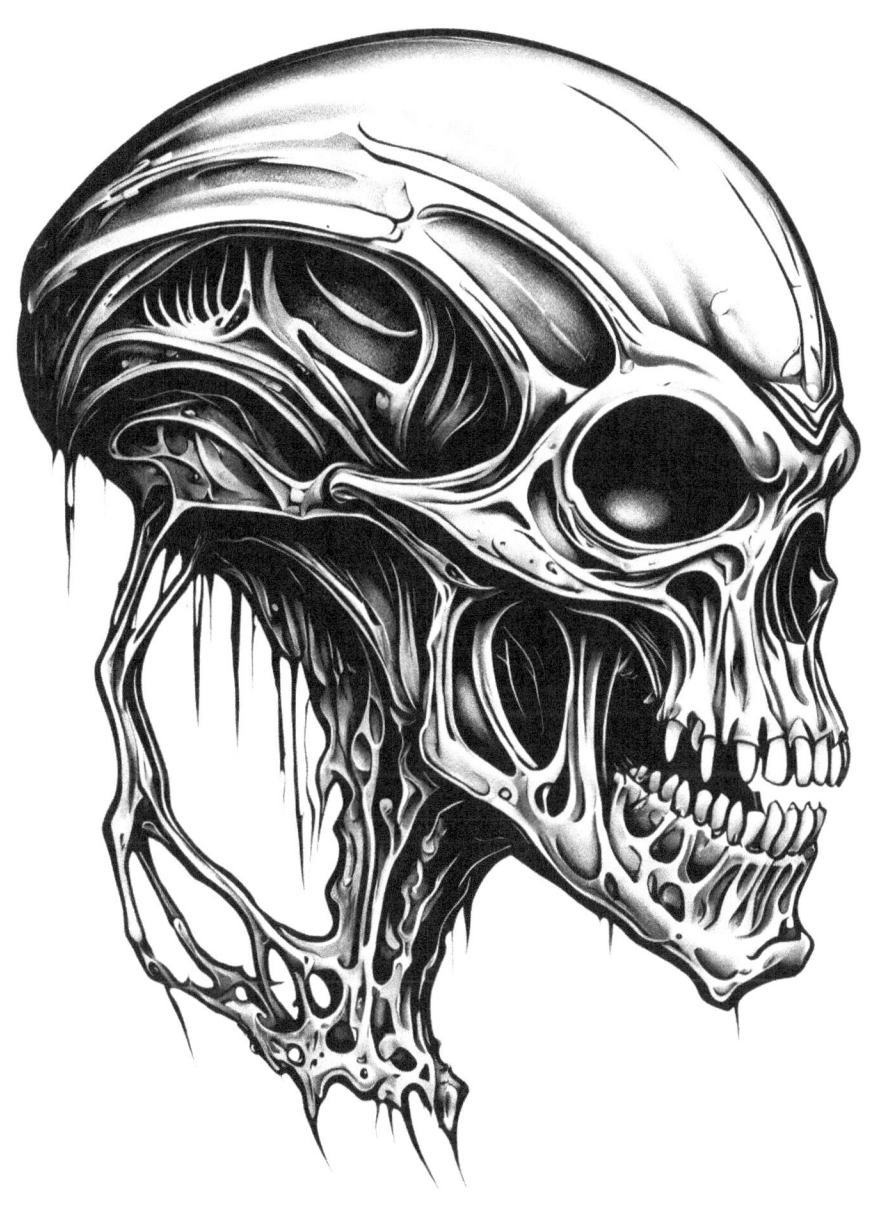

ALIEN SKULL TATTOOS

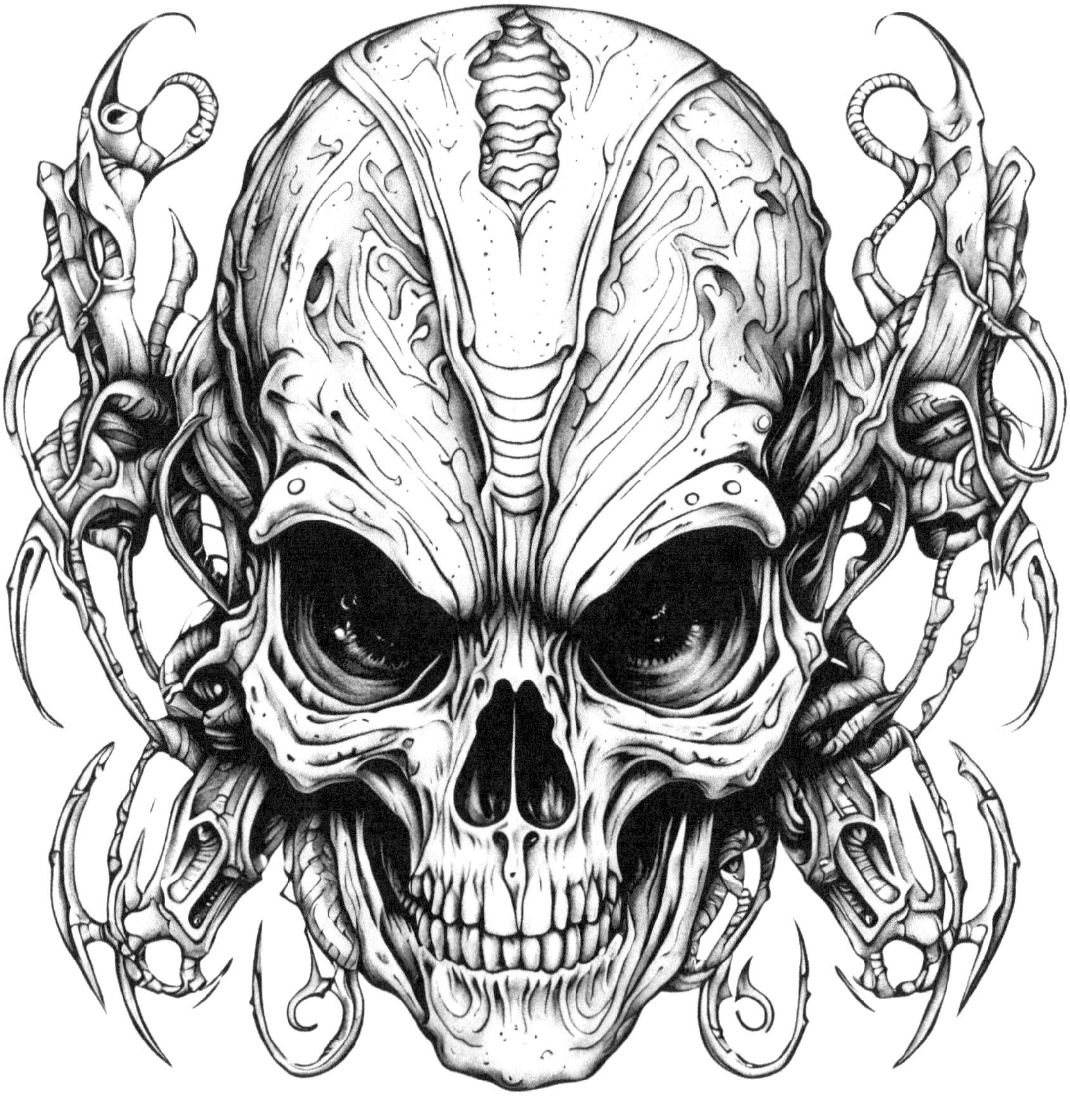

ALIEN SKULL TATTOOS

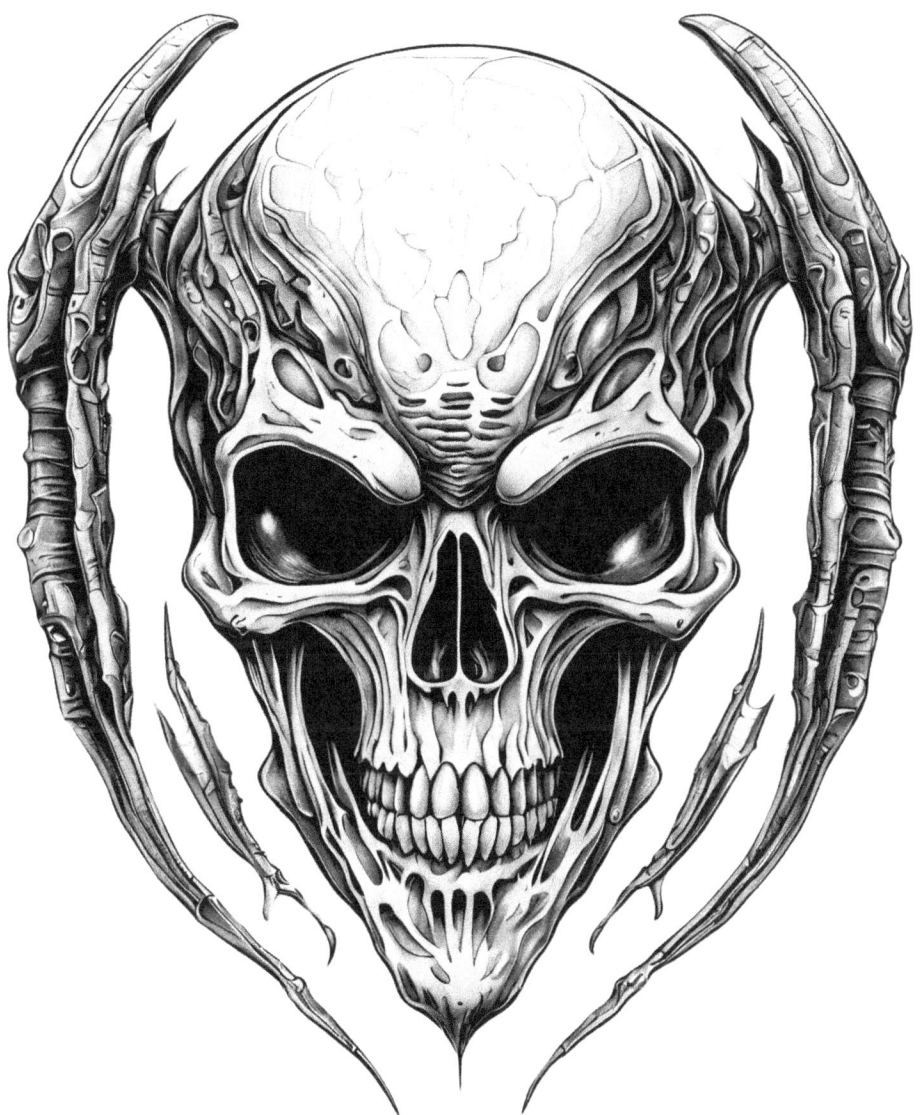

ALIEN SKULL TATTOOS

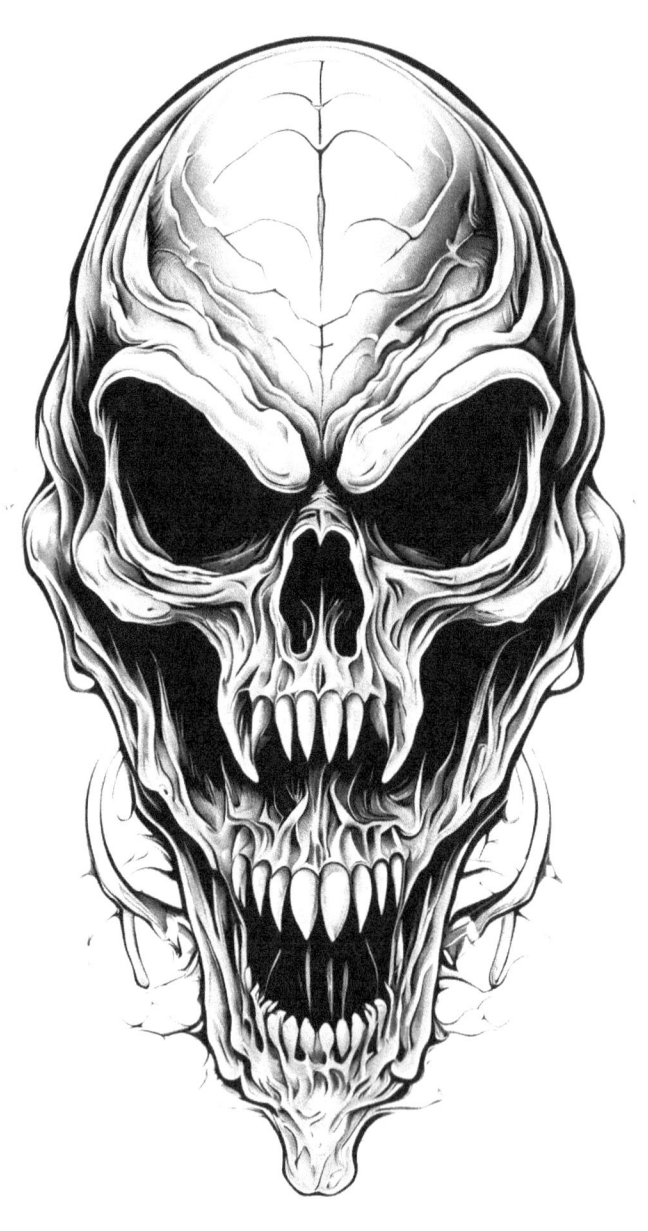

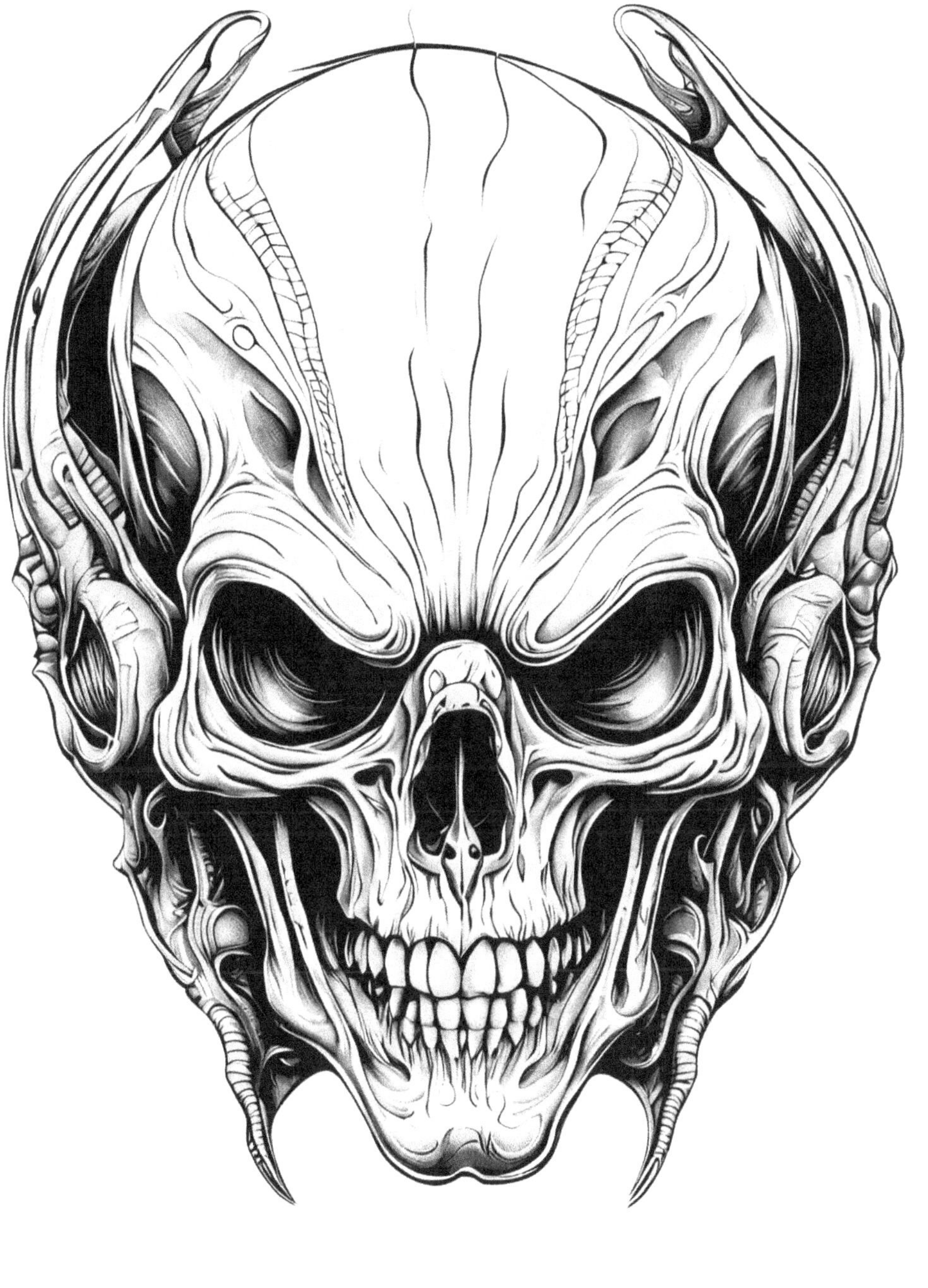

ALIEN SKULL TATTOOS

ALIEN SKULL TATTOOS

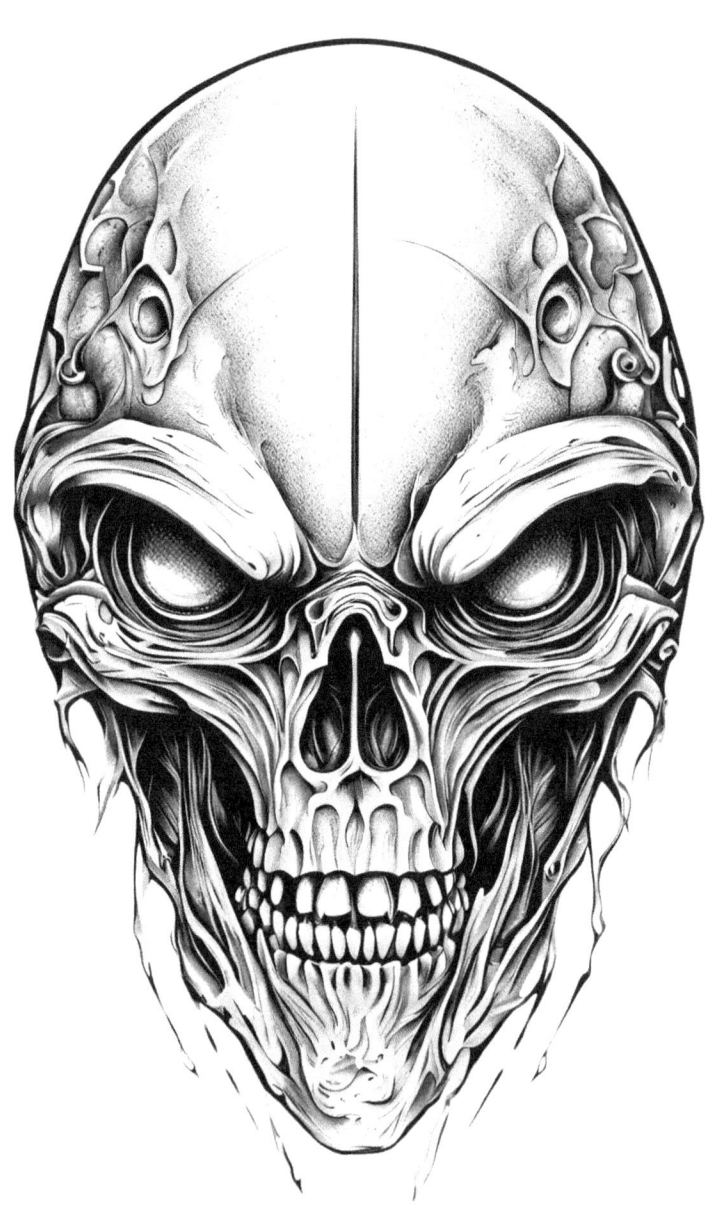

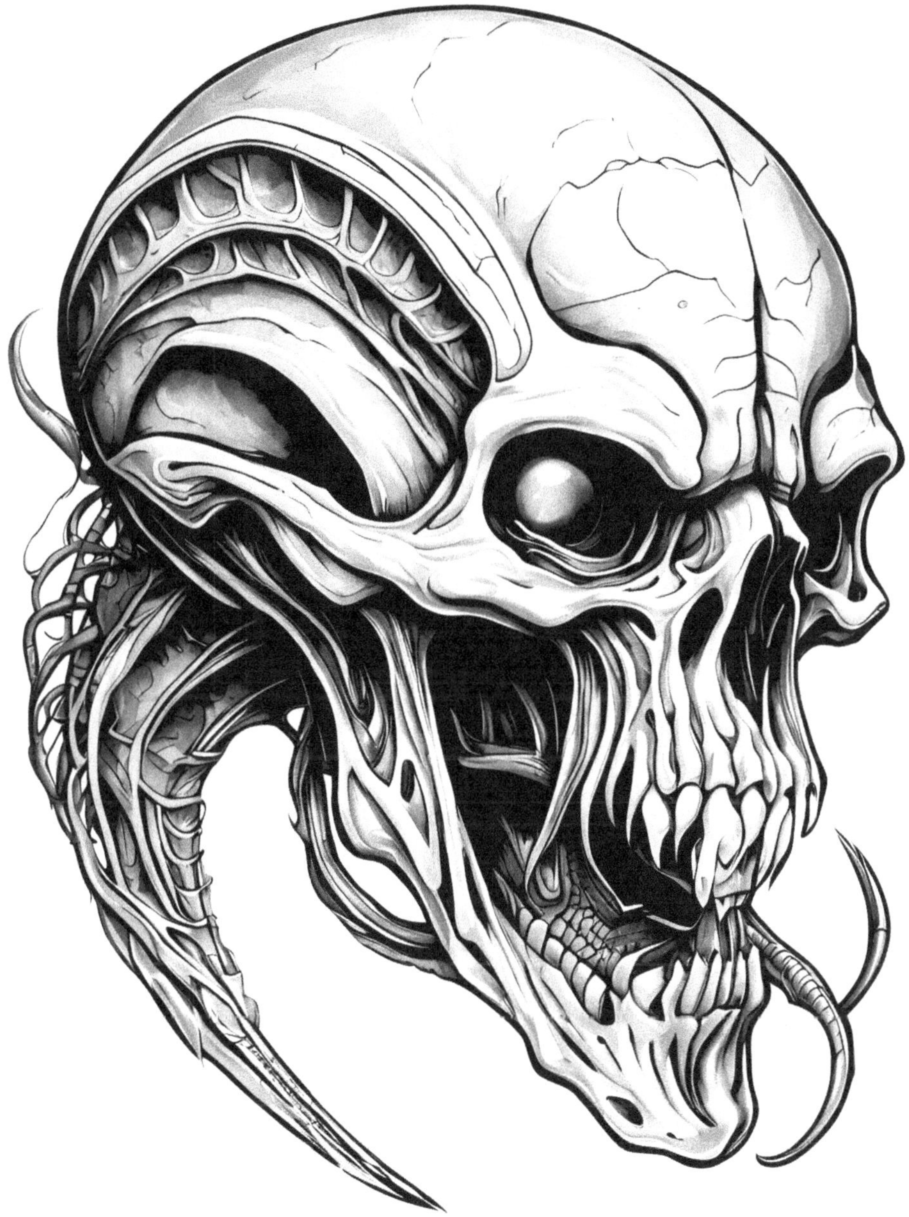

ALIEN SKULL TATTOOS

ALIEN SKULL TATTOOS

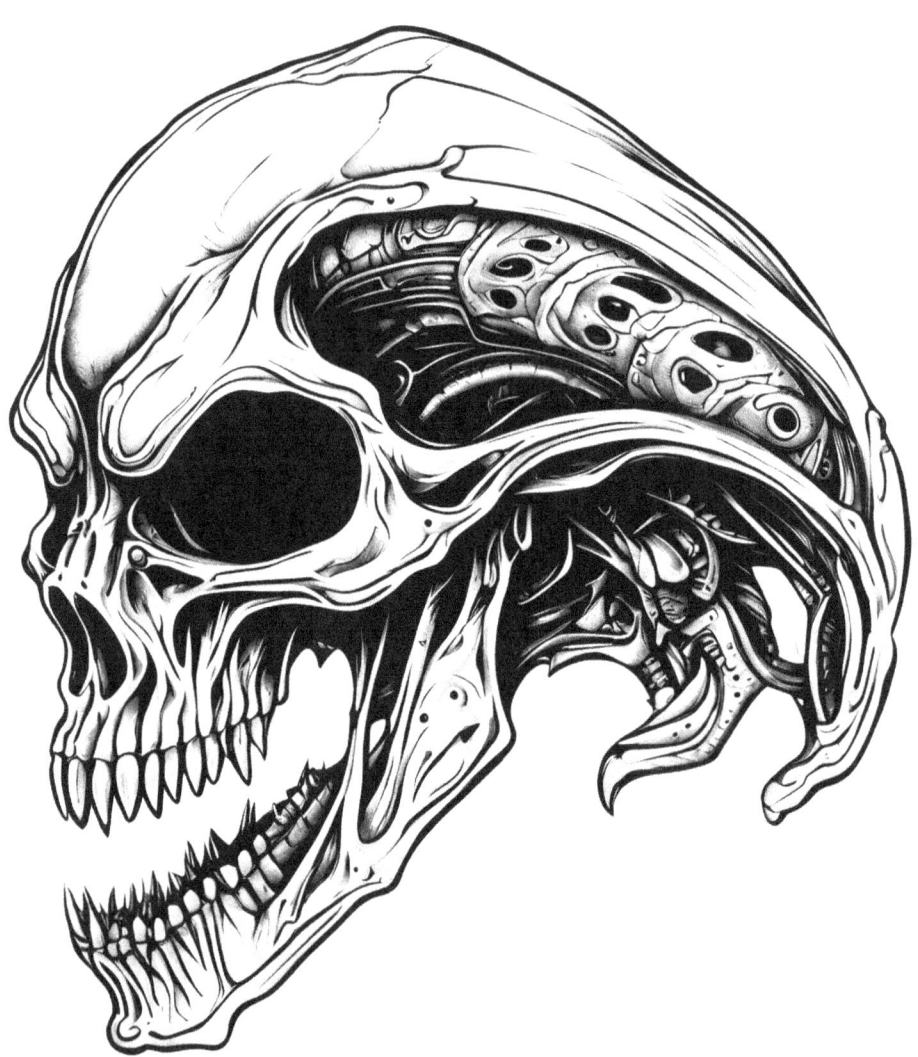

ALIEN SKULL TATTOOS

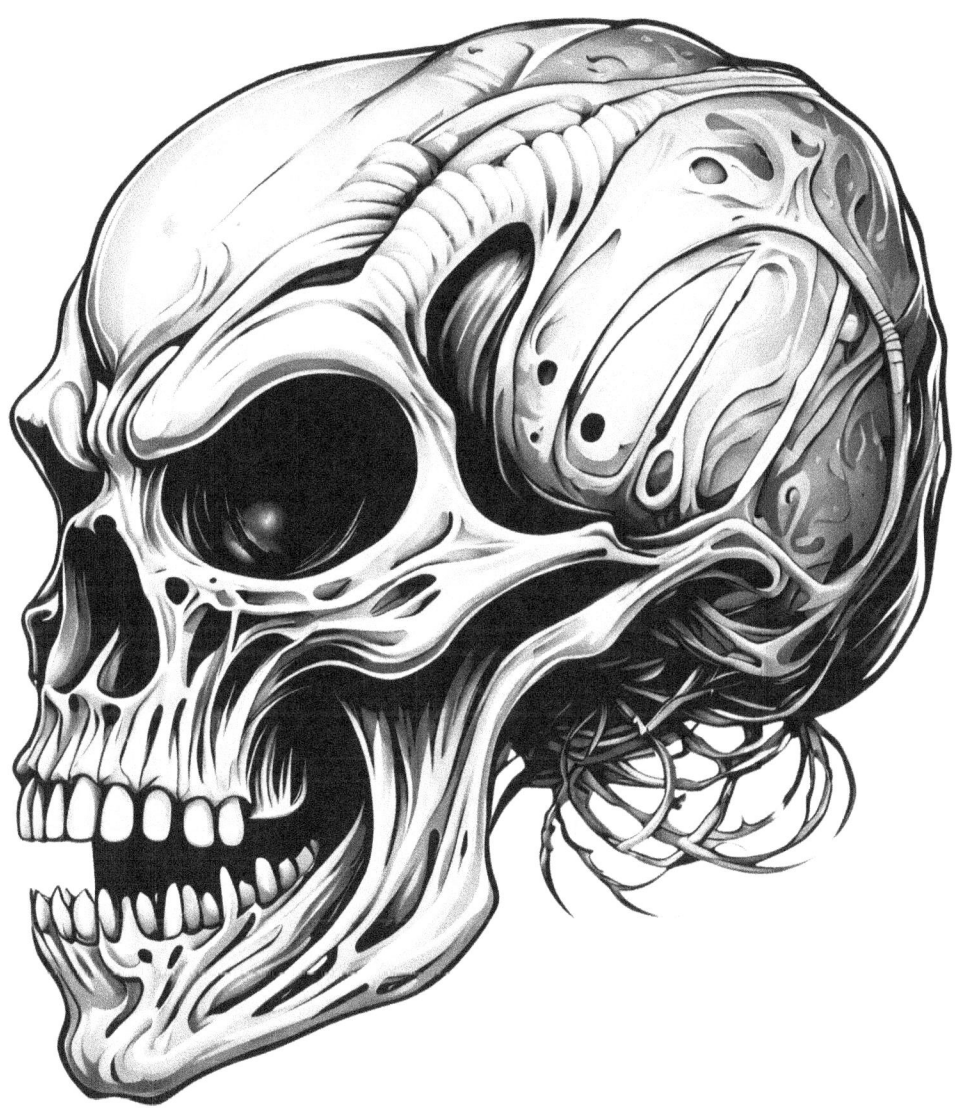

ALIEN SKULL TATTOOS

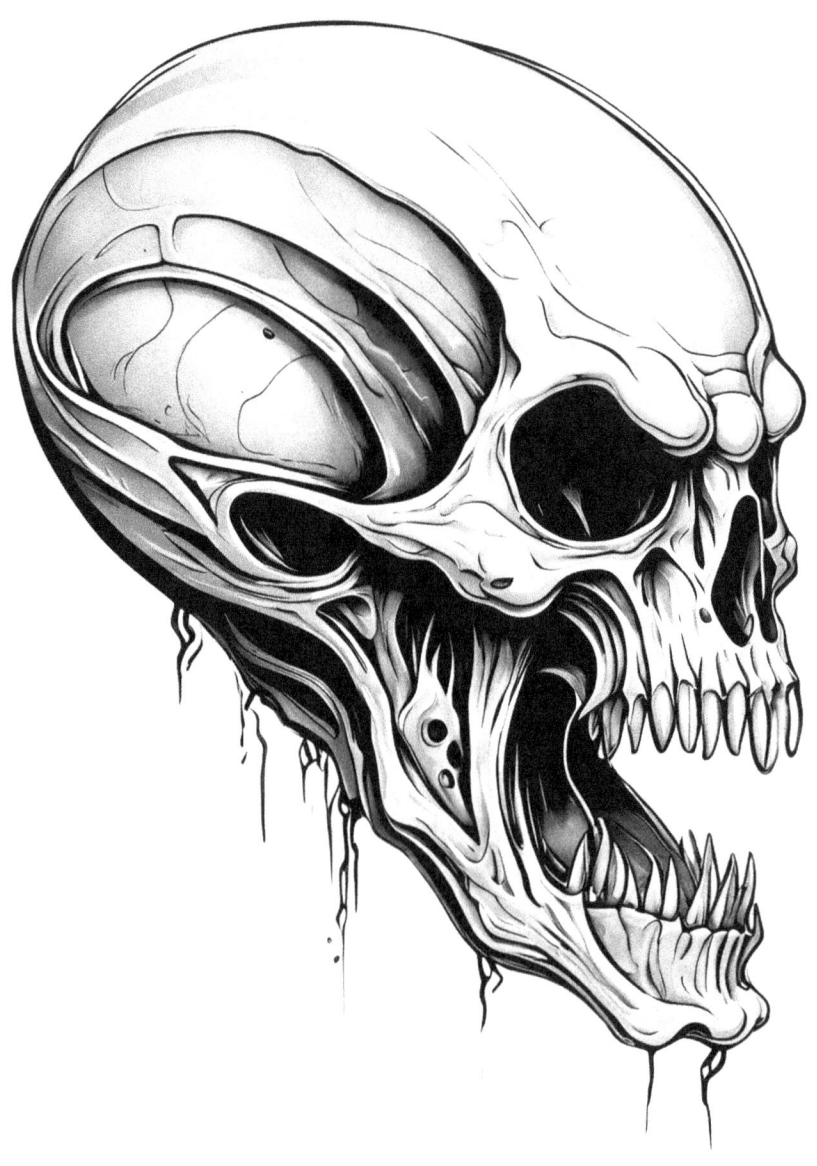

ALIEN SKULL TATTOOS

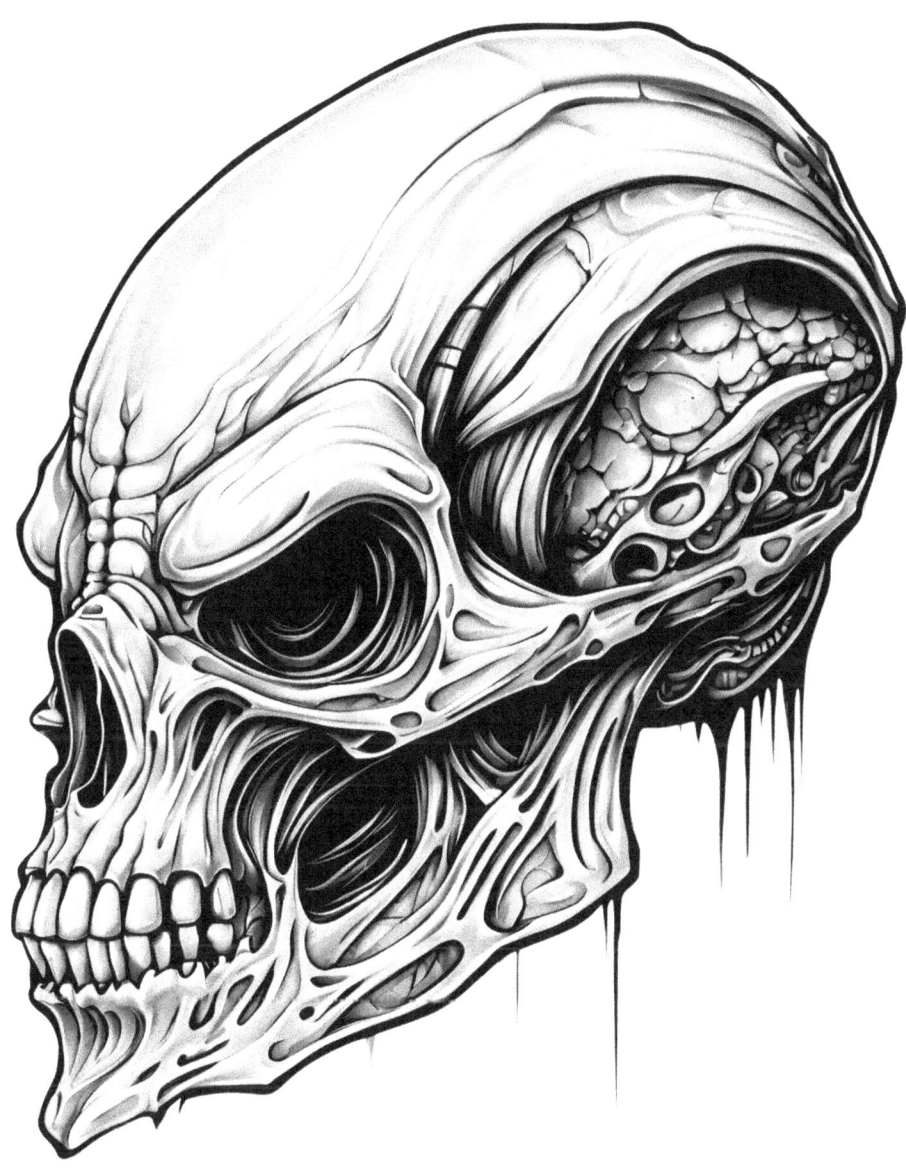

ALIEN SKULL TATTOOS

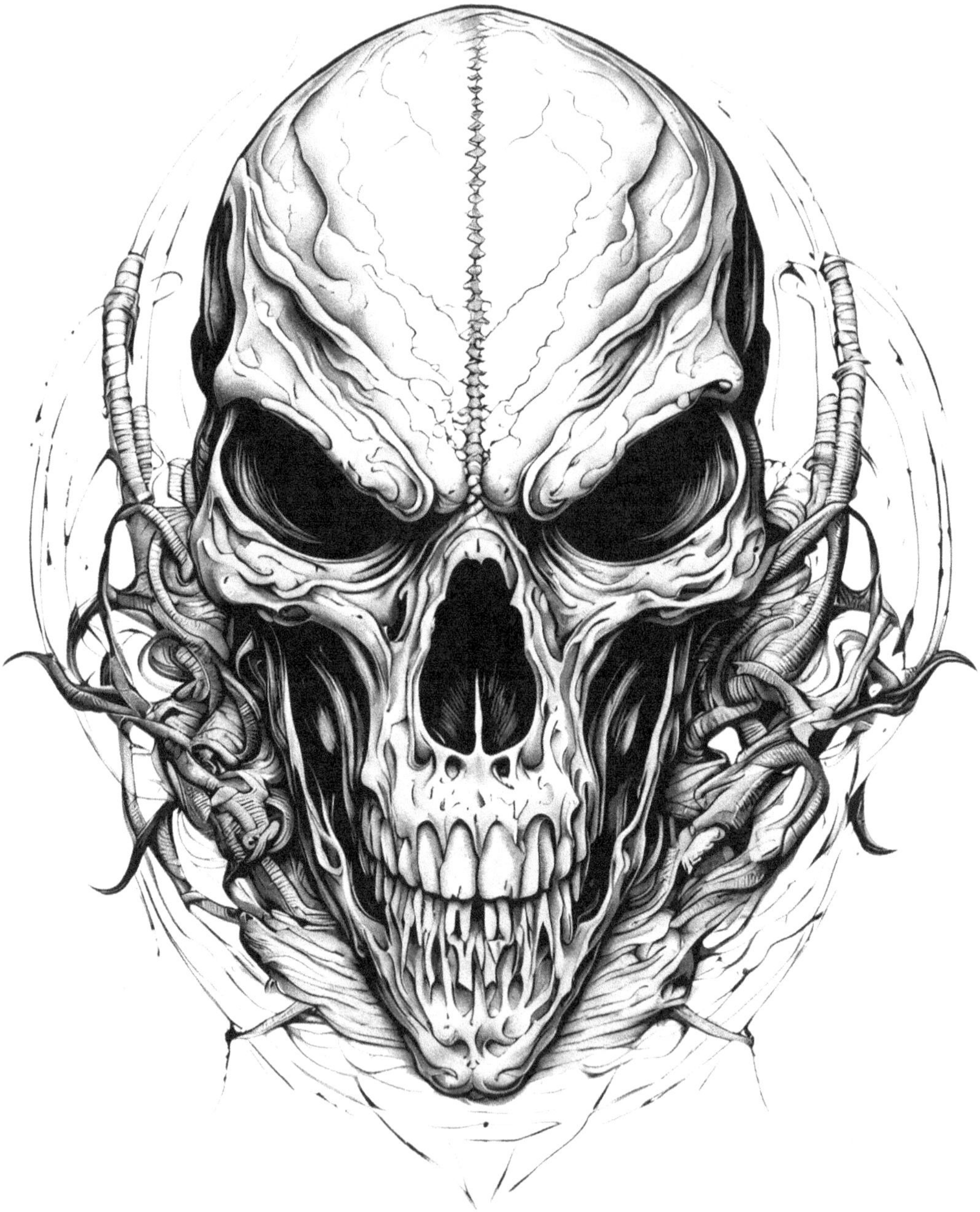

ALIEN SKULL TATTOOS

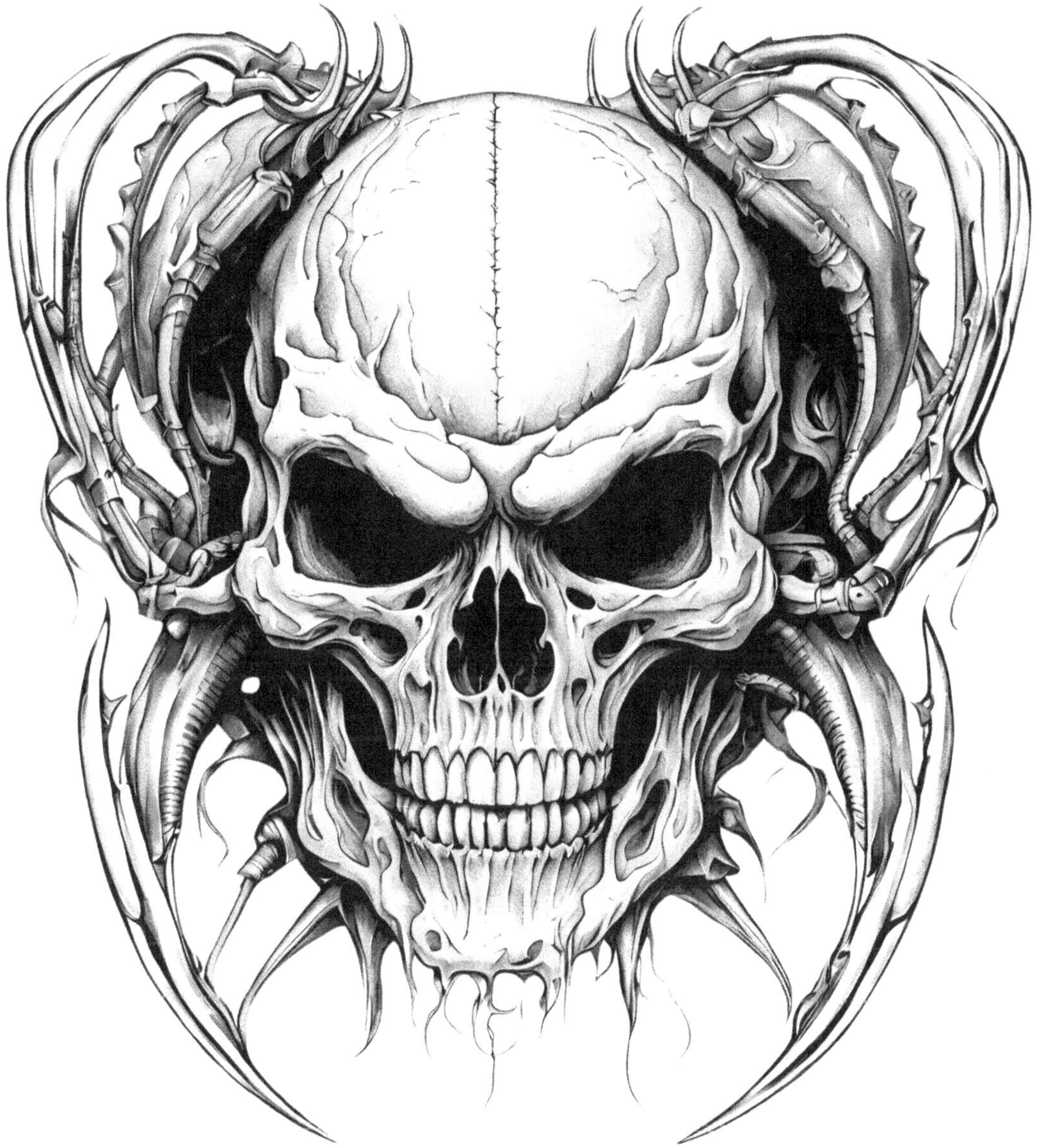

FINAL THOUGHTS

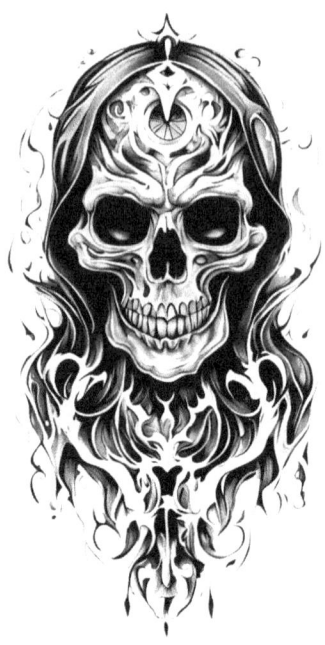

Thanks for purchasing this book, be sure to check out my other books on my author page including;

BLACK AND WHITE TATTOO DESIGN BOOK

If you enjoyed this book I would greatly appreciate a positive review.

Many thanks

Harley Ray

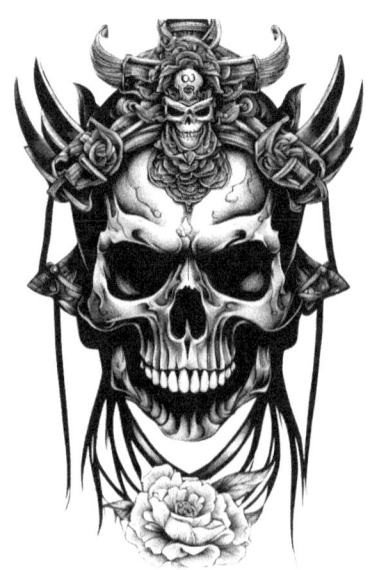

www.ingramcontent.com/pod-product-compliance
Lightning Source LLC
Chambersburg PA
CBHW082203220526
45470CB00010B/3028